D1393864

WOMEN WANDERERS AND THE WRITING
OF MOBILITY, 1784–1814

In the last days of the Scandinavian journey that would become the basis of her great post-Revolutionary travel book, Mary Wollstonecraft wrote, "I am weary of travelling – yet seem to have no home – no resting place to look to. – I am strangely cast off." From this starting point, Ingrid Horrocks reveals the significance of representations of women wanderers in the late eighteenth and early nineteenth centuries, particularly in the work of women writers. She follows gendered, frequently reluctant wanderers beyond travel narratives into poetry, gothic romances, and sentimental novels, and places them within a long history of uses of the more traditional literary figure of the male wanderer. Drawing out the relationship between mobility and affect, and illuminating textual forms of wandering, Horrocks shows how paying attention to the figure of the woman wanderer sheds new light on women and travel and alters assumptions about mobility's connection with freedom.

INGRID HORROCKS completed a doctorate at Princeton University before taking up a job in her native New Zealand. She has been a Commonwealth Scholar, and in 2009 she was awarded a prestigious Marsden Fast-Start Award by the Royal Society of New Zealand. She is the author of a travel book as well as of articles published in journals including *Studies in Travel Writing*, *Studies in Romanticism*, and *ELH*. She is also the editor of an edition of Mary Wollstonecraft's only travel book, co-editor of an edition of Charlotte Smith's poems, and author of the pre-1840 chapter of a new *History of New Zealand Literature* (2016).

CAMBRIDGE STUDIES IN ROMANTICISM

This series aims to foster the best new work in one of the most challenging fields within English literary studies. From the early 1780s to the early 1830s a formidable array of talented men and women took to literary composition, not just in poetry, which some of them famously transformed, but in many modes of writing. The expansion of publishing created new opportunities for writers, and the political stakes of what they wrote were raised again by what Wordsworth called those "great national events" that were "almost daily taking place": the French Revolution, the Napoleonic and American wars, urbanization, industrialization, religious revival, an expanded empire abroad, and the reform movement at home. This was an enormous ambition, even when it pretended otherwise. The relations between science, philosophy, religion, and literature were reworked in texts such as *Frankenstein* and *Biographia Literaria*; gender relations in *A Vindication of the Rights of Woman* and *Don Juan*; journalism by Cobbett and Hazlitt; poetic form, content, and style by the Lake School and the Cockney School. Outside Shakespeare studies, probably no body of writing has produced such a wealth of comment or done so much to shape the responses of modern criticism. This indeed is the period that saw the emergence of those notions of "literature" and of literary history, especially national literary history, on which modern scholarship in English has been founded.

The categories produced by Romanticism have also been challenged by recent historicist arguments. The task of the series is to engage both with a challenging corpus of Romantic writings and with the changing field of criticism they have helped to shape. As with other literary series published by Cambridge, this one will represent the work of both younger and more established scholars, on either side of the Atlantic and elsewhere.

For a complete list of titles published, see end of book.

WOMEN WANDERERS AND THE WRITING OF MOBILITY, 1784–1814

INGRID HORROCKS

Massey University, Wellington

CAMBRIDGE
UNIVERSITY PRESS

CAMBRIDGE
UNIVERSITY PRESS

University Printing House, Cambridge CB2 8BS, United Kingdom

One Liberty Plaza, 20th Floor, New York, NY 10006, USA

477 Williamstown Road, Port Melbourne, VIC 3207, Australia

4843/24, 2nd Floor, Ansari Road, Daryaganj, Delhi – 110002, India

79 Anson Road, #06–04/06, Singapore 079906

Cambridge University Press is part of the University of Cambridge.

It furthers the University's mission by disseminating knowledge in the pursuit of education, learning, and research at the highest international levels of excellence.

www.cambridge.org
Information on this title: www.cambridge.org/9781107182233
DOI: 10.1017/9781316856109

First published 2017

Printed in the United Kingdom by Clays, St Ives plc

A catalogue record for this publication is available from the British Library.

ISBN 978-1-107-18223-3 Hardback

For my parents

Contents

Illustrations

All illustrations are from Charlotte Smith, *Elegiac Sonnets and Other Poems* (London: Printed for T. Cadell, Junior, and W. Davies, 1797), Rare Book Division, Department of Rare Books and Special Collections, Princeton University Library. Figures 2.1–2.4 first appeared in the 1789 edition of the work. Figures 2.5–2.6 first appeared in the two-volume edition of 1797.

Acknowledgments

I am immensely grateful to all those who have helped me in the rather long journey involved in the writing of this book.

This project had its genesis long ago in a master's dissertation on women travel writers written at the University of York under the supervision of Harriet Guest and Jane Rendall, and a doctoral dissertation written at Princeton University under the supervision of Claudia Johnson, Sophie Gee, and James Richardson. I am incredibly grateful for the time and insights they each dedicated to my work and the various inspiring models they provided of what it means to be a scholar and writer.

I received a number of grants that made the initial research possible and I would in particular like to thank the British Council for the award of the Commonwealth Scholarship that began this journey and Princeton University for a doctoral grant to continue it. A Marsden Fast-Start Award from the Royal Society of New Zealand then encouraged and enabled its reconceptualization into this new project and its completion as it now stands. I am very grateful for this. I also owe a debt of gratitude to Massey University, and in particular the School of English and Media Studies, for providing me with an academic home on my return to New Zealand, and for a number of years of financial, departmental, and collegial support. I have also been supported by a number of Massey University Research Fund Awards.

For generous assistance over the years I would like to thank the library staff and curators at the following institutions: the British Library; Bodleian Libraries, University of Oxford; the Carl H. Pforzheimer Collection of Shelley and his Circle, New York Public Library; the Alexander Turnbull Library, National Library of New Zealand Te Puna Mātauranga o Aotearoa; Princeton University Library; and Massey University Libraries in Wellington and Palmerston North.

For insights, stimulating conversations, thoughtful readings, encouragement, advice, and friendships that have contributed to the making of this book, I thank Abby Bender, John Barrell, Linda Bree, Kerry Bystrom,

Deirdre Coleman, Thom Conroy, Nadia Ellis, Hannah Gerrard, Ian Goodwin, Joe Grixti, Abigail Heald, Evan Horowitz, Jocelyn Harris, Hannah Johnson, Suvir Kaul, Claire Knowles, Jonathan Lamb, Sinead MacNamara, Barry McCrea, Tina Makereti, John Muirhead, Alexandra Neel, Michael Newton, Bridget Orr, Peter Otto, Sean Phelan, Laura Sayre, Kim Stern, Esther Schor, Bethan Stevens, Philip Steer, Natasha Tessone, Heidi Thomson, Bryan Walpert, Deborah Weiss, Susan Wolfson, Miriama Young, and Wesley Yu. I thank in particular those who have read and commented on parts of this manuscript in its various iterations and also the two exceptionally helpful peer reviewers for Cambridge University Press. At various points I was also helped by three excellent research assistants, Pip Adam, Alexandra Paterson, and Tessa Pratt, as well as an indexer, Damian Love.

Special mention needs to be made of my academic writing group in Wellington: Elizabeth Gray, Nikki Hessell, and Sarah Ross. This book wouldn't have been written without you. Finally, my partner, Tim Corballis, deserves thanks for his unstinting support of all aspects of my life and work, as do my twin daughters, Lena and Natasha, for disrupting my life in all the right ways.

This book is dedicated with love to my parents, John and Virginia Horrocks, who taught me to love literature and to think about what it contributes to the world – to the original wanderers in my life, who have, nonetheless, always given me a great sense of home.

*

I would also like to thank the Rare Book Division, Department of Rare Books and Special Collections, Princeton University Library, for permission to use the images from their copy of Charlotte Smith's *Elegiac Sonnets*. An earlier version of the sections of Chapter 1 focused on James Thomson and Oliver Goldsmith was previously published as Ingrid Horrocks, "'Circling Eye' and 'Houseless Stranger': The New Eighteenth-Century Wanderer," *ELH (English Literary History)* 77.3 (Fall 2010): 665–87. It is reprinted with the permission of Johns Hopkins University Press. An earlier version of parts of Chapter 3 appeared previously in, Ingrid Horrocks, "'Her Ideas Arranged Themselves': Re-membering Poetry in Radcliffe," *Studies in Romanticism* (Winter 2008): 507–25. It is reprinted with permission. Small parts of Chapter 4 are adapted from the Introduction to *Letters Written during a Short Residence in Sweden, Norway, and Denmark*, by Mary Wollstonecraft, edited by Ingrid Horrocks (Peterborough, ON: Broadview, 2013). These are reprinted with the permission of Broadview Press.

Abbreviations

Em	Charlotte Smith, *The Emigrants. Charlotte Smith: Major Poetic Works*. Ed. Claire Knowles and Ingrid Horrocks. Peterborough, ON: Broadview, 2017.
ES	Charlotte Smith, *Elegiac Sonnets. Charlotte Smith: Major Poetic Works*. Ed. Claire Knowles and Ingrid Horrocks. Peterborough, ON: Broadview, 2017.
Task	William Cowper, *The Task. The Task and Selected Other Poems*. Ed. James Sambrook. London: Longman, 1994.
TMS	Adam Smith, *The Theory of Moral Sentiments*. Ed. Knud Haakonssen. Cambridge: Cambridge University Press, 2002.
Tr	Oliver Goldsmith, *The Traveller, or a Prospect of Society. The Poems of Thomas Gray, William Collins, and Oliver Goldsmith*. Ed. Roger Lonsdale. London: Longman, 1969.
Sp, Su, A, W	James Thomson, *Spring, Summer, Autumn, Winter* in *The Seasons*. Ed. James Sambrook. Oxford: Clarendon, 1981.

Introduction
Reluctant Wanderers

In the last days of the Scandinavian journey that would become the basis of her great post-Revolutionary travel book, Mary Wollstonecraft wrote, "I am weary of travelling – yet seem to have no home – no resting place to look to. – I am strangely cast off." This sentiment reverberates through her writings, as she repeatedly casts herself as a solitary wanderer.[1] Wollstonecraft is not alone in depicting movement as troubling. "Forlorn," "unhappy," "helpless," "harassed," and even "terrified" women wanderers populate British writing of the late eighteenth and early nineteenth centuries, especially women's writing. These are not travelers as we know them, adventuring out to explore the world, but unwilling pained figures, moving not because they choose to but because they have no choice. One of Ann Radcliffe's orphan heroines shudders at the mere possibility of becoming "a wanderer in the wide world; without friends to protect, or money to support her; the prospect was gloomy – was terrible!"[2] This book examines what these early women wanderers can show us about the terrors of leaving home. At the same time it explores what is exciting and expansive about such journeys beyond the familiar.

To be a wanderer is not quite the same as being a traveler: wandering assumes neither destination nor homecoming. The wanderer's narrative tends to work by digression and detour rather than by a direct route. Wanderers, and their narratives, are always in danger of becoming lost. A wanderer is also someone who moves from place to place encountering a series of different people, making her a natural vehicle for literary explorations of sympathy and sociability, social exclusion and loneliness.

The wanderer became a valuable metaphorical figure in the eighteenth century as writers encountered the implications of a more mobile and urbanized society, in which journeys beyond the domestic home or the town where one was born were becoming increasingly common. From the picaresque hero to the sentimental traveler or "man of feeling," to the iconic

I

traveler of Romantic writing, the male wanderer is a recurrent and familiar figure in texts of this period, while his journey is written into the DNA of the novelistic *Bildungsroman*. This book alters the familiar critical picture of an explosion in interest in wanderers in the late eighteenth century by finding an unexpected concentration of wanderers in women's texts. It also finds that women wanderers tend to bear the worst consequences of wandering. I focus on works by four key women authors, Charlotte Smith, Ann Radcliffe, Mary Wollstonecraft, and Frances Burney. Here we find the haunting opposites of the pleasant meanderings of Henry Fielding's Tom Jones or Samuel Johnson's Rasselas, the leisurely travels of Laurence Sterne's Yorick, or even the burdened, but ultimately consoling, movements of William Wordsworth's traveler-poets. The female wanderers I look at typically inhabit more marginal social positions than their predominantly male predecessors or Romantic descendants – my authors are interested in a kind of deep homelessness, both physical and emotional. The structure of excursion and return that gives more familiar traditions of wandering a frame of security is distinctively lacking here: these pained wanderers are indigent, unpatronized poets dependent on the market; wives separated from abusive husbands; orphans whose guardians prey upon rather than protect them; unmarried mothers; unhoused widows; and émigrés in flight. Typically they lack a home, and in some cases never had one. Nor is the dignifying or glorifying romance model of the quest available to them. In these writings, travel is not what sociologist Georg Simmel described as an "adventure," a kind of "island in life," but the landscape of life itself.[3] An examination of these vulnerable wanderers makes movement in what is often seen as the first "great age of travel" look rather more frightening than has previously been understood. It also subtly shifts understandings of the history of both sympathy and mobility.

If this book is about travelers, poetic speakers, and characters in novels who wander not because they choose to but because they have no choice, it is also about texts that wander as much as their human subjects: it is about sonnet sequences that seem unable to stop; novels that digress endlessly from plot, stray from prose into verse, or quote other texts obsessively; and travel narratives that seem incapable of reaching a homecoming. Wandering can be productively understood as a formal trait of these texts as much as an activity that takes place within them. By reluctant wandering, evoked in the title phrase of this introduction, I mean literal movement that resists its own forward progression – and texts which seem to represent that resistance formally. My most ambitious objective in this book is to find ways of understanding wanderings (digressions) in writing we are only just learning to reread, and to ask what can be said about the formal aesthetics of texts that cannot or do not choose to chart a clear path forward. Throughout, I foreground the symbiotic relationship between wandering protagonists who cannot direct their routes and the formally wandering texts that they inhabit.

In approaching the question of how the aesthetics of texts of this period might be linked to their recurrent narratives of homelessness, I examine manifestations of literal and textual wandering within different genres. I start with the long poem, a poetic form especially useful for charting shifts in metaphorical depictions of the human figure in the landscape because of its focus on landscape descriptions and its accompanying meandering structure. Here I discuss a number of texts, written by both women and men, in particular, the long poems of James Thomson, Oliver Goldsmith, William Cowper, and Charlotte Smith. I then examine figurations of women's wandering in Smith's evolving sonnet sequence, *Elegiac Sonnets, and Other Poems* (1784–1800); Radcliffe's most digressive gothic novel, *The Mysteries of Udolpho* (1794); Wollstonecraft's only travel narrative, *Letters Written During a Short Residence in Sweden, Norway, and Denmark* (1796); and in Burney's last sentimental novel, *The Wanderer; or, Female Difficulties* (1814). I close the historical frame by means of an analysis, focused on Wordsworth, of what the tradition of the Romantic wanderer learns, and what it suppresses, from this female tradition. *Women Wanderers and the Writing of Mobility* identifies and explicates a cross-genre mode of writing and in doing so makes an argument for the formal distinctiveness of the literature of the late eighteenth century in general, literature that is still too often treated as merely transitional, or subsumed into pre-Romanticism. A significant body of new interdisciplinary thinking about mobility has for some time been reshaping scholarship across a number of fields. In exploring the story of an overlooked literary tradition of writing about movement, I aim to further expand the ways in which we are able to think through the relationships between travel, mobility, gender, social interaction, and literary form.

Wandering Sympathies

What roles do women wanderers play in more familiar traditions of wandering? To demarcate what the tradition of the reluctant woman wanderer involves, it will be helpful first to distinguish it from other traditions of writing about movement. While my focus is largely on women's wanderings in female-authored texts, to open up the landscape more generally I want to set this within a wider literary and cultural conversation drawing on both male- and female-authored writings.

To start with, figurations of the reluctant woman wanderer are distinct both from the male wanderers central to the eighteenth-century tradition of the sentimental journey and from the more easily passed over women bit players in this predominantly masculine tradition of writing about travel. In the quintessential male-authored texts of sentimental literature, gender serves a strategic structural function in demarcating and separating out the different aspects of the experience of mobility. Following on from the Grand Tour and associations of Enlightenment travel, opportunities for adventure and sympathy are predominantly linked to male travelers in works by Samuel Johnson, Laurence Sterne, and Henry MacKenzie. In tandem, the most dire effects of exposure and the potential to become lost – the disquieting resonances of movement more associated with wandering than travel – tend to be projected onto female figures. This is already a complication of the archetypal Odysseus and Penelope narrative. There the male traveler's journey is enabled by a woman who stays stationary – functioning both as a metonym of home and as a point of origin to be left and returned to – and who becomes linked to the nineteenth-century trope of the domestic woman as angel of the house.[4] In their sentimental and Romantic formations, frequently mobile female figures enable the male traveler's journey by absorbing, and voicing, the more troubling aspects of mobility itself.

In *Rasselas* (1759) it is Johnson's woman wanderer, not his traveler prince, whom he uses to register the shock of the move from the security of the domestic, or the stationary hilltop view, to the potential vulnerability of the nomadic. When the little troop ventures out of the Happy Valley – Johnson's dystopic Eden – to begin their wanderings about the world, the prince, Rasselas, anticipates "all the pleasures of travel." By contrast,

> The princess and her maid turned their eyes towards every part, and, seeing nothing to bound their prospect, considered themselves as in danger of being lost in a dreary vacuity. They stopped and trembled. 'I am almost afraid, said the princess, to begin a journey of which I cannot perceive an end, and to venture into this immense plain where I may be approached on every side by men whom I never saw.' The prince felt nearly the same emotions, though he thought it more manly to conceal them.[5]

What is revealing about this particular familial tableau of the emotional division of labor is that Johnson suggests, somewhat humorously, that

Rasselas experiences "nearly" the same feelings as his sister despite his seeming excitement. The distinction, Johnson implies, is one of expression. While both travelers feel "unmanly" anxiety about beginning a journey, it is, by implication, Nekayah's "womanly" task to voice fear of the unknown – like Milton's Eve, to lament the move to "wander down / Into a lower World, to this obscure / And wilde ..."[6] In a reversal of conventional discourses of aesthetics, it is women travelers who are made to anticipate the sublime terrors which face a wanderer in the world outside the home – the sense of exposure, lack of direction, and perhaps most importantly, loneliness and fear in a wide world inhabited by strangers. It is as though the more troubling aspects of the journey are so threatening that a female voice becomes necessary as a vehicle for both expressing and dismissing these threats. The distinction made by Johnson is a contained version of the poetic examples I discuss in Chapter 1, where "the Man of philosophic Eye," to use James Thomson and William Cowper's terms, is carefully, and often anxiously, demarcated along class and gender lines from those exposed to the "horrid Prospect" and "formless Wild" where "comprehension wanders lost" (*A*, 1133, *W*, 281–83, *Task*, 4.75). Mobility, Johnson and others imply, if looked at – or spoken – directly, would endanger manliness itself.

Mobility might also endanger one's sanity, as Sterne suggests by means of the figure of Maria of Moulines in his hugely popular fictionalized travel narrative, *A Sentimental Journey through France and Italy* (1768). In perhaps the most iconic tableau in sentimental literature, Sterne's satirical hero, Yorick, meets Maria "wandering somewhere about the road." While he has only been traveling for a matter of weeks, she tells him she has already

> stray'd as far as Rome, and walk'd round St Peter's once – and return'd back – that she found her way alone across the Apennines – had travell'd over all Lombardy without money – and through the flinty roads of Savoy without shoes.[7]

Sterne links the different journeys Maria has taken with dashes in a way that accentuates their stuttering, random, and directionless quality, as though she can no more narrate her wanderings than she can understand them. "Poor Maria" as "disorder'd maid" embodies a nightmare version of that state Nekayah fears in such an unmanly way: Maria has become lost, both literally and psychologically, on a journey without end. Yorick's pity for this fellow wanderer is precisely what insulates him from the vulnerability that identification with her, and with the aspects of wandering she represents, might bring. Yorick, and so Sterne, depicts Maria's vast travels as "weaknesses and wanderings," implicitly constructing the equivocal masculinity of the sentimental traveler – and the onward movement of his journey – on the foundation of the extremity of her vulnerability and lack of direction. When Yorick jauntily "journieth on his way" at the end of their tear-fueled encounter, he leaves Maria literally standing in the public marketplace, as much on the road as ever, and more dangerously so than he ever will be.[8]

Three decades later, as part of what Susan Wolfson calls Romanticism's "fascination of male poetics with female formations,"[9] William Wordsworth also turns repeatedly to depictions of women wanderers, from the beggar in *An Evening Walk* (1793), to the vagrants of the Salisbury Plains poems and *Lyrical Ballads* (1798 and 1800), to distressed Margaret in *The Ruined Cottage* (1798) and Book I of *The Excursion* (1814). I will return to this with particular reference to the work of David Simpson later in this introduction, and in more detail in the coda at the end of the book. Wordsworth's women wanderers also tend to bear the worst consequences of wandering; indeed, these consequences are frequently fatal. At the same time, as in sentimental literature their stories are often bracketed by being told to an interlocutor of some sort, frequently another traveler who meets her on the road. This bracketing traveler and narrator is again usually male and in his most iconic form can "*afford* to suffer / with those whom he saw suffer," implying both emotional and economic resources the women wanderers in these encounters lack.[10]

Without overemphasizing the continuity between Sterne and Wordsworth, in whose work such encounters become radically more troubling, the persistent recurrence of this figure of the woman wanderer across decades and across literary forms suggests its general usefulness and centrality to efforts in this period to think through, and at times to diffuse, the unsettling implications of a more mobile society. As exemplified in the Sterne example, these female figures of abjection and loss are often sighted, engaged with, and moved on from – being left with startling frequency to madness or death. Yet the recurrent presence of these women wanderers within male wanderers' stories suggests that in this period they in some sense work as the emblematic means of constructing the male wanderer's condition. One of the questions I pose is whether wandering men in this age are themselves always potentially in a female subject position, or whether female wanderings are categorically different from male wanderings in texts of this period. Either way, the condition signified by female wandering itself is never fully addressed in these male-authored texts; it is always (even if only obliquely) contained within a wider narrative, rather than being the subject of narrative itself. The women wanderers who appear in these sentimental texts, and who reappear as the countless female beggars, gypsies, and grieving widows of Romanticism, are suggestive of the deep homelessness explored by the women authors whose work is examined in this book, but they fail to fully represent it. Smith, Radcliffe, Wollstonecraft, and Burney are certainly working in conversation with these traditions, but they take on the riskier project of making the vulnerable figure of the woman wanderer their start and end point, in the process taking up all the potential for psychological and narrative crisis this move suggests. In a very real sense, the women poetic speakers, travelers, and characters depicted at the center of these female-authored texts cannot afford to suffer with those they see suffer, feeling persistently threatened by the task of encountering the wide world from a socially and economically unstable position.

The divergent imagining of the journey brought forward in these female-authored texts has especially important implications for our understandings of sympathy in the period in which it was theorized. Sympathy, broadly conceived as the "social passion" of "fellow-feeling," to use Adam Smith's terms, played a key role in imaginings of sociability and civil society in the eighteenth century (*TMS*, 47). In Smith's theorization of imaginative sympathy in *The Theory of Moral Sentiments* (1759–1790), which first appeared just under a decade before Sterne's sentimental journey (and which I will turn to in more detail shortly), the figure of the "spectator" is central. This figure is imagined engaged in the act of watching others suffer and working to participate in what other people feel. As James Chandler draws out in *An Archaeology of Sympathy: The Sentimental Mode in Literature and Cinema* (2013), what Sterne and the subgenre of writing about travel he influenced did with Smith's theorization was to make the journey through the world the central metaphor or "vehicle" for imaginings of sympathy. Sentimental travel literalized the series of encounters involved in engaging imaginatively with others, figuring this through actual movement through the world and as actual encounters with people. In the activities of the traveling spectator of the sentimental journey, writers fused physical mobility with virtual or emotional movement into other people's points of view, making the spectator a figure in motion, defined by his "capacity to move and be moved."[11] As I show in my first chapter, this shift can also be seen pictorially through the shift in landscape aesthetics that occurred over the century, from a privileging of the centralized, generalizing, raised prospect viewer to the emergence of the earthbound and open wanderer as a key figure for imagining social relations.

As a number of scholars have shown, sympathy in sentimental literature involved not just a "feeling for" others but often a "feeling down," or as Adam Smith puts it, a kind of "candid condescension and indulgent humanity" by the privileged classes (*TMS*, 29). Performances of sympathy require objects of sympathy, who in the literature of sensibility and of sentimental travel take a number of forms, from suffering women of various kinds, to slaves, to wounded soldiers and the rural poor displaced by enclosure. As Julie Ellison notes, the central texts of sensibility and sentimentality are not unaware of the potential embarrassments of these exchanges.[12] Nonetheless, scenes of sympathy in these texts, whether built on literal encounters or purely imagined ones, typically work by means of a hierarchical emotional exchange that posits an upper-middle-class man, or less often woman, as the idealized subject of sympathy, to be observed and admired in a transitory moment of feeling for someone else. The peculiar pleasures associated with such moments are exemplified by the "undescribable emotions" Sterne's Yorick feels as a result of weeping with Maria, which make him feel no less than "positive [he has] a soul."[13] In such moments, the ability to sympathize becomes a virtue in itself, "both a character trait and an intellectual performance enacted before an audience of friends and acquaintances" —and readers.[14]

In a shift from earlier critical understandings of sentimentality and sensibility, which saw them predominantly as enabling female expression, much has now been written about the heterosocial nature of what G. J. Barker-Benfield first dubbed the "cult of sensibility."[15] Claudia L. Johnson and others have argued that the sentimental "men of feeling" from Sterne through Edmund Burke frequently reduce women to being the objects of male tears by themselves occupying formerly feminine gender traits, while Ellison has delineated a longer political history of the predominance of "male tender-heartedness."[16] Wollstonecraft's own critique of sensibility in her two *Vindications* has played a vital role in this reassessment, as has her travel writing in the more recent critical shift, discussed in Chapter 4, that favors the view that women writers nonetheless managed to co-opt the language of sensibility and sentimental travel for their own ends.

If Sterne's sentimental traveler and Henry MacKenzie's "man of feeling" are emblematic of a way of imagining and exploring sympathy through a series of hierarchical encounters, then a divergent tradition of writing about movement must also involve a recalibration of conceptions of sympathy. Revealing things happen when a female political philosopher (Wollstonecraft's traveler in *A Short Residence*) or a highly educated female emigrant (Burney's Juliet), or even a gothic heroine (Radcliffe's Emily), takes the place of a mad Maria or a doomed female vagrant on the road. The bare fact of their refusal to (quite) go mad or die, and in the process to enable or make safe someone else's somewhat less troubled movements, makes new narratives of wandering and the individual mind necessary. Rather than splitting the wanderer figure in two – into its "male" and "female" attributes – these texts work to develop a figure that combines a Yorick and a Maria (spectator and sufferer, subject and object), concentrating vision and abjection in a single figure. The distress of women as depicted in sentimental literature is real, these women's revisions of the sentimental journey suggest, but we need to think harder about the social, political, and economic causes of those distresses – and about their wide-ranging effects.

Evocations of women's wanderings at the center of texts by authors such as Charlotte Smith, Wollstonecraft, and Burney, I argue, while by no means completely displacing the hierarchies at work in much sentimental literature and in much Romantic writing, nonetheless complicate the power relations implicit in traditions in which the suffering female is frequently figured as an object of a male protagonist's, and so a reader's, pity and concern. Once sympathy is no longer rendered safe by being understood as an interaction based on social inequality – of which gender is one of the clearest markers – it becomes exponentially more difficult to regulate and manage. As I discuss, Wollstonecraft has sympathy rise "to anguish" for her homeless traveler in *A Short Residence*; while "horror" at what someone else has done "occup[ies]" the mind of Radcliffe's gothic heroine.[17] The moment in Wollstonecraft amounts to a kind of emotional invasion of a too present awareness of the suffering of multiple others, that in Radcliffe to an eerie, haunting level of emotional vulnerability. Burney shows her homeless protagonist, Juliet, reduced to the condition of a kind of human automaton as a result of the unrelenting demands of others on her time, her labor, and her feelings. In presenting the female figures at the center of their texts as fitting awkwardly into the categories of either subject or object of feeling these writers challenge the structure on which sentimental literature is based.

More widely, the movements of women wanderers at the center of these works unsettle models such as Adam Smith's of a society bound by sympathy. In imagining the primary exchange of sympathy through the figure of the "impartial spectator," Smith is working within the tradition of a theory of moral judgment also found in the work of fellow Scottish

philosophers Francis Hutcheson and David Hume. In Smith, this spectator is conceived of as taking on, and in the process judging, the feelings of
others by means of explicit acts of the imagination. Smith writes, here as is
often the case signaling his posited spectator through the universal first
person plural, "we can form no idea of the manner in which they [the party
concerned] are affected, but by conceiving what we ourselves should feel in
the like situation." This involves an act of the imagination by which "we
place ourselves in his situation" and only once his feelings have been
"brought home to ourselves, when we have thus adopted and made them
our own" do they "begin at last to affect us" (*TMS*, 11–2). In *A Philosophical
Enquiry into the Origin of our Ideas of the Sublime and Beautiful* (1757),
Burke uses a similar formulation of emotional movement to Smith's
"imaginary change of situation" when he describes sympathy "as a sort of
substitution, by which we are put into the place of another man, and
affected in many respects as he is affected" (*TMS*, 26).[18] What Smith
particularly stresses is the act of "bringing home" others' feelings to
ourselves and testing them against what we would feel in the same
situation.

However, as D.D. Raphael has emphasized, such acts of imagination
explicitly do not always lead to sympathy in Smith's account, and Smith
makes sympathy (and the withholding of it) an essential component of his
theory of judgment and social relations. As Raphael summarizes of the
position of the spectator in Smith:

> If his own imagined feeling is the same as the actual feeling of the agent, he is
> 'sympathizing' with the agent, and his awareness of the sympathy (fellow-
> feeling) is given expression in approval, declaring that the action is appro-
> priate (right). If, on the other hand, his own imagined feeling differs from
> that of the agent, he lacks sympathy with the agent, and his awareness of this
> is given expression in disapproval, declaring that the action is inappropriate
> (wrong).[19]

Adam Smith proposes that the feeling of a suffering agent must be able to
accord with that of the spectator; otherwise, "when, upon bringing the case
home to himself, he finds that they do not coincide with what he feels, they
necessarily appear to him unjust and improper, and unsuitable to the
causes which excite them" (*TMS*, 20). To work as a system of moral
judgment, such a model is dependent on accepting a general idea of
humanity, and a generalizable "disinterested" or "impartial" spectator
who can act as a kind of template against which to judge, to use Smith's
terms, the "suitableness or unsuitableness," the "propriety or impropriety,"

and the "decency or ungracefulness" of people's actions and feelings (*TMS*, 22). To fall outside the bounds of sympathy in Smith, then, is also to fall outside the bounds of moral approval.[20]

That which only applies *partially* has little place in this system based on feelings that are communicable in a general sense. Smith repeatedly emphasizes that we cannot sympathize with the particular in others. "Even of the passions derived from the imagination," he writes, "those which take their origin from a peculiar turn or habit it has acquired, though they may be acknowledged to be perfectly natural, are, however, but little sympathized with" (*TMS*, 38). Smith figures the very expression of strong emotions that "arise from a certain situation or disposition of the body" (including "violent hunger" and one might assume gender) as an example of bad manners and as actually "indecent" and the object of "peculiar disgust." Even "to cry out with bodily pain" he describes as "unmanly and unbecoming" because it is "disproportioned" to what can be felt by an observer (*TMS*, 33–5). It is telling that here, as in Johnson, the expression of pain or fear is figured as "unmanly." The fact that Smith's generalized spectator is clearly male, while women are associated with embodied particularity and so not even quite able to participate fully as objects of sympathy, is suggested by his statement that "To talk to a woman as we would to a man is improper" (*TMS*, 34).

Smith's friend and mentor Hume's solution to situations and emotions that potentially transgress the limits of sympathy is that as "[e]very man's interest is peculiar to himself," in order to enable sociable sympathetic exchange people should use a "general language" formed for "general use" and that develops "a general point of view."[21] Smith's impartial spectator is elaborated from this basis in Hume, and like Hume, Smith repeatedly sets the "peculiar" up in contradistinction to this notion of the "general." This again mirrors the conceptions of landscape aesthetics and the prospect view discussed in the early parts of my first chapter. In that context, the general view, imagined as being removed from particularity, party politics, or profession, is prized as the only correct way to assess and present society as a whole. In the case of these models of sympathy and of landscape aesthetics, however, the notion of who can access the general is also clearly imagined in a curtailed way. Although Hume, for instance, suggests his collective is universal, his model of sympathy in fact is assumed only to operate within polite society or small social circles within that, imagined as a "Club or Knot of Companions."[22]

Smith adds an important additional element to Hume's solution to the problem of the particular or individual in relation to generalized sympathy: Smith turns, in what Raphael sees as his major original contribution to moral philosophy, to the "*effect on the agent* of the reactions of spectators."[23] Just as spectators work to "assume the circumstances of the person principally concerned," Smith argues, the person principally concerned must "in some measure" work "to assume those of the spectators." In order to produce the "concords" of shared feelings on which Smith suggests the very "harmony of society" is dependent, Smith argues that a sufferer should "flatten" or "bring down his emotions to what the spectator can go along with" (*TMS*, 27, 29). Smith puts a new emphasis on "constancy," "patience," and "endurance" in suffering itself (*TMS*, 37). This is the basis of Smith's stoic objection to the expression of strong or "excessive" passions: passions should be neither too high nor too low, he suggests, but should aim for a certain, communicable "mediocrity" (*TMS*, 32). As Raphael observes, if the spectator's virtue in Smith is the Christian one of humanity, what he demands of the sufferer or active agent is the stoic virtue of "self-command."[24]

Through his notion of the "supposed impartial spectator" Smith then extends this model in a way that makes it relevant also to how people conceive of their own feelings and behavior, whether or not there is a bystander present to observe them. In later versions of *The Theory of Moral Sentiments*, as the notion of self-control becomes paramount, Smith argues that moral agents should learn to only feel for themselves as they imagine others might feel for them.[25] By this point Smith's model sets out to account not just for how people judge others but also for how they judge and monitor their own actions and feelings through a theory of imagined sympathy and an internalized imagined spectator. We "examine our own conduct as we imagine any other fair and impartial spectator would examine it," Smith writes (*TMS*, 310, 129).

Besides being dependent on accepting the notion of a generalizable spectator, as David Simpson points out in *Wordsworth, Commodification and Social Concern: The Poetics of Modernity* (2009), this model of social relations and self-assessment is entirely dependent on an acceptance of sympathetic communication as achievable and as a good in itself.[26] "How are the unfortunate relieved when they have found out a person to whom they can communicate the cause of their sorrow?" Smith asks rhetorically, assured he knows the answer to be affirmative (*TMS*, 18). For Simpson, in Adam Smith, "Sympathy is a function of a desire for sympathy, or the desire for consensus . . . a mediated formation whereby the subject seeks to produce itself into an exchangeable item."[27] He argues that this makes Smith primarily a theorist of the normative and of normalization, a branch of moral philosophy inherited by thinkers such as Simmel and Jürgen Habermas and in more recent imaginings of civil society.[28] Smith's sense of the need to "flatten" one's emotions to a level of communicable mediocrity finds echoes, for instance, in Simmel's version of "pure interaction" in his essay "On Sociability" (1910), in which his "*artificial*" or play world of sociability is "made up of beings who have renounced both the objective and the purely personal features of the intensity and extensiveness of life in order to bring about among themselves a pure interaction, free of any disturbing material accent."[29] As Simpson observes, theories such as Adam Smith's have little to say about what happens when the unfortunate do not feel relieved by actual or imagined sympathetic exchange, when a desire for sympathy or "concord" is not present, or when this desire disappears or has broken down.[30]

Failures of sympathy are central to the literary evocations of the reluctant woman wanderer in the women's text I examine, as Simpson argues they become in Wordsworth's poetry, where figures such as the Old Cumberland Beggar are repeatedly presented in ways that break with the "Smithian circle," marked by reciprocal desires for emotional exchange.[31] Indeed, the women I write about anticipate the move Simpson suggests is original to Wordsworth's poetry. Simpson reads Wordsworth's work as refusing to adhere to either the stoical-Smithian or sentimental versions of sympathy. In his account, rather than presenting the expected tableaux of sympathetic interactions restorative of social relations, Wordsworth repeatedly stages encounters between people that "dramatize alienation rather than community" and failed connections rather than sympathy realized. In these interactions in Wordsworth, Simpson argues, which are markedly without celebration of dialogue or mutual accommodation, "the sufferer makes *no* effort to adjust his or her self-presentation in order to allow for the comfortably empathic reaction in the spectator."[32] Writing of Wordsworth's use of female figures such as the "hunger-bitten girl," whom Wordsworth writes of meeting in France in 1792 and Margaret of *The Ruined Cottage* among other moments, Simpson concludes: these are not "the standard picaresque or charitable interaction in which some bond is established between strangers that models or presages the initiation of a social contract. Instead, the poem[s] presents an anatomy of how hard it can be to take that step."[33] The women writers discussed in *Women Wanderers and the Writing of Mobility* anticipate Wordsworth's move, and as I explicate across the following chapters and address more explicitly in my coda, in placing women at the center of their texts rather than as secondary figures in sentimental tableaux as tends to happen in Wordsworth, foreground the particular, or peculiar, of individual experience, and the difficulty of communicating this. One might see these as interactions in which the "disturbing material accent" and "intensity and extensiveness of life" that Simmel alludes to cannot be set aside.

I am interested in this book, then, in where a system of sympathetic exchange such as that of Adam Smith leaves those who cannot for whatever reason generalize their stories so that they appear as more than individual sufferings – as more than Maria's "weaknesses and wanderings." I am interested in where it leaves partial stories, as well as sufferings that may seem excessive, perverse, mad, or self-inflicted. These texts question how such human beings and literary speakers are to take part in the sociability of sympathetic exchange, as either subjects or objects of feeling. They explore what changes when Adam Smith's "he" is a "she." As feminist and postcolonial scholarship has so extensively shown, a marginal voice is inherently a voice which does not automatically have access to the implicitly political power to generalize.[34] The texts foregrounded in my book show that the gendered hierarchies of sympathy cannot simply be reversed: because we do not automatically see a woman writer (or traveler), for example, as speaking with the voice of tradition, what we tend to see before us (still), "with painful clarity," is the "individual woman ... rather than the representative man" or often, not even the representative woman.[35] Such seemingly individual voices can all too easily be dismissed as presenting themselves as objects of feeling "merely" asking for pity, and for that very reason not even meriting compassionate sympathy, a problem of which all four women writers at the center of this study are acutely aware. The movements of women wanderers at the center of these works, then, unsettle circulating models of sympathy in three central ways: they destabilize the hierarchies assumed within these model, they highlight the limitations of both the idealized figure of the disinterested spectator and of the sentimental traveler, and they make way for explorations of encounters in which sufferers refuse or are unable to modulate their suffering in the way theorists argued they must in order to enter acceptably into the sociable system of sympathy. Even Adam Smith's basic organizing metaphor—based on the "bringing home" of feeling to oneself—becomes ironic and troubling in relation to gendered, mobile subjects who are *homeless* both on literal and psychological levels. Characteristically, when the reluctant woman wanderer takes up the position of the subject of sympathy, it is as an involved and *partial* rather than as impartial spectator. And she frequently falls outside the recognized bounds of objects of sympathy. In returning again and again to the figure of the woman wanderer, these texts stress the fundamental danger of sympathetic inter-action for some, and the psychic as well as practical implications of that danger. Given the centrality of such imaginings of sympathetic exchange to imaginings of civil society, repeated representations of failures of feeling evoke radical ruptures in the social fabric. If sentimental travel and its descendants literalized the imaginative encounters central to philosophical understandings of society such as Adam Smith's, then the encounters enacted in narratives of pained, gendered wandering highlight the con-tingencies of that imagined world.

Before moving on, the tradition of the reluctant woman wanderer needs to be distinguished from one further set of familiar associations of wandering, those that link women's wandering directly to error and moral fall. This connotation of wandering is taken to its most exaggerated form in the period my book focuses on in novels such as Charlotte Dacre's gothic work, *Zofloya, or the Moor* (1806), and the two novels by Percy Bysshe Shelley it influenced, *Zastrozzi, A Romance* and *St Irvyne; or, The Rosicrucian: A Romance* (1810–1811). These are novels of rampant female desire – startlingly so after the more muted texts of the previous decade – and in them "wandering" is assigned markedly gendered and moral associations. The original sin in *Zofloya* is the "wanderings" of the mother's affections away from her husband and children, and the general moral given that a guard "should be constantly checked over the wander-ings of the heart," and in particular of female hearts. As the daughter, Victoria, herself moves further and further from the paths of virtue, her ideas and eyes increasingly frequently "wildly wander[]," and she wanders into the "pathless forest," both literally and metaphorically. At the end of the novel, Victoria confronts her mother with her crime: "Thy heart wandered from its allegiance to thy husband, my heart wandered from mine."[36] Both women's crimes lead directly to their husbands' deaths. Such wanderings in the "trackless forests" are repeated and exaggerated through Shelley's character of Matilda in *Zastrozzi*, herself also a textual descendant of Matthew Lewis' sexually voracious Matilda in *The Monk: A Romance* (1797). Shelley's Matilda's wanderings in search of the man she loves involve "casting off all sense of decorum" and outstepping "the bounds of modesty."[37] Jane Austen's *Mansfield Park* (1814) provides a more confined example of this kind of female wandering in the charged scene on Mr. Rushmore's estate in which Maria Bertram ventures with

Henry Tilney around the edge of the garden gate and into the park beyond.[38] Again, this first act of wandering proves fatal to Maria's future marriage.

The (im)morality of female characters' wanderings in Dacre's and Shelley's novels, in particular, is made more marked by the fact that wandering tends to be used quite differently in the depiction of the activity of the male characters in these novels. In *Zofloya*, Victoria's brother Leonardo, for instance, also becomes a wanderer as a result of his mother's actions. However, Leonardo is presented as a traveler and a victim of circumstance, akin to a hero of romance on trial, while the moral lapse is, at least at first, kept squarely in the realm of the mother: when Leonardo is forced to "once more resume[ ] his wanderings," he laments, "now I am again an outcast on the wide expanse of creation, no friend, no home, nor a prospect of obtaining bread for tomorrow's subsistence: Oh mother!"[39] By contrast, in the reluctant movement concentrated in women's texts the misery associated with the act of woman's wandering is explicitly separated from moral fault. Instead this condition of distress is represented as being the result of social circumstances rather than of either moral failing or choice – and this condition is represented as only being exacerbated by mistaken social assumptions that, as Burney puts it, a person's "misfortunes" must be "the effect of their crimes."[40] These texts challenge us to think more about the reasons some people become displaced, the material and psychological difficulties that follow, and why they might need to tell their stories in the way they do.

Framing Mobilities

The time span this book covers is a wartime one.[41] The first edition of Smith's *Elegiac Sonnets*, which I read as the germinal text in this tradition of writing about reluctant women wanderers, appeared in 1784 shortly after Britain's abandonment of their claim to North America after nearly a decade of warfare. This year also saw the completion of William Cowper's important transitional text, *The Task* (1785), which responds directly to the national and global upheavals of the 1780s, and which I discuss in the opening chapter. The two great texts of wandering with which the book closes, Frances Burney's *The Wanderer; or, Female Difficulties* and William Wordsworth's *The Excursion*, were both published in 1814, the final year of the war between Britain and France that was fought almost without interruption from 1793. Within this wider time frame, the most sustained literary explorations of the figure of the woman wanderer are concentrated in the turbulent 1790s, the period of extreme social, political, and economic upheaval in Britain that followed the French Revolution and the declaration of war. In this decade, literal wanderers, from discharged soldiers, to emigrants, to war widows, to the growing ranks of the homeless, became more literally visible on the landscape. Literary texts that figure troubled wanderers in this period are in part responding to this historical reality.

Representatively, the 1790s saw the arrival of thousands of French refugees on the stretch of coastline from Dover to Southampton, who came in increasing numbers following the September massacres in France in the autumn and winter of 1792. For the next 10 years, it is estimated that around 12,000 émigrés arrived in Britain per annum.[42] While many were members of the ancien regime elites, bringing with them their class privilege and at least part of their wealth, others arrived in need of the most basic assistance, coming in open boats with little but the clothes they wore.[43] A periodical such as the *Analytical Review*, as well as a flurry of pamphlets, shows debates within Britain about how to regard and treat these new arrivals taking place with similar heat to debates about the wisdom of war, and about broader questions of rights raised in works such as Thomas Paine's *Rights of Man* (1791). For some, the displaced emigrants should be treated as "*strangers in distress*," while for others they could be divided between Nobility and "respectable Citizens" opposed to the Revolution in France, and "Adventurers and vagabonds" come to ferment revolution within Britain, that is, as "vermin who were so much the more dangerous as they were in perpetual motion."[44] The controversial Aliens Act passed in 1793 made way for unprecedented levels of surveillance and control of the movements of foreign nationals in Britain and, despite being opposed by the Whig opposition as breaching basic human rights, was passed in an atmosphere of political and social panic.[45] The demands of these new arrivals and the economic and emotional toll taken by the ensuing war, along with disastrous harvests in the 1790s and resulting food scarcity, led to hugely increased levels of poverty and homelessness.[46] As the crisis intensified, all those with an "unsettled way of life" came to be seen as potential sources of political and social unrest. As Quentin Bailey has shown, harsh new penal measures were brought in that altered the 1744 Vagrancy Act, bringing in tighter regulations on vagrants, peddlers, beggars, discharged soldiers, and travelers and wanderers of all kinds, and making the lack of a home or ostensible livelihood a crime worthy of newly severe punishment.[47] *Habeas corpus* was suspended in mid-1794, allowing for detention without trial and by the end of 1795 two repressive "Gagging Acts" – the Treasonable Practices Bill and the repressive Seditious Meeting Bill – became law, effectively crushing the reform movement and placing ever tighter controls on people's movements and freedom of expression.[48]

Smith's poem about the emigrants and Burney's story of a female refugee, in particular, address themselves directly to the emigrant crisis of the 1790s, using it to hold up a mirror to Britain's internal political and affective economy. Both authors situate those displaced by war at the center of their texts, staging complex engagements with questions of how far social sympathy does and should extend, and arguing forcefully for the social causes of displacements of all kinds and their attendant anguishes. They place uprooted foreign women, thrust into "unprotected poverty" by circumstance, as well as their British female counterparts, at the heart of this discussion.[49] Wollstonecraft declares that in the climate of the 1790s women do not even have a nation, for "the laws of her country – if women have a country – afford her no protection or redress"[50] and she figures herself in *A Short Residence* not so much as a British traveler in Europe, than as a woman socially and perpetually exiled on some basic level. While Radcliffe approaches these debates rather more obliquely, the question of who gets to move and speak and who doesn't, as well as who controls that movement and speech and the effects of that control, are crucial to her work. While the 1790s, also of course the decade of *Lyrical Ballads* (1798 and 1800), is the locus of all the key texts I discuss in this book, the longer time frame of my study allows me both to situate the figure of the wanderer in its eighteenth-century context and to explore some of its nineteenth-century developments.

Notwithstanding its end date and focus on the 1790s, however, this is importantly an eighteenth-century project. Over the historical period this book covers the literary associations of wandering were being transformed, shifting from connections with *travail*, that is, labor, toil, and sorrow, to Romantic notions of freedom. Histories of walking and vagrancy by literary historians such as Anne Wallace have shown that in medieval and early modern periods, moving without direct purpose outside prescribed geographical bounds was conceived of both as a kind of suffering and as literally criminal.[51] However, by the mid eighteenth century mobility had been separated from its necessary roots in criminality (something the reactionary moves in the 1790s sought to partially reinstate) and was only slowly becoming detached from an association with suffering. In his 1755 dictionary, Samuel Johnson still traces *to travel* to its derivation in *travail*, but separates this suffering from the verb's modern meanings, noting that in its modern sense "to travel" signals more properly "to journey" than "to labour." He links this activity, especially when conceived of as a "journey of curiosity or instruction," directly to the Enlightenment project of enlargement of the mind and a greater understanding of society.[52] By contrast, at this mid-century juncture Johnson assigns no such value to the act of wandering, which retains all the older negative associations gradually being detached from travel proper, and in its troubling uncertainty and lack of direction runs contrary to the emerging definitions of acceptably destination-orientated movement. Johnson defines *wandering* as "uncertain peregrination," and the accompanying example from Joseph Addison directly equates such "wand'rings" with "toils." To the verb *to wander*, uniquely among its near synonyms, *to rove, to ramble, to walk*, and *to travel*, Johnson assigns exclusively negative connotations. His definition, "To rove; to ramble here and there; to go, without any certain course," is glossed, "It has always a sense of either evil or flight, and imports either idleness, vitiousness, or misery."[53]

Yet just over half a century later it was wandering that had become the Romantic activity *par excellence*, associated with sympathy and vision and almost inextricable from explorations of the Romantic subject. Wordsworth's walks around the lakes and further afield are specifically constructed as acts of wandering rather than travel, and in them the process of the journey became newly central as distinct from the destination. Johnson's own *Rasselas* as well as Sterne's *A Sentimental Journey* played a role in making way for this transformation. Romantic notions of wandering, and more widely travel, as a vehicle of self-discovery have proved hugely influential on subsequent imaginings of mobility. Most scholarly histories of wandering, with varying degrees of skepticism, take Romantic conceptions as their watershed moment and as their starting point. Over the past two decades, a number of book-length studies have been published on "walking," "vagrancy," and "homelessness" in late eighteenth- and early nineteenth-century literary culture.[54] In all cases, these scholars of movement take Wordsworth as their touchstone and demonstrate the influential, and consequential, equation made between movement and freedom of choice in what Anne Wallace and Robin Jarvis term the Romantic "peripatetic," and Celeste Langan terms "Romantic vagrancy."[55] Freedom of choice is even central to Carl Thompson's model in *The Suffering Traveller and the Romantic Imagination* (2007), built on the basis of a masculine agenda of the Romantic canon as traditionally conceived, which he argues places "misadventure" at the center of travel in part in an effort to remasculinize the journey at a point when travel was becoming more accessible to women.[56] One might expect the recurrence in Romantic texts to figures of homelessness and vagrancy, so often women, to collapse the positive associations of mobility, but as Langan in particular illuminates (and questions), "Romantic vagrancy" is based on a construction of an analogy of equivalent freedom between all wanderers.[57]

In the woman's texts I write about, movement continues to be figured as strongly associated with work or suffering, and is often experienced as relentless motion rather than, as later texts have taught us to expect, enabling liberating moments of vision, sympathy, or insight. Movement is frequently constituted as the opposite of freedom. Part of the work *Women Wanderers and the Writing of Mobility* does is to direct attention to texts that remind us of older, darker associations of movement at precisely the moment these were first being obscured from literary view. While in much Romantic literature, especially in its post-1790s forms, the margins become paradoxically central and authoritative, the journeys of the women wanderers I look at, as I have begun to suggest, illuminate what it means to wander here below, without access to authority or the ability to universalize one's feelings of isolation.

In directing attention to this overlooked, cross-genre body of texts that illuminate precisely the kinds of difficulties suppressed by some Romantic reimaginings of movement as freedom, this book steps into the space opened up by work such as Langan's which has denaturalized this Romantic equation. This is a similar move to that performed by Michael Wiley in *Romantic Migrations: Local, National, and Transnational Dispositions* (2008) and Toby Benis in *Romantic Diasporas: French Émigrés, British Convicts, and Jews* (2009), who redirect the critical gaze to the presence of forced migrations and diaspora in the texts of this period, starting from the founding observation that although the trope of the exile may be central to the self-imagining of poets such as Byron, and to a lesser extent Samuel Taylor Coleridge and Percy Bysshe Shelley, "[y]et for many, exile was not an aesthetic or a political pose, but a brutal historical reality."[58] Where my approach differs from that of Wiley and Benis is both in my focus on the gendering of difficult movement rather than the movements of mass migrations, and in bringing forward a tradition that I read as primarily eighteenth century rather than Romantic. Although the tradition of the reluctant wanderer arose just before, and even concurrently with, that of the Romantic wanderer, it is most revealing when read in the context of eighteenth-century conceptions of sympathy, interiority, and formal drifting, and in an intellectual space in which wandering was not necessarily already annexed to freedom. Benis, though, shares my interest in how to read relationships between specific kinds of movements and social situations on the one hand, and specific literary forms on the other. She asks "how the structure of these Romantic-era narratives are shaped, and destabilized, by the awareness and experience of diaspora."[59] My research aims to take seriously the failures of transcendence enacted in a different body of literature, and the personal and political desolations these authors seek forms to represent. The title phrase of this introduction, "reluctant wanderers," is meant to allow for a recoupling of wandering with its more disquieting roots – for a reassociation of wandering with "unwillingness," "disinclination," "hesitation," or in the now rare meaning of reluctant, offering opposition.[60]

Most broadly, my approach operates in conversation with, and aims to contribute to, new interdisciplinary work being done on travel and mobility. Influenced by critics such as Edward Said, James Clifford, Sara Mills, and Elizabeth Bohls, most scholars of travel now tend to emphasize and explore the way in which travel means different things to different people. Such work consistently reaches beyond what Clifford calls the "travel myth" of the traveler as "someone who has the security and privilege to move about in relatively unconstrained ways," to take in movements such as those involved in captivity narratives, economic migrations, or the experiences of refugees.[61] Work on mobility is now exploring the movements of people and things, the meanings, metaphors, and ideologies attached to mobility over time, and also attempting to develop a new set of analytical tools adequate to the complexity of various mechanisms of movement. Even more than the expanded emphasis of scholarship on travel, the new methodologies associated with the "mobilities paradigm" in the social sciences bring into view a whole new range of human movements *as* movement, and provide ways of exploring what happens to people and things (and feelings) in the spaces in between places, when subjected to persistent or enforced mobility, or simply in the mundane movements of everyday lives. This work has extensively demonstrated the many ways in which, on the contrary to being associated with freedom, mobility is frequently associated with, and reinscribes, social and economic inequalities of all kinds.[62] The range of literal and metaphorical mobilities discussed in this book adds to the kinds of overlooked forms of movement the "mobilities turn" in scholarship aims to make available for exploration. The specific instances of complex engagements with mobility I discuss might be seen as a strongly literary contribution to the "microhistories of 'displaced' things and persons" Stephen Greenblatt calls for in his edited collection of new approaches to thinking about mobility, *Cultural Mobility: A Manifesto* (2010).[63] Mobilities research has in turn informed my readings in the chapters that follow, providing vocabularies and approaches for foregrounding and connecting different kinds of mobility and for thinking about the ways in which "socially produced motion" is experienced and represented.[64] A concept such as "network capital," for example, which sociologist John Urry argues can be set alongside Pierre Bourdieu's analysis of forms of economic and cultural capital, and incorporates such things as having the travel documents that make travel safe, to "movement capacity" such as being able to walk distances, proves useful for thinking about what is so immensely difficult about a situation such as that of Burney's refugee protagonist.[65]

Work in this new interdisciplinary field has highlighted the importance of complex understandings of historical traditions of movement because it consistently locates mobility as central to Western modernity *and* as rooted in late eighteenth- and early nineteenth-century shifts in social and political economy and corresponding conceptual shifts. Key theorizations of the field in the social sciences, such as Urry's *Mobilities* (2007), and cultural geographers Tim Cresswell's *On the Move: Mobility in the Modern Western World* (2006) and Peter Adey's *Mobility* (2010), begin from the assumption and develop the claim that "mobility is central to what it is to be modern."[66] This correspondence is exemplified in the key figures for the modern (and subsequently postmodern) subject in art and theory: the *flâneur*, the valorized nomad, the tourist, and the exile.[67] As Simpson notes, "We are seemingly obsessed with theorizing refugees, nomads and displaced (and sometimes resurgent) multitudes as the governing figures of a global postmodern condition."[68] Within historically grounded, field-shaping theorizations of mobility such as Urry's, Cresswell's, and Adey's, the late eighteenth century frequently stands as the period in which it is possible to locate the initial shift to "a way of thinking in terms of mobility – a metaphysics of mobility that is distinct from what came before it."[69]

Within the actual histories of the conceptual shift that recur in these studies, however, the intellectual contribution of the eighteenth and early nineteenth century still tends to be focused on the influential annexation of mobility to freedom. Cresswell cites Thomas Hobbes's equation between human mobility and freedom along with eighteenth-century English jurist William Blackstone's argument that the right to personal liberty is " 'loco-movement'," consisting of the ability of " 'changing situation, or removing one's person to whatsoever place one's own inclination may direct'."[70]

Urry draws extensively on Jarvis and Wallace and their histories of the emergence of male leisure walking both in the country and in the new spaces of the modern city, where footpaths were first introduced in the eighteenth century.[71] The very acknowledgment of the problems associated with women's access to such modes of movement in accounts such as these has the unintended, but inadvertent, effect of seeming to reconfine women (along with other subjects without access to at least middle-class male privilege) to a stationary position. I would argue that this is the inevitable, persistent effect of how we have conceived of the history of movement in this era, based on our inheritance of the ideological connection between travel and freedom. It is an effect that obscures the very real frequency with which women occupy the doubly disenfranchised position of coerced wanderer.

The direct influence over the past decade of new critical understandings of mobility can be seen in work on the literature of the eighteenth and early nineteenth centuries such as that by Wiley and Benis, as well as by Miranda Burgess, Alan Bewell, Kevis Goodman, James Chandler, and Wolfram Schmidgen. Critics such as Burgess and Bewell, in particular, along with scholars working in adjacent areas such as Jonathan Lamb, are engaged in the work of constructing a more nuanced picture of the new global "conditions of mobility" that emerged in the eighteenth century and the ways in which these irrevocably altered imaginings and representations of society and of the human subject.[72] One of the contributions of new approaches to mobility is that they provide ways of investigating mobility on different scales alongside one another, including the literal with the abstract or metaphorical, and the physical with the emotional.[73] New work focused in this period has paid close and fruitful attention to voyages of exploration, patterns of emigration, and to the depopulation caused by enclosure; to rapid changes in global transportation systems for people, goods, plants, and mail; and to developments in inland navigation within Britain through the extension of the canal system, followed by the compression of space with the rapid development of the railways.[74] At the same time, this work challenges us to consider how the fundamental philosophical, intellectual, and literary shifts that occurred in this period can be understood as directly responding to these transformations in social, economic and political economy, and, most significantly, as structured in their very conception by issues of mobility.

Of especially, direct relevance to my book is the way this recent critical work has illuminated the extent to which the new conditions of mobility (of goods as well as people) became central to imaginings and metaphorical constructions of sympathy, something we will see at work in Wollstonecraft and Burney's writing, for example, where the limits of sympathy are tested against the new demands of finance capitalism. Eighteenth-century theorizations of sympathy are a natural starting point for both affect studies and mobility studies because of a shared concern with the mobility of emotions and with imagining community across distance. This was a period in which the likelihood not only of moving oneself, but of daily encounters with people, goods, and information from elsewhere, increased exponentially. The fact that Sterne popularized Smith's imaginings of sympathy through the metaphor of the journey at this particular historical juncture is not coincidental. Burgess, in particular, argues that "the analysis of mobile affect that emerges in the later part of the eighteenth century is part of a broader contemporary analysis of mobility over distance, which intersects, in turn, with the history of literary thought."[75] In Burgess's account, which focuses on the shift from Hume to Adam Smith, the new awareness of global mobility and the "global scope of feeling" that emerged in the later eighteenth century is experienced and expressed as anxiety, while in Lamb's and Goodman's accounts (albeit in different ways), it is expressed as a chronic form of eighteenth-century nostalgia, or motion sickness.[76] For Burgess and Goodman, especially, textual evocations of a sense of interpersonal anxiety or general unease are not just reactions to (symptoms of) an increasingly mobile world, but its medium: "a way of imagining the world-historical present, otherwise beyond the grasp or view of any single body."[77]

Earlier scholarship on the emotions published over the past two decades has already demonstrated the radical shift that occurred in the understanding of feeling and sympathy in the later eighteenth century. Literary critics such as Adela Pinch and Deidre Lynch and historians such as Dror Wahrman influentially argued that an interest in feelings as inward, or private, was a distinct social development of the period and formed part of an effort to imagine "an inner consciousness" at precisely the moment in which the circulation, mobility, and contagiousness of feelings between people became newly visible and newly troubling.[78] In Hume, for instance, in particular in his early *A Treatise of Human Nature* (1739–1740), emotions appear as rapidly mobile and as "so contagious, that they pass with the greatest facility from one person to another, and produce corresponding movements in all human breasts."[79] In his essay "Of National Characters" (1748), sympathy and "Contagion" are at points presented as synonymous.[80] Even in his later, somewhat more circumspect, *An Enquiry Concerning the Principles of Morals* (1751–1777), he still allows for the occasional moment of "immediate sympathy" preceding judgment, when feelings "transfuse themselves" from one person to another.[81] However, Hume simultaneously insists, as Pinch illuminates, that society depends on individuals who can rely on the personal authenticity of their own emotional responses.[82] Other critics have also drawn attention to the way in which Hume gradually works to assign sympathy reduced significance, increasingly emphasizing for instance that our concern for ourselves is stronger than our concern for others.[83]

It is Adam Smith who most consistently reconceives of feeling for others as a problem – something we need a deliberate act of the imagination to engage in.[84] This allows Smith to limit sympathy even among friends of different professions, until, directly invoking Hume's "knot of companions," Smith can write, "A philosopher is company to a philosopher only; the member of a club, to his own little knot of companions" (*TMS*, 41). Burgess and Mary Fairclough suggest that Smith's emphasis on the role of the imagination in sympathetic exchange might be understood as a "masterstroke of displacement" by which Adam Smith inserts "judgment" as a controlling device to deal with new anxieties annexed to both the communicability of feeling and the new conditions of mobility in which sympathy was conceived.[85] In the process Smith works to confirm boundaries around an individual subjectivity: he inoculates his "impartial spectator" against contagion from others' mobile emotions by conceiving of him as a controlling viewer who through acts of the imagination works, in Smith's carefully controlled terms, to "judge of the propriety or impropriety of the affections of other men" as well as his own (*TMS*, 20). As Burgess also points out though, even as Smith sets up a structure that defends against it, he acknowledges in his very language (in particular in the recurrent metaphors of "transport" and "bringing home") the tendency of feelings to travel.[86] Work such as Burgess', as well as, for instance, Mary Favret's discussions of literary response to global warfare as reported in the newspaper and Fairclough's on anxieties about sympathy as a medium of communication within mass collectives in the 1790s, allows us to situate literary and philosophical developments within the context of wider eighteenth-century engagements with mobility and expansiveness, as well as of anxieties about how society and self could work under new conditions.

Again, questions remain about partial or permeable subjects, who may become either isolated from sympathetic exchange or hauntingly exposed to the emotions of others. Both situations are potentially exacerbated by mobility, by which a person becomes isolated from an assumed community and is subjected to repeated encounters with strangers. At times, in the works discussed in this book, protagonists themselves function like things or goods, locked in ceaseless, painful circulation. If we are to understand the full range of eighteenth-century engagements with affect, and especially engagements with affect in the pivotal 1790s, we also need a richer understanding of the full range of mobilities through which they were imagined. Collectively, the body of work discussed in this book presents an underexamined, and radically troubling, range of responses to what was conceived of in this period as a new mobility of both bodies and emotions.

Gendering Movement

The arguments made in this book also speak directly to the ongoing reassessment of the intellectual and formal contributions of women writers to literary and cultural history, and show how an understanding of the workings of texts by women necessitates new understandings of the literary culture of this period as a whole, as well as of those that followed. In the process of shifting our understanding of the history of thinking about women's movements, it should also alter our understandings of the history of women's lives. In the past decades, major new works on women's writing in this period have appeared, most notably Paula Backscheider's *Eighteenth-Century Women Poets and Their Poetry: Inventing Agency, Inventing Genre* (2005), Susan Staves's *A Literary History of Women's Writing in Britain, 1660–1789* (2006), and Stephen Behrendt's *British Women Poets and the Romantic Writing Community* (2009).[87] Each still presents itself as a preliminary reassessment that builds on three decades of recuperative feminist scholarship, with much still to be done. This scholarship is exciting because it consistently argues for the need for an "alternative aesthetic" and for developing new ways of interpreting the messiness of eighteenth-century texts (what Claudia Johnson calls the "bizarre and untidy"), which the achievements of Jane Austen on the one hand, and the great age of Romantic poetry on the other, have made difficult to approach.[88] As Backscheider writes in her reassessment of women's contribution to eighteenth-century poetics, "Expressions of new meanings and different realities often generate new forms."[89] My book contributes to this developing critical conversation by bringing forward a trope that highlights the nonlinear, the undirected, and the distressed in literary texts authored by women, and showing how formal difficulties can be used to represent literal ones.

My arguments also draw on critical work specifically on the history of women's travel writing, such as Elizabeth Bohls' still unsurpassed study,

Women Travel Writers and the Language of Aesthetics, 1716–1818 (1995), and continue the work of shifting criticism of women's writing and women's lives beyond an earlier focus on the private sphere. At the same time, my wider emphasis on "wanderings" and "mobility" rather than the narrower notion of "travel," along with a focus on depictions of women's movements within a range of genres, involves an expansion of which women we think of as mobile. The resultant focus on less self-directed forms of women's movement helps to shift the study of women's mobilities beyond the exceptional woman narrative that has been a feature of much critical work on women's travel until relatively recently.[90] Emphasis on the exceptionality (and frequently also the eccentricity) of famous female travelers such as Lady Mary Wortley Montagu, Isabella Bird, Mary Kingsley, or even Wollstonecraft herself, can have the unintentional effect, once again, of confining the vast majority of women to the imagined stationary space of the domestic. Moving beyond this involves not only setting aside choice as a defining feature of "real travel" (the phrase is Paul Fussell's) but renewed attention to the question of how desire and intention affect how movement is experienced and greater sensitivity to "the baggage that the traveler carries," to "not simply whether or not movement is carried out with determination, but who or what makes that determination."[91] The tradition of "reluctant wandering" represents important early thinking about how crucially different the experience of mobility is for different people in differing circumstances: as Caren Kaplan, theorist of more recent discourses of displacement, sums up in a distinctly unromantic formulation, "all displacements are not the same."[92]

Gender creates a particular set of complications (baggage) for the late-eighteenth- and early-nineteenth-century woman on the move, however she is defined. She seldom sets out on a self-directed journey, is seldom alone, and if she is alone, her motives are more likely to be misconstrued. As Wallace writes in her study that focuses specifically on traditions of walking from the late eighteenth century into the nineteenth, but which can be applied more widely to women's movements, "sexual content seems to preserve fearful reactions to women's walking even when favourable interpretations of men's walking have become standard, not only in literary texts but in experience."[93] This is something Burney explores at some length in *The Wanderer*. My approach to these texts is based on the grounding assumption of current work on women's travel writing and on mobility more generally, of "gender as a factor which consistently makes a difference (although not always in the same way)."[94] The crucial factors of frequent lack of choice and a heightened sense of exposure are what often lead to a maintained connection with the misery or toil of earlier associations of wandering. My readings of these texts suggest that the figure of the woman wanderer both serves as emblematic of women's peculiarly exposed position in this period, and also, as more generally representative – that is, as a valuable general entry point for explorations of what feels most unanchored and troubling about mobile, modern subjectivity.

I focus on women wanderers in female-authored texts also for the simple reason that there are so very many of them in this period, and they are so very miserable, and this invites further examination. For a preliminary approach to broad questions of conceptual and linguistic shifts, the new methodologies of the digital humanities are helpful, in particular, as the authors of one multiuniversity, multidatabase project put it, those approaches which progress beyond treating newly available digital texts "as book surrogates and move towards the exploration of the potential that emerges when you put many texts in a single environment."[95] A preliminary "distant reading" (the term and approach stemming from Franco Moretti), based on a content analysis of uses of the term "wander" and its lexical roots in a corpus of just under 200 novels, confirms critical understandings that there was a sharp rise in interest in wanderers in literary texts of the final two decades of the eighteenth century. The corpus was compiled from multiple databases in an effort to give a representative cross-section of texts from the period.[96] "Wander" and its lexical roots features four times more frequently in the corpus of novels published between 1786 and 1820 than it does in a corpus of those published between 1720 and 1785. By contrast, "travel" and its corresponding lexical roots do not change across the period, suggesting that we are mistaken if we think of wandering as automatically linked to traveling. The emergent sample of novels – some predictable, some less so – that feature wandering on a purely linguistic level with the most frequency is revealing. In a sample of the twenty-six novels with the highest frequency of use, the only novels published before 1777 to feature are Eliza Haywood's *Adventures of Eovaii, Princess of Ilaveo* (1736) and Samuel Johnson's *Rasselas* (1759).[97] Although early eighteenth-century literary figures such as the heroes of the picaresque have elements of what we would think of as wanderers, it is not until the second half of the eighteenth century that movement, in novels at least, begins to be frequently denominated *as* "wandering." The early century novels that one might expect to feature a high incidence of words for wandering turn out to display a conspicuous lack of interest, at least in the term: from *Robinson Crusoe* (1719) to *Moll Flanders* (1722) to *Gulliver's Travels* (1727); from *Clarissa* (1747–1748) to *A Sentimental Journey* (1768) to *The Man of Feeling* (1771). Most surprisingly, perhaps, of the novels that use the term with the most frequency, the vast majority are written by women, including works by Radcliffe and Wollstonecraft, as well as by Mary Hays, Mary Robinson, Sydney Owenson, and a number of less well-known women authors of the period. This discovery alone challenges assumptions of wandering as a masculine literary tradition. Characters described as wandering are also at least as often female, something that is certainly not true of traveling. The novels by the male authors that feature in this sample – by Johnson, MacKenzie, William Beckford, Percy Bysshe Shelley, and Charles Maturin – cluster at either end of the period in which "wandering" becomes a noticeable key term in novels, leaving an interlude of over 20 years from 1787 to 1810 in which a number of novels feature "wandering" prominently, all of which, at least in this corpus, are written by women.

This schematic analysis brings to the surface a surprising and striking dominance of women authors, and to a slightly lesser extent, of women wanderers in this new literary preoccupation. In addition to the examples cited in my opening paragraph to this Introduction, multiple examples that link the literary activity of wandering to an evocation of a state of unanchored suffering emerge: Wollstonecraft's eponymous heroine of her first novel, *Mary; A Fiction* (1788), reaches crisis point as a "forlorn wanderer"; Hays's Emma, in *Memoirs of Emma Courtney* (1796), faces becoming "a comfortless, solitary, shivering, wanderer, in the dreary wilderness of human society"; while the adjectival phrase "unhappy wanderer" repeats like an epithet through Smith's *The Old Manor House* (1793). "[D]esolate wandering Cava" of Augusta Amelia Stuart's *Cava of Toledo; or, the Gothic Princess* (1812), wanders "a wretched pilgrim, destitute of parents, of friends, of a home, where I could pass, in safety and without molestation," and appellations of wandering become repetitive to the point of being comical in Anna Maria MacKenzie's *Irish Guardian, or, Errors of Eccentricity* (1809), in which the heroine, Almeria, wanders as a man in an effort to escape a forced marriage. Another of Radcliffe's heroines, Julia in her *A Sicilian Romance* (1790), faints at the suggestion that there are only two options in life: marry the person she is told to "or quit this castle for ever, and wander where you will."[98] Burney's *The Wanderer; or, Female Difficulties*, then, in which the homeless heroine wanders through five volumes in flight from her forced marriage, finding again and again that she must "be again a wanderer," is only the longest, most iterative, exploration of this involuntary state.[99]

Text in Motion

Women Wanderers and the Writing of Mobility is a cross-genre study because these wanderers move across genres to appear in poetry, gothic romances, and sentimental novels, as well as travel narratives. While Toby Benis charts the stress of social upheaval and the emigrant situation on the structure of the novel and Robin Jarvis would have blank verse as the poetic medium of the peripatetic, like Miranda Burgess and Alan Bewell's work, my book explores a kind of mobile form as it moves across genres.[100] Rather than setting aside formal concerns, this cross-genre scope allows for a more acute awareness of the peculiar and distinctive reworkings of form in general in the texts of the period and asks us to consider what these formal shifts register and evoke. The difficulties of these wanderers' movements are represented by difficult texts – the accounts of their uncertain journeys and threatened subjectivities turn out to be each in their way as difficult to narrate and depict as that of Sterne's Maria, whose story can only be told in disjointed, dash-marked, phrases.

As already noted, recent assessments of women's writing of this period express the need for new interpretative frameworks, and for new, revisionist aesthetics for accounting for the workings of these texts. In part as a result of the ways in which attention to women's texts has changed our understanding of the period as a whole, scholars of eighteenth-century literary culture have begun to place a renewed emphasis on the open-ended and the inchoate qualities of literary texts in general, and on what Ina Ferris calls in relation to travel writing, "formal drifting."[101] The strong formal turn in the past few years, especially in scholarship on the eighteenth-century novel, opens out into the kinds of enquiries called for in a 2011–2012 Special Issue of *Eighteenth-Century Fiction*, for which John Ricetti posed as its guiding question, "How can we talk in more or less formal terms about works of prose fiction that are opportunistic and improvisatory and do not seem to adhere to any particular formal pattern? What sort of critical terms might be employed to explain how such fiction possesses a sustaining structure that provides coherence and meaning?"[102] Stephen Behrendt contends that "The emerging 'modern' novel whose roots we see in the late eighteenth and early nineteenth centuries is 'realistic' precisely to the extent that it moves toward a world-view characterized by unresolved inconsistencies, contradictions, ambivalences, and 'dead ends' of sorts."[103] New books on the history of the eighteenth-century novel by Sandra Macpherson and Jessie Molesworth demonstrate that useful new critical terms with which to approach eighteenth-century fiction are "accident" and "chance."[104] Macpherson and Molesworth argue that these concepts are frequently elevated above intention or agency in the prose works of the period and they situate their approaches to the novel by contrast to understandings based on the *Bildungsroman* model. In the *Bildung* model, the novel is understood, in Georg Lukács' classic formulation, as an "adventure of interiority," featuring, "the soul that goes to find itself, that seeks adventures in order to be proved and tested by them, and, by proving itself, to find its own essence."[105] Critical work such as Macpherson's and Molesworth's, which builds on earlier scholarship by Deidre Lynch in particular, develops new ways to move beyond conceptions of the eighteenth-century novel influenced by the novel's nineteenth-century developments. These understandings of the novel run critically in parallel with Romantic-influenced understandings of poetry as a "drama of consciousness" and travel writing as the "adventure of the self" free from context.[106] Still more recent critical work has suggested that the best way to move beyond assumptions about eighteenth-century literature based on the influential "rise of the novel" paradigm (coupled with a theory of the modern based on interiority and boundedness), may be to more consistently read different genres alongside one another.[107]

In addition to being useful across genres, like "chance" and "accident," the term "wandering," especially when combined with the negative desire implied in the term "reluctant," challenges notions of an isolated interiority founded on agency. The literal – and corresponding formal – movements I use the term "wandering" to describe, come much closer to being dictated and shaped by chance or accident or by the demands of another, than they do to being shaped by any specific desire on the part of the individual poetic speaker, novelistic protagonist, or traveler. On the contrary, I would suggest that the "sustaining structure" across this range of texts might be described as one defined not only by directionless wandering but also by the kind of negative desire signaled by the term *reluctant*. The structure evoked here is somewhat similar to that explored by Andrea Henderson in her study of what she calls the "painful pleasures of modern life," in which she asks, "What attracted writers devoted to the idea of social progress and even revolution to representations of suspense and delay?"[108] The related question I ask is, what attracted these writers to depictions of relentless, seemingly endless, often repetitive, motion, in which the subjects must either leave their direction to chance – Burney's ceaselessly mobile heroine must "commit to accident, since she had no motive of choice, the way she should go"[109] – or move reluctantly at someone else's command almost every step of the way? I propose *wandering* as another new critical term to be productively employed not only to explore the "sustaining structure" of late eighteenth-century prose fictions but also the idiosyncratic, and often apparently random formal movements of texts across a range of genres in the eighteenth century. In order to approach the formal strangeness of the texts of this period, we need to first take account of the narrative and psychological difficulties of the situations they depict.

In parallel to new formalist developments in studies of the novel, in the past two decades travel writing has attracted increasing, and much needed, formal analysis. Wollstonecraft's travel memoir, *A Short Residence*, is an illustrative example: now frequently considered her masterpiece, it had to wait until the twenty-first century even to attract widespread critical attention.[110] In Wollstonecraft's case, this neglect is also in part the result of the way in which germinal accounts of early women's writing tended to focus either on the most explicitly feminist texts or on women's novels, domesticity, and the private sphere.[111] As a result, travel writing and the traditions of wandering associated with it remained for a long time largely limited to men's travels, which themselves only relatively recently began to be treated seriously as literature.

As Ferris puts it in her resonant work on travel writing and print anxiety in the eighteenth century, travel writing was not so much a genre at this point as a "generic possibility," "a frontier discourse, a quasi genre on the edge of the settled literary field."[112] As I have argued elsewhere, as a prolific reviewer of travel writing for the *Analytical Review* Wollstonecraft herself played a key role in shaping the emerging discourse.[113] Like the late eighteenth-century reviewers whom Ferris' work surveys, we have struggled to find a critical vocabulary for talking about the formal ambiguities of travel writing. One approach is suggested by current understandings of the achievement of *A Short Residence*, which focus on its hybrid nature, and the way in which, to quote one Bakhtinian reading, it fuses a "great variety of generic forms and discursive styles in a polyphonic simultaneity."[114] However, this still tends to emphasize the intentionality and ultimate rhetorical success of a project like Wollstonecraft's, despite the fact that the text constructs a narrative of devastating bleakness and vacillation, and finally seems to collapse in on itself. Ferris argues for an alternate way of approaching the disorientation involved in reading eighteenth-century travel writing. Using a comparison between Mary Louis Pratt's reading of Alexander von Humboldt and contemporary reviews of Humboldt's travel writings, she suggests that Pratt's reading "exemplifies how our later eyes tend most to notice what makes these voluminous writings coherent – the 'view' that comprehends the world – but contemporary eyes were overwhelmed by their sheer quantity and inchoateness." Ferris suggests, in a gesture similar to that made by John Ricetti in his call for new work on the eighteenth-century novel, that we might usefully focus, instead, on "the implications of such formal drifting."[115] Work such as Jonathan Lamb's on accounts of voyages to the South Seas and his more recent *The Things Things Say* (2011), also shift attention far from Pratt and others' "imperial eyes," to the discontinuities and exhibitions of the profoundly unsettling in eighteenth-century travel narratives.[116] This is not so much about the "view" as it is about those lost within the landscape. Such focus on formal drifting immediately challenges – in both the novel and travel writing – any simple anachronistic reading of the eighteenth-century journey as narrative of self-discovery. I am interested in what happens if we accept travel writing as the most digressive, discursive, open ended of genres, even more so than the novel or the long poem, and then transfer this understanding, by means of the figure of the wanderer, back into other literary forms. This opens up new ways of understanding the central place of literal, metaphorical, and emotional mobility in the texts of this period.

Throughout this book I also pay attention to moments in which wandering takes on textual manifestations, down to the level of sentence structure and intertextuality. I am especially interested in the wider applicability of, to use Ferris again, travel writing's "notorious intertextuality, which confounded the distinction between one text and another, between what was properly one's own and what belonged to someone else."[117] Again, it seems no coincidence that texts about literal mobility also most acutely evoke an analogous restlessness of both text and feeling. Just as frequent quotation from poetry, prose, and previous travelers' writings is an established feature of eighteenth-century travel writing, it is also a feature of each of the key texts examined in this study, reinforcing an understanding of travel writing as a useful template for this cross-genre mode. Wollstonecraft's traveler in *A Short Residence* reads the countries she visits as much through Shakespeare as through the landscapes she encounters; the speakers in Smith's poems quote to such an extent that her contemporaries accused Smith of plagiarism; and Radcliffe's novels are so full of literary allusion that she has been described as the most "secondhand" of important novelists.[118] I am interested in what we might learn from seeing quotation as itself a form of mental wandering – as what Ralph Waldo Emerson calls a "travelling of the mind"– deeply related to concerns about sympathy, the mobility of emotion, and the ways in which we move in and out of others' thoughts and feelings.[119] I conclude that these writers' practices of allusion play a key role in their evocation of the pain of subjects who cannot direct their own movements – or frequently, direct their own thoughts. These subjects frequently experience interaction (literal, metaphorical, and textual) as involuntary, binding, or limited: they are often peculiarly and at times frighteningly involved with the feelings and expressions of other people; or, on the contrary, are painfully exiled from full citizenship in a sympathetic literary community of the mind. These wanderers suffer from a kind of restlessness of mind, which often becomes something either *more* or *less* than sympathy. I find that Charlotte Smith and Wollstonecraft both evoke the inadequacy of quotation to represent the feelings they seek to express and they use this inadequacy to highlight a sense of social isolation. For Radcliffe, quotation itself is more unequivocally positive, but she evokes a sense of isolation and pain by having quotation, with all its potential for sympathetic identification and mobile release, disappear at key gothic moments in her work. In the case of Burney, it proves revealing to read *The Wanderer* as drawing on a wider form of allusion, as she quotes on the level of scene from touristic experience, repeatedly marking her wanderer's pained and frightening exclusion from this conventional experience by invoking it. If Harold Bloom was, and continues to be, primarily interested in how what he calls "strong poets" deal with their precursors, my very different focus brings forward the distinctive ways in which liminal or marginal authors and characters – wanderers – engage with others through quotations and allusions, and the painful difficulties they use allusion to represent.

The central role understandings of literary interaction have come to play in the critical reassessment of the workings and contribution of women's writing in this period, in particular, is signaled in instances such as a 2013 special issue of *Women's Writing* on influence, intertextuality, and agency in eighteenth-century women's work. As the editor of the issue Jennie Batchelor notes, in the past decade Backscheider, Behrendt, and Wolfson have placed the terms "community" and "interaction" at the forefront of discussions of the literary culture of a period on which criticism was once dominated by ideas of the individual author working in splendid isolation.[120] This is analogous to the shift from place and identity to mobility and interaction in wider scholarship. For the most part in this book, but not in all cases, I favor Wolfson's term "interaction" over "intertextuality" or (Bloom's) "literary influence," because it allows for more acknowledgment of the human subjects who author and are depicted in texts. However, Wolfson in *Romantic Interactions: Social Being and the Turns of Literary Action* (2010), like most recent critics on this aspect of women's writing including Backscheider and Behrendt, is primarily interested in interaction as the way in which authors come "to self-definition as 'author' in connection with other authors – whether on the bookshelf, or in the embodied company of someone else writing."[121] I am more concerned with the role practices of allusion play within the construction – and interruption – of the subjectivities of speakers and characters within texts. Behrendt and Wolfson both use Charlotte Smith's copious and persistent practices of allusion as a case study for demonstrating the necessity of "recognizing this frank acknowledgement of a writing *community*" in the texts of this period.[122] For Wolfson, Smith offers "a virtual seminar on interactions" in her long poem *The Emigrants*, as she stacks up allusion after allusion in order to summon, as Wolfson puts it, the "traditionally masculine epic authority to advance her strongest, most passionate claims."[123] However, the persistent and overt use of quotations in these texts amounts to more than an effort by women authors to bolster their cultural authority by borrowing from canonical texts – or to acknowledge their participation in a wider community. My focus on how allusion is used in evocations of pained and reluctant wandering works to highlight what Wolfson acknowledges as the "shadow-story" of interaction, which "lies in interactions that agitate and alienate."[124] Quotation can as easily signal trauma and hauntings in these texts as it can sympathetic consolation, and I use the figure of the wanderer to develop ways of reading for both.

Itineraries

My argument in this book, then, is that the element of subjective crisis concentrated on figures of abject women wanderers has distinctive and important intellectual and textual effects. These effects can help us better understand the "metaphysics of mobility" that emerged toward the end of the eighteenth century and that we still live within today.[125] Each of the five chapters focuses on depictions of wandering in a single, if fluid, genre in order to make this argument on the level of form as well as trope. I begin, in Chapter 1, by using the long poem from Alexander Pope and James Thomson through Charlotte Smith to situate the gendered late eighteenth-century literary mode within a longer historical context. I argue for the emergence in the eighteenth century of the figure of the wanderer as social observer out of a reimagining of the prospect overview. This is not just a rhetorical and aesthetic shift, involving an exchange of favored literary personae but a conceptual shift that registers the very real social upheavals of the second half of the eighteenth century and the uncertainties that came with them. In order to bring out the radical transformation in the identity of the observer that had occurred by the 1790s, I pay particular attention to Smith's inheritance and subsequent reimagining and regendering in *The Emigrants* of Oliver Goldsmith and William Cowper's figures of the poet-observer as exiled wanderer. In seeking a figure adequate to the crisis of the 1790s, Smith shifts the poet-observer from the hilltop or the parlor, to the coastline, placing her face-to-face with a group of real, historically situated wanderers whose homelessness is greater than her own. This relocating of both subject and object of sympathy represents a crucial reimagining of the literary figure of the wanderer, as well as of the uses to which it could be put.

In Chapter 2, I turn my attention from the long poem to the sonnet sequence. Unlike the long poem, in large part due to Smith herself, the sonnet became associated with women poets in the 1780s and 1790s. Along with Backscheider, I read Smith's sonnets as establishing the melancholic, rootless wanderer as her influential signature persona. But I then depart from this to analyze the progressive darkening of the wanderer figure over time in Smith's sequence and the way in which Smith registers through this ceaselessly mobile figure a profound sense of personal and political loss in the wake of the bloodying of the French Revolution and the British declaration of war with France. I argue that the form of this repetitive, self-referential, and potentially endless sonnet sequence itself replicates the theme of deep literal and psychological homelessness evoked in the individual sonnets. Expanding and psychologizing the ideas at the heart of her more obviously political *The Emigrants*, in *Elegiac Sonnets* Smith uses the form of the sonnet sequence to cultivate an aesthetics of endless wandering. In the process she challenges idealized imaginings of all-inclusive social sympathy, presenting speakers with no one to hear them but the dead.

I then turn in Chapter 3 to an examination of the textual practices of quotation and interpolation of poetry in the most famously meandering of gothic novels, Radcliffe's *Udolpho*. This may seem like an outlier text in a book about wanderers, but once we expand the parameters of what we consider as mobility, the gothic heroine becomes recognizable as an especially coerced wanderer. In this chapter, I draw out the relationships between literal, textual, and imaginative wandering, and the isolating compulsions of the gothic text. Political debates about the freedom of the imagination and critical discussions of both the construction of the gothic subject and of the poetic novel in the 1790s contribute to my discussion in this chapter, especially as set in motion by Favret, Leah Price, Deidre Lynch, and G. Gabrielle Starr. The placement of quotations, poetry, and lyric moments in prose in *Udolpho*, I argue, is much less random than previously understood, and is deeply interconnected with how metaphors of stasis and movement work within the text, and to Radcliffe's exploration of the conditions under which sympathy might become blocked.

Chapter 4 turns for the first time to an actual travel narrative. In *A Short Residence*, Wollstonecraft develops and complicates the political thought of her two *Vindications*, staging her most complex engagement with sympathy through a reimagining of the sentimental journey. It is surely no coincidence that Wollstonecraft's most eloquent work is structured around a woman wanderer. Indeed, the centrality of thinking about movement to the history of feminist action is suggested by the now completely naturalized phrase, "the woman's *movement*." In *A Short Residence*, the voice of the wanderer gains its resonance from combining a figuration of women's emancipation with one of women's suffering, suggesting how difficult it is to separate one from the other. By embracing and performing her real situation as a woman without a place, Wollstonecraft enacts a failure of genre, building toward a sense that mobility such as hers is not as it should be, and refusing to enact the homecoming that gives more conventional travel narratives a frame of security. Wollstonecraft's text deals centrally, and with unprecedented eloquence, with the problems facing a marginal subject feeling, speaking, and moving in new ways, making it an essential text in any history of thinking about mobility.

In the final chapter, I take up Frances Burney's great novel of wandering as the belated culmination of this cross-genre tradition of writing about movement. This chapter seeks to account for the strangeness of Burney's voluminous sentimental novel by refocusing attention on the equivalence implied within its full title, *The Wanderer; or, Female Difficulties*. I put the geographical distances covered by the refugee heroine, Juliet, as she seeks to find a place to live and work, in close relation to the (immense, digressive) distance traversed between the first cover of this five-volume novel and the last. Reading Juliet's lack of direction, even as she embarks on a standard tourist itinerary, within the context of recent critical work on the eighteenth-century novel, I explore ways in which Juliet's wanderings provide a troubling alternative to understandings of the figure of the wanderer as a self-exploring subject. I show how Burney writes the reluctance associated with enforced movement into her novel's very sentence structure so that the very length of this text, along with its convoluted plot and its unwieldy extended sentences, are all part of the novel's performance of "female difficulties." The alternate, parallel tradition of wandering discovered in *Women Wanderers and the Writing of Mobility* allows for new readings of the workings of digressive narratives and a refocusing of attention on the most unsettled and unsettling forms of mobility evoked in (and by) literary texts.

CHAPTER I

"Circling Eye" to "Houseless Stranger"
The Shifting Landscape in the Long Poem

A standard concept in eighteenth-century studies is that the metaphor of the prospect view, as developed in poems such as Alexander Pope's *Windsor Forest* (1713) and James Thomson's *The Seasons* (1726–1730), based its authority on the notion of being able to present what John Barrell first labeled an "equal, wide survey" of society as a whole from a single, stable, and elevated position.[1] This position, which claimed to encompass everything, was annexed to the position of the "disinterested" gentleman in retirement and was a fiction born out of a real sense that society was becoming more difficult to comprehend and describe. In prospect poems the poet is imagined as standing alongside this idealized gentleman, at once playing a role in bringing him into being and, through assuming his view, endeavoring to present a survey in poetic form of the landscape, the nation, and the empire. Until recently this metaphor has dominated understandings of the eighteenth-century poetic observer.

In this introductory chapter I take the prospect view as a starting point for an examination of the alternative, more ambiguous literary figure of the wanderer, a figure that emerged as important precisely as this stabilizing fantasy was becoming more difficult to sustain. The notion that the poet came to be associated with the melancholic wanderer in the mid-century is a critical commonplace.[2] What I show here, instead, is how this figure developed out of a reimagining of the prospect overview itself. I use the long poem as the textual ground on which to explore this shift. Rather than standing and surveying from on high, this new observer is imagined as moving through the world, assembling a view of society from multiple fragmentary sights and interactions. The shift involves a kind of stepping down, in both literal and figurative terms, of the writer and the imagined poetic observer from the hilltop to the fields and the town. Eclipsing the metaphor of the prospect viewer, the wanderer is a vitally modern figure, approaching vision not through stability but through mobility, not through detachment but through sympathy. Mary Wollstonecraft is drawing on a by then well-established tradition, and at the same time expressing her own somewhat uneasy, gendered relation to that tradition, when she writes in the 1790s, "I descend from my height, and mixing with my fellow-creatures, feel myself hurried along the common stream ... The world cannot be seen by an unmoved spectator, we must mix in the throng, and feel as men feel before we can judge of their feelings."[3]

I propose that the poetic wanderer becomes *the* figure for what Kevis Goodman describes as a shift around the mid-century from the observer as a "contemplative, closed subject, aspiring to a 'philosophic eye,' " to the observer as an "open, vulnerable and dependent being."[4] Poets such as Thomas Gray, Oliver Goldsmith, William Cowper, and, in particular, Charlotte Smith, present the viewpoint of a wanderer who moves through the landscape as the only basis upon which sympathy, and so a new idea of community, can be developed. But the mobility on which these wanderers stake their very claims to vision brings with it the possibility of alienation from any place or position. These poets repeatedly return to the idea that a visionary wanderer is still, ineluctably, a "houseless stranger" (*Tr*, 4). As a result, the wanderer emerges as an ambivalent figure – ideally connoting vision through vulnerability, but potentially signaling either vision *or* vulnerability. The figure is developed by these poets in an effort to imagine how a rapidly decentering, as well as more mobile and extensive, society could still be represented as a connected whole. Nonetheless, the figure carries with it into the very structure of its new identity elements of the anxieties that made it necessary in the first place. These difficulties are particularly evident when the figure is understood as a descendant of the authoritative prospect viewer.

In the first part of this chapter I demonstrate the ambivalent emergence of this figure first through examination of a specific moment of transition: the shift from the elevated perspective of Pope and especially Thomson's prospect poems to the wanderer narrative embodied in Goldsmith's *The Traveller, or A Prospect of Society* (1764). Goldsmith's poem started life as "A Prospect of Society," and only later in its composition was the original title demoted to a subtitle.[5] The complete title could be followed by a question mark: can the vantage point of "the traveller" provide a new, more egalitarian "prospect of society"? My analysis highlights the difficulties Goldsmith encounters as he seeks to transform Thomson's "benighted Wretch" – his own "houseless stranger" – into a figure through which to reimagine the possibilities for a wide view (*At*, 1145, *Tr*, 4). Goldsmith's figure of the traveler or wanderer is then taken up and developed in the 1780s and 1790s, notably in the long poems of Cowper and Smith, the focus of the second half of this chapter. Cowper makes mobility central not so much literally as Goldsmith does, but on the figurative level of language, metaphor, and poetic form, so that even when he is not writing about actual movement, the language and feel of movement is present; in *The Task* a feeling of instability and exile return from abroad to haunt even the domestic home. A decade later, Smith takes as her subject a real community of homeless wanderers, the refugees from the French Revolution arriving on the coasts of Britain. The inheritances and 1790s innovations of *The Emigrants* come sharply into focus when the poem is placed within this longer history of the emergence and development of the figure of the wanderer in the long poem across the eighteenth century. As literary historians such as Paula Backscheider and David Fairer observe, the integration of women's writing into the literary history of eighteenth-century poetry has lagged behind that of British Romanticism and the eighteenth-century novel.[6] Backscheider cites the fact that even women writers who are "recognized as excellent poets," such as Anne Finch, Countess of Winchilsea, and Smith, have not yet been integrated into the history of eighteenth-century poetry as evidence of "the need for a new explanatory model."[7] The new approach to figurations of wandering offered in this chapter provides one such model.

Considered chronologically, the poems examined here provide a way of approaching an evolution in tropes of mobility, inflected in the later part of the century as Britain's empire began to seem more unstable, by growing anxiety about finding a position from which it would be possible to speak of, or to, society. They increasingly locate the vulnerability of the modern subject, as represented through movement, at the center of any hope for achieving such a position or acquiring a new overview. And crucially, as the century draws to an end, this position becomes one based on the guiding principle of sympathy. In this chapter I use the long poem to sketch out a history of the shifting nuances attached to the figure of the traveler or wanderer as emblematic of developing ideas about modern subjectivity and the globalized world. In the process the chapter sets up some of the reasons why this ambiguous figure proved such a rich and complex resource for women writers of later decades. The wanderer is malleable enough to suggest both authority and fragility, and indeed he or she makes fragility – wandering – a precondition for wide vision itself. If the prospect overview tended to be gendered male, the gender of the figure of the wanderer, even when explored by male writers, was much more open to contestation.

"The Circling Eye": The View in Thomson's *Seasons*

To begin with the prospect, then. In *The Seasons* James Thomson steps away from Alexander Pope's tightly controlled couplets into blank verse, but in many other ways remains standing on an eminence alongside his predecessor, in particular in his conception of how society should be imagined and represented. It is worthwhile remembering how the basic structure of the prospect view is understood before turning to how the movement of a "dark way-faring Stranger" emerged as an alternative metaphor for observation (*W*, 179). *The Seasons*, like Pope's earlier *Windsor Forest*, is imagined through a series of prospect views from aristocrats' rural estates, which explicitly or implicitly place the poet beside a landowner or patriot.[8] So Pope describes the relationship between patriot landowner and poet in *Windsor Forest*:

> Happy the man whom this bright court approves,
> His sovereign favors, and his country loves:
> Happy next him, who to these shades retires,
> Whom nature charms, and whom the Muse inspires[.][9]

The line leads directly from court and sovereign, through the landowner whom court, sovereign, and nation "loves" to the poet, he whom "the Muse inspires." The closeness of identification between poet and landowner is apparent in the ambiguity of "Happy next him": "him" at first seems meant to be read as the happy landowner himself, beside or next to whom the poet stands; only as the sentence moves on through the attributes of this "him," does it become apparent that the subject of the second clause is actually the poet himself. In moments like this Pope attempts, through positioning himself in such close proximity to the fiction of the All-comprehending Gentleman he helps to evoke, to assume the mantle of an overseer of the landscape and of society. Likewise, in *The Seasons*, Thomson blends his voice with that of public figures in retirement, or assumes their perspectives. *Autumn*, for instance, is built upon homage to Arthur Onslow, Speaker of the House of Commons, whose "Patriot-Virtues" "distend" his very thoughts (*A*, 13). The distension of Onslow's thought is what gives license to the poet's own claims to "boundless" and "swell[ing]" vision (*A*, 7–8). This poetic speaker's specific, static location within the landscape is his essential defining characteristic and at times he even seems to stand alongside God himself, possessing what Thomas Nagel calls in a discussion of John Milton, a "view from nowhere."[10] As John Sitter writes in his work on "literary loneliness," such visions from retirement are not easy to sustain: "This is a complex stance, something achieved by living not merely in the country but close enough to the metropolis to be part of it (a sort of Connecticut of the soul); it must be achieved again and again in poem after poem, a vocal vision carefully and naturally 'cultivated.'"[11]

From this stable and centralized position, the poet-viewer in prospect poems figuratively moves outward to roam across the landscape and around the globe. The words "excursive," "extended," "unbounded," and "distended" are like a refrain in *The Seasons*, applied either to the activities of the eye, or less often, of the mind. Viewing Hagley Park through the "Eye" (*Sp*, 956) of the statesman, landowner, and poet, George Lyttleton, in *Spring* Thomson writes in one of the most frequently discussed passages in *The Seasons*:

> Meantime you gain the Height, from whose fair Brow
> The bursting Prospect spreads immense around:
> And snatch'd o'er Hill and Dale, and Wood and Lawn,
> And verdant Field, and darkening Heath between,
> And Villages embosom'd soft in Trees,
> And spiry Towns by surging Columns mark'd
> Of household Smoak, your Eye excursive roams:
> Wide-stretching from the *Hall*[.]   (*Sp*, 950–7)

This entire scene, built up by a litany of "Ands" and encompassing hills, fields, villages, and towns, is produced purely as that across which the landowner and poet's prospective "Eye excursive roams." In extended readings of these lines John Barrell shows how the reader's attention is moved through the landscape and into the distance, so that as the reader's eye "traverses the landscape, so it will register, though it will not dwell upon, the structure of that landscape."[12] What most sharply distinguishes such prospective scenes from later scenes of wandering is the investment they make in presenting this world view as centralized and stationary as much as extensive and mobile: hence the constant necessity for the emi-nence – the piece of land from which to view. This centralization continues to dominate in Thomson despite the fact that, as David Fairer puts it, he "brought a dynamic mode of seeing into engagement with an ever-shifting nature" so that after Thomson, "movement and change were inextricably part of the natural scene."[13] Following on from poems such as Pope's *Windsor Forest*, Thomson also made communication, comparison, and networks of global mobility inextricable from this scene, but again, always from a centered position.[14] The world across which Lyttleton and the poet's eye roam is imagined as fanning out –"wide-stretching" – from the central "Hall," which Lyttleton owns. Similarly, in *Autumn*, the poet, having neatly annexed himself to Onslow, looks out across

> A gayly-checker'd Heart-expanding View,
> Far as the circling Eye can shoot around,
> Unbounded tossing in a Flood of Corn.   (*A*, 40–2)

While the heart and eye shoot "far" beyond themselves here, even becoming figuratively one with the tossing corn, the eye is nonetheless "circling," so by implication always moves from and in relation to an origin, a center. Such conceptions of a stabilized public center are vital to the figuration of the prospective eye in Thomson and his predecessors. But more than this, this origin – this centralized position – has the appearance of holding an unstable world together. The entire globe in Thomson is imagined as only extending as far as the mental eye can reach. It is nonetheless the globe, not just the nation, that Thomson feels the need to have his poem imagine.

As many critics whose work builds on Barrell's have shown, the fiction of the disinterested prospect view obscures much. Tim Fulford, Jacqueline Labbe, Suvir Kaul, and Rachel Crawford, each from a different angle, illuminate the assumptions about gender, empire, and nation, as well as class, which the eighteenth-century idea of a centralized, extended vision bolsters and the sublimations this vision necessitates.[15] In recent years, this work has in turn enabled a move beyond the paradigm so influentially established by Barrell, so that the prospect now tends to be seen as having always been to an extent unstable and compromised. Indeed, even in Barrell's account, the assertions of authority of the prospective view often struggle with the instability of their claims. Twenty-first-century criticism of *The Seasons* favors terms such as Dennis Desroches' "rhetoric of disclosure," and Kevis Goodman in particular argues for a shift in attention away from the apparent thematic "smoothness" of these kinds of poems and the "socio-historical contradictions that the poem's aesthetic strategies attempt to resolve," toward what those very strategies "unleash."[16]

When we shift our focus away from the prospect view and look more closely at what *The Seasons* seeks to still or diffuse, we find a more embodied wanderer already there in shadow form. The extensiveness of the prospective eye in fact keeps producing its own ghostly opposites, benighted and bewildered wanderers who find themselves lost within the landscape. The sheer frequency with which *The Seasons* returns to figures who are lost within the "maze" of life, society, or landscape indicates an anxiety that invites us to pay attention to these lost figures, of whom the wanderer is only the most literal (*A*, 16). Thomson distinguishes his generalizing poetic speaker from women, workers, drunkards, and foreigners, as well as from wanderers, whose limited viewpoints work in these passages as what Labbe calls the prospect's "disempowered complement."[17] Thomson's characteristic practice is to evoke these others as absorbed in the detail of their own lives, and then to distinguish their narrow, partial, outlook from the wide vision of figures associated with the poetic speaker himself. Predictably, there are a number of women who become companions to walkers in the poem and bolster the male "roving Eye" precisely by themselves moving with "downcast Eyes" (*Sp*, 507, 485). These female figures characteristically shoot out beauty from their eyes rather than perceiving with them, and so remain unaware of the direction they are taking.[18] A georgic passage in *Autumn* depicts a group of reapers as being involved in "rural Scandal," "rural Jest," and "rural Talk" to pass the time, in contrast to the "Master," with whom the poet blends his own voice and view, who is "conscious, glancing oft on every Side / His sated Eye" (*A*, 158–64). In contradistinction to the conversation of drunk laborers, which moves "In endless Mazes, intricate, perplex'd" (*A*, 542), the potentially similar "Maze of Eloquence" through which the statesman Onslow's wisdom "devolves" is carefully embedded within a structure – "A Rowl of Periods" (*A*, 16–17).[19] Most tellingly, this distinction between those within society and those overseeing it is played out in terms of knowledge and is heightened by the encounter with something new and beyond the local or every day. When meteors are seen in *Autumn* as "All Ether coursing in a Maze of Light," the resulting panic is personified as a communicable disease passing "From Look to Look, contagious thro' the Croud" (*A*, 1114–15). This is a textbook account of David Hume's earliest ideas about passions as a kind of "contagion" by which feelings move rapidly from one person to another. It exemplifies the kind of communication of sympathy through a crowd that would increasingly trouble theorists and writers as the century went on, in particular in the revolutionary context of the 1790s.[20] Meanwhile, in Thomson, outside this confusion, as though this contrast were the reason the scene is evoked, stands the stable observer, "the Man of philosophic Eye," who "Curious surveys" nature directly (*A*, 1133, 1135). Elsewhere described as one of "th' enlighten'd Few, / Whose Godlike Minds Philosophy exalts" (*Su*, 1714–15), this figure of understanding is assigned a position in which he is able to separate the "Maze of Light" into "Causes, and Materials" (*A*, 1136), reestablishing order from apparent chaos through his ability to comprehend the complicated workings of nature and society. This figure is a progenitor of what turned into Adam Smith's "impartial spectator," who also stands apart, using his judgment rather than being subject to immediate contagion from the emotions of others. Like Smith's figure, Thomson's observer also seems to be brought into being by an encounter with a wider, more mobile, and rapidly shifting world and by a pressing apprehension of the potential for loss and panic.

The figure of the wanderer is the most concrete embodiment of these "others" in Thomson, figures liable to become so lost in the moving maze of the landscape that they cannot claim any control over it. Soon after the "Man of philosophic Eye" has sought to establish his supremacy in *Autumn*, the poem falls into a threatening account of night, in the darkness of which "Order confounded lies; all Beauty void; / Distinction lost; and gay Variety / One universal Blot" (*A*, 1141–3). The prospective eye invested in "Order," "Beauty," "Distinction," and "Variety" is powerless here, leaving behind only an isolated man, walking in darkness:

> Drear is the State of the benighted Wretch,
> Who then, bewilder'd, wanders thro' the Dark,
> Full of pale Fancies, and Chimeras huge;
> Nor visited by one directive Ray,
> From Cottage streaming, or from airy Hall.   (*A*, 1145–9)

This figure, who "wanders thro' the Dark" is "bewilder'd," lost in incomprehensible details. Rather than letting his eye wander out from the hall as Lyttleton does in *Spring*, he is stuck within the landscape, distant from the Hall, which does not even grant him a "directive Ray" which might rescue him from his wandering.[21] In Thomson, getting lost, wandering, or losing track of one's center are not to be taken lightly. At times this recurrent, straying figure is lost even in daylight. In *Winter* snow – like darkness – confounds distinction, so that the "swain" no longer understands even his own fields:

> As thus the Snows arise; and foul, and fierce,
> All Winter drives along the darken'd Air;
> In his own loose-revolving Fields, the Swain
> Disaster'd stands; sees other Hills ascend,
> Of unknown joyless Brow; and other Scenes,
> Of horrid Prospect, shag the trackless Plain:
> Nor finds the River, nor the Forest, hid
> Beneath the formless Wild; but wanders on
> From Hill to Dale, still more and more astray;
> Impatient flouncing thro' the drifted Heaps,
> Stung with the Thoughts of Home; the Thoughts of Home
> Rush on his Nerves, and call their Vigour forth
> In many a vain Attempt. How sinks his Soul!
> What black Despair, what Horror fills his Heart!   (*W*, 276–89)

Lacking all identifying marks, only "unknown," "other," "trackless," "formless," the landscape through which the swain wanders is a kind of inverted or "horrid prospect." The stuttered repetition of "thoughts of home" highlights that the pain associated with this state comes from a loss of center or direction: the swain clearly no longer knows the direction in which home lies. His wandering is defined, in fact, by his distance from any position from which he could acquire a view, suggesting that for Thomson "home" and "view" amount to the same thing. Being distant from either tends to be not only fearful but literally fatal in *The Seasons*: so potently representative of loss of perspective and loss of control, these figures are often abandoned by the poem as lost, with no choice but to "wander" ever onward, "still more and more astray."

The identification of Thomson's wanderer's movements with a kind of "horrid Prospect" is vital in terms of the later history of the figure. Rather than moving only with a "circling eye," this straying figure is forced to traverse the landscape physically, moving from "hill to dale," from eminence to valley and across new and unknown worlds. But as this reading of Thomson's poem shows, the wanderer's movements none-theless in some way mimic those of the prospective eye, which likewise moves out across the landscape. The wanderer contains within him the mobility of the prospect view – like the prospective eye the wanderer ventures outward from the Hall. Earlier critics such as Fulford have shown how consistently Thomson confines the "apprehension of chaos" suggested by such figures to "set pieces" in *The Seasons*, which "provide vicarious experiences of human misery without seriously threa-tening the comfort of the reader's position."[22] They work as a kind of sentimental tableau. What continues to make the figure of the wanderer so haunting, though, is the fact that he embodies a nightmare, inverted, version of prospective boundlessness: the lost wanderer represents what the prospect might become were it to lose its center and elevation. In addition to being embodied, the element of choice and the stability of the center disappear when the observer becomes mobile. This makes for a related, but vitally different figure.

Even in prospective moments *The Seasons* at times exhibits a fear (or premonition) that it will not be able to sustain itself in the expansive open spaces it wants to encompass. There are times when, as critics observe, Thomson's eye cannot "compose the landscape" (Barrell) or "organize the scene" (Zoë Kinsley).[23] In *Summer* the poem depicts its muse (and so presumably the prospective eye she transports) flying through the "torrid zones" and only just managing to maintain her height above all she sees and describes. Above a river in South America

> Scarce the Muse
> Dares stretch her Wing o'er this enormous Mass
> Of rushing Water; scarce she dares attempt
> The sea-like *Plata*[.]   (*Su*, 840–3)

Thomson's repeated use of the word "scarce" here suggests that his muse is at any moment in danger of losing confidence and falling, to be overwhelmed by the sublime vastness of all the poem describes, literally drowned in "rushing water." Kaul suggests that we might read the "convolutions of argument and image" in such moments as evidence of the sheer difficulty of Thomson's position as "poet of empire."[24] We might extend this reading far beyond empire's culpability to the immense complexity of being connected to so many people and so many places over such vast distances. It is telling that at this moment the extensiveness of the prospective flight is feminized, as though to emphasize the muse's (and so the poem's) vulnerability. Not only water, but land too, often threatens to dissolve and so engulf the beholder and in the process the poem. At one point, imaginatively looking out across a vast savannah, suddenly "the wandering Eye, / Unfixt, is in a verdant Ocean lost" (*Su*, 692–3). In such moments the landscape becomes as featureless as the "formless," "trackless" place through which the wanderer stumbles. Without signposts to "fix" it, the eye is in danger of losing sight, both of how the scene is organized and of its own center, and without a center to hold it, the prospective eye, already a kind of wanderer, is in danger of becoming "lost."

In these moments *The Seasons* displays surprising and suggestive affinities with another, often overlooked, long poem of the period, *The Wanderer: A Poem* (1729). In *The Wanderer*, by Thomson's friend and contemporary Richard Savage, the prospective eye and the lost wanderer frequently become one, bringing into focus the potential dangers of the prospective eye's wanderings:

> Still Fancy waft me on! deceiv'd I stand,
> Estrang'd, advent'rous on a foreign Land!
> Wide and more wide extends the scene unknown!
> Where shall I turn, a *Wand'rer*, and alone?[25]

In the course of these four lines the imagined eye of fancy actually becomes a wanderer; faced with the extensiveness of "the scene unknown" the prospective waftings of fancy are translated into the more troubling act of embodied wandering.

Paying attention to figures of wandering in long poems like Thomson's reemphasizes how, for all the long poems of this period's claims to authoritative, wide-ranging vision, their very extensiveness and mobility make them vulnerable. The observant eye contains within it the shadow figure of a lost wanderer, a figure more dependent on his surroundings than the detached, centered eye of the prospect, which sweeps across the landscape, the nation, and the empire from on high. Once the prospect itself fails the decentered wanderer, already unleashed, would be taken up by later poets and recuperated as a new and more egalitarian means to vision. Inevitably, however, this new observer takes into its new role many of the difficulties associated with it when it existed only as the prospect's dark shadow.

"The Houseless Stranger": Goldsmith's New Prospect of Society

Being "lost" in Thomson's *The Seasons* – being within the landscape rather than looking down on it – is transformed in the work of later poets including Goldsmith, Cowper, and Charlotte Smith, into the only grounds on which sympathy, and so a new idea of community, could be developed. What made it possible, and in fact necessary, for Thomson's "dark way-faring Stranger" to become precisely the figure that would be taken up by mid-to-late-century poets as the embodiment of the poet's voice? Goldsmith's *The Traveller, or A Prospect of Society* is at once a critique of the authoritative prospect of earlier poets and an elegy for the passing of the seeming authority of the position from which they spoke. The central question Goldsmith asks in *The Traveller* is how a poet could, from a marginalized, decentered position, still hope to claim a universal voice or a new prospect of society.

By the 1760s and 1770s, when Goldsmith wrote this and his more famous *The Deserted Village* (1770), the reasons for the unbounded vision of the prospect poem becoming more difficult to assume included changes in the landscape and changes in the societal position of the poet. As explored by critics such as Barrell, Crawford, Goodman, and of course earlier by Raymond Williams, between the 1730s and the 1760s ideas about the British landscape shifted, and along with them the uses to which a poetic construction of the landscape could be put. This was brought about by the Enclosure Acts, increasing censure of the expansion of private estates into formerly public lands and new skepticism about the wisdom of imperial expansion. The unbounded prospect of the earlier century – aligned then with the expansionist empire and with an idealized notion of centralized British liberty – by the second half of the century came to be associated with oppression and the excesses of luxury. This shift in notions of social relations within the landscape is evident in the contrast between Thomson's and Goldsmith's depictions of a "Master." While in Thomson the "Master" benevolently watches the work of the village reapers with a "conscious" eye, providing a necessary and passive overview, in Goldsmith the "master" moves a "tyrant's hand," seizing the land from the village laborers – "One only master grasps the whole domain."[26] Fairer observes that at the center of Goldsmith's poetry "is an aching void where georgic might be ... We are presented not with an economy, but with unreconciled extremes of luxury and want."[27] Through *The Deserted Village* Goldsmith was to become the most famous critic of enclosure: here, and in his novel *The Vicar of Wakefield* (1766), which begins with an eviction, he explicitly condemns the landowner's unbounded view by drawing attention to the cost at which it is acquired. Within such a framework, the landowner's prospect is no longer an ethically viable place from which to view the world poetically. It fails to represent a prospective social vision – a developmental trajectory for the landscape – to which Goldsmith would want to subscribe or to endorse.

The prospective view was also difficult to assume by the 1760s because not only were landowners no longer such easily positive figures for the poet to associate himself with, but poets less often lived by their patronage. Pope and Thomson are crossover figures, at once patronized and independent. Although sometimes considered the first professional poet, Pope's addressing of verse epistles to Bolingbroke, Cobham, Bathurst, Burlington, and others corresponds to equally impressive subscription lists to many of his volumes, and he continued to benefit from many of the traditional advantages of private patronage. Thomson similarly dedicated parts of *The Seasons* to various public figures, among them George Lyttleton, who subsequently arranged a government pension for him.[28] Goldsmith, by contrast, like many of his contemporaries, including Thomas Gray and Edward Young, lived in the city, and, like his close friend, Samuel Johnson (and like Charlotte Smith, Frances Burney, and Mary Wollstonecraft), supported himself largely by his writing. He explicitly laments that "the link between patronage and learning ... now seems entirely broken." The language Goldsmith uses – authors, he suggests, are now "kept pretty much at a distance" – implies much more than a loss of funds, evoking an image of authors pushed to the periphery in the widest possible sense.[29] While he hoped there were still men whom the muse calls upon "not like a creditor, but a friend," he did not count himself among them.[30] Not being able to afford a prospect, even if he had wanted one, Goldsmith turned to the figure of the wanderer instead.

In *The Traveller*, Goldsmith challenges the claim that the stationary landowner, whatever his ethics, even possesses an overview. The poem continues to align a stationary position with patriotism, but redefines patriotism as a state that, by its very certainty and self-confidence, leads to a limited and particularized rather than an extended vision. *The Traveller* was, as Dustin Griffin in his work on poetry and patriotism says, "plainly offered to eighteenth-century readers as a critique of uncritically patriotic assumptions."[31] Goldsmith wants to chart and evoke a specific change in the meaning of the word "patriot," from someone associated with a stationary, but powerful position, to someone associated with a limited, biased view. In *A Comparative View of Races and Nations*, which appeared in *The Royal Magazine* as a series of letters in 1761, Goldsmith expresses a desire to create a kind of cosmopolitan mind or generalizing world view, free of national or particularized bias: "I should esteem it my greatest happiness," he writes, "could I enlarge one mind, and make the man who now boasts his patriotism, a citizen of the world."[32] Hope for an enlarged mind, and by implication an extended vision, can here only be achieved through the abnegation of patriotism. *The Traveller* proceeds to present a series of patriots who, by blindly praising the little world they know, show themselves to be incapable of looking beyond their own situations: "The shuddering tenant of the frigid zone / Boldly proclaims that happiest spot his own"; "The naked negro, panting at the line, / Boasts of his golden sands and palmy wine" (*T*, 65–6, 69–70). This is a marked shift from Pope and Thomson's wise patriot-landowners, who disappear almost entirely in Goldsmith's poetry.

In *The Traveller*, such figures are deliberately set in contradistinction to the now literally mobile poet who declares, in one of the central arguments of the poem, that "Though patriots flatter, still shall wisdom find / An equal portion dealt to all mankind" (*Tr*, 77–8).[33] This balanced line that begins with "Though patriots" and is broken by a caesura sets the stationary patriot on the wrong side of the Thomsonian contrast by which only some possess the "wisdom" needed to "compare" and "estimate" states other than their own. The rest of Goldsmith's poem places his mobile figure on the right side of this binary. The full extent of the claim annexed to the new mobility of the poet had been summed up by Johnson a few years earlier in *Rasselas* (1759). There Imlac describes how, having decided to become a poet, he "ranged mountains and deserts" in search of "[w]hatever is beautiful, and whatever is dreadful," for, he explains, a poet "must divest himself of the prejudices of his age or country." The grandiosity of Imlac's claim is nicely undercut by Rasselas's response that in that case "no human being can ever be a poet."[34]

Goldsmith's particular effort to separate the poet from the stationary observer leads to the paradox that structures *The Traveller*. His prizing free of the subject from any one location or nation is undertaken precisely in order to re-enable a return to the stable and authoritative "circling eye" of the conventional prospect. The poem itself comes out of a moment of stasis rather than movement: his traveler-poet "sit[s] me down a pensive hour to spend" (*Tr*, 32). Critics have suggested that Goldsmith's traveler-poet is not a traveler at all, as the poem itself comes out of a moment of respite from what there is of a journey. Pat Rogers notes that "Unlike Cain, or the Wandering Jew, or the Ancient Mariner . . . this traveller is allowed, if not to rest, at least to escape his curse long enough to take stock of the places he has visited."[35] For most of the poem Goldsmith's traveler-poet, just like Pope and Thomson's patriotic prospective poets, in fact only travels by means of the eye, like them moving from a stable, elevated center. From this stationary position in "Alpine solitudes" (*Tr*, 31), he considers the mixed blessings of the nations imaginatively spread out below him – Italy, Switzerland, France, Holland, and finally, with ascending confidence as "genius spreads her wing" (*Tr*, 317), Britain herself. Indeed, it would be to deny much of the impulse of the poem not to acknowledge that it was, as was Johnson's *The Vanity of Human Wishes* (1749), in large part an experiment in whether the authority of the conventional prospect was sustainable under new conditions. But while the stability of the prospective authority is retained, in Goldsmith it emerges in a new form. Some of the differences are obvious, not least the fact that in Goldsmith the prospect is no longer safely centered in Britain with the world fanning out around it. But what is most significantly new is that the structure of *The Traveller* suggests that a viewer must first be detached from any single spot, home, or nation, before he can approach the familiar but subtly new position from which vision is possible. This new foregrounding of a mobile subject makes a significant difference to the concept of an overview.

The voice of an embodied and apparently individualized traveler dominates Goldsmith's poem for 300 lines before the prospective eye is able to leap into disembodied, depersonalized flight. W. B. Carnochan writes illustratively of John Denham's efforts in various drafts of the foundational prospect poem, *Coopers Hill* (1642), to get his poet to the hilltop without

having him climb it. As Carnochan puts it, "an earthbound activity like
climbing them [mountains] could only be an embarrassment." Denham's
solution is to have the poet borne upward by the force of his own
imagination, eliding the moment of climbing: "Exalted to this height,
I first look downe."[36] Thomson's solution is similar – "Meantime you
gain the height" (*Sp*, 950) – as is that of his contemporary, John Dyer, in
Grongar Hill (1726). Robin Jarvis, who makes a more teleological version of
my own argument about the gradual introduction of the "figure-in-the-
landscape" or the "subject-in-motion" across the century in poetic form,
suggests that in Goldsmith the "process of the poet's wandering steps is
[still] invisibilised because the main thrust" of the poem is situated
elsewhere.[37] However, by starting with the traveler, Goldsmith's poem,
in contrast to that of his predecessors, reminds us of the hill that must be
climbed to reach the "exalted" height of the prospect and of the embodied
labor that must be exerted.

The Traveller opens with the vulnerable rather than the authoritative
aspect of the figure:

> Remote, unfriended, melancholy, slow,
> Or by the lazy Scheldt or wandering Po;
> Or onward, where the rude Carinthian boor
> Against the houseless stranger shuts the door;
> Or where Campania's plain forsaken lies,
> A weary waste expanding to the skies:
> Where'er I roam, whatever realms to see,
> My heart untravelled fondly turns to thee;
> Still to my brother turns, with ceaseless pain,
> And drags at each remove a lengthening chain.　　(*Tr*, 1–10)

"Remote" is a startling word with which to begin a poem, and an even
more startling word by which to begin to define a subjectivity. Initially
unmodified, in not being remote from anything in particular, the word and
those which follow it float as negative psychic conditions of distance from
everything. The alternate landscapes introduced by "or" in the following
lines, which culminate in the "expanding" waste of Campania, extend this
effect by placing the poem and poet in no place in particular, just a number
of desolate possible landscapes. This is very different from the many
catalogues accumulating through the series of "Ands" over which the
"eye" in Thomson's poem "excursive roams." The effect here is that the
landscape of the poem, although in fact gradually filling with details, has
the feeling of being emptied out before the "Where'er I roam" is
introduced.[38] The speaker – the poem's "traveler" – thus moves through

a landscape that, with its "forsaken" and "weary" expanses, comes close to the "formless" spaces to which Thomson's wanderers are abandoned.

The reason for the landscape appearing this way in *The Traveller* only becomes clear once we realize that the speaker is actively turning away from it, back toward his brother at home, rather than fully inhabiting where he is at any single moment. This gesture is similar to the decentering that occurs at the opening of Gray's "Ode on a Distant Prospect of Eton College" (1747) that begins with a view of the "distant spires" from which the poet is irrevocably separated.[39] In *The Traveller*, this turning back is precisely the gesture of the patriot abroad, whose "first, best country ever is at home" (*Tr*, 74). But while later in *The Traveller* Goldsmith calls this dismissively, although not without complications, the "patriot's boast" (*T*, 73), at the start it is experienced as the inevitable and painful condition of the traveler, never either at home nor free of thoughts of home.[40] This feeling, along with the opening lines of the poem, resonates through the century. There is an inherent contradiction in this position in Goldsmith, which signals both freedom and loss. There is also an echo here of Richard Savage, which once heard becomes hard to miss. The heavy, distinctive cadence of Goldsmith's opening line, "Remote, unfriended, melancholy, slow," seems to answer the opening to one of Savage's poems, "Hopeless, abandoned, aimless and oppress'd," suggesting an identification on Goldsmith's part with a poet who, at least in Johnson's account in the *Life of Savage* (1744), cast himself as representative of the homeless and the oppressed.[41]

The Traveller, like Savage's poetry but with more control, demonstrates an awareness that the balance is precarious between travel as metaphor for enabling detachment and travel as mere unceasing motion. The threat of the traveler-poet becoming like the lost swain in *The Seasons*, who simply "wanders on" "Stung with the thoughts of home" – or like the figure of the gypsy, the Wandering Jew, or the vagrant – does not haunt the vision of *The Traveller* so much as possess it. The poem proceeds through a series of complex positionings in which the poet alternately yearns for a home prospect, or a "happiest spot," and realizations that such a spot can only ever be a fiction. His homebound brother inhabits the spot from which we might expect a traditional prospective view to be possible. However, the new logic of Goldsmith's poem insists on the limitations of this position. The poem suggests that, having made a choice to love a particular spot, the brother cannot love the world at large; conversely the poet, by rejecting a limited scope and instead choosing to look at the world at large, becomes incapable of loving any single spot. The complex irony that the poem tries to hold onto is that knowledge of the blindness of the self-satisfied patriot does not make the condition of the mobile subject any less difficult. Despite his praise of detachment, Goldsmith's speaker admits to a wish "to find / Some spot to real happiness consigned, / Where my worn soul, each wandering hope at rest / May gather bliss" (*Tr*, 59–62) and laments that "My fortune leads [me] to transverse worlds alone, / And find no spot of all the world my own" (*Tr*, 29–30). He is both "remote" from anywhere, and leaning back toward his brother. The poem suggests that once one realizes that there are multiple possible perspectives it may become impossible to settle or be content with any single view. As Roger Lonsdale puts it, "The irony turns inadvertently back on the disabled poet-philosopher: to travel in search of happiness is only to equip oneself to assess the limitations of the happiness of others, and to lose one's own capacity for it."[42] The traveler may have generalizing vision, but he is also defined by where he is not, pained always by an idea of "home" and condemned with "steps unceasing" to a "life in wandering spent and care" (*Tr*, 25, 24). The condition of the traveler is described as one of "ceaseless pain."

A peculiar and suggestive echo of Pope's *Eloisa to Abelard* (1717) is contained in the terms in which Goldsmith's speaker's brother's happy home is praised: "Eternal blessings crown" the brother (*Tr*, 11). This phrase alludes to the passage in Pope's poem in which Eloisa compares her own breathing passion and experience of the world with the "Eternal sunshine of the spotless mind!" possessed by vestal virgins.[43] That Goldsmith was thinking of Pope's poem here is reinforced by his use of Pope's exact word pair, "Eternal sunshine," in *The Deserted Village* in a description of a parallel figure to the brother in *The Traveller*.[44] In *Eloisa to Abelard*, those who possess such blessings are quietly set aside in ultra-regimented, balanced lines: they, "The world forgetting, [are] by the world forgot" (209). Indeed, the underlying themes of *The Traveller* and *Eloisa to Abelard* are similar – both express the competing attractions of the security that comes from retirement from the world versus the more dangerous pleasures of the involvement and experience associated with wandering. This comparison helps to bring out the way in which the conventional position of removal and control attached to the older prospect – which of course became synonymous with Pope's own later voice – is reconfigured in *The Traveller* as not only limited but in some way barren or infertile. Eloisa's experiences in the world, her wanderings, make even her confinement very different from that of those who have always been so confined. But if only the vestal virgins are truly limited, only she is truly pained, as is also true reciprocally of the traveler's brother left behind in the domestic home and the traveler alone on the road. Eloisa's fragile, aching, crucially female voice is an especially telling one for Goldsmith to align his decentered poet with rather than the stately, centralized, and more authoritatively masculine voice Pope assumed in his later poetry. The alignment suggests a disruption of gender identity as authority becomes more uncertain.

Only in the final stanzas of *The Traveller* does the poem discover the wider possibilities for travel as suffering: through the generalized figure of the exile, mobility opens the way for the wanderer to feel for, or with, others. In the end, this enabling of sympathetic engagement is perhaps the point of the new figure. The prospect view that dominates *The Traveller* ends with a description of Britain descending into the grips of rampant commercialism, afflicted by personified "opulence" and its counterpart, "depopulation" (*Tr*, 393–412). "Forced from their homes" to stray through the wilds of North America, exiled villagers at the end of *The Traveller*, who will become the subject of *The Deserted Village*, are doubles of the "houseless," mobile poet himself, and like him are credited with the ability to see beyond their own situations. The poet imagines that "Even now, perhaps" (*Tr*, 413)

> The pensive exile, bending with his woe,
> To stop too fearful, and too faint to go,
> Casts a long look, where England's glories shine,
> And bids his bosom sympathize with mine.   (*Tr*, 419–22)[45]

Like the traveler-poet, the "pensive exile" is trapped in a state of perpetual movement; like him, he casts a "long look" back toward England. The existence of a longed for and shared stationary place is essential to the sympathy enabled in this passage. Here, the only act of sympathy in the poem occurs between wanderers, or exiles, joined by their communal looking back to their former, or desired, home and nation. The exchange might be understood as a long-distance instance of Adam Smith's "mutual sympathy," by which the "passions of the person principally concerned are in perfect concord with the sympathetic emotions of the spectator" (*TMS*, 17,20), and even akin to David Hume's idealized celebration of the kind of "*immediate* sympathy, which men have with characters similar to their own."[46] It is an example of sympathetic interchange that serves to establish a bond between strangers and so suggest community reforged. What the moment in Goldsmith highlights, of course, is the very strangeness and strains on such imagining of mobile emotion, by which the feelings about mobility of far-flung victims of the Enclosure Acts and of forced evictions can be figured as being in "perfect concord," to use Adam Smith's terms, with those of a mobile and somewhat homesick traveler-poet touring the Continent. This imagining of a kind of emotional concord can only be achieved through setting aside the actual difference in the material conditions in these very different life experiences. Whatever its problems, however, in this pivotal moment in Goldsmith a feeling of dispossession becomes the shared, potentially general or universal, condition which allows for an imagined sympathetic leap from one bosom to another.

This act of communal nostalgia for a lost place that binds speaker and exile can usefully be seen as a temporal as well as a spatial gesture in line with what Williams and Crawford describe as a mid-century interest in generating an "innocent space" of the past, associated with "one's youth, Eden, with England's Golden Age," through which to express anxieties about, or dissatisfaction with, the present, and at the same time to bring a new idea of the English nation into being.[47] In the process, as Deidre Lynch puts it, "home becomes a structure of feeling focused on what it once meant to belong."[48] As I explore shortly in relation to Charlotte Smith and in more depth in subsequent chapters, even the potential of this binding innocent space of the past becomes uncertain in the face of the revolutions of the 1780s and 1790s. But for the moment, Goldsmith's exiled villager's "long look" toward "where England's glories shine" is nostalgic both in the word's eighteenth-century sense of missing a place in the present and in its modern sense of missing something past.[49] This builds on Goldsmith's use of Pastoral to set the present against a lost English past, evoking an idealized age in which all lived in harmony in the landscape as much as it does any yearning for the contemporary nation the exile has just left. The evicted exile's historically contextualized longing for an earlier situation, then, adds a general and a temporal dimension to all the yearnings in the poem for "some happy spot" – for a stable place which no longer exists, but which is imagined as having once been possible. In seeking to imagine how a new society of alienated modern subjects might work, then, Goldsmith makes sympathy vital for holding such a diverse, far-flung body of people together, and ironically forms this mutual sympathy from nostalgia for precisely the fictional community they imagine they have left behind.

This new vision of society is qualitatively different from that imagined when the prospective "genius takes flight" and sweeps on high across the scene as it does in the traditional prospect. Decentered and unstable, this is a community based on dispossession. By reflecting his traveler-poet in the exiled villagers, Goldsmith creates a kind of elegiac community (and even nation) of wanderers – creating a community of all those without any "happy spot" to call their own, those exiled from the past, and those who are, so to speak, no longer at home in the village. Here, and in *The Deserted Village*, modern collective experience comes to be expressed through figures of wandering and exile – in those who know how to miss something and how to suffer. Mobile subjects take center stage. Having reconfigured the patriot as one with a troublingly narrow vision, Goldsmith replaces him with a rootless wanderer and poet who seeks to see, comprehend, and sympathize with the happiness and misery of all.

Perhaps the most evocative (and circular) aspect of Goldsmith's community of wanderers is its configuration of the pensive exile as the poet's distant reader. How else can the exile literally perform the function of sympathizing with the poet, except by reading his poem and so learning of his pain? The odd formulation in which Goldsmith's exile "bids his bosom sympathize with mine," seems to work on Adam Smith's assumption that the sharing of distress automatically has the capacity to "alleviate the weight" of suffering (*TMS*, 18). But perhaps Goldsmith is also presenting his traveler-poet as a kind of template from which a sense of exile might be expressed and measured. To return to the idea of exile as distant reader, though, specifically then, literature in Goldsmith's text is what enables communication beyond a particular situation and thus the formation of a fictional, global community of the dispossessed. Text is what is mobile. Counterintuitively, the poet's greatest act of sympathy is not only in imagining those who will be capable of sympathizing with him, but also of reading him. Indeed, the literature of the rest of the century is full of echoes of Goldsmith which do precisely this. The poem's evocation of a solitary, nostalgic wanderer became a touchstone in prose travel narratives from the 1760s onward and Wollstonecraft refers to Goldsmith in more desolate moments in her travel writing.[50] Lines from *The Traveller* are also echoed by Smith in her *Elegiac Sonnets* (1784–1800), in which the sonnet-speaker moves, "Alone, reluctant, desolate, and slow" in tandem with an "Unhappy pilgrim" (*ES*, 52.10, 1), and are quoted by Radcliffe in *The Mysteries of Udolpho* (1794) as her own heroine begins a journey.[51] The community of wanderers – or the dispossessed – is for Goldsmith also a community of readers and writers, each claiming vision through a shared experience of homelessness. By its conclusion, *The Traveller* is as much addressed to other exiles as it is to the poet-traveler's brother at home.

"Wand'rers, Gone Astray": Cowper's Task

While Goldsmith made his poet a literally mobile "houseless stranger," Cowper is famous for his poet-speaker being very much at home. *The Task* (1785), published in six books, returned the site from which to imagine a connected world to rural Britain, but in an altered form from that around which Thomson structures *The Seasons*. Instead of using a series of aristocrats' seats, Cowper builds his long poem around the daily activities of middle-class rural life and of the domestic home. Leonore Davidoff and Catherine Hall have shown that *The Task* was the most popular work in family libraries through into the nineteenth century and the poem is often discussed in terms of its influential role in placing ideas of middle-class domesticity at the center of new ideas of Britishness.[52] Cowper addresses "Domestic bliss" as the "only bliss / Of Paradise that has surviv'd the fall!" (*Task*, 3.41–42). Yet, despite Cowper's emphasis on stasis and domesticity, the view of the world assembled in *The Task* is as dependent on metaphorical and structural conceptions of wandering, mobility, and the global as is *The Traveller's*. In the past decade, *The Task* has been subjected to vital reinterpretation, most notably by Kevis Goodman and Mary Favret, whose work highlights how Cowper's version of domestic retreat functions not so much as a shutting out of the elements, a "keeping out" of the national and global upheavals of the 1780s, but as "a bridge" (Favret) or "passageway" (Goodman), ideally as useful for "communication with" as it is for "fortification against" the violence of the wider world.[53] This critical work creates a space for a reading of the way in which Cowper's vision of domestic retreat needs to be understood not so much as a rejection of the wide range of the prospect view but as an updating and reconceiving of the mobility already inherent in it.

While Goldsmith only discovers the potential of sympathy between wanderers near the end of *The Traveller*, such "long-distance sympathy," to use Julie Ellison's term, is the ground on which Cowper's wide view is based.[54] *The Task* was written in 1783 and 1784 in the immediate wake of the loss of the American colonies after nearly a decade of war and in the context of troubling developments in the empire in India. In it, Cowper works to evoke the feeling of a connected world through developing a sense of universal sympathy in suffering and a sense of existential exile. If we each, including the poet, are "wand'rers, gone astray," each, "in his own delusions ... lost" (*Task*, 3. 124–5), the thematic and structural logic of the poem runs, "How then should I and any man that lives / Be strangers to each other?" (*Task*, 3.

200–1). This familiar Christian poetic conception forms the basis for Cowper's arguments for universal humanity, and for such specific political agendas as the abolition of the slave trade. It is the foundation – and the reason – for the six books poem's wide range. As Marshall Brown puts it, *The Task* is a "congenitally restless" poem, its very randomness "calculated to reflect both the homelessness and the universal fellowship of man."[55] I argue that Cowper repeatedly uses images of travelers and the language of mobility to alert his readers to the strangeness of what it might actually mean emotionally to "sit in sorrow for mankind," as Goldsmith puts it (*Tr*, 100). Through these images, Cowper explores what might be required by the kind of constant sympathetic leaps from the mind of one stranger to another – often over vast distances – imagined at the conclusion to *The Traveller*. *The Task* asks and further explores how such a kinship, such a linking of exiled self to exiled other, such a binding of the world by multiple, wide-ranging interactions between mobile strangers, is to work.

Cowper views the world from his stationary position in *The Task* not by means of a Thomsonian excursive eye but through descriptions of a series of travelers. Book One begins in a Thomsonian mode with the poet as country walker, experiencing the familiar uplift to the "speculative height" of prospective vision (*Task*, 1. 289) and distinguished from a list of the usual suspects lost in their own movements and incapable of taking in the view: a downward gazing "boorish driver leaning o'er his team"; a thresher incapable of pause; a city dweller "self-imprison'd" in "proud saloons"; and a "tim'rous mate," who although allowed out on the first walk, with the arrival of Winter finds that "female feet / Too weak to struggle with tenacious clay, / . . . are best at home" (*Task*, 1. 298, 414, 214–17). However, the poem soon shifts to lengthier accounts of specific wanderers who function, as Sarah Houghton-Walker observes, as much as analogues of the poet-speaker as contrasts, moving outward from Crazy Kate, a former serving maid who now "roams / The dreary waste," to an ambiguously depicted group of gypsies, imagined as "houseless rovers of the sylvan world," to Omai, the Tahitian brought to London and back by James Cook (*Task*, 1. 546–7, 588).[56] All these figures share a sense of existential homelessness, and in the case of Omai, especially, it is difficult to know exactly where the narrative of these more literally houseless wanderers ends and that of the "pensive wand'rer" in rural Britain aligned with the poet begins (*Task*, 1. 761). Omai functions as an uncanny Crusoe-like figure in the poem, evoked as a kind of castaway even on his own home island, "straying on the beach" looking longingly back toward England in an exaggerated version of the condition of Goldsmith's "pensive exile" (*Task*, 1. 654; *Tr*, 419).

The most explicit example of viewing the world through the eyes of a traveler in *The Task* comes in the now much-discussed scene of reading the newspaper in Book Four, "The Winter Evening."[57] Cowper repeatedly figures anxieties about how much one can be moved by accounts of others' sorrows, and how far the self is capable of extending beyond its center without losing track of that center, through scenes of reading. In these scenes, text stands in both for the landscape of the world, and, as in Goldsmith, as the only thing that binds parts of a global society together. Sitting quietly at home and at the same time encountering the "map of busy life" through the newspaper, which seems made of "Heav'n, earth, and ocean plunder'd of their sweets" (*Task*, 4. 55, 82), the reader-observer claims that:

> Thus sitting and surveying thus at ease
> The globe and its concerns, I seem advanc'd
> To some secure and more than mortal height,
> That lib'rates and exempts me from them all.
> It turns submitted to my view, turns round
> With all its generations; I behold
> The tumult and am still.   (*Task*, 4. 94–100)

Here the updated but still very Thomsonian concept of the observer as a stabilized (and stabilizing) center is accentuated by the globe itself being what turns, submitting and revealing itself to the beholder's all-encompassing view. Elevated and stationary, involved in the analytical task of "surveying," this perspective allows the spectator to make claims to being "secure," "liberated," "exempt," and emotionally "still." The scene functions as a reworking of the "speculative height" evoked in Book One, which by being resituated from the viewer on the hilltop to the reader of the newspaper, accentuates the stillness of the position. Then in this passage from Book Four, as in Book One, Cowper modifies his vision by adding in figures of embodied traveling. Rather than continuing to imagine the world primarily from a centered position, Cowper here transforms his textual prospect into an act of what Goodman calls "virtual" or "sofa-travel,"[58] in which the reader-observer moves figuratively in tandem with a distant voyager:

> He travels and expatiates, as the bee
> From flow'r to flow'r, so he from land to land;
> The manners, customs, policy of all

> Pay contribution to the store he gleans;
> He sucks intelligence in ev'ry clime,
> And spreads the honey of his deep research
> At his return, a rich repast for me.
> He travels and I too. I tread his deck,
> Ascend his topmast, through his peering eyes
> Discover countries, with a kindred heart
> Suffer his woes and share in his escapes,
> While fancy, like the finger of a clock,
> Runs the great circuit, and is still at home.   (*Task*, 4. 107–19)

Again the metaphor, this time of the mobile viewer as fertilizing bee, is Thomsonian (*Su*, 759–60). However, as happens so frequently in *The Task*, and almost never in *The Seasons*, Cowper evokes a distant "he" who travels as distinct from the "I" who stays at home. Rather than soaring on high above the sea like Thomson's prospective muse (*Su*, 841–3), Cowper's poet-viewer sees the world by means of a "kindred heart" looking through an embodied traveler's eyes, suffering his woes, sharing in his escapes, and even climbing his topmast. The traveler offers not only knowledge but experience, accessed through a sympathetic leap of imagination. As David Higgins writes in his work on what he calls Cowper's "glocal vision," by which it is possible to be simultaneously both at home and abroad, the effect is to give a "ground-level global perspective, rather than an elevated prospect view."[59] What we get both here and in the Omai passage in Book One, is an extended view of the way in which the retired brother in Goldsmith's poem might view the world by means of the traveler-poet's account: "He travels and I too." In Cowper reading allows the stationary man at home to assemble a view of the world by figuratively moving over vast regions in the company of a literally mobile, if only imagined, traveler. We might read the scene of reading the newspaper in *The Task* as a democratized, middle-class prospect of the world.

Even as the poet-speaker imaginatively traverses the world, however, Cowper directs attention to the gap between the viewer and all he sees. The unexpected short, summary sentence, "He travels and I too," separates the observer from the traveler as much as it connects him. The image of the globe flattened into a clock face around which fancy "runs" also draws attention to the deep strangeness of circumnavigating the earth while simultaneously remaining both "still" – that is stationary, but also potentially emotionally unmoved – and "at home." As Anne Wallace observes, "Fancy does not fly here but runs, and in the most curious fashion . . . This is not departure and return in true excursive (or expatiatory) fashion, but the mock excursion of a fancy circumscribed by time and domesticity, its flight grounded in the perspectives of actual human travellers."[60] Favret suggests that Cowper's recourse to the newspaper and the clock needs to be understood as "not simply a medium for an increasingly far-flung spatiality . . . [but] here works to dampen, if not finally still, the noise of that violent world."[61] If there is something chilling about this attempt to, as Favret puts it, "dampen" response, the poem presents this as a necessary effort to comprehend a newly present, extensive world, without being overwhelmed. The figure of the traveler as mobile double of the stationary viewer functions in this moment in a similar way, playing a structural role in introducing the distance the poet needs to "see . . . / . . . and not feel," to "hear the roar" of the world at "a safe distance" (*Task*, 4. 89–92). The embodied traveler, who is separate from the viewer, both enables a vision of the world through sympathy, and suggests the futility – and indeed the terror – of such an endeavor.

The kind of engagement – figured as movement – that Cowper fears is suggested by the description of reading the newspaper that occurs in the long version of this passage. The reader finds that having "long[ed]" and even "burn[ed]" to read the paper, once begun he enters into a "wilderness" where he is bound to read on, "Fast bound in chains of silence" made of his own "inquisitive attention" (*Task*, 4. 33–4, 52–3).[62] Both meanings of "fast," as connoting rapid movement and as being firmly fixed in place, are active here, and the "chains of silence" make the reader into a kind of laboring slave to the newspaper he reads. Such addiction to the newspapers, or "newsmongering," had been a subject of concern and satire since the seventeenth century, going back to Addison and Steele's *Tatler* and *Spectator* projects and Daniel Defoe's *Review*.[63] Addison and Steele satirized those addicted to the news as "Wanderers" lost in columns of "Tautology" and "Contradiction," of "saying and unsaying" and "interpretations of indifferent Actions" without discrimination. These satirized coffeehouse consumers of the news are driven into a kind of lunatic frenzy of novelty about international political events to the explicit detriment of domestic interests closer to home, entering into a state of indiscriminate confusion analogous to that feared by Cowper.[64]

Cowper's scene of reading enacts at a figurative level a similar problem to that facing Goldsmith's traveler-poet when, in his most pained incarnation, he moves from place to place without volition or understanding, "Impell'd with steps unceasing" (*Tr*, 26). Like Goldsmith's traveler, Cowper's virtual voyager is unable to return home no matter how much he wants to. Most troublingly, rather than a masterful prospect emerging from all this mental movement, instead, at least momentarily, "forests of no-meaning spread the page / In which all comprehension wanders lost"(*Task*, 4. 75). The landscape of the newspaper across which the reader in *The Task* moves, "spread[s]" uncannily out before him, leading the reader on to a point at which he has no choice but to wander on, "lost," transformed from visionary and mobile overseer of the world back into Thomson's straying traveler.

The experience of reading the newspaper is only one of many scenes of reading and writing in *The Task* in which Cowper depicts subjects traveling rapidly from one topic to the next without fully engaging with anything – seeming "exempt" from them all. Perhaps most explicitly, in a passage in Book Six, "The Winter Walk at Noon," Cowper depicts reading as involving a kind of infatuating forward momentum which moves rapidly beyond the grasp of comprehension, holding "an unthinking multitude enthrall'd" (*Task*, 6. 100). As with the "forests" of the newspaper, the text is active within this passage not the reader, who is "lead" passively onward, unwittingly entering a treacherous landscape of "labyrinths and wilds / of error" "without pause or choice" (*Task*, 6. 103–4, 107). Elsewhere in the poem, Cowper depicts this kind of mental motion as being something like passive tourism, in which the mental tourist, though he "travels far," moves so rapidly that he merely views "ev'ry idle thing," rather than entering into the kind of engagement of "blood" so prized elsewhere in the poem (*Task*, 4. 234, 241; 3. 204). Cowper adds a new element to Goldsmith's sense of sympathy developed through mobility, then, suggesting that quick, wide-ranging mental movements from engagement with one person or topic to the next, often figured through something like Hume's model of contagious sympathy, might turn into a sort of torturous, and potentially meaningless (even politically dangerous), series of reactions.

The question, then, is what exactly does Cowper present as "the task," from which the poet or subject is being distracted when they stray into indifferent details, or move too rapidly? If an act such as reading the newspaper – which so clearly fascinates Cowper – inevitably involves the reader in a complex and potentially compromised situation, what does *The Task* set up as an alternative model of vision? Part of why this is hard to pinpoint is the way in which Cowper enacts the challenges of his poetic task in the very workings of his poem. Houghton-Walker goes further than Brown's declaration that *The Task* is a "congenitally restless" work, describing it as a "wandering poem in content and form," in which "subtle complexities are important because it is just this refusal to fit into the patterns and conclusions it seems to draw for itself, its gypsylike ability, that is, to sustain a connotative wandering as a poem (and in doing so to mimic Cowper's inability to settle as a narrator), that makes Cowper's *The Task* a great work."[65] The poem is the medium for its consciousness of mobility and endless restlessness. Cowper repeatedly represents his poem as in danger of going astray, and as in danger of moving too far and too fast as are the subjects he depicts. "Roving as I rove, / Where shall I find an end, or how proceed?" he asks, in a characteristic gesture in which the speaker appears unsure where he is going (*Task*, 4. 232–3). The poem works by lurches into the wider world and efforts to pull back when its movements and range become in some way excessive. After a number of declarations on public affairs at the end of Book Two, Book Three deliberately, and self-consciously, returns to the topic of nature, beginning with a description of the poet as wanderer who until this point has been "long in thickets and in brakes / Entangled, winds now this way and now that / His devious course uncertain, seeking home" (*Task*, 3. 1–3). The mistaken readers in Book Six are similarly invited to return to the slower movements of nature, and in particular of winter, which enable "wisdom" and "truth" to "seize at once / The roving thought, and fix it on themselves" (*Task*, 6. 114, 116–7).[66] Cowper figures the long poem, like the newspaper (and life itself), as a perilous landscape through which both writer and reader wander, seeking moments of vision and sympathy, but in constant danger of becoming lost. On the contrary to presenting himself as writing away safely at home, venturing out occasionally to indulge in well-regulated sympathetic encounters or reveries, the poet in *The Task*, and the poem itself, is much more often evoked as struggling, "As he that travels far," moving from "slough to slough" "half despairing of escape" (*Task*, 4. 234; 3. 5, 6).

Despite the poem's wide range, quiet rural retreat is nonetheless a recurring motif in *The Task*, while at its most insular retreat is praised for helping to "secure" the mind: "A faithful barrier, not o'erleap'd with ease" (*Task*, 3. 681). As emblematic of the poem as the sentiment that we all are wanderers "gone astray" is the domestic tableau in Book Four, beginning, "Now stir the fire, and close the shutters fast, / Let fall the curtains, wheel the sofa round / . . . So let us welcome peaceful evening in" (*Task*, 4. 36–7, 41). As Goodman and Favret explore, such pauses in Cowper allow for the kind of thought that makes way for a deeper comprehension of the lives of others – for the kind of thought that allows for the development of that connection between exiled self and exiled other which the poem seeks. In Cowper's "Brown Study," in Book Four, which became the basis of Samuel Taylor Coleridge's "Frost at Midnight," the poem explicitly evokes a kind of mental pause, a "vacuity of thought," in which "the understanding takes repose" (*Task*, 4. 96–7). Goodman suggests this "contemplative" consciousness as "an aperture, a medium – a loophole – through which the world's strangeness enters," in the poem (*Task*, 4. 80).[67] The poet's "waking dream" in this passage of a world of towers, churches, and faces as he gazes into the fire, allows him to see "strange visages express'd," and to feel "some stranger's near approach" more successfully than all the endless, busy variety of activities presented to him by the landscape of the newspaper (*Task*, 4. 287–8). For Goodman, this amounts to a surrendering of the view of the spectator in exchange for that of the historically "dispossessed or vagrant subjects," associated with "the risks, gains, and culpabilities of transoceanic conquest."[68]

What continues to trouble such readings, even of this scene, is the fact that this opening seems only realizable within the security of retreat, from which we might imagine nothing *but* spectatorship is possible. Even as he opens up a space for an apprehension of the mobile lives of others, Cowper does so in a way reminiscent of Adam Smith's simultaneously opening and closing down of the possibilities for direct emotional engagement. Retreat exists only by contrast to the knowledge of what it excludes:

> How calm is my recess, and how the frost
> Raging abroad, and the rough wind, endear
> The silence and the warmth enjoy'd within!   (*Task*, 4. 308–10)

This evocation of the wonderfully active "Raging" frost transmutes into an "unfelt" snowfall, which "Assimilate all objects," casting a kind of "veil" over the earth (*Task*, 4. 324, 329, 333). When the poet turns to an actual traveler outside in this assimilating landscape, as he inevitably does, it is to reinforce his own sense of refuge and the distinction between inside and outside, as much as to open up any space for sympathy with an actual "stranger":

> It seems the part of wisdom, and no sin
> Against the law of love, to measure lots
> With less distinguish'd than ourselves, that thus
> We may with patience bear our mod'rate ills,
> And sympathize with others, suffering more.
> Ill fares the trav'ller now   (*Task*, 4. 336–41)

This traveler becomes so much a part of the undifferentiated outside landscape that his cart "appears a moving hill of snow" (*Task*, 4. 346). We are back in the vicinity of Thomson's haunting swain, who is at once lost in a "trackless," "formless," snowy landscape, and carefully distanced from the poetic-speaker and his readers, although in the Cowper passage the need for a response is at least raised (*W*, 280, 282). As Favret comments, though, in Cowper the poet "responds to the frozen man with oddly impeded feeling"[69]:

> Oh happy! and in my account, denied
> That sensibility of pain with which
> Refinement is endued, thrice happy thou,
> Thy frame robust and hardy, feels indeed
> The piercing cold, but feels it unimpair'd.   (*Task*, 4. 357–61)

The curious self-reflexivity of that phrase "in my account" awkwardly invokes a kind of Smithian "mediating imagination" as Miranda Burgess and David Simpson describe it, which detaches feeling from being properly that of either subject or object of sympathy, or of being fully mobile between them.[70] There is also a sense here that because the traveler's suffering takes its origins from what Adam Smith calls a "certain situation or disposition of the body" which here rises to "bodily pain," it does not quite reach the speaker even in imagination. As the poet does not share the traveler's pain, he cannot, to use Smith's terms, "go along with" his feelings of suffering (*TMS*, 33–5). The account itself has the effect of simultaneously anesthetizing the poet and imagined suffering traveler (who exhibits Smith's requisite virtues of "patience" and "endurance"), while the former seems to need to drain the image of immediate feeling in order to continue with his narrative.

At the end of *Paradise Lost*, when Adam and Eve "with wandering steps and slow, / Through *Eden* took their solitarie way," they have been assured that they will find "A paradise within."[71] A "paradise within" is precisely what Cowper seeks to create in *The Task*, but it is a fragile, anxious paradise for which a particular setting is necessary. Cowper develops his "paradise within" best when he is safely within a "snug" parlor: like Milton's Eve and Samuel Johnson's Nekayah, he is afraid (with reason) of "the frost / Raging abroad" (*Task*, 4. 308–9), of the world beyond, "obscure / And wilde."[72] At the same time, the very need to find a paradise within that drives *The Task* is resonant and expressive of an apprehension of the "global scope of feeling" becoming newly confronting in this moment.[73] Finding a place in which paradise within is possible is a problem faced in all the texts discussed in the following chapters – and it becomes a political problem. If Charlotte Smith, Ann Radcliffe, Mary Wollstonecraft, and Frances Burney all agree with Goldsmith that the traveler is the emblematic modern subject, the person who through suffering is rendered capable of mobile sympathy and vision, then they also agree with Cowper that this is a potentially perilous situation for that subject. Although the domestic is precisely the problem in many of the texts I examine, Cowper's retreat to the domestic is nonetheless part of an acknowledgment of fear of a wider, boundless, mobile world, and therefore it reflects an important moment in the development of the figure of the reluctant wanderer. Indeed, as Andrew Elfenbein shows, Cowper's association with the domestic led him to being characterized as feminine or womanly.[74] At the same time, this space of the domestic is depicted as inaccessible to women wanderers in works by women writers with surprising frequency, suggesting that, like Thomson's prospect and Goldsmith's unrestricted travels, Cowper's vision from domestic retreat is still founded on an element of unacknowledged authority and security.

"The Emigrants": Charlotte Smith's Radical Unhousing

When, in the early 1790s, Charlotte Smith set out to write the long blank verse poem, *The Emigrants* (1793), "in the way of the Task," she took up William Cowper's questions about the ethics of retreat, the limits of sympathy, and the possibilities for a new wide view.[75] To do so, she placed a phalanx of real-life wanderers center stage, the emigrants from Revolutionary France arriving in Britain in increasing numbers. In historical terms much, of course, had changed in the period of less-than-a-decade between the compositional periods of the two poems. The historical moment of 1783 and 1784, although reverberating with the recent loss of the American colonies, is still essentially different from that of the composition of *The Emigrants*, which appeared not only post the storming of the Bastille in 1789, but post the September massacres of 1792, post the regicide in January 1793, and post the February 1793 declaration of war between France and England. Book One of Smith's two-book poem is dated November 1792, in the first winter months of the influx of emigrants following the worsening of conditions in France; Book Two is dated April 1793.[76] During the months Smith was writing it the British Parliament was debating the controversial Alien Bill, designed to allow the government to monitor and restrict the movements of foreign nationals, a debate Smith is likely to have been following closely given the allusion in her *Preface* to Charles James Fox's parliamentary speeches.[77] In returning to *The Task* as a model, Smith was forced to address both the utility and the (in)adequacy of its poetic position in relation to a new historical reality.

Smith began writing *The Emigrants* shortly after spending 2 weeks in a short-lived, communal literary retreat with Cowper in August 1792 at the Eartham home of their mutual friend, William Hayley.[78] She was already famous for her endlessly-popular *Elegiac Sonnets* (1784–1800), the subject of my Chapter 2, but her correspondence nonetheless repeatedly advertises the fact that her new poem was to be "corrected" by Cowper, and it appeared in May 1793 with a long dedication to him.[79] Critics have noted the way in which Smith carefully aligns herself in her dedication with Cowper, as well as James Thomson and Fox, in their defense of "Liberty" – a term which of course meant something rather more radical by 1793 – and associates her poem with Cowper's nonpartisan, pacifist politics.[80] It is precisely Cowper's language of universal sympathy in suffering developed in *The Task* that Smith lays claim to in her dedication when she describes her subject – the emigrants – as having "pressed upon an heart, that has learned, perhaps from its own sufferings, to feel with acute, though unavailing compassion, the calamity of others."[81] Her putative aim in *The Emigrants* is that her representation of the "painful exile" of the emigrants "may tend to humanize both countries, by convincing each, that good qualities exist in the other."[82]

Cowper's response to Smith's poem, expressed in a series of letters to Hayley, suggests what is belied by Smith's careful self-positioning as his heir. Unlike Smith's reviewers, Cowper clearly detected what Susan Wolfson calls the "acid" in Smith's descriptions in the poem.[83] He neither saw it as nonpartisan nor considered it ought to be: he thought, rather, that it should contain less "severity" toward the emigrants and more "righteous invective against the National Convention."[84] Uncertain of whether Smith's (or Hayley's) views would coincide with his own, Cowper returned the draft of the poem uncommented on ("unmark'd with any proof of the particular attention I had given it"), and when Smith sent him the finished work he thanked her for the dedication but made no mention of *The Emigrants* itself.[85] Cowper's unease about Smith's politics is not, however, enough to fully account for his discomfort about the poem. As late as September 9, 1792, acquainted with the first of the August and September massacres in France, he had found in her novel *Desmond* (1792), generally understood to be her more radical work, "nothing" to which he "could not heartily subscribe."[86] He repeatedly praised her *Elegiac Sonnets* and *The Old Manor House* (1793). What then, made *The Emigrants*, in particular, so troubling to its dedicatee? I argue here that it was Smith's poetics as much as her politics that troubled Cowper – and in particular her repositioning of his version of the poet-observer as exiled wanderer. I read the two poems in tandem in order to bring into focus Smith's important and specific contribution to the recasting of the literary figure of the wanderer for the 1790s.

To begin, then, with what Smith inherited from Cowper in writing what Stuart Curran calls "the finest piece of extended blank verse in English" between *The Task* and *The Prelude* (1799).[87] As frequently noted, the most direct claim Smith makes for her ability to sympathize with the French emigrants' feelings comes in her allusion to the fact that she has experienced exile herself. This claim to mutual sympathy is based on time she spent in Normandy in 1784–1785 with her children in order to escape from her husband's debts. "I mourn your sorrows," she writes in Book One, implying a direct causal link between the similarity of her own experience and her ability to sympathize, "for I too have known involuntary exile" (*E* 1.155–6).[88] Creating for her earlier self a position structurally similar to that of Oliver Goldsmith's "pensive exile" looking back toward England, and to Cowper's Omai, Smith continues:

> and while yet
> England had charms for me, have felt how sad
> It is to look across the dim cold sea,
> That melancholy rolls its refluent tides
> Between us and the dear regretted land
> We call our own –   (*Em*, 1. 156–61)

As with both Goldsmith's and Cowper's images of exiles, this sets off a kind of mirror house effect, in which outcasts double each other, gazing back and forth endlessness across bodies of water, and entering each other's experience through their shared sense of displacement wherever they happen to be situated. In the opening of Book Two of *The Emigrants* especially, invoking Milton as well as Cowper,[89] Smith explicitly extends this experience of displacement to take in a generalized sense of existential exile and suffering:

> Mournful and slow, along the wave-worn cliff,
> Pensive I took my solitary way,
> Lost in despondence, while contemplating
> Not my own wayward destiny alone,
> (Hard as it is, and difficult to bear!)
> But in beholding the unhappy lot
> Of the lorn Exiles;
>   . . .
>   They, like me,
> From fairer hopes and happier prospects driven,
> Shrink from the future, and regret the past.   (*Em*, 2. 4–10, 14–16)

Both hope, and later memory, prove equally unable to offer respite in *The Emigrants*. As at the end of Goldsmith's poem, this failure adds a temporal dimension to spatial displacement, as both poet and emigrants miss not only a happier location but also a happier past. For both speaker and émigrés in Smith's poem a gap emerges, as Smith scholar Jacqueline Labbe puts it, between "the preparation for life and the living of it, exploring the very definition of alienation."[90]

Much of the political bite of *The Emigrants* comes from Smith's representation of her female poet-wanderer, even when located in England, as no less exiled and unhoused than the emigrants she observes. In linking herself, as Amy Garnai observes, "socially, politically and psychologically" to the emigrants, Smith departs from the approach taken by contemporaries such as Hannah More and Frances Burney, who in writing pamphlets on the emigrant's situation emphasize their separate identity as members of a privileged class and nation.[91] Charlotte Smith sets aside this conventional and secure hierarchical structure of sympathy. 1790s readers would have been familiar from the prefaces to her *Elegiac Sonnets* with Smith's own story of descent from gentility to relative poverty. The reality of her position in this period was even more acute than her references to it within her poems and prefaces imply. Sometime in February 1793, her books and furniture were seized by one landlord for failure to pay her debts, and she was refused entry – presumably with many of her twelve children, most of whom were still at home – to new lodgings by another landlord.[92] But the speaker in *The Emigrants'* sense of exile and alienation is political as much as personal, as Smith makes clear in the untranslated epigraph from Virgil's *Georgics*, ending, "sævit toto Mars impius orbe" (Uncaring Mars savages the whole world).[93] As in Cowper, a shared sense of loss forms the foundation for the community of displaced exiles which the poem develops, but the devastation of the 1790s, which creates the possibility for a more direct connection between poet-observer and the victims of historical forces, makes this shared sense of loss more palpable.

From this shared foundation, then, Smith necessarily departs from Cowper's poem in important ways. As we have seen, for Cowper, counterintuitively, being at home is essential for the apprehension of the plight of the literally unhoused. As I have suggested, Cowper's view of the world, although founded on sympathy and involvement – and on a metaphorical concept of exile – still, paradoxically, maintains a locatedness and centeredness akin to that of the prospect view. For quite practical reasons, this is not an option for Smith. Garnai makes a similar observation, writing that, despite Smith's appeal to Cowper's "understanding of a common, shared humanity," the

> conception of a virtuous retirement is not feasible for Smith, neither in her own life, with its endless economic struggle, nor in her poem, whose landscape of despair precludes the possibility of both interior growth and external physical cultivation. Compelled by the urgency of the emigrants' situation and the dramatic events of the Revolution itself, Smith cannot adopt the leisurely particularity of Cowper's contemplations of his garden nor his desultory digressions on matters of the world in general.[94]

For Smith, retreat is not only impossible, but untenable. She instead adopts Cowper's metaphor of a world of existential wanderers and literalizes it: she places her poet-observer outside the home and on the move. For the first time female, the embodied poet-wanderer in *The Emigrants* is herself depicted as literally houseless and placeless, wandering along clifftops on the edge of the land buffeted by wind. In *The Emigrants*, as is also the case in most of Smith's sonnets, there is no parlor to return to. In tandem, the houseless stranger with whom the poet-speaker identifies and sympathizes in *The Traveller* and *The Task* is particularized in *The Emigrants* and brought back home to Britain. This relocating of both subject and object of the poem involves a fundamental revolution in imaginings of the position of the poet-observer, as well as in uses to which the literary figure of the wanderer could be put.

The Emigrants opens with an explicit rejection of the location of retreat as a place from which to view or feel. Despite the scene of the poem being set "*on the Cliffs to the Eastward of the Town of Brighthelmstone in Sussex*," elevated eminence, mountain top, and gentleman's seat are also all equally absent from the poem as sustainable positions. Dominant readings of *The Emigrants* continue to interpret it, at least in part, as a prospect poem and, in the case of Kari E. Lokke for example, as a poem that valorizes detachment.[95] However, Smith carefully links retreat and prospect view in the opening lines of the poem and presents them as equally desirable and equally untenable. Having introduced the scope of the generalized miseries of humanity in the opening lines of the poem, from the heavy, alliterative drumroll of "doubts, diseases, abject dread of Death," to "Fancied or real wants; and wounded pride," Smith tells us that from all this her speaker's "weary soul recoils" (*Em*, 1. 15, 17, 35):

How often do I half abjure Society,
And sigh for some lone Cottage, deep embower'd
   ...
There do I wish to hide me; well content
If on the short grass, strewn with fairy flowers,
I might repose thus shelter'd; or when Eve
In Orient crimson lingers in the west,
Gain the high mount, and mark these waves remote
(Lucid tho' distant)   (*Em*, 1. 42–3, 48–53)

The desire to be "deep embower'd" in some "lone cottage" associates this desire for retreat both with Milton's bower and, more specifically, with what would have been the familiar emblem, somewhat simplified here, of Cowper's idealized domestic cottage, a version of which is introduced in Book One of *The Task*, likewise "hidden" and "remote" (*Task*, 1. 228).[96] The final two lines I quote then subtly shift ground, metaphorically conflating a desire for "shelter'd" retreat with the yearning for a detached, elevated prospect view – a "high" view that might render the world safely contained, "remote / (Lucid tho' distant)." Smith's punctuation works to bracket and frame the world, and to quieten the "troubled waves" that feature in the opening lines of the poem (*Em*, 1. 2); the word "lucid" here conjures a sense that in distant prospect the world becomes luminous, able to be viewed with a reasoned clarity. When we see domestic retreat as developed by Cowper as an updating of the prospect view, it becomes clearer that in such passages Smith is invoking (and rejecting) not only a way of life but also a position to view from.

This perspective of illuminating withdrawal from, and containment of, the human world, is not allowed to stand for long in *The Emigrants*, and is within a few short lines reduced to blindness. The position is introduced in the past tense and conditional voice now so that we know it has failed:

For I have thought, that I should then behold
The beauteous works of God, unspoil'd by Man
... less affected ..., by human woes
I witness'd not.   (*Em*, 1. 55–8)

"Tranquil seclusion" (*Em*, 1. 65), these lines suggest, would amount to a failure to witness "human woes." Shifting ground again, Smith then presents such a withdrawal from consciousness of suffering – such willing blindness – as impossible anyway. Over fifteen lines Smith enumerates all the possible locations in which such seclusion might be sought only to deny them as places of seclusion: not the Cowper-like "Cot sequester'd," or a "more substantial farm," or any "buildings, new and trim, / With windows circling" – a reference to dwellings of the newly rich clustered in the neighborhood of the Prince of Wales' Royal Pavilion – the poem enumerates, "Can shut out for an hour the spectre Care" (*Em*, 1. 75, 78, 87–8, 90).[97] Suspended syntax delays the introduction of the allegorical figure of Care into the essentially realist descriptions of a range of buildings, making the entrance of this ghostly "spectre" created by the human mind all the more haunting and seemingly inevitable. No building can shut out the mind's consciousness of its own or other's sufferings, the lines suggest, making Care itself into a kind of wanderer entering the home and mind from outside. The figure of Care functions here as somewhat like the haunting stranger in Cowper's "Brown Study," but whereas there it functions as a figure for sympathetic engagement, here it signals *only* care. In Smith, retreat offers neither view nor consolation.

Not coincidentally, it is in this moment that Smith locates her own poet-speaker in the scene for the first time. She is specifically not in the parlor by the fire but is located outside the rows of windows, walking (*Em*, 1. 88). In almost the same moment Smith also introduces her group of historically specific wanderers. This has the effect that the poet-observer, now figured as literal wanderer, is positioned in much closer proximity to a set of wandering others than happens in earlier long poems from *The Seasons* to *The Task*. The gap between subject and object has narrowed. Smith first introduces the emigrants as they literally "approach" her poet speaker, "Behold, in witness of this mournful truth, / A group approach me" (*Em*, 1. 94–5). The scene, again, is possibly a deliberate, relocating, echo of Cowper's "Brown Study," which Mary Favret describes as Smith's "cue" for *The Emigrants*, "where the poet wanders from himself and 'home' to encounter strange visages and the stranger's near approach."[98] At the very least the scene radically refigures what a stranger's "near approach" might involve. It is worth noting that during the period in which Book One of the poem is dated, Smith was sheltering a group of emigrants in her home, one of whom her daughter later married.

In Book Two, Smith develops this sense of intimate engagement by giving direct evidence of the emigrants having spoken with the poet-speaker, an action unimaginable in *The Task*, *The Traveller*, or *The Seasons*, making Smith's emigrants among the first of the multitude of wanderers and exiles who tell their framed stories in poetry throughout the 1790s:

> Shuddering, I view the pictures they have drawn
> Of desolated countries
>
>   . . .
>
> Oft have I heard the melancholy tale,
> Which, all their native gaiety forgot,
> These Exiles tell –   (*Em*, 2. 216–217, 239–41)

In a letter of November 1792 – the same month in which she dates the first book of *The Emigrants* – Smith wrote of being appalled by the "hideous picture which a friend of mine, himself one of the most determined Democrates I know, has given of the situation of the Emigrants."[99] This is sympathy imagined as a profoundly visual act, with the effect of distributing or circulating feeling among multiple people.[100] In the poem, the emigrants' stories become a part of the poet's wide view: she "views" the "pictures" they draw. Smith's emphasis on the physical presence and proximity of the emigrants achieves a quite different effect from Cowper's travels by means of the newspaper, or his sense of "some stranger's near approach," apprehended while the poet gazes into the fire on a winter evening, "myself creating what I saw" (*Task*, 4. 290). It is not so much that Smith's interaction between poet and stranger is more realist: as Michael Wiley points out, most emigrants did not actually stay on the Sussex coast – and certainly not on the actual seashore – but quickly moved on to London.[101] Nor that it is necessarily more successful: in a later rewriting of the poem, "The Female Exile," Smith has her speaker lament that she does not have the "affluence," to "warm the cold heart of the wretched."[102] Nor, finally, as Wiley again shows, is the hierarchy between viewer and what they view that is such a feature of the prospect entirely set aside.[103] Rather, the shift in location of both poet and wanderer is representative of a shift in understanding of how a community of exiles should be constructed. She and the exiles are face to face.

Part of why Smith needs to set aside the perspective from retreat or prospective distance – still so desirable as a position – is so that she can stage a political rejection of a claim that, as Cowper phrases it in *The Task*, it is a "part of wisdom" to "measure lots," with those who suffer more than us, and so "with patience bear our moderate ills" (*Task*, 4. 336–9). In his *A Philosophical Enquiry into the Origin of Our Ideas of the Sublime and the Beautiful* (1757), Edmund Burke frames this as a kind of "satisfaction" we feel in sympathy on encountering the distresses of others, from "the contemplation of our own freedom from the evils which we see represented."[104] In direct opposition, Smith's poet-speaker states that, "never yet could I derive relief, / . . . / From the sad thought, that others like myself / Live but to swell affliction's countless tribes!" (*Em*, I. 61, 63–4). Smith refuses to comfortably make the kind of distinction that Cowper's call for wisdom demands, or Burke suggests we find pleasure in. Later in *The Emigrants*, it is the "lowest poor" within Britain, the "Poor vagrant wretches! outcasts of the world!" who are tentatively invited to engage in this form of consolation (*Em*, I. 312, 303). The complex later passage conjectures that the exiled nobles on the beach, "must feel / More poignant anguish" than the more inured poor such as the "solitary Shepherd shiv'ring," who is as a result invited to, "if the sight / Of wide-extended misery softens yours / Awhile, suspend your murmurs!" (*Em*, I. 311–12, 299, 306–8). The stretch required for this move, which in light of the earlier declaration in the poem of its inefficacy amounts to a logical lapse, provides a clue to why Smith is so focused on setting the perspective of retreat aside in the first place. She wants to evoke, both for her wandering-speaker and her readers, a closer identification with the literally houseless than allowed for in the relationship of seemingly stable, comparative lots of Adam Smithian or Burkean sympathy. In *The Emigrants*, Smith works to invoke something closer to the "substitutability" David Simpson puts forward as a way of understanding the dynamics of Wordsworth's poetry, which Simpson suggests is "based on a simpler and much more threatening equivalence: it says that each of us could be in the place of the other without doing anything at all to assist in the exchange," and in its absolute form portends "nothing less than the end of social and economic classes and of all such distinctions."[105] If in Cowper the suggestion is that all might be potentially exposed, while actually maintaining a stable position for his poet-speaker, then in Smith all – including the poet – are exposed. The poor, perhaps, can measure lots with new exiles because they are already literally on the same level; they may derive comfort from seeing that all are potentially exposed to such sufferings as theirs.

The political intent of Smith's passage becomes clear when she then turns her speaker's address from the most wretched within Britain, to the rich, "Fortune's worthless favourites!" (*Em*, I. 315). She offers the emigrants to them not as a consolation but as a "lesson" from which Britain's more fortunate citizens might "learn" (*Em*, I. 332–3). Such a lesson is precisely what is also offered to the wailing self-obsessed poet of the opening of the poem, who wishes for a retreat (*Em*, I. 74). The lesson itself is an unequivocally Revolutionary one brought home from across the channel, and for it to work Britain's own houseless poor, increasingly under pressure in the 1790s, need to be brought into the frame:

> trembling, learn, that if oppress'd too long,
> The raging multitude, to madness stung,
> Will turn on their oppressors; and, no more
> By sounding titles and parading forms
> Bound like tame victims, will redress themselves!   (*Em*, I. 333–7)

As Labbe puts it in her reading of this passage, "Having approached, identified with and then defamiliarized the unhoused emigrants, Smith uses their situation to 'other' Britain itself, presenting it as a version of pre-Revolutionary France."[106] Smith plays a double game in her use of the metaphor of universal exile here. She creates the experience of the "ill-starr'd Exiles," "Banish'd for ever" to "wander" "Thro' the wide World unshelter'd," as one to which all could under certain circumstances be exposed, and so as the basis for the poem's seemingly benign call for "pure humanity!" (*Em*, I. 354, 97, 101, 103, 368). She simultaneously, however, critiques the exiled priests and gentry and those like them, and presents their situation as in part self-inflicted. My emphasis on Smith's critique here builds on Wolfson's and Labbe's readings of the "acid" in Smith's descriptions of the emigrants, as opposed to readings such as those by Lokke and Stephen Behrendt, which argue for the poem's creation of the kind of "internationalist consciousness" set up in Smith's Dedication to Cowper.[107] The syntax of the poem's many summary sentences exemplifies the double valance of Smith's descriptions of the emigrants' sufferings: "Whate'er your errors, I lament your fate"; "Still, as Men misled / By early prejudice (so hard to break), / I mourn your sorrows"; "Who suffer for their conscience, have a claim, / Whate'er that principle may be, to praise" (*Em*, I. 107, 153–5, 352–3). Asylum should be offered to the victims of the Revolution, in other words, because their situation demands it; but their reason for needing that asylum should not be forgotten. Neither should the fact that it makes a difference whether one is literally exposed to hardship, or still safe at home just imagining it. This is a lesson for those who are not yet houseless – it is an invitation to fully imagine an exposed situation and to try to close the gap between one's own condition and that of the unhoused other. Cowper's "raging" frost and Smith's "raging multitude" are entirely different propositions. For Smith, to evoke a newly urgent sense of exposure her poet-observer needs to place herself in a location of greater vulnerability than that allowed for in a vision such as Cowper's (or Thomson's). Smith's "severity" toward the emigrants to which Cowper objected is essential not only to the historical politics of the poem but also to its poetics. Favret, in her brief comparison of the two poems, suggests that the relationship between individual and context disintegrates in both

Cowper's "Brown Study" and Smith's *The Emigrants*, so that both "un-house[ ] the self altogether, opening it to strange and foreign sensibilities."[108] This is certainly true, but it is also true that the kind of context through which each poet imagines the possibility for such opening out is fundamentally different – Cowper's poet in the home and Smith's poet wandering the margins of the sea.

In Smith's evocation of the very poor as "Poor wand'ring wretches! whosoe'er you are, / That hopeless, houseless, friendless, travel wide" (*Em*, 1. 296–7), she sounds, as Wolfson observes, "the shock of Shakespeare's newly banished Lear confronting the world outside the castle walls":[109]

> Poor naked wretches, wheresoe'er you are,
> That bide the pelting of this pitiless storm,
> How shall your houseless heads and unfed sides,
> Your looped and windowed raggedness, defend you
> From seasons such as these?[110]

Smith's lines also, in their very cadence, evoke Goldsmith's "houseless stranger" who moves, "Remote, unfriended, melancholy, slow" (*Tr*, 1). However, Smith's overlaying with Lear is symptomatic of the 1790s shift in perspective that structures *The Emigrants*. Lear's shock, and subsequent unhoused insight, comes not just from contemplating the sufferings of the poor but from his own literal, as well as psychological, expulsion onto the heath. Smith's poet-speaker is not as literally unhoused as Lear – at least we are given no specific information to suggest she is – but any space of retreat and stability is essentially absent from the poem. Instead of taking up any of the well-established locations from which to view, and rejecting Cowper's fragile but present comforts, Smith places her poet-speaker in close proximity to the literally "houseless" exiles around which she structures her poem, and she makes the logic of the poem annex a kind of deep and present homelessness to both – and so to all.

The shock of Smith's Lear-like exposure reverberates through the chapters that follow in this book, shaking Smith's own sonnet-speaker, Radcliffe's gothic heroines, Wollstonecraft's melancholic traveler, and Burney's eponymous female wanderer, herself a 1790s refugee from Revolutionary France.

CHAPTER 2

The Desolations of Wandering
Charlotte Smith's Elegiac Sonnets, 1784–1800

Having reached the 1790s, I want to linger here for the next three chapters in order to analyze how the pressing concerns of this decade are exhibited and evoked through mobility in three texts in three different genres, starting with Charlotte Smith's own immensely influential sonnet sequence. Almost a decade before Smith published *The Emigrants* (1793) she had established her reputation and trademark poetic persona in *Elegiac Sonnets* (1784–1800), a work she developed and published in installments over 16 years. She is now, as she was in her lifetime, not only recognized as one of the major figures in the literature of the late century, but as Stephen Behrendt puts it, as being "without question the most important figure" in the sonnet revival that would become so associated with Romanticism.[1] *Elegiac Sonnets* is increasingly read as developing in range and sophistication over time, in a shift from earlier critical work which treated the sonnets as largely unchanging, and understood Smith's more political and distinctively 1790s work as happening in her longer poems and in her novels.[2] What remains a challenge is to treat a text like *Elegiac Sonnets*, which was published in nine ever-expanding and ever-popular editions, as a single work with its own internal consistencies and developments, and to simultaneously remain sensitive to the distinct moments of the composition and publication of different sonnets. The difficulties of analyzing long poems such as *The Seasons* and *The Task* because of their length and lack of clear determining structure (their formal mobility) are frequently commented on.[3] Considering a work such as *Elegiac Sonnets* as an aggregate or a sequence rather than as a collection of discreet poems poses similar interpretive problems – and because of its publication over time brings up new ones. Simply put, besides the obvious financial incentives, what did Smith gain as a poet by continuing to add sonnets to this sequence? How might we find ways to read Smith's *Elegiac Sonnets* as making of, as Neil Fraistat writes of Dante's *La Vita Nuova* and Petrarch's *Canzoniere*, "the sonnet's contracted tensions a more expansive statement, elaborating and exploring concerns that as a single unit the sonnet could only imply"?[4] Mobility, I argue, is both the subject of those concerns and the medium of their exploration.

While in *The Emigrants* Smith compares her poet-speaker's condition to that of real-life exiles, in the ninety-two poems that come to make up *Elegiac Sonnets* she fashions a largely rhetorical and literary community of the displaced, invoking such a community's inadequacies even as she brings it into being. Charting the shifting tropeic and formal resonances of wandering across the sequence provides a way to approach *Elegiac Sonnets* as an evolving, historically situated, and potentially open-ended text. Unanchored mobility is central to Smith's *Elegiac Sonnets*, it is there from the outset, it transforms over the course of the sequence, and most important for my argument, it can be understood to do work on the level of form as well as trope. This chapter shows ways in which an expanding text can evoke a kind of accretion of loss, represented in Smith's case through repetition and intensification of images of ceaseless difficult movement "without pause or choice" (*Task*, 6. 107).

I am certainly not the first person to be interested in the repeated use of figures of wandering in *Elegiac Sonnets*. Over two decades ago, Stuart Curran influentially described "rootless exile" as the "constant theme" of the sonnets.[5] Paula Backscheider, in *Eighteenth-Century Women Poets and their Poetry: Inventing Agency, Inventing Genre* (2005), argues for the perspective of "the lonely wanderer" as a key unifying device in *Elegiac Sonnets* and attributes Smith's success and influence in large part to the way in which she uses this figure to take "the great mood of the poetry of her century and turn[ ] it into a cycle." Smith's sonnets, Backscheider argues, "explore all the moods of melancholy, just as the great sonnet cycles of Spenser, Sidney, and Shakespeare did those of love."[6] I take this discussion in several new directions. On the level of trope, I am interested in Smith's development of a much darker figure of the wanderer (and female poet) than that of the melancholy national bard "who can travel and *see*" suggested by Backscheider and others.[7] The figure of the bard, like Oliver Goldsmith's traveler-poet, assumes a collective authority even from a position of social marginality. By contrast, as Smith's sequence accumulates she thematically and formally resituates her own mobile speaker's increasingly isolating, and frequently violent, experiences as irrevocably separate from those of "Melancholy's votaries" (*ES*, 80.2).[8] "I delight to stray" (*ES*, 4.2) is transformed to "desolate I stray" (*ES*, 62.10). Smith sets aside the traditional figure of melancholic wanderer in *Elegiac Sonnets*, I believe, just as surely as she does the view from either retirement or retreat in *The Emigrants*. In the process, her strategic translation of the figure of the wanderer in *Elegiac Sonnets* deepens our sense that mobility could signal a state much more alienated than the figure's initial recognizable poetic mood of melancholy – and could be used to register a sense of personal and political loss too deep (and blank) for either nostalgia or for successful imaginings of sympathetic community in exile. The development in the trope across the sequence can be seen most graphically represented in the expensively produced plates that were added in 1789 and 1797 (Figures 2.1–2.5), which together work as a kind of flip-book, setting the woman wanderer in increasingly isolated, painful, and wild motion.

The repetitive and self-referential form *Elegiac Sonnets* takes on over time then replicates and extends the sequence's themes of deep literal and psychological homelessness. Smith always added new sonnets to the end of her sequence, and even when she signaled a new direction in the work with a second volume, Volume Two, this new volume was still published alongside a reissue of Volume One. Her contemporary (and competitor) Anna Seward dubbed *Elegiac Sonnets* "a perpetual dun on pity," while one of her many imitators, Anne Bannerman, expressed concern about the potential for "tedium and monotony attending the perusal of a numerous collection of small, unconnected pieces of fourteen lines."[9] Tedium, monotony, unconnectedness, boredom. A sense of perpetuity or endlessness. Whatever Smith's sonnets' many strengths, this remains part of the experience of a reader encountering *Elegiac Sonnets* for the first time. To ask a more specific version of my previous question, then, what might monotony, repetition, a failure to move forward, a wandering rather than developing narrative structure, be able to express? I am interested in how an endless form might become a medium for registering and expressing a general sense of dislocation and movement without end. In this chapter, wandering is understood as something wider than moving from place to place, becoming associated with a pervasive textual mode and feeling.

Smith's well-rehearsed biography is helpful for setting up the tropeic and textual wanderings in *Elegiac Sonnets* because of what Melissa Sodeman calls Smith's "profound sense of exile from her own story."[10] As Smith reminds her readers in the increasingly lengthy prefaces to each edition of *Elegiac Sonnets*, she had plenty of reasons to see herself, like the speakers in her sonnets, as one of the "sufferers of the earth" (*ES*, 4.9). Born into a landed Sussex family, she was married off by her father at the age of 15, or, as she saw it in later life, "sold, *a legal prostitute*."[11] She prepared her first sonnets for publication in 1783 in debtors' prison, where her husband's spending habits had him confined, and after she finally left her marriage of 20 years she moved constantly from one temporary lodging to the next, struggling to support her twelve children by producing nearly a novel a year. William Cowper characterized her as "Chain'd to her desk like a slave to his oar," inviting a suggestive comparison between her as slave to writing and those in *The Task* who risk becoming slaves to reading, their attention constantly in motion.[12] The analogy between slavery and writing (or reading) popular novels is only deepened by the fact that Smith's efforts to make a living by writing were hampered by her husband's continued legal claims upon her independent earnings.[13] Sodeman rightly observes that the autobiographical stand-ins Smith repeatedly uses in her fiction are "numbingly repetitive," but suggests that this is possibly because in the 1790s there was no resolution on offer for problems such as Smith's – no historical reality on which she could base a different plot for her female characters.[14] Smith repeatedly figures her own situation of being stuck without a home or place of rest, as well as those of characters and poetic-speakers associated with her, as a form of ceaseless mobility. She also frequently elevates a condition of ceaseless mobility to mythic levels: the speaker in *The Emigrants* evokes a sense of endless activity, endless repetition, and endless futility not only through the emigrants themselves but through comparisons of herself to a "baffled wave" beating against the beach; to the daughters of Danaüs, condemned to forever draw water in a sieve; and to Sisyphus, eternally pushing his stone (*Em*, 1.71, 68–70). In the endnote to a late sonnet Smith compares her situation to that of King Lear figuratively bound on a purgatorial "wheel of fire." In this instance, the direct comparison Smith draws is between Lear's perpetual torture and her own inability to find relief from "common business and forms of life," making it clear that the mental distresses Smith was concerned with representing were as much about the everyday self-exile of preoccupation and labor as they were with the drama of the heath (*ES*, 79, note).[15] *Elegiac Sonnets* is characterized by similar painful repetitiveness. In the preface to the sixth edition, published in 1792, Smith writes, "can the *effect* cease, while the *cause* remains? . . . I have unfortunately no reason yet, though nine years have elapsed, to *change my tone*" (55).

At the same time, the biographical reading of Smith's evocations of exile and exclusion should not be overemphasized nor should the sense of stuckness in her writing be conflated with stasis. Her representation of her sense of exile is certainly gendered, especially in her prose works and paratextual writing around her poems. In *Elegiac Sonnets*, she played a germinal role in making the conventionally male persona and perspective of the wanderer available to women writers – and indeed in some ways to making it seem peculiarly useful to the evocation of a gendered subject position. This regendering of the trope of the wanderer is as much part of Smith's contribution to late eighteenth-century literature as her regendering of the sonnet itself, and it is a regendering that further unhouses the melancholic figure in important ways. But as Alan Bewell argues of John Clare's "discovery" two decades later of the social and political implications of taking up the position of a poet of class for evocations of his sense of homelessness and loss, I would argue that the identity of the gendered wanderer is not just one thrust upon Smith by circumstance. It is a position she adopts and extends across her *Elegiac Sonnets* as a critical strategy through which to grapple more generally with contemporary geographical, social, and political unsettlements.[16]

"Alone and Pensive, I Delight to Stray": The First Edition

Before a "*tone*" can be repeated, of course, it must first be established. The sixteen sonnets in the first and second editions of *Elegiac Sonnets*, published first in 1784 as *Elegiac Sonnets, and Other Essays*, establish the tropes and images Smith then reworks and reimagines over the next decade and a half as she adds to the sequence – and as the historical situation changes. The poetic-speaker as wanderer is already central in these poems, appearing in the light of the moon, on cliffs overlooking the sea, or walking across the Sussex Downs. The poems also introduce Smith's cast of lost pilgrims, shipwrecked mariners, and exiles, all of whom function as (often inadequate) substitutes for the emotional state of the sonnet-speaker herself. Smith introduces the first edition as a collection of "little Poems," each expressive of a "single Sentiment." She explains that "Some very melancholy moments have been beguiled by expressing in verse the sensations those moments brought" (53). When Coleridge refers to Smith and William Bowles in his "Introduction to the Sonnets" (1797) as having established the rules of the English sonnet it is toward this statement and these poems that he gestures, defining the sonnet as a "small poem, in which some lonely feeling is developed," preferably "deduced from, and associated with, the scenery of Nature."[17]

As I did with the prospect in the previous chapter, I want to spend a moment sketching out how the template of this sentimental form works before moving on to how Smith reimagines it through shifting figures of wandering as the sequence developments. The chief trope of the melancholy or sentimental moment is the pause in walking, conducive to sympathy and poetic creativity. In Smith's first sonnets of the 1780s, wandering is centrally characterized by periods of reflection conducive to a generalized sense of communality in suffering, and so to consolation. The wandering such moments evoke is reminiscent of the sympathetic wandering undertaken by sentimental travelers such as Oliver Goldsmith's poet traveler, or Laurence Sterne's and Henry MacKenzie's men of feeling, but with a more Romantic focus on encounters with nature rather than people. The overlap comes from a shared structuring by the pause within movement and the feeling of connection and sympathy it is presented as enabling. So, in Sonnet 4, "To the Moon," a regular English sonnet, Smith's speaker declares that she "delight[s] to stray," "[a]lone and pensive" in the light of the moon, which is praised for shedding "a soft calm" upon her "troubled breast":

> Queen of the silver bow! – by thy pale beam,
>   Alone and pensive, I delight to stray,
> And watch thy shadow trembling in the stream,
>   Or mark the floating clouds that cross thy way.
> And while I gaze, thy mild and placid light
>   Sheds a soft calm upon my troubled breast;
> And oft I think – fair planet of the night,
>   That in thy orb, the wretched may have rest:
> The sufferers of the earth perhaps may go,
>   Released by death – to thy benignant sphere;
> And the sad children of Despair and Woe
>   Forget, in thee, their cup of sorrow here.
> Oh! that I soon may reach thy world serene,
> Poor wearied pilgrim – in this toiling scene!   (*ES*, 4)

Here the speaker evokes a sense of calm in the first quatrain as a result of her wanderings in the "placid light" of the moon. Smith's suspended syntax makes the words "Alone and pensive" first modify the moon, and then the "I," joining pensive poet to hanging moon. Out of this suspended moment, the speaker expresses a troubled longing for "rest," "release," "forgetfulness," and "serenity," although for now this is only "perhaps" available to the "sufferers of the earth," and is explicitly not yet available to her. The intimation that the poem comes from a moment of stasis within wandering rather than from wandering itself is picked up in the engraving by Richard Corbauld, included along with a number of other plates from the 1789 edition onward.[18] This plate became iconic of the sequence, presenting an attractive image of what a "melancholy moment" might

Figure 2.1 Sonnet 4, "To the Moon" accompanying image: "Queen of the Silver Bow." *Elegiac Sonnets*, Volume One. By R[ichard] Corbould, engraved by Milton. January 1, 1789.

look like, and in some ways it continues to influence our understanding of Smith as a lyric poet. Corbauld's image stabilizes the poem, presenting a solitary and idealized image of a woman who seems to have just stopped walking, the folds of her dress angled slightly to suggest recent motion, and who is now absorbed in a peaceful moment of contemplation (Figure 2.1).

Sonnet 12, "Written on the Sea Shore. – October, 1784," added in the third edition of 1786, presents a comparable moment in which a woman pauses in the act of wandering, and even more than is the case with Sonnet 4, this sonnet is explicitly presented as coming from a moment in which the speaker has stopped during a walk of some kind, this time "musing," to take a "solitary seat" upon an outcrop above the sea.

> On some rude fragment of the rocky shore,
>   Where on the fractured cliff the billows break,
>   Musing, my solitary seat I take,
> And listen to the deep and solemn roar.
>
> O'er the dark waves the winds tempestuous howl;
>   The screaming sea-bird quits the troubled sea:
>   But the wild gloomy scene has charms for me,
> And suits the mournful temper of my soul.
>
> Already shipwreck'd by the storms of Fate,
>   Like the poor mariner, methinks, I stand,
>   Cast on a rock; who sees the distant land
> From whence no succour comes – or comes too late.
> Faint and more faint are heard his feeble cries,
> 'Till in the rising tide the exhausted sufferer dies.   (*ES*, 12)

Again it is this image of the solitary thinking or composing woman that is illustrated in 1789, this time by Thomas Stothard (Figure 2.2).

Here, however, the engraving acknowledges the paradoxical communality of the solitary moments of melancholy depicted in these sonnets, showing the female wanderer holding a book. The book could be Edward Young's *The Revenge, A Tragedy* (1721), which is endnoted to line 8 and echoed in the poem, and which provides the template for its mood as well as the original of the storm suited to "the gloomy Habit" of a speaker's "soul."[19] The communality of the speaker's melancholy in the seashore sonnet works on multiple levels: it is reflected in nature; doubled in the feelings of the dying "mariner ... / Cast on a rock," much as Goldsmith's is in the feelings of the "pensive exile"; and it activates the poetic tradition of isolation and melancholy. The seemingly solitary moments depicted in the early sonnets, enabled

Plate 2.   Sonnet 8.

Stothard del.   Neagle sculp.

Published January 1.st 1789, by T. Cadell Strand.

On some rude fragment of the rocky shore.

Figure 2.2 Sonnet 12, "Written on the Sea Shore" accompanying image: "On some rude fragment of the rocky shore."*Elegiac Sonnets*, Volume One. By [Thomas] Stothard, engraved by Neagle. January 1, 1789.

by the pause in wandering, work as portals to a sense of generalized human suffering. Smith's creation of this space for a gestation of feeling, which in turn enables the creation of poetry, is what "beguiles" melancholy in these moments and is what creates the early sonnets' sense of consolation through wandering.

It is worth acknowledging, though, that the illustrations and dominant images of the speaker of the poems are actually belied by the agitation on the level of language even in these early sonnets, as well as by the accompanying darkness and morbidity of the communal consolation offered. The actual location of the composition of these "moments" was the King's Bench Prison: Smith's solitary evening walker is pure fiction. The "soft calm" of Sonnet 4 is counterbalanced by the "troubled breast" which needs calming and which is then reflected in the "troubled sea" of Sonnet 12. The seashore sonnet is dominated by the sounds of the sea's "solemn roar," the "wind's tempestuous howl," and seabirds' "screaming," while the speaker's location on a "fragment" of "fractured cliff" looking outward could not be more marginal and exposed. The wider world is very much present. Meanwhile, the images of release this speaker conjures are in every case deathly: the sufferers of the earth's best hopes are in being "Released by death"; when "no succour comes – or comes too late" to the exhausted castaway, he is left with no option but death (*ES*, 4.10, 12.12). Such morbidity necessarily lends a bleak undertone to the "delight" in a moment of straying evoked in Sonnet 4 and to the "charms" of the "gloomy scene" in Sonnet 12. If we read the offered consolation back into the poems, the illustrations become images of a woman thinking about her own death and the deaths of others. The real call for relief, even in these early sonnets, is a call for the cessation of this tormented consciousness. As Sarah M. Zimmerman writes, "the sonnets develop an account of the most private of relationships, to one's own mortality."[20] What is most curious about this, however, is just how publicly and communally this seemingly private relationship is imagined at this point in the sequence. Only later will Smith turn this literary communality back in on itself, charting a poetics of alienation from one's own poetic voice. It is precisely these more chronically alienated aspects of the earlier sonnets that come to the surface and become politicized as the sequence expands. When Smith invites readers to treat her wandering speaker as an ideal sentimental object of sympathy (a chaste Maria), she at once claims her readers' sympathy for appealing generalized moments of sorrow – inviting them to take voyeuristic pleasure in the melancholic instants of the poems – and begins to interpolate them into a specific narrative that dramatizes isolation and despair.

"The Wild Blast, Rising from the Western Cave": Revolutionary Imaginings, 1789

Figures of dissatisfaction that develop across *Elegiac Sonnets* darken as the sequence advances and as Smith adds more sonnets over time. In the late 1780s, the sonnets' consolation becomes ever more tenuous. Having drawn her readers' sympathies in, Smith begins to depict wider wanderings and to push wandering itself further and further toward the painful "steps unceasing" that Oliver Goldsmith's poet-speaker had feared his travels might become (*Tr*, 24). Sonnet 36, for instance, which closes the expanded fourth edition of 1786, makes loss of both poetry and rest or respite part of the depletions of wandering:

> Should the lone Wanderer, fainting on his way,
>   Rest for a moment of the sultry hours,
> And tho' his path thro' thorns and roughness lay,
>   Pluck the wild rose, or woodbine's gadding flowers,
> Weaving gay wreaths beneath some sheltering tree,
>   The sense of sorrow he awhile may lose;
> So have I sought thy flowers, fair Poesy!
>   So charm'd my way with Friendship and the Muse.
> But darker now grows life's unhappy day,
>   Dark with new clouds of evil yet to come,
> Her pencil sickening Fancy throws away,
>   And weary Hope reclines upon the tomb;
> And points my wishes to that tranquil shore,
> Where the pale spectre Care pursues no more.   (*ES*, 36)

Initially, Smith's speaker imagines a "lone Wanderer," "faint" like the poor mariner of the seashore poem, seeking a situation in which his "sense of sorrow he awhile may lose." The relationship of this lone Wanderer's search and that of the speaker is not simply analogous here, but homologous, sharing the structure of moments of creation plucked during a journey along a "rugged path" (*ES*, 1.2) of "thorns and roughness" (*ES*, 36.3). By the end of the second quatrain the activity of the wanderer, "Weaving gay wreathes," emphasized by its combination of assonance and alliteration and reminiscent of the "fantastic garlands" of the sequence's opening sonnet (*ES*, 1.4), functions as a metaphor for Smith's own acts of poetic composition – and so too for her sequence of interwoven sonnets.

At the beginning of the sestet the turn, "But darker now grows life's unhappy day," then begins the consolidation of the despairing note of the poem, rejecting all possibility of consolation. The Richard Corbauld plate that accompanies this poem, again from the 1789 edition onward, in contrast to the plates for the earlier moon and seashore sonnets, takes up the darker second half of the sonnet, underlining that this is where the emotional energy of this slightly later poem lies (Figure 2.3). The personified image of "weary Hope" reclining "upon a tomb" in both poem and plate echoes and embodies the yearning for death elided in the illustrations to Sonnets 4 and 12. In this case, though, even hope for death is depicted as having become listless and weak herself, almost fading out of the image. The "sheltering tree" of the first half of the poem, reminiscent of the first sonnets and subsequently of the "fairy flowers" and the desire to be "shelter'd" associated with retreat in *The Emigrants*, has little place in this darkening landscape.

As there is no spot for a wanderer to rest after the turn in this sonnet, or for Fancy to write of rest, there may, in fact, be no room for writing at all. This sense is underlined by Smith's invocation of a series of allegorical agents, which move the poem away from a metaphorical invocation of a state of mind to an allegorical state already detached from this world. Rather than depicting poetry as a strangely hopeful invocation of death, then, this sonnet suggests that even imagining or imitating the rest of death is something that poetry may not be capable of doing: Fancy no longer provides such easy solace. The lone Wanderer when "fainting on his way" may eventually just have to keep on wandering, and in such circumstances poetry might no longer be possible.

The strangest instance of "sickening Fancy" and fading "Hope" comes when the quiet desire for consolation in death of poems such as Sonnet 4, "To the Moon," develops into the poetic wanderer's envy of the dead. This finds its most bizarre deployment in Sonnet 44, "Written in the Church Yard at Middleton in Sussex" (dubbed by Stuart Curran the "grotesque forty-fourth")[21] and in its accompanying "Elegy."[21] Both poems were first published in the illustrated 1789 edition which appeared soon after Smith's move to Brighton ("Elegy" among the "other poems" placed at the end of the volume). Both are situated, as *The Emigrants* would be, on the edge of the coast just across the channel from Revolutionary France (44, note; *Elegy*, note). In them the generalized rocky shore of the seashore poem becomes a specific churchyard where the sea wall has caved in, allowing waves to pull the remains of human bodies and bones into the sea. The terms of the speaker's envy of the dead, worked through in the final,

Figure 2.3 Sonnet 36 accompanying image: "Her pencil sickening fancy throws away." *Elegiac Sonnets*, Volume One. By [Richard] Corbould, engraved by Neagle. January 1, 1789.

tightly-rhymed sestet of Sonnet 44, are tortured in their counterintuitiveness. The sonnet works to suggest that while the dead neither feel nor hear the "winds and waters rave," and the tug and pull of the violently "warring elements" of which they have become a part, the speaker, by contrast, is left standing feeling all the violence which the dead are spared.

> Press'd by the Moon, mute arbitress of tides,
>   While the loud equinox its power combines,
>   The sea no more its swelling surge confines,
> But o'er the shrinking land sublimely rides.
> The wild blast, rising from the Western cave,
>   Drives the huge billows from their heaving bed;
>   Tears from their grassy tombs the village dead,
> And breaks the silent sabbath of the grave!
> With shells and sea-weed mingled, on the shore
>   Lo! their bones whiten in the frequent wave;
>   But vain to them the winds and waters rave;
> *They* hear the warring elements no more:
> While I am doom'd – by life's long storm opprest,
> To gaze with envy on their gloomy rest.   (*ES*, 44)

The full rhyme on "opprest" and "rest" in the final couplet emphasizes the poem's bizarre directing idea that no matter how turbulent and gloomy the situation of the bones in the sea is, it is restful (as well as enviable) by comparison with the situation in which the speaker lives, "opprest" – the opposite of rest.

Critical work on Sonnet 44 has tended to emphasize Smith's manipulation of comparison and contrast between her speaker and the skeletons tossed in the sea, with the effect that, as Adela Pinch concludes, "the poem threatens the repose of the dead only to further emphasize their utter remoteness from strife and pain."[22] However, even though Sonnet 44 declares the situation of the "village dead" restful and impenetrable, the poem's actual energy lies in its evocation of the violent unrest even of the dead themselves. The sea moves in strong violent verbs – driving, tearing, heaving, and breaking – so that it is not simply depicted as laying siege to the land and to the graveyard, but as attacking them. The violence of Smith's poem's language is emphasized by contrast with the factual, descriptive language of her endnote which gives an account of the sea's more gradual "continual encroachments," and "approaches" (*ES*, 44, note). Within the sonnet Smith seeks to imitate the "wild blast" of the storm, straining, and not quite being contained within, the strict constraints of the sonnet form. If Smith's "village dead," as Esther Schor argues in a persuasive reading of this sonnet as a rewriting of Thomas Gray's "Elegy Written in a Country Churchyard" (1751), are an echo of Gray's "rude forefathers" who relieve him of his sense of isolation, then Smith's sonnet might be read as a violent assertion of her "gendered exclusion" from any such peace. As Schor comments, in this poem Smith is impossibly separated from "Gray's cult of sympathy for the patriarchal dead," and from the authority and associated consolations of this masculine literary tradition, and a feeling of communality with the past.[23] The peace of these dead – of this past – is precisely what the insistent turmoil of the poem disrupts. By giving the moon and the tides with which the speaker associates herself the strength to pull the graves into the sea, Smith assigns to herself agency to unsettle this tradition. The sad and seemingly resigned tone of the sonnet's final couplet is entirely undercut by the poem's brutality in beating the skeletons it describes against the sand, trying to make them feel the pain which the speaker suffers. Sonnet 44 might be understood as akin to what Diana Fuss dubs a "corpse poem," and in particular as part of a line of those "political corpse poems" that seek to right a social injustice by deflating "those corpses that have been culturally canonized."[24] Smith's humbling of figures from the past takes a peculiarly violent form. Notably, their punishment is mobility. The dead's very unrest, which Sonnet 44 seeks to evoke, in turn makes the dead difficult objects for the speaker to see as images of release: the speaker's effort simultaneously to envy and punish the dead creates the struggle of the poem, and indeed constitutes its most dire form of restlessness.

There is not actually much in Sonnet 44 itself, as is the case with many of Smith's sonnets, to directly assert the gender of the speaker. Jacqueline Labbe in particular has shown that the gender of Smith's sonnet speakers is frequently fluid. For Labbe, the sonnets in which Smith's speakers are engaged in what Labbe terms the traditionally male activity of wandering are especially strong examples of how Smith uses a layering of gender in *Elegiac Sonnets* in a way that disturbs gender boundaries.[25] However, the parallels between Sonnet 44 and the accompanying "Elegy" (although the two poems clearly have different speakers), encourage us, instead, to read the act of wandering in Smith's sonnets as embodying a specifically female, and specifically politicized, mode. The voice of the seventeen-stanza "Elegy" is that of the female indigent, or a "widow'd wanderer," whose richer lover has been lost at sea, leaving her to be "Forth to the world, a widow'd wanderer driven" (*Elegy*, 29). Smith's endnote to the poem places it "in the church-yard mentioned in Sonnet the 44th" then particularizes this location even further, making it the site of the tomb of the lover's father who had opposed the marriage. In the process, the patriarchal dead become the direct cause of the speaker's material and emotional sufferings. The poem also more generally transforms the anonymous graves of Sonnet 44 into explicit monuments to oppression: here, "Avarice finds a quiet grave!" and the "proud aggressor's tomb" is raised (*Elegy*, note, 12, 67). In her 1797 preface to Volume Two of *Elegiac Sonnets*, Smith would also describe as "aggressors" those responsible for her own financial situation and for the "dreadful misfortunes" it has led to – including the necessity for two of her sons to enter the army (99).[26] The dead are no longer objects of sympathy as they are in Gray, but rather examples of those whose financial and emotional economies have failed people like this female speaker, who becomes their "living victim" (*Elegy*, 24).

By "Elegy," Smith has made the woman wanderer on an outcrop above the sea an explicit image not of charming and accepting melancholy but of intense, mobile, and furious social alienation. Again, this contributes to Smith's radical remaking of the figure of the poetic wanderer. We are no longer invited to imagine this figure returning to a comfortable, middle-class home at the end of a contemplative walk, or finding relief in imagining those who have suffered like her. This is wandering as loss and as ongoing homelessness without emotional or financial resources. It is also a far cry from the leisure walking that is more familiarly associated with women's movements in this period, as it is by Rebecca Solnit and John Urry, for instance, when they use Jane Austen and Dorothy Wordsworth as their exemplars for discussing women's movements in the period in their histories of mobility.[27] Smith's gendered figure tears apart (rather than merely unpicks) what was in the process of becoming a Romantic equation between movement and freedom, in which women's movements too, were implicated.

While Smith's speaker stands alone at the end of Sonnet 44 gazing in impotent envy and rage on the tossing bones, the "Elegy," in contrast, enacts the kind of wish-fulfillment reminiscent of the very early sonnets. Only this is now combined with a revenge fantasy such as that desired by Sonnet 44 and hinted at in the form of radical substitutability in *The Emigrants*. Rather than being an observer only implicitly associated with the upheaval of the elements, the speaker in the "Elegy" calls the sea up over the land. In a gothic scene of "terrors" and "shrieks of horror," the elegy's speaker climbs on a tomb, "Invoking vengeance on the dust below" (*Elegy*, 5, 14, 20). In a stormy speech once again reminiscent of the anger of

Lear on the heath, this "widow'd wanderer" cast upon the world incites the "Spirits of the Tempest" to come, calling,

> Loud and more loud, ye foaming billows! burst;
> Ye warring elements! more fiercely rave,
> Till the wide waves o'erwhelm the spot accurst   (*Elegy*, 9–11)

Echoing the "warring elements" and the "rave" of the waves in the sonnet (*ES*, 44.11–12), the speaker here becomes their commander; she speaks with their angry voice. The dramatic climax of the poem comes only in the final stanza:

> The Ocean hears – The embodied waters come –
> Rise o'er the land, and with resistless sweep
> Tear from its base the proud aggressor's tomb,
> And bear the injured to eternal sleep!   (*Elegy*, 65–8)

Here the speaker, along with the village dead, is taken into the sea: generalized once more as "the injured" she is granted the rest she desires and achieves "eternal sleep." The syntactically necessary condition that allows her to stop wandering is the destruction of the "proud aggressor's" tomb. The physically necessary condition is that the land itself disappears. Both poems are radically placeless, being situated on literally crumbling ground. By this stage the sequence has moved far from "moments" of melancholy, to poems which collectively stage confrontations, albeit morbid ones, with those Smith feels are responsible for inflicting pain and thus for the necessity of wanderings in the widest sense.

The shift from the melancholy state of the first sonnets to that expressed in these later poems of the Revolutionary period is again graphically represented in another Corbauld plate, this one appearing opposite the "Elegy" from the 1789 edition onward (Figure 2.4). This plate could equally illustrate Sonnet 44 and it depicts a wild, moving version of the pensive figure of the early illustrations. This female figure no longer sits in quiet and appealing contemplation, with the sea unobserved in the backdrop, but is the moving center of a storm. The wind tears at her hair and the sash of her dress, and she is caught in a moment of dashing toward the sea, leaning so far forward she looks as though she is about to fall. In motion, vulnerable, exposed to the elements, she presents a striking image of what mobility might come to mean for some. These poems of the late 1780s are at once despairing in their sentiments and defiant – even revolutionary – in their tumultuous imagery.

Figure 2.4 "Elegy" accompanying image: No Title. *Elegiac Sonnets*, Volume One. By [Richard] Corbould, engraved by [James] Heath. January 1, 1789.

"Desolate I Stray": Elegiac Sonnets, Volume Two, 1797

Volume One of *Elegiac Sonnets* found its final form in the sixth edition of 1792, after which Smith turned her poetic focus to *The Emigrants*. When Volume Two appeared in 1797, it contained twenty-five new sonnets (Sonnets 60–84), as well as a number of other poems, including "The Female Exile," which extracted and rewrote a key moment from *The Emigrants*.[28] In the edition of 1800, this was expanded to thirty-three sonnets, bringing the sequence as a whole to its final length of ninety-two sonnets. As a result of the critical understandings of the sonnets that saw its story as largely finished by the 1790s when Smith began to use her novels and long poems in interesting political ways, the poems in Volume Two were for a long time overlooked altogether, let alone treated as a distinct moment in the publication history of *Elegiac Sonnets*. The proliferation of different editions contributed to this critical oversight, making it difficult to get a clear sense of which poems were added when. The publication of the first modern edition of the sonnets edited by Stuart Curran in 1993, complete with their prefaces but without the engravings, despite its immense value, created its own issues, as once the poems were taken from their original settings it became difficult to gain a sense of edition breaks at all. This has been somewhat resolved only in very recent editions.[29] However, Volume Two represents a distinctly new moment in Smith's evolving use of the sonnet sequence and an extension of her meditation on the difficulties of wandering.

Smith's growing affinity with English radicals during the years between the completion of Volume One and the publication of Volume Two is underscored by her novels, in particular *Desmond* (1792), as well as in the political bite of *The Emigrants* itself. During these years, Smith became increasingly intimate with public figures such as the radical Joel Barlow and Thomas Erskine, the lawyer who famously defended Thomas Hardy, Thomas Paine, and other radicals on charges of treason.[30] As we have seen in relation to *The Emigrants*, the arrival of thousands of French refugees on the south coast where Smith lived literalized her previously general and abstracted sense of the omnipresence of pained wanderers, exiles, and those shipwrecked in various ways, both literal and metaphorical. At the same time, like so many of her contemporaries Smith became increasingly pained by political developments as the French Revolution became bloody, government within Britain became increasingly authoritarian, and both countries found themselves engaged in a war with no foreseeable end in sight. She seems to be expressing something close to her own views when her narrator in *The Banished Man* (1794) observes of the English character, Ellesmere, "His thorough conviction of what it [the Revolution] might have been, only encreased the concern and disgust he felt in reflecting on what it was."[31] Soon after completing *The Emigrants* Smith herself very quickly and very directly felt the personal effects of war when in September 1793 her 20-year-old son, Charles, was wounded at Dunkirk and came home with one leg amputated – "mutilated for life" as Smith put it in a letter – and once again dependent on his writer mother for support.[32]

In her preface to Volume Two, Smith puts her new poems forward as capable carriers of "opinions" which may even be shocking to "liberal-minded personages" (101), inviting readers to see in her sonnets such political opinions as had been widely criticized in her novels and even inviting them to reread the earlier poems. In what is Smith's strongest statement of the reach of her 1790s sonnets, the contained "moments" of melancholy of the first editions is translated into something akin to global tragedy – to the "tragedy in real life," and "the extensive and still threatening desolation, that overspreads this country, and in some degree, every quarter of the world" (102). This echoes the preface from Virgil with which she had opened Book Two of *The Emigrants* and in the context of *Elegiac Sonnets* it amounts to a shift from a kind of poetic melancholy to what Jacqueline Labbe calls in a reading of the connections between Smith and Wordsworth's "war poetry," "the real."[33] Wandering in the final movement of Smith's sonnets is a key trope through which she registers her growing sense of the potential failure of social sympathy, evocatively extending the translation she has already begun of wandering into a metaphor for alienations of all kinds – from a figure of contemplation and embodied sympathy to a sign of alienation. From an activity characterized by the pauses within it to a sign of ceaseless mobility. But *Elegiac Sonnets* was already a lengthy work by this point, and these new poems work in conversation with the "melancholy moments" that still come at the opening of the sequence in which they appear.

Smith's later sonnets stage some of her most challenging attempts to explore the relationship between the personal and the political, and the personal and the general, increasingly depicting the difficulty of finding space for a self capable of sympathetic identification, even of the face-to-face kind represented in *The Emigrants*, in a political landscape which she sees as becoming increasingly bleak. Sonnet 80, "To the Invisible Moon," which comes near the end of the sequence and directly addresses Sonnet 4, "To the

Moon," is useful for visualizing Smith's evocation of both political loss and self-alienation in the 1790s. Before the sonnet even begins, Smith's endnote to the title underwrites the political desolation and confinement of the poem's position by triggering the context of Milton's *Samson Agonistes* (1671):

> *... I address the Moon when not visible at night in our hemisphere. "The Sun to me is dark, / And silent as the Moon / When she deserts the night, / Hid in her secret interlunar cave." Milton. *Samson Agonistes* [lines 86–9]

This reference, of course, activates much more than an astronomical explanation of the situation of the sonnet. The quoted lines come from the famous opening of Milton's work, in which Samson laments his loss of sight, light, and hope, and his subsequent isolation from human community. In Milton, the image of the invisible moon forms part of a politically situated figuration of a kind of "living death" in the face of loss of personal and political options. Milton's evocation of a speaker who sees himself as only different from the dead in that he still feels pain chimes with the feelings of Smith's sonnets from Sonnet 44 onward, and prepares the way for the deeper resonances of psychological and political loss of late sonnets such as Sonnet 80. Milton's Samson laments:

> Scarce half I seem to live, dead more than half.
> O dark, dark, dark, amid the blaze of noon,
>   ...
> To live a life half dead, a living death,
> And buried; but O yet more miserable!
> My self, my Sepulcher, a moving Grave,
> Buried, yet not exempt
> By priviledge of death and burial
> From worst of other evils, pains and wrongs [.][34]

Allusion here underscores the potency of Smith's extreme sense of alienation and loss on both a personal and political level.

By contrast to signaling an imagined escape from suffering, in the increasingly bleak political landscape of the 1790s, wandering in *Elegiac Sonnets* comes to invoke painful motion without reprieve, and, most devastatingly, without hope of reprieve. Wandering in these later poems is characterized by negatives. One sonnet which appeared near the beginning of Volume Two begins, "While thus I wander, cheerless and unblest, / And find in change of place but change of pain" (*ES*, 62.1–2).[35] The speaker in Sonnet 52, "The Pilgrim," which comes near the end of Volume One does not move "Alone and pensive" as is the case in very early sonnets, occasionally stopping to "muse," but instead journeys, "Alone, reluctant, desolate and slow" (*ES*, 4.2, 12.3, 52.10).[36] This echoes the iconic opening line of Oliver Goldsmith's *The Traveller*, "Remote, unfriended, melancholy, slow," but rather than invoking Goldsmith's community in exile joined by a shared imagining of a lost past, Smith's speaker is confined to the painful present, while her heart "trembling at the past – recoils from future woe" (*Tr*, 1, *ES*, 52.12).[37] Meanwhile, the once "serene" moon, so associated with poetry, now throws only a "wan" and "cold" light, which specifically fails to lead to community: the "unblest" wanderer reproaches the moon as the, "pale Eye of Evening, thy soft light / Leads to no happy home" (*ES*, 4.13, 62.1–14).

The desolation of these 1790s sonnets is dependent for its full evocation on their placement at the end of a sequence which in its opening poems continues to evoke precisely those feelings that the speaker declares are now inaccessible to her. Underscoring this is the fact that the moving, alienated subject in this darker landscape tends to be separated not only from others but also from versions of her former self as depicted in earlier sonnets, who at least had some hope that consolation through poetic wanderings might be possible. Sonnet 80, "To the Invisible Moon" is full of allusions to the situation of Smith's earlier sonnet speakers, which forms a point of contrast rather than comparison (as is the case with the Milton allusion) with the bleak new situation depicted in the later sonnet. The violence of the images upon which Smith's solitary figure in Sonnet 80, isolated again on a "steep rock" on the very edge of the land, now chooses to look is startling:

> Dark and conceal'd art thou, soft Evening's Queen,
>   And Melancholy's votaries that delight
> To watch thee, gliding thro' the blue serene,
>   Now vainly seek thee on the brow of night –
> Mild Sorrow, such as Hope has not forsook,
>   May love to muse beneath thy silver reign;
> But *I* prefer from some steep rock to look
>   On the obscure and fluctuating main,
> What time the martial star with lurid glare,
>   Portentous, gleams above the troubled deep;
> Or the red comet shakes his blazing hair;
>   Or on the fire-ting'd waves the lightnings leap;
> While thy fair beams illume another sky,
> And shine for beings less accurst than I.   (*ES*, 80)

Here the "martial star," the star of war, glares above the "troubled deep" of the ocean; a red comet seems to shake in anger; and lightning leaps across waves. In other poems which come late in the sequence, there are literal signs of war on the waters, and the ocean itself becomes red with the blood of the "mangled dead" (*ES*, 83.12). The "warring elements" of the church-yard sonnet and "Elegy" become the speaker's whole world in these later sonnets, and the poems do not even try to suggest that the dead are spared this violence, making the clean, white, fleshless bones of the earlier church-yard sonnet seem almost peaceful in retrospect despite their being beaten against the shore. Images of consolation become impossible in this now literally battle-shaken world; the political "Hope" of the late 1780s and early 1790s, already under stress in poems such as *The Emigrants*, is no longer tenable. Death itself is now resolutely violent: the silver reign of the early moonlit scenes has been replaced by darkness and by the morbid red of blood and warfare.

The hopefulness of "Melancholy's votaries" of the moon who might still even bother searching for a "world serene" through poetry, wandering, and a fantasy of peaceful death, is rejected in the rhyme of the final couplet of Sonnet 80, "To the Invisible Moon," which moves from "other sky" to "I." These worshippers exist in a world so separate from that of the speaking subject that they live under another sky and another moon from that on which she gazes – metaphorically, they are a hemisphere away. While the poem quotes the former state of the speaker – bringing back diction from earlier poems such as "serene" and "delight" – the "I" in the poem declares herself to be quite separate from the versions of her earlier self with which such words and feelings are connected. "Melancholy's votaries" are grouped among "beings less accurst than I." Sonnets like these show versions of the speaker's former self – and quote her images and diction – but they do not quite connect these to the speaker. Smith, then, suggests a break in sympathy between even her former and present self: this newly mobile speaker fails even to be able to generalize her present situation as related to her former one. The "invisibility" of the moon in the title signals the invisibility of the state of the initial sonnets – and crucially also of the hopes. The speaker at the end of Sonnet 80 seems capable only of gazing on what is before her now, as if transfixed. Nor will Smith exercise the "self-control" and "endurance" in suffering demanded within Adam Smith's model of sympathy in order to make her experience generalizable and so communicable to others. She does not so much seem to be seeking sympathy (including that of the reader) in these late sonnets, as represent-ing exclusion from its affective economy.

This exclusion is figured in part as an inability to fully achieve the sympathy suggested by quotation. Smith's frequent use of quotation and allusion throughout her sonnets has contributed to her being placed in work such as that by Stephen Behrendt and Paula Backscheider at the center of discussions of the inherent sociability of the sonnet, as well as of sentimental verse in general, with its complex manipulations of the interplay between personal feelings and their conventional and literary associations.[38] Formally, of course, sonnets are always a kind of quotation. At the same time, however, Smith's overt practices of allusion in *Elegiac Sonnets* continue to challenge understandings of allusion that see it predominantly as a marker of belonging, or of communal consolation – or as a matter of summoning the authority of a masculine literary tradition in what Susan Wolfson calls "Romantic interaction."[39] Smith's practices of quotation in *Elegiac Sonnets* fit at least in part, as do Wollstonecraft's as discussed in Chapter 4, into Wolfson's "shadow-story" of Romantic interaction, marked by interactions that "agitate and alienate."[40] In Smith, quotations as often function as marks of alienation, exile, and failed connection, as they do of belonging. As Melissa Sodeman puts it in her work on Smith's novels, "Rather than providing a window into a greater literary context, Smith's quotations . . . serve as marks of her exile from the 'community of the mind' within which [Samuel] Johnson claimed quotations circulated."[41] For Adela Pinch, in the "echo chambers" of English poetry that Smith has *Elegiac Sonnets* become, Smith shows us from her opening sonnet that writing within a (masculine) literary tradition can make one melancholy because one must always be quoting someone else.[42]

I want to build on this body of critical work on the more alienated side of Smith's practices of quotation by suggesting that Smith's late sonnets express an exacerbation of this situation. In her late sonnets, in addition to quoting more and more extensively from others, Smith develops a form of self-referential textual interaction within the sequence, based on comparisons with a former self of the early sonnets from whom the later speaker has now become irretrievably separated. If quoting someone else who is explicitly not oneself is melancholy, then how much more troubling and how much lonelier must it be to quote a former version of oneself, whose feelings are no longer accessible?

An especially overt manifestation of the speaker's condition of confinement in her own difficult, and all-too-present, experience is visually represented in the engraving that accompanies another sonnet from Volume Two, Sonnet 70, descriptively entitled, "On being cautioned against walking on an headland overlooking the sea, because it was frequented by a lunatic" (Figure 2.5). This was part of the group of four new

Figure 2.5 Sonnet 70, "On being cautioned against walking on an headland" accompanying image: "In moody Sadness on the giddy Brink." *Elegiac Sonnets*, Volume Two. By R[ichard] Corbould, engraved by J[ames] Heath. May 15, 1797.

images included in the new volume, along with a new frontispiece, and it illustrates starkly the speaker's separation from others. It is possible to miss the woman in the image altogether. She hovers in the background behind the figure of the "lunatic," a "solitary wretch," who, seeming to represent a version of the speaker's former self, now stands between her and the sea. The caption to the engraving, which quotes the sonnet it accompanies, reads, "In moody sadness, on the giddy brink, / I see him more with envy than with fear." The "giddy brink" recalls the "giddy height" that the "unhappy Pilgrim" journeys along in Sonnet 52 (*ES*, 52.4–1).

When in this sonnet the speaker is reduced to envying the misled "lunatic," the thought that release from the present and from the isolated self might be possible becomes the product of an unstable mind:

> *He* has no *nice felicities* that shrink
>   From giant horrors; wildly wandering here,
> He seems (uncursed with reason) not to know
> The depth or the duration of his woe.   (*ES*, 70.11–14)

Unlike Smith's speaker, whose very need to keep adding to her sequence performs the duration of her woe. Envy, it is worth remembering, is not the same as sympathy, but involves a dissonance between experiences. The image in the poem is further complicated by the conventional association between the "lunatic" and the poet – the speaker stands in this case at a remove from herself as poet, as well as from someone capable of feeling and sympathy (even if that sympathy is only sympathy in a shared sense of despair). The link between poet and "lunatic" is premised on the ability of both to in imagination become other beings – to move free from the circumscribed limits of reality. But while the idea that poetry itself is only an illusion of release is reinforced by the association of poet and lunatic, in these late poems Smith depicts herself as no longer even able to access that illusion. Goldsmith's twinned exiles have become twinned lunatics, now not even bound by mutual sympathy, but projecting a confronting image of isolation and failed sympathetic engagement.

The woman depicted in this engraving is also clearly older, and more careworn than in any of the images yet shown in *Elegiac Sonnets*, and resembles Smith herself as depicted in the frontispiece to Volume Two more than she does the young women of the 1789 illustrations, reinforcing the separation between the two volumes (Figure 2.6).[43] The caption to the new portrait in Volume Two reads, "Oh! Time has changed me since you saw me last. / And heavy Hours with Time's deforming Hand / Have written Strange Defeatures on my Face," directly describing the self-alienation the sonnets evoke. Rather than being a generalized and appealing figure as in the earlier images (Labbe calls them "young love-lies"), or becoming like Wordsworth's idealized, representative, if questionable, "Being made / Of many Beings," Smith is here simply a disappointing version of herself, marked by the "deforming Hand" and "Defeatures" of her particular, relentless biography.[44] She is just an old woman as Lear on the heath is just an old man, "the thing itself; unaccommodated man."[45] She presents as neither conventional, easily integrated object of sympathy, nor as a subject capable of initiating sympathetic exchange. This is a political as well as an aesthetic statement: in the climate of the late 1790s, Smith suggests, there is little hope of change of situation, no easy way to comprehend through sympathy, let alone alleviate suffering in this way, and little option but to look on a difficult world. How different the figure of the melancholy wanderer becomes if we understand this uncompromising engraving as an image of one.

What then is left? The answer proffered by Sonnet 80 and Sonnet 83, "The Sea View," is in part a scene of violence – and in particular of warfare – which possesses its own energies and responsibilities. This is similar to the scene Smith begun the work of witnessing in *The Emigrants*, resituating the poet-speaker from the home or the inland hilltop to the edge of the land. An endnote to "The Sea View" explains that the sonnet was "Suggested by the recollection of having seen, some years since . . . an engagement between two armed ships, from the high down called the Beacon Hill, near Brighthelmstone," situating the sonnet-speaker in the same location just outside Brighton as the speaker in *The Emigrants* (*ES*, 83, note). The sestet of this sonnet breaks in upon the tranquil pastoral scene of the octave, reminiscent of the earlier sonnets, with:

> When, like dark plague-spots by the Demons shed,
> Charged deep with death, upon the waves, far seen,
>   Move the war-freighted ships; and fierce and red,
>   Flash their destructive fire – The mangled dead
> And dying victims then pollute the flood.
> Ah! thus man spoils Heaven's glorious works with blood!   (*ES*, 83.9–14)

The flash of light against darkness is man-made in this sonnet, and its "destructive fire" brings only death. There is a messy fleshiness at the heart

P. Conde sculp.

Oh! Time has Changed me since you saw me last,
And heavy Hours with Time's deforming Hand,
Have written strange Defeatures in my Face.

Published May 15th 1797. by Cadell and Davies Strand.

Figure 2.6 Frontispiece: "Oh! Time has Changed me." Volume Two, *Elegiac Sonnets*. By Pierre Condé, after John Opie. May 15, 1797.

of the sonnet that is entirely different from the image of the bones tossed by the sea in Sonnet 44, and which brings warfare closer to home than is the case even in *The Emigrants*. The dead here are "mangled" or still in the bloody process of dying, while the whole scene is associated with apocalyptic biblical imagery of plague, pollution, and spoil. Smith's late 1790s sonnets are in part a lament that politics and history do not, as it had seemed they might in the early 1790s, provide a model for personal hope, and in part an effort to represent what this new historical present looks and feels like. This in turn connects with the more important answer to the question of what is left once the movement of history itself comes to seem authoritarian, and once what the benign consoling light of the moon represents has becomes inaccessible. What is left, Smith suggests, is the isolated subject with which so many of her sonnets end, who by the close of the sequence has only one choice: to look again and again on a world she finds alienating and violent and to give up her fantasies of calm release through consoling communality in suffering. This relinquishment of fantasy, along with the rejection of retreat explored in *The Emigrants*, provides one answer to why Smith makes political horror enter so palpably into her seemingly private sonnets. This seems to be what she means by representing the "tragedy in real life."

In the late 1790s sonnets placed at the end of her sonnet sequence, Smith makes wandering, like the prospect view or the "Cot sequester'd" of retreat in *The Emigrants* (*Em* 1.75), fail to function as an image of release, transforming it instead into a figure for difficult, continued, and confusing involvement – into a figure for labor and for endless and meaningless motion. The "I" inhabited by her wanderer is forever fractured by being separated from its former self, and forever stuck in the singular solitariness of its being in the present moment. This is as significant a challenge to positive imaginings of mobility and sympathy as that posed by *The Emigrants* – and more formally complex. The solitary and isolated subject in Smith's late sonnets is reminiscent of, but bleaker than, the Wordsworthian conception, say, in "Lines Written a Few Miles above Tintern Abbey" (1798). In a poem like "Tintern Abbey," Wordsworth seeks some kind of consoling, interior wandering and sees consolation as at least partly possible through a doubled self – in the "then" and the "now," and the realization that the "now" itself is broken in two through recollection, with memory a "dwelling-place / For all sweet sounds and harmonies."[46] What Smith misses, finally, in her late sonnets is fully accessible, and recoverable, "recollection," and without this there can be no hope of tranquillity.

Painful repetition is all that is left. We might remember the speaker in Sonnet 52, "The Pilgrim," who is represented "trembling at the past" and equally "recoils from future woe" (*ES*, 52.14). By its end, Smith's *Elegiac Sonnets* is not quite elegiac. This trembling, exposed location in the in-between is what separates Smith's reluctant wanderer most drastically also from both Goldsmith's and William Cowper's communities of exiles: her late sonnet-speakers are unable – and unwilling – to turn to the past, in whatever form, for consolation. This desolate position also separates her poetic-speaker from the figure of the national bard. As Stephen Behrendt puts it, for many women writers, "There *were* no 'good old days' for them; any good days that were to be had necessarily lay in the future."[47] As later chapters explore, the political and aesthetic problem of exile without nostalgia for some past is also central to Mary Wollstonecraft's and Frances Burney's work, playing a key role in ima-ginings of dire forms of homelessness.

Smith's poetry in the end gets its energy from an intense sense of alienation and loss, despite the fact that her sonnet sequence appears on the surface to be a staging of a series of melancholy moments of consola-tion in Nature, and despite many editions using the "To the Moon" image as frontispiece, suggesting that this works as an emblem for the whole. The shift enacted in *Elegiac Sonnets*, both over time and within the sequence itself, presents two challenges: to think about whether suffer-ing – both personal and political – necessarily makes room for sympathy, an assumption that is as central to *The Traveller* and *The Task*, as it is to Adam Smith's *The Theory of Moral Sentiments* and sentimental literature in general; and to think about whether continued motion might be debilitating as often as it is enabling. Smith's is a poetry in which "mangled corpses" lurk beneath the surface from the very beginning. In the political climate of the 1790s, unable to believe in the fantasy consolation of a "world serene," her sonnet-speaker finally declares, "But *I* prefer . . . to look / On the obscure and fluctuating main" (*ES*, 4.13, 80.7–8). This is a preference, she makes clear, born out of necessity and out of a particular historical moment. This "look" is what produces her version of the abject wanderer – a figure who comes to speak of, to borrow Wollstonecraft's phrase, "a world in ruins," in which everyone seems as dispossessed as they are unable to transcend their suffering through sympathetic feeling.[48] The very form of Smith's repetitiveness and the "perpetual" feel of *Elegiac Sonnets* itself replicate and deepen the theme of literal and psychological homelessness at its heart. As the sequence evolves through each addition, the poetic speaker's loss – the impossibility of her finding consolation or of moving forward – become part of what Smith's *Elegiac Sonnets* as a whole works to perform. Each new installment on the same theme is a declaration of continued and deepening homelessness – each subsequent repetition of images of exile and wandering by their very repetition effects a deepening of alienation.

CHAPTER 3

"The Irresistible Force of Circumstances"
The Poetics of Wandering in Radcliffean Gothic

> they should never catch me going on my travels any more! I must
> think it a fine thing, truly, to come abroad, and see foreign parts!
> I little thought I was coming to be catched up in an old castle, among
> such dreary mountains, with the chance of being murdered.
>
> *The Mysteries of Udolpho*, 297.

> She frequently took a volume of Shakspear or Milton, and, having
> gained some wild preeminence, would seat herself beneath the pines,
> whose low murmurs soothed her heart, and conspired with the visions
> of the poet to lull her to forgetfulness of grief.
>
> *The Romance of the Forest*, 261.

In Ann Radcliffe, we meet not just wanderers but great travelers. Adeline in
The Romance of the Forest (1791) travels all over France and sails up the
Rhone to Switzerland; Emily St. Aubert in *The Mysteries of Udolpho* (1794)
wanders with her father from their native Gascony to the shores of the
Mediterranean, visits Venice, and sojourns in the Italian alps; while Ellena
di Rosalba in *The Italian* (1797) travels back and forth from Naples and
spends time in a house on the Adriatic Sea. As Ellen Moers observes in her
landmark essay, "Traveling Heroinism: Gothic for Heroines," the gothic
novel in Radcliffe's hands became "a device to send maidens on distant and
exciting journeys."[1] Radcliffe's heroines are, of course, also coerced travelers – the term *reluctant* rather understates the case here. Adeline makes her
first appearance with a man "leading, or rather forcibly dragging" her
along, and demanding that another man "convey" her elsewhere; Emily
sets out "in obedience to the will of a stranger," is threatened with a forced
marriage in Venice, and imprisoned in the villainous Montoni's mountain
castle for much of the novel; and Ellena's travel starts when she is
kidnapped from her home.[2] For Moers, these plot elements function as
mechanisms by which Radcliffe has her heroines embark with propriety on
their wide-ranging adventures. Other critics have also tended to focus on
the enabling aspects of the actual journeys in Radcliffe's texts.[3] But

traveling in the Radcliffean mode of the gothic involves escalating threats of loss, violence, and madness. Subject to repeated terrors, Radcliffe's wandering heroines risk becoming as psychologically homeless as they are literally displaced.

If we shift our attention from travel to mobility, understood within Tim Cresswell's formulation as all "socially produced motion," it becomes easier to see that Radcliffe's novels are about those without the capital or social autonomy to direct their own movements and about how it is possible to survive such conditions of disempowerment.[4] Such a shift in focus helps to make more visible the mechanisms by which a gothic heroine's mobility and stasis is produced, and in the process what these conditions represent. As media and cultural theorist David Morley writes, drawing on Doreen Massey's notion of "power geometry" to explain the relationship between mobility and power: "The ultimate issue is not who moves or is still, but who has control. ... It matters little whether the choice is exercised in favour of staying still or in favour of movement."[5] Whether a gothic heroine is imprisoned or traveling widely, she seldom has control over where or when she goes or where and when she stays.

This chapter turns to Radcliffe's gothic heroines as reluctant wanderers because the twinned tropes of the imposed journey and of imprisonment are so central to evocations of gothic terror. This helps to demonstrate the consequences of mobility when it does not signal William Blackstone's ideal of personal liberty but rather, by its association with coercion, narrates liberty's opposites. The gothic presents the implications of reluctant wanderings in their most starkly realized incarnations. Radcliffe was also the chief proponent, along with Charlotte Smith, of the poetic novel – the novel that incorporates actual verses and lyric passages in prose. Many of Smith's sonnets reappeared, or appeared first, in the pages of her novels. This additional formal innovation allows these authors to set an alternate mode of movement against the terrorizing journeys their novels narrate. In relation to Radcliffe, critics have noted that much as she rushes her traveling heroines along, her novels are also marked by digressions from plot – digressions that contribute as much to the atmosphere of Radcliffe's gothic as does her mastery of suspense.[6] These digressions, I argue in this chapter, are formal or textual as well as thematic and literal. Radcliffe's heroines, as indeed do many of Smith's, love to wander through mountainous landscapes, to read and paint, to look at the view, and to dwell on the past. They also have a tendency to lapse into offset quotations, to imaginatively wander into other worlds, and to compose poems that break up the text of these novels. They are, in other words, drawn to enter the kinds of lyric pauses evoked in Smith's early sonnets. Rather than separating out and focusing either on the terrors of the journey in Radcliffe's work or on its enabling aspects, here I investigate the relationship between the compulsions of the gothic journey and Radcliffe's interest in wandering form as developed through landscape description, quotation, and interpolated original verses. I argue that Radcliffe fuses the gothic with the poetic novel in a way that at once demonstrates the fragility of imaginative or digressive wanderings and their necessity and resonance.

As will be becoming clear, this chapter is somewhat an outlier in this book as a whole, in part because wandering emerges in Radcliffean gothic, surprisingly, as a somewhat less abject physical and mental state than we see represented in the texts I discuss in other chapters. This difference is in part a result, I believe, of Radcliffe starting from a given that a gendered relationship with mobility is troubled and then moving toward an effort to find sources of consolation within that. She refuses to focus on her heroine's suffering with quite such unrelenting consistency as a novelist like Frances Burney, whose piling of troubles on her heroine in *The Wanderer; or, Female Difficulties* is only an extension of her practice in her two immediately preceding novels. Radcliffe's somewhat lighter tone (if one can only call it that by contrast with Smith, Wollstonecraft, and Burney) may also be a result of genre difference, stemming from the necessity of offering a reader some variety as release from the pressures of the gothic. However, Radcliffe remains an important writer for a history of the woman wanderer, in particular for her exploration of the relationship between physical and mental mobility. In my own book about bleak, troubled texts, it is perhaps fitting that the central chapter should offer some respite.

Radcliffe's staging of a contest between two textual modes of wandering (and experience) – one gothic, the other poetic or lyric – takes a particularly potent and suggestive form in *Udolpho*, around which I focus this chapter. In parts of *Udolpho* Radcliffe has quotation – from authors ranging from Shakespeare and Milton to James Thomson, William Collins, Thomas Gray, and Charlotte Smith – occur so frequently her characters can seem like permeable, porous beings who could as easily think the thoughts of another as their own. By contrast, while a proliferation of quotations and original poems frames the period of Emily's confinement in the castle of Udolpho – the point at which her enforced journey becomes actual imprisonment – there is only one inset quotation and no original poetry whatsoever in the imprisonment section of the novel itself.[7] As discussed in the previous chapter, Smith in her later, post-Revolutionary editions of

Elegiac Sonnets uses literary allusion to signal her wandering speaker's growing sense of exile from a sympathetic community of the mind. In Radcliffe's mid-1790s text, she has her heroine, when the pressures of the journey reach crisis point, become isolated from the space of the literary community altogether. Both authors use a form of exclusion from this imagined community to evoke moments when a mobile subject becomes too pained or isolated to engage, and both situate such moments in the context of a wider sense of political and social crises. Reading *Udolpho* through scenes that stage the blocking and enabling of literary interaction, however, also suggests that if Radcliffe represents the nadir of the gothic journey as isolation from literary interaction, the structure of her novel works to show that to remember, to read, and to write literature in some sense signals movement free from isolation or confinement.

The Poetic Novel as Wandering Form

Udolpho and *The Romance of the Forest* both carry the subtitle, *Interspersed with some Pieces of Poetry*. These subtitles are dropped from modern editions and bibliographies, but they ask us to pay attention to "interspersed" poetry as a distinctive aspect of these novels' forms. As one contemporary reviewer puts it, "The verses which are interspersed are announced in the title-page, and are consequently intended to be pointed out to particular notice."[8] Whether they receive particular notice is, however, questionable. In 1810, Anna Laetitia Barbauld wrote anxiously about the tendency of readers to skip over poems interpolated into Radcliffe's novels:

> It ought not to be forgotten that there are many elegant pieces of poetry interspersed through the volumes of Mrs. Radcliffe. . . . The true lovers of poetry are almost apt to regret its being brought in as an accompaniment to narrative, where it is generally neglected . . . and the common reader is always impatient to get on with the story.[9]

In his review of *Udolpho*, Samuel Taylor Coleridge succumbs to the opposite temptation of excising and quoting a full poem out of its narrative context – detaching it from its role as "accompaniment" to narrative – while also like Barbauld lamenting that "poetical beauties have not a fair chance of being attended to, amidst the stronger interest inspired by such a series of adventures."[10] I am interested in what it means to read this kind of poetic novel as Barbauld's "true lover of poetry" would. What happens if we take seriously the idea that this does not mean excising poetry and digressive moments from the novels in which they appear, nor skipping over them as we concentrate on the plot, but instead reading them as a vital complement to the more linear prose narrative? If we accept, as Mary Wollstonecraft suggests in a review of Smith's early poetic novel, *Emmeline, the Orphan of the Castle* (1788), that it is impossible for the poetic descriptions and poetry in such novels to be "separated from the woven web without injuring them," these novels read very differently.[11] How these woven "webs" entangle both characters and readers emerges in new ways. *Udolpho* as poetic novel, I want to suggest, offers a lesson in reading the alternative aesthetics of wandering texts – a lesson built on the idea that the gothic is a genre most expressive when seemingly most inarticulate.[12]

Precedents for the practice of placing poetry within novels are few and far between. The practice is not a feature of any of the eighteenth-century novels we know well and, until the 1780s, seems to have been largely confined to works by Jane Barker and Charlotte Lennox.[13] Barker is particularly interesting because she frames what she terms her "Patch-Work" novels as distinctively female productions distinguished from her contemporary Daniel Defoe's "HISTORIES." This implies a distinction between the more linear approach of male novelists, and Barker's more fragmentary, wandering one. In her preface to one novel, Barker makes a faux-modest reference to the preface's lack of poetic interpolation, *"One tongue is enough for a Woman."*[14] The mixed-genre production which follows is a demonstration that one tongue (one genre) may be enough for a woman, but Barker, at least, thought two tongues (two genres) was better. Her literary descendants, in particular Radcliffe and Smith, seem to have agreed. Radcliffe also introduced the practice of using poetic quotations as epigraphs at the beginning of each chapter, in an unprecedented act of what E. J. Clery calls "literary kleptomania."[15] By the time she published *Udolpho*, Radcliffe's reviewers were identifying her use of interspersed poetry as part of a contemporary "fashion."[16] Other 1790s writers who use verses as well as a proliferation of quotations in their novels include Thomas Holcroft, Matthew Lewis, and Mary Robinson, all novelists who were also notably concerned with delineating the many, often conflicting, meanings of mobility.

This interpenetration of genres has come to be seen as central to a moment of intense generic experimentation in the 1790s.[17] Innovative critical work on the poetic novel has made important contributions to a shift in readings of *Udolpho* in particular over the last two decades, helping to liberate it from an earlier critical fascination with the "so-called Gothic core" of the text.[18] Initial research by Mary Favret, Leah Price, and G. Gabrielle Starr suggested that the placement of lyric poems within eighteenth-century novels tends to be "chaotic," "parenthetical," or "episodic," performing, if anything, the difference between lyric and narrative, often at the expense of lyric.[19] In an effort to account for the peculiar structure of these novels, Price makes the provocative suggestion that eighteenth-century anthologists trained readers to pace themselves, cultivating a notion of distinction between two kinds of reading – "a leisured appreciation of beauties, and an impatient, or efficient, rush through plot" – and that by the 1790s this created a taste for novels which would themselves act in a similarly bipartite manner. Radcliffe's contemporary popularity and influence, she argues, came from her novels' presentation to her readers of a choice of discourses or paces of reading.[20] In the wake of Radcliffe's great poetic novels, Robinson in *Walsingham, or, the Pupil of Nature* (1797) and Lewis in *The Monk, A Romance* (1796) go so far as to provide an "Index to the Poetry," inviting readers to approach their texts as poetry collections as much as novels.[21] Revealingly, Price explains these texts' concern with "pacing" and "choice" through kinds of movement, mapping different paces by analogy with guidebooks, which presented travelers with "anthology-pieces designed to be savored once the tourist reached a picturesque stopping-place" and more "prosaic instructions about how to get most efficiently from one point to another."[22] Poetry, poetic quotation, and landscape descriptions are imagined here as voluntary stopping-off points within a narrative journey. More broadly, in an argument I turn to at the conclusion of this chapter, Miranda Burgess in particular has shown how the debate about reading that became intense in this period can be understood in the context of metaphors of movement and more general concerns about mobility. As with Cowper, thinking about kinds of reading was one way of thinking about kinds of movement, and vice-versa.

Attention such as Price's to the "stop-and-go rhythm" of blended texts has provided a template for new ways of approaching the apparent pauses or digressions within novels such as Radcliffe's. Recent critical work does not so much challenge arguments for the peculiarly parenthetical nature of poetic moments in 1790s novels, as reassess the effect of this performance of difference.[23] In the context of this book on reluctant wanderers, I am interested, in particular, in the way in which the "stop-and-go rhythm" could in fact be used to demonstrate the *lack of choice* facing particular people – especially women – in certain circumstances. Gaining access to the parts of life akin to pauses within a journey (narrative) is a privilege which those who are not the directors of their own journeys (and stories) cannot always afford. Heroines such as Smith's Emmeline or Geraldine and Radcliffe's Adeline or Emily frequently find it difficult to stop long enough to read or compose poetry and are constantly being called in from the garden or disturbed during moments of contemplation. This connects with ideas developed within mobility studies scholarship about the "pausibility" of particular places. As John Urry writes, some places seem naturally to invite or are actively designed to allow for moments of pause and notice and for activities such as slow walking. However, as he also notes, even such places can work to reinscribe hierarchies, highlighting inequities of access to such pauses within movement.[24] A house garden in an eighteenth-century novel would seem to be the epitome of a "pausible" place, a fact that only highlights the frequency with which women in Radcliffe's gothic and Smith's sentimental novels are not even allowed to occupy or move freely in these locations. As readers, once psychologically in the grip of a Montoni, we may also find it hard to stop long enough to read the poetry these characters do write or to linger over Radcliffe's or Smith's celebrated landscape descriptions, even when they do become possible within the text itself. Yet this act of pausing, I would argue, is precisely what Radcliffe works to have her readers see and do.

By paying localized and specific attention to the labor to which Radcliffe puts poetry, quotation, and landscape description in *Udolpho*, I want to contrast the relationship of Price's and Burgess's idea of choice and judgment in reading and imagination in the period to the compulsions of the gothic text. For Radcliffe, the presence and absence of poetry in particular becomes a tool for exploring – and resisting – the implications of the gothic itself. Collectively, lyric interludes in *Udolpho* work not so much as isolated episodes, or as "static, atemporal, self-contained passages," to use Price's formulation,[25] but as the spaced out installments that give meaning to the text. In work on Amelia Opie, Shelley King has usefully suggested the more active and centralizing term "integral lyric" to replace Price's "inscribed lyric" and Starr's "absorbed lyric."[26] In *Udolpho*, both quoted and original poetry provide vital companionship and support to isolated individuals and single voices within the gothic narrative. Lyric's intermittent, but integral, development in Radcliffean gothic may amount to the alternative mode which her texts are primarily invested in exploring, even while demonstrating that mode's vulnerability. Radcliffe's poetic novels, in which lyric moments never stand alone, but are always broken in upon by narrative, play an important, if easily overlooked, role in Radcliffe's explorations of where a person stands within her own story and within her own journey.

"Horror Occupied her Mind": The Gothic Journey and Its Affects

Soon after her father dies Emily St. Aubert is taken by Montoni, her new guardian by virtue of having recently married her aunt, from her home in France to Venice and then on to Udolpho, Montoni's fortress in the Apennines. The famous scene in which Emily lifts the mysterious black veil that hangs in a chamber of the castle, sees what she thinks is a corpse, takes this as evidence that Montoni is a murderer, and promptly faints, is emblematic of this frequently analyzed section of *Udolpho*. The imaginative as well as physical constraints Emily experiences while imprisoned in Udolpho, I argue, are the logical apotheosis of the compulsions involved in her journey toward Montoni's realm. They are the novel's most potent representations of Emily's lack of control over her own mobility, including, to use a phrase from Morley again, her "capacity to withdraw and disconnect."[27]

When Emily comes to from her faint, we are told, "Horror occupied her mind, and excluded, for a time, all sense of past, and dread of future misfortune" (249). Horror here overwrites all other experience – both past and future – for a time limiting the subject to a single terrorizing idea. Later in the same section of the novel, when Emily prematurely thinks she has discovered that Montoni has killed her aunt also, the psychological oppressiveness of her situation is figured as an "intolerable weight" by which she is "compelled to bear" the "horror of the secret" to the point where "her reason seemed to totter" (350). Not knowing what will happen to her next is compared to being "condemned to . . . torturing suspense!" (243). The effect of Emily's situation in such moments is a gothic version of the experience of the sublime as Edmund Burke describes it, when, "the mind is so entirely filled with its object, that it cannot entertain any other, nor by consequence reason on that object which employs it."[28] In her own posthumously published treatise on the difference between horror and terror, Radcliffe conceives of this version of the sublime as gothic horror, which, rather than awakening and expanding the faculties, "contracts, freezes, and nearly annihilates them."[29] In *Udolpho*, she represents such a moment of extreme horror as only survived by a momentary and symbolic extinction of mind and voice – a death in narrative terms. Between Emily's dropping to the floor in the veil scene and her recovery, her consciousness vanishes from the text, as she moves away from a horrified and intolerable selfhood into a self-protective blank, a narrative nothingness: she faints rather than thinks. This celebrated gothic scene suggests that when something puts unremitting or unbearable pressure on a subject, the most that subject can hope to do is disappear.

Such signature moments in *Udolpho* contribute to a general consensus among theorists of the gothic from Eve Sedgwick to Robert Miles that "the Gothic represents the subject in a state of deracination, or the self finding itself dispossessed in its own house, in a condition of rupture, disjunction, fragmentation."[30] The problem the gothic constantly faces is how to represent or imagine such a subject. While the veil scene and the moment of horror that dominates the unpoetic core of *Udolpho* represents an exclusion of a subject from her own subjectivity, the absence or exclusion of poetry throughout the Udolpho section is a milder representation of this same self-alienated condition. In this condition, a subject can neither remember nor think beyond the pressures of the immediate moment – a situation in which the whole of her life, and even her thought, is controlled by another. That one of the effects of such gothic overwriting is isolation from the consolations of sympathy invoked through literary experience is highlighted by Radcliffe's staging of a number of scenes in which Emily finds that she cannot even read in her mountain prison.[31] Such scenes place *Udolpho* in a long, developing, history of explorations of sympathy through scenes of reading.[32] Toward the end of the novel's gothic section, Emily's failed attempts at reading culminate in an extended meditation on the prisoner's stymied ability to connect to others through literature:

> Emily sought to lose the sense of her own cares, in the visionary scenes of the poet; but she had again to lament the irresistible force of circumstances over the taste and powers of the mind; and that it requires a spirit at ease to be sensible even to the abstract pleasures of pure intellect. The enthusiasm of genius, with all its pictured scenes, now appeared cold, and dim. As she mused upon the book before her, she involuntarily exclaimed, 'Are these, indeed, the passages, that have so often given me exquisite delight? Where did the charm exist? – Was it in my mind, or in the imagination of the poet? It lived in each', said she, pausing. 'But the fire of the poet is vain, if the mind of his reader is not tempered like his own, however it may be inferior to his in power'. (383)

Reading is constructed here as communication between the reader's mind and the mind of the poet – which Angela Wright identifies as Shakespeare – between which the text stands as a kind of "charm," linking the two minds and "living" in each.[33] This is not a surprising formulation of how literature works, resembling Burke's account of the "pleasure" of the "social affections" by which "poetry, painting, and other affecting arts, transfuse their passions from one breast to another."[34] What is notable, though, is the concern expressed in the passage with how such sympathetic communication can become obstructed. The anxiety that occupies (overwrites) Emily's mind during the most gothic parts of *Udolpho* is represented as horrific precisely because it isolates her from other texts and minds. In the formulation of this passage the "fire" of "the poet" is made to appear "cold, and dim" not by any intrinsic lack of feeling or capacity for sympathy in the temper of the subject's mind but rather by the "irresistible force of circumstances." All too conscious of "her own situation" and in a constant state of terror for her life, Emily becomes isolated in the most profound sense in Udolpho. In Chapter 5, I return to an analogous situation in Burney's novel of wandering in more detail, in which Burney, too, works to evoke the affects of such unrelenting pressure on a subject. Whereas Burke, Adam Smith, and Hume all present examples of objects who for various reasons fall outside the bounds of sympathy, here it is Radcliffe's traveling subject (as is also the case in Burney) who herself becomes unable to engage. Invaded or overwhelmed subject rather than impartial spectator, Emily becomes preoccupied by the passionate demands of another in a way that places her beyond the more benign, consoling form of sympathetic engagement represented by reading. To use and reverse Adam Smith's terms, "upon bringing the case home" to herself while reading, and finding that the feelings she encounters do not "coincide" with her own, she does not question the justice of the other's feelings but is rather forced to reflect on the reduction in her own capacity to feel (*TMS*, 20).

The specific isolating paralysis developed by Radcliffe in *Udolpho*, and also evoked in varying ways in the texts I discuss by Charlotte Smith, Wollstonecraft, and Burney, marks a development from scenes of literary interaction in mid-century texts such as Charlotte Lennox's *The Female Quixote* (1752). In Lennox, in the moments of most distress the heroine finds comfort in "ransacking her Memory" for examples of women she has read about and "adapting their Sentiments, and making Use of their Language in her Complaints" (although Lennox's novel, too, is concerned with the limited usefulness of such support).[35] Even in Mary Robinson's contemporary *Walsingham*, poetry is described and depicted as that which never fails "to visit ... under the pressure of calamity."[36] Robinson's eponymous poet hero is almost comically resilient in his capacity to compose and quote poetry anywhere and everywhere:

As I have before remarked, the muse never forsook me, when fortune was most severe: I no sooner entered my prison than, with no light but that which a grated window afforded, I wrote the following little ode . . .[37]

By contrast, the more psychological forms of imprisonment Radcliffe is interested in representing are underscored by Emily's inability to read or compose while imprisoned, which become symbolic of a confinement far more debilitating than castle walls. Emily's failure to find release and consolation through literary interaction in parts of *Udolpho* participates as much in Radcliffe's exploration of the affects of the gothic as does the veil scene itself. By displacing external texts from sections of her novel, Radcliffe demonstrates how confined the imagination can be made by a restrictive or repressive social environment.

Emily is always looking out the window while imprisoned, and landscape description, which is such a distinctive feature of all Radcliffe's novels, functions as a slightly less futile attempt to find even transitory relief from the anxieties of the gothic present. In *Udolpho*, landscape description, like poetry, is explicitly represented as being sought "to relieve her [Emily's] mind from the busy ideas, that tormented it" (241). It often succeeds in "soothing" Emily's emotions in the very same moments in which reading fails to. Leaning from her casement window, or walking on the heavily patrolled ramparts, Emily's eye gains a certain kind of liberation. This is her first view on waking up in Udolpho:

> She rose, and, to relieve her mind from the busy ideas, that tormented it, compelled herself to notice external objects. From her casement she looked out upon the wild grandeur of the scene, closed nearly on all sides by alpine steeps, whose tops, peeping over each other, faded from the eye in misty hues . . . From these her sight wandered over the cliffs and woods into the valley . . . a thin dusky vapour, that rose from the valley, overspread its features with a sweet obscurity . . . it was delightful to watch the gleaming objects . . . in the valley – the green turf – dark woods – little rocky recesses – a few peasants' huts – the foaming stream – a herd of cattle, and various images of pastoral beauty . . . while the mountains, gradually sinking in the perspective, appeared to shelve into the Adriatic sea, for such Emily imagined to be the gleam of blueish light, that terminated the view.
>   Thus she endeavoured to amuse her fancy, and was not unsuccessful . . . and her mind recovered its strength. (241–2)

Here Emily's mind, or at least her sight, moves, as it was unable to in the scene of failed reading, outward beyond herself and the "busy ideas" that are a torture to her. Her sight seems to be projected out of herself to wander across the very landscape which in fact castle walls block her access to. "From her casement she looked out" begins the move outward, moving free of Udolpho and its torments, even as the mention of the "casement" reinforces the constraints and limits – the frame – within which this movement occurs. Her gaze continues onward as, "From these [the mountains] her sight wandered over the cliffs," and takes note of various "objects" or "images" in the valley. In this scene and others like it in *Udolpho*, landscape description seems to function not as a way to achieve the prospective dominance aimed at by poems such as James Thomson's *The Seasons*, nor of constituting a self as might happen in William Wordsworth for instance, but as a way of deconstituting a self in intolerable pain. Finding the thoughts occupying her consciousness too tormenting, Emily compels herself simply to notice "external objects," enacting a melancholic evacuation of self. As in the veil scene, she makes of her inner self a protective blank, finding relief this time in noticing and letting her eyes wander over only what is outside herself. In addition, an important part of what facilitates this imaginative evacuation of self through landscape is the "fading" of the actual features of the landscape, making even the landscape's particular identity indistinct under a "thin dusky vapour" of "sweet obscurity."

That landscape description is possible in Udolpho when poetry is not is, I believe, indicative not of the weakness of poetry to penetrate the walls of Udolpho but of the important social powers ascribed to literary community in Radcliffe's novels, powers that are explicitly put into abeyance when a subject lives under a state of tyranny. The structuring of *Udolpho* around the presence and absence of poetry suggests that landscape description in prose is possible because its function is limited in a way poetic quotation or composition is not. The distinction between the way in which landscape description functions in *Udolpho* and the way in which poetry does is analogous to a distinction made by W. B. Carnochan between the scope of a single eye, and the imaginative flight that the prospective eye seeks to rise to, which allows the prospect to be extended, imaginatively, to far beyond what could be encompassed by any single person.[38] Carnochan is referring to moments, like that in *The Seasons*, when Thomson claims a yet wider view for his poem: "The Muse expands her solitary Flight; / And, hovering o'er the wild stupendous Scene, / Beholds new Seas beneath another Sky"(*W*, 891–3). This imaginative flight draws on and encompasses a collective knowledge of other worlds. In landscape description, Emily can evacuate herself to an extent, and her vision can indeed wander widely, but it takes poetry (and the freedom it requires) to become fully disembodied in a way that allows imaginative and sympathetic mobility across space and time, and between people, analogous to imaginative flight. Radcliffe has Emily, while imprisoned in Udolpho, almost able to see the Adriatic but unable to quite imagine the entirely "new seas" Thomson claims to encompass. Such "abstract pleasures" are depicted as a locus of sympathy to which Emily cannot make herself available at this point (383). If we think about this in terms set up by Oliver Goldsmith and Charlotte Smith, Radcliffe represents Emily as not quite able to pause long enough in her painful mental journey – which has here become a painful imprisonment – to make of her suffering any kind of collective experience. As happens in Charlotte Smith, but never in Goldsmith, even while looking outside herself, Emily remains isolated, while melancholy does not necessarily allow her to transcend her individual experience.

Unlike poetic quotation or composition, landscape description is not explicitly intertextual and does not invoke any prompter or listener, but it can itself form a kind of basic quotation. Radcliffe's dependence on writers of landscape aesthetics such as William Gilpin, and paintings by Salvator Rosa and Claude Lorrain rather than on direct experience, has contributed to her reputation as what George Dekker calls the most "secondhand" of important novelists.[39] Radcliffe also, like Smith, has a great capacity to repeat (quote) her own descriptions so that as Coleridge and other contemporary reviewers observed, an element of "sameness" emerges across her many landscapes: "the pine and the larch tree wave, and the full moon pours its lustre through almost every chapter."[40] Despite its undeniable linguistic and repetitive nature, however, landscape description in the Udolpho section of the novel is nonetheless not quite presented as referential reflection – no matter how much Radcliffe's prose itself works within a preestablished generic frame, Emily's consciousness is not presented as allusive. In looking out the window, she is not processing or communicating; she is just registering. Landscape description functions primarily as a step away from an oppressive overwriting of self by gothic horror to "the green turf – dark woods – little rocky recesses." The landscape descriptions that persist through the most gothic parts of *Udolpho* represent the faintest echo of literary imagination that is possible for a "spirit [not] at ease," a mind occupied by "busy thoughts" that threaten at any moment to turn into occupation by gothic horror. Emily cannot sympathize with other people, only with dumb nature. Nonetheless, this ability of the self to evacuate the mind from suffering, to make of her already alienated subjectivity an absence – to look out the window – is developed as vital to surviving the condition of crisis represented by the most gothic sections of the novel. This conception of the alienated subject goes some way toward accounting for the novel's peculiar evasion of interiority – an evasion that we will see exaggerated in Burney's novel of wandering. The more gothic parts of *Udolpho* attempt to theorize trauma in a way that engages with problems in the constitution of the subject, and the availability of a radically unhoused subject to engage in acts of sympathy.

Quoting Britannia: Ghostly Voices and the Communitarian Self

What happens, then, in those moments in which Emily, or the text, *can* read, remember, or compose poetry, and what are we, as readers ourselves, missing if we read over or past them? While quotation might be understood to participate in the gothic mode of representing a "fragmented" subject dispossessed in "its own house," in *Udolpho*, quotation's role in this dispossession takes a primarily recuperative rather than threatening form. Whereas horror dominates the mind in the Udolpho section of the novel, Radcliffe develops poetry as expanding beyond an individual consciousness in a way that is creative, constructive, and relies on a communitarian concept of selfhood. She is, in this regard, more hopeful than her contemporaries Smith and Wollstonecraft and in particular less troubled than Wollstonecraft by the idea of a generalized self. As Ann Wierda Rowland has shown in work on the relationship between Romantic poetry and the Romantic novel that develops on Leah Price's arguments, when a character in a novel quotes from another text he or she draws on a shared literary archive recognizable to the novel's readers, with the effect that quoted poetry in novels takes on a social function.[41] Through quotation, in other words, the single voice of the character or text joins other voices, so quotations within Radcliffe's novels, and perhaps in all novels, engage with an idea of sympathy or community. Radcliffe is not troubled by membership in this community or literary tradition in the way that Smith and Wollstonecraft are. This runs parallel to the fact that she is also more content to evoke a nostalgic sense of a home, in geographical, temporal, and political senses, that can be yearned back toward. Meanwhile, an understanding of quotation as communitarian has specific implications within the context of the gothic.

The poetic epigraph that opens Volume Two of *Udolpho* and so inaugurates Emily's journey away from the literal community of her home and toward the homelessness of Montoni's realm is a quote from Oliver Goldsmith's ubiquitous *The Traveller, or A Prospect of Society* (1764) – "Where'er I roam, whatever realms I see, / My heart untravell'd still shall turn to thee" (Tr, 7–8, *Udolpho*, 161). This in turn evokes a previous moment of leave-taking and quotation from Goldsmith earlier in the novel when Emily sets off on her first journey with her father who looks behind him:

> till the haziness of distance blended his home with the general landscape, and St. Aubert seemed to
>
> Drag at each remove a lengthening chain.   (27)

Through moments like these, Radcliffe claims a place for her uprooted characters in Goldsmith's paradoxical community of solitary wanderers, constructing her protagonists like Goldsmith's poetic speaker as exiles possessed by bouts of homesickness and joined by their yearning for home. By signaling her characters' departures through quotation, Radcliffe perpetuates Goldsmith's communitarian effect of endless, sympathetic echo so that Emily sets off like St. Aubert, who is exiled like Goldsmith's poetic speaker, who reflects his own experience in that of the "pensive exile" in the wilds of America, whom he in turn hopes will bid "his bosom sympathize with mine" (*Tr*, 419, 422).

If *Udolpho* has a poetic mascot besides the ever-present Shakespeare, however, it is James Thomson, and if it has a chorus, it is his *Britannia, A Poem* (1729).[42] This ties Emily's experience into a situation wider and more specific than simply that of the homesick exile. A particularly suggestive scene in which Radcliffe evokes Thomson occurs when Emily sails from Venice on a barge with Montoni and her aunt shortly before they set out for Udolpho. This scene begins as Emily moves from the confined cabin to the deck of the barge, "anxious to escape" to the "benevolence of nature" which will allow her "the quiet which Montoni had denied her elsewhere" (210). Here we have the standard Radcliffean set up of gothic occupation versus escape through nature. In this case, a dissolving evening landscape and a whole auditory community of unseen speakers prepare the ground for the movement of the text from observations on the evening scene into quotation:

> The vessel glided smoothly on: amid the stillness of the hour Emily heard, now and then, the solitary voice of the barge-men on the bank, as they spoke to their horses; while, from a remote part of the vessel, with melancholy song,
>
> The sailor sooth'd
> Beneath the trembling moon, the midnight wave.   (210)

Emily hears oddly, but suitably, at once the singular and plural "solitary voice" of the "barge-*men*" (emphasis added) on the shore as well as the melancholy song of the sailor. Meanwhile, the song of the sailor in the scene is also rendered plural by Radcliffe's narrator (somewhat awkwardly) describing it in the voice of Thomson's *Britannia*, recounting another sailor's song. In this moment, in the same way that the sailor dissolves into something other than himself, so do character and text. Through quotation both heroine and narrator vanish into a multiplicity of voices – becoming blurry and difficult to locate like the evening landscapes which facilitate such moments – so that Emily's thoughts, Radcliffe's narrative, and Thomson's poetry all equally speak the moment. This transparency of voice is what both makes such moments soothing and speaks their creative power. Unlike in landscape description, memory is essential here: for Emily and the text to be "reminded," Thomson's poetry must be remembered from some previous time. As prose and verse, self and other, dissolve into each other, a chorus of whispered voices is brought into being in a powerful, if momentary, evocation of sympathetic sociability.

At other moments, a feeling for poetry more explicitly links different people together within the novel. In the opening chapter, Emily's connection with her father is expressed through a joint feeling for books and poetry. As father and daughter wander together in the woods near their home, St. Aubert talks of "that high enthusiasm, which wakes the poet's dream," paraphrasing what Emily has said to herself just a few pages earlier, to which Emily responds, "how exactly you describe what I have felt so often, and which I thought nobody had ever felt but myself!" (15,5).[43] As Emily's exclamation suggests, poetry in *Udolpho* provides a space for people to experience the same feelings as each other – or to wander into each other's feelings.

The importance Radcliffe attaches to the kind of sympathetic chorus provided by poetry in her text, a chorus which has the effect of making Emily feel connected to something wider than herself even when alone, is reinforced by the novel's frequent return to *Britannia*. Through quotations from *Britannia*, Emily's desires and need for release from the pressures she is under are aligned with the needs of Britain itself. In Thomson's poem, the passage in which the sailor soothes "the midnight wave" describes the soothing activities of Peace, which Britannia seeks and which Thomson describes as "thou Source, and Soul of *social* Life" (emphasis added).[44] Like Thomson's "Peace," the "quiet" that Emily is denied by Montoni's tyrannies, becomes the precondition for social life – and so for quotation.

Thomson's political poetry, in particular *Liberty* (1735–1736), became newly popular and "readable" in the wake of the French Revolution and the subsequent beginning of war with France, reinforcing the significance of Radcliffe's use of *Britannia*. John Barrell and Harriet Guest have shown that Thomson's patriotic account of political virtue, and the consequences of a lack of it, was drawn on extensively by those calling for reform of all kinds in the 1790s, from those more narrowly concerned with political corruption to such radical figures as Robert Thompson, author of the anthem "God save the – RIGHTS OF MAN." Charlotte Smith is by no means alone when in both *Desmond* (1792) and *The Emigrants* (1793) she enlists Thomson on the side of "rights and liberties," implying that there is a consonance between the politics of Thomson and those of Thomas Paine and other Revolutionaries.[45] A few pages earlier than the quotation I have just been discussing, Radcliffe has Emily's thoughts merge with those of Thomson's Britannia at the exact moment near the opening of his poem in which Britannia mourns the degeneration of her empire into a state of warfare and represents herself as being under siege. Radcliffe has the quotation appear in a moment in which Emily, in parallel to Britannia, begins to mourn her own loss of a view of the open sea:

> Emily gave a last look to the Adriatic, and to the dim sail,
>
>   That from the sky-mix'd wave
>   Dawns on the sight,
>
> and the barge slowly glided between the green and luxuriant slopes of the river. (208)[46]

Radcliffe sets up a parallel between Emily's vulnerable and defeated situation and that which Britain finds herself in, much as Smith does when she alludes to Milton's figure of the defeated Samson in her desolate Sonnet 80, "To the Invisible Moon." Neither writer is unaware of the political implications of their invocations of these particular moments in these particular poems. In such moments of precise quotation, Radcliffe's text does not simply claim to speak with numerous voices but claims to dissolve or extend into an idea of Britain in need of liberation from pressing and threatening difficulties. Her text speaks in unison with a specific idea of a wider public, specifically the public of a nation engaged in an on-going war, as Britain was in 1794.

By analogy, if one of the effects of Montoni's regime of terror is to create a profound sense of isolation, this in turn produces a situation that needs to be counteracted by a whole chorus of other voices. Deidre Lynch has written evocatively about the curious effects that come from the haunting of gothic texts by citations – that is by voices from entirely outside the text itself. She writes, for instance, that Shakespeare can become, "a haunting presence, [who seems] to have *stolen* into the character's reveries."[47] Lynch's language is indicative of her reading – there is something disturbing, she suggests, something illicit about the occupation of a gothic character by the words of a dead poet, which "steal" into thought. In Radcliffe, however, and to an extent also in Smith's novels, I would argue that quotation goes in the opposite direction. In Radcliffe's work, quotations may seem, and in fact become, disturbing, but their most central function is that of releasing the subject. They work as a form of sympathetic expansiveness and appropriation: Emily is enlarged by Thomson, not occupied by him. That is, rather than stealing *into* a character's reveries, much as the horror represented by Montoni does, quotations momentarily release a character *out* of their own reveries into the "visionary scenes of the poet" (383) and into stories wider than the one they are trapped within. Quotation, like landscape description, functions in Radcliffe's gothic as something like the inverse of Austenian free-indirect discourse: it takes us further outside, rather than inside, the character's mind, thus releasing that mind from the trauma the gothic plot inflicts.

What for Lynch underlies gothic intrigue – that is literary haunting or being occupied by another voice – I believe is depicted in Radcliffe as being made necessary by the gothic itself. Through quotation and poetry, then, Radcliffe redirects gothic dispossession from the self in an alternate, more nurturing direction. We might call this a "wandering subject" as opposed to a "fragmented" one – a subject who seeks to move beyond dispossession toward (re)constituting a virtual home in the realm of the communal. Here my reading of Radcliffe also diverges from writers on the gothic such as Robert Miles who writes that Radcliffe's heroines, "caught on the threshold of subjectivity," do not "gaze outward for clues capable of solving the mysteries of her puzzling situation, but inward, to the topography of waking dreams" and, as a result, "the narrative as a whole becomes a drama of the interior."[48] Quotation in Radcliffe works, instead, in a similar way to Goldsmith's conception of the wanderer as one whose vision is not limited by being tied to any particular "spot": wandering into quotations from others allows both Emily's thoughts and Radcliffe's text to move beyond any particularity of identity or voice and so to achieve a generalization of (but not from) self. As Rowland observes, using the example of Orlando Somerive in Smith's *Old Manor House* (1793), quotation in these novels creates interiority as a communal construct.[49] What I seek to add to Rowland's formulation – and what Radcliffe, and also Smith at her most gothic, adds to Goldsmith's formulation – is the therapeutic aspect of such imaginings of a communal rather than individual self. Characters in gothic novels *need* to wander, both literally and imaginatively. And this is not always possible. Radcliffe's figuration of the generative effects of movement outward in moments of liberty in the text makes the novel's strongest case against the gothic mode of domination and for some kind of mobility of the imagination.

To return to the political context in which Radcliffe was writing, it is worth remembering that imagination was precisely what was coming under attack in the years in which *Udolpho* was completed and published. In 1794, reformers were put in the strange situation of being charged with "imagining or compassing the King's death" as a result of proposing changes to the parliamentary system.[50] Only recent biographical and critical work on Radcliffe has changed the previous consensus of her as a political conservative, so it is worth holding onto an image of her and her husband meeting with William Godwin a number of times right in the middle of the Treason Trials of 1794, and as Godwin recorded in his diary, "talk[ing] of morals & fortitude."[51] This conversation over tea occurred a matter of weeks before *habeus corpus* was suspended. Radcliffe's precise use of quotation, and of *Britannia* in particular, at this political and historical juncture builds the critical case for Radcliffe's novels working to critique rather than reinforce what Godwin describes in the title to his own gothic intervention as, "things as they are."[52] Angela Wright comes to similar conclusions about the politics of Radcliffe's use of allusions, locating Radcliffe's mapping of a crisis of imagination through reference to Shakespeare firmly in the wider political crises of the 1790s.[53] Radcliffe's investment in testing the limits of a particular relationship between self and society, developed through quotation and allusion, was of pressing social and political importance in the moment in which she wrote.

Up until this point, I have focused on the content of quotation, but the mere presence of quotations is equally important, as they function just as strongly structurally within *Udolpho* as they do thematically. In fact, often the thematic content is what Lynch might describe as threatening, but the quotation still performs a preliminary comforting or liberating function on a basic structural level. For instance, when Emily is released from Udolpho, her new freedom immediately makes it possible to remember and to shift her thoughts into those of others. Literal mobility enables mental mobility. This functions as a kind of relief, despite the fact that this particular quotation, from Thomas Gray's "The Bard," does no less than dwell on the idea that the chambers of Udolpho may be "With many a foul, and midnight murder stain'd"(407).[54] This also, of course, evokes the context of *Hamlet*, which underwrites the castle sections of the novel.[55] Invoking such morbid images is certainly a peculiar form for comfort to take (as it is also in Smith's early sonnets), but Emily's ability to quote seems nonetheless to be a sign of her release. In a similar way, in the two moments of quotation from *Britannia* discussed earlier, as well as those from Goldsmith's *The Traveller*, even without their deeper content these quotations add an accompaniment to the previously isolated voice of both character and narrator.

Scholars have suggested that in an effort to bolster the novel form, poetic novels deliberately display the redundancy of the lyrics they quote or the original poems they insert by preempting them in prose descriptions.[56] But in the case of *Udolpho*, this apparent redundancy or parenthetical nature is paradoxically precisely what makes these inserted lyrics play such a very important role. They demonstrate that another mind thought (and expressed) precisely what the character at this moment in the novel is feeling, and thus, the character is not only not alone but also has someone else on to whom they can project the expression of their feelings. Inserted quotations and lyrics transform the novel into a kind of palimpsest, over-laying the feelings of the text and the subject, and becoming an intrinsic part of the depth of both. The apparent redundancy of double-thinking between prose and lyric is quite the opposite of redundant: it is central to the alleviation of feelings of isolation and curtailed possibilities that so often threaten both the subject and the text, and it forms part of the pattern of repetition and echo that are so much a part of the texture of Radcliffe's work.

Radcliffe's deliberate placement of quotation and poems in *Udolpho* invites us to pay particular attention to the workings of quotation in other prose works by her contemporaries. The literature of the second half of the eighteenth century is as full of great quoters, particularly in women's texts, as it is full of great wanderers. Frequently, they are one and the same. Smith's fast-moving, Revolutionary-era novel, *Desmond* (1792), contains two interludes that mark extended periods of respite from the onward trajectory of the narrative, one in Herefordshire and one in Meudon in France. The tone of these parts of Smith's epistolary novel is very different from that of other parts of the text in which her heroine, Geraldine, is generally terrorized and forced to move from place to place by her abusive husband. The Herefordshire and Meudon sections of the novel, by contrast, repeatedly return to words such as "reflection" and "reverie" and to sounds that "soothe" the mind; they are characterized by "solitary walks," descriptions of having "wandered," "uninterrupted tranquillity," and the constant presence of Geraldine's lover nearby watching her, even when she is not aware of him.[57] It is no coincidence that the three letters from Geraldine during the Herefordshire interlude are also markedly filled with quotations, and she composes the only interpolated poem in the novel in Meudon. One leisurely description of the "delicious" landscape through which Geraldine "wanders," for instance, is punctuated by quotations from William Cowper, Goldsmith, Gray, and Smith's friend William Hayley, as well as Petrarch and the French author Madame des Houlieres. In the next letter, Milton and Shakespeare are added to this accumulating anthology.[58] A number of moments in these letters also implicitly echo *Elegiac Sonnets*, as when Geraldine writes of how she is soothed by the song of a nightingale, the addressee of three of Smith's sonnets, which Geraldine fancies to be "the spirit of some solitary and deserted being like myself."[59] Geraldine's transient freedom to wander through a landscape of her own choosing in these sections of *Desmond* enables, and is marked by, imaginative wanderings into other texts and other thoughts. Like Emily in the barge-scene but not when imprisoned, and Smith in her early sonnets but not in her later ones, Geraldine is soothed by the presence of a sympathetic community of allusion in the less oppressive sections of *Desmond* and loses touch with this community as soon as she is hurried along again.

Jane Austen's heroines quote too, just not in quite the same way as Radcliffe's or Smith's in that Austen seldom uses direct quotations.[60] Austen's playful awareness of the necessity and difficulty of allusion under certain circumstances is suggested by the consoling as well as haunting role played by *Udolpho* in *Northanger Abbey* (1818). Catherine is a descendant of Charlotte Lennox's Female Quixote, Arabella, as much as she is of Radcliffe's Emily, but Austen is at least half serious in her description of Catherine's training to become a heroine consisting of reading "all such works as heroines must read to supply their memories with those quotations which are so serviceable and so soothing in the vicissitudes of their eventful lives."[61] How allusion works for Austen is encapsulated most directly in the famous scene of quotation – or failed quotation – from *Persuasion* (1817), which as in Smith and Radcliffe is associated with a leisurely kind of walking. Having been overlooked by her former suitor Captain Wentworth on a country walk, Anne Elliot finds that, "Her pleasure in the walk must arise from the exercise and the day, from the view of the last smiles of the year upon the tawny lawns, and withered hedges, and from repeating to herself some few of the thousand poetical descriptions extant of autumn." However, as in Radcliffe and Smith, even quotation is not proof against pain when it presses too close. "She occupied her mind as much as possible in such like musings and quotations," the passage continues, but finds this is "not possible" when she gets too close to Wentworth and Louisa Musgrove, between whom there seems to be a growing attachment.[62] In a similar moment of painful realization in *Mansfield Park* (1814), Fanny Price finds herself unable to read.[63] In the scene from *Persuasion*, Anne finds that she:

> could not immediately fall into a quotation again. The sweet scenes of autumn were for a while put by – unless some tender sonnet, fraught with the apt analogy of the declining year, with declining happiness, and the images of youth and hope, and spring, all gone together, blessed her memory. She roused herself to say, as they struck by order into another path, 'Is not this one of the ways to Winthrop?' But nobody heard, or, at least, nobody answered her.[64]

This scene as a whole is illuminating on a number of levels. It illustrates in compressed form that although Austen is interested in exploring a different kind of pain from that evoked by the gothic, issues of loneliness and exclusion from a circle of social sympathy are no less present and are just as linked to the potential communality of literary interaction as they are in Radcliffe and Smith. In the first part of the scene, any of "the thousand" "lines of feeling" that Anne might choose to repeat to herself while walking are depicted as equally able to offer her a form of companionship and pleasure in her solitariness. In the second half of the scene, even this mental companionship – this dissolving of a single pained individual into a wider communality of feeling – fails; simultaneously, even the "sweet scenes of autumn" by which Anne is literally as well as imaginatively surrounded seem to become inaccessible to her. What returns is a more muted and limited form of literary consolation, contained in what sounds like a description of a late Smith sonnet, which only reflects back her own desolation rather than providing release from it. Austen's sophisticated exploration of the vital but limited efficacy of allusion comes surprisingly close to Radcliffe's, working to underline the literal sense of social isolation and of a search for consolation that such scenes evoke.

Arise!: Emily as Poet

Radcliffe's original poems in *Udolpho* extend still further the idea that ideal selfhood entails access to communitarian modes of thought and that this can become blocked. The poems Radcliffe ascribes to Emily tend to be introduced with something to the effect of, "her ideas arranged themselves in the following lines" (73), as is also the case in *The Romance of the Forest*, in which Adeline is also a poet. While a lack of agency so deliberately and repeatedly marked might seem peculiar in novels in which Radcliffe seeks to give her heroines an active role in evoking a new, mobile community through the composition of poetry, it taps directly into eighteenth-century idealizations of literature, and of poetry in particular, as springing naturally from a communal past or a communal landscape. To use a phrase from William Collins, whom Radcliffe admired: "Thou need'st but take the pencil to thy hand / And paint what all believe who own thy genial land."[65] Radcliffe's description of the original poetry in *The Romance of the Forest* and *Udolpho* as lines merely "arranged" stakes a claim for these poems coming from, and giving shape and language to, some kind of shared consciousness – possibly a particularly British one, given the close associations of this idea to the formation of a national identity in mid-to-late century poetry.

Through poetry, both Radcliffe's characters and Radcliffe's text construct and are constructed by something that is simultaneously theirs and not quite theirs. We might read Radcliffe's displacement of agency as an assertion of the power to create a language for community through poetry. For my reading, Radcliffe's depiction of her own (and Emily's) poems as kinds of cultural quotations suggests that interpolated poetry, like quotation, work to take us further outside the subject, rather than further inside. The poems themselves are characterized by a marked freedom of movement, allowing their authors to, in imagination, wander far away from themselves into a wider world.

A notion of original poetry existing in a communal realm is particularly evident in the way that the poems in *Udolpho* echo and re-echo each other, seeming to communicate through the fabric of the text, and having the effect of alleviating the apparent loneliness of any particular moment. The twenty-five stanza poem, "The Sea-Nymph," which reverberates through the novel after Emily composes it alone in her room in Venice, is a particularly notable example of the mobility of poetic images within the text. If evening landscapes suggest blurring of boundaries, water takes this notion of a dissolving external landscape to a tactile level.

"The Sea-Nymph" as a fantasy of liberation, imaginative mobility, and connection is signaled in the opening stanza, which takes pleasure in the thick, dissolving quality of water and extends the nymph's field of action to the entire globe:

> anxious to escape from serious reflections, she now endeavoured to throw her fanciful ideas into a train, and concluded the hour with composing the following lines:

> THE SEA-NYMPH

> Down, down a thousand fathom deep,
> Among the sounding seas I go;
> Play round the foot of ev'ry steep
> Whose cliffs above the ocean grow   (179)

In the body of the poem, both the depth and the breadth of the ocean are explored to the very feet of the cliffs that surround it. The opening of the poem with the double stress on "Down, down," and the way it leads straight on from prose that describes Emily's effort to "throw" herself into something different from "serious reflection," has the effect of giving Emily's imagination the same mobile freedom as the nymph to wander and play in infinite regions of space. Radcliffe's emphasis on unfathomable deep, which suggests that as a figure of the poetic imagination the nymph is journeying into some kind of depths or unconscious, is extended into cultural knowledge by the echo, noted by Anna Laetitia Barbauld, of Ariel's "five fathom deep" song from *The Tempest*.[66] The remarkable "sounding seas," defining the medium through which the nymph moves *as* sound, makes her verse which moves "among" these sounds also seem to come from them. The sea – that which is beyond the self – becomes a coauthor of the poem. Far from achieving the expression of distinct identity which post-Romantic definitions of lyric subjectivity might lead us to expect, or being, "personal and private, documents of the self for itself," as Gary Kelly, for instance, describes the poems in Radcliffe, Emily's poetry extends her solitary voice into a generalized one.[67] We might remember the strange "gleam of blueish light" which Emily "imagined" to be the sea when she looks out across the landscape from her room in Udolpho (242). Here she successfully dissolves into this yearned-for element.

In one of the previous scenes where we saw Emily identifying with Britannia, Emily leant on the deck of a ship listening to the sounds around her, from the voices of sailors and bargemen to the voice of a dead poet

conjured through quotation. In "The Sea-Nymph," the scene of aural sociability enabled by unconfined movement which the poem develops is the barge
scene's mirror image: as nymph-speaker Emily herself becomes the active,
unseen voice who whispers soothing sounds to a lonely subject, this time the
sailor himself withdrawn to the deck of his ship for a moment of reverie:

> And oft at midnight's stillest hour,
> When summer seas the vessel lave,
> I love to prove my charmful pow'r
> While floating on the moon-light wave.

> And when deep sleep the crew has bound,
> And the sad lover musing leans
> O'er the ship's side, I breathe around
> Such strains as speak no mortal means!   (179)

Like the voice of the bargemen, the sea nymph is capable of sounding both
a "single note" and of calling forth a plurality of watery "choral voices."
And this "potent voice" is credited with the power to save sailors in storms
and to soothe their fears. This localized mirroring reflects a more general
development between quotation and composition of poetry in *Udolpho*: in
"The Sea-Nymph," Emily (and Radcliffe) moves from participant in
a communal voice to originator of this voice and in the process the voice
of sympathetic connection gains strength. It is fitting that in the final
stanza of this poem the reader of Radcliffe's text should be invited to
participate in the ghostly community that moves beneath the surface, or
against the onward momentum, of the gothic plot. "Come," play, sings the
communal poetic voice, "Whoe'er ye are that love my lay" (181).

Emily composes "The Sea-Nymph" shortly before she is imprisoned in
Udolpho, and it is answered on the other side of that poetic void by
"To a Sea-Nymph," a song sung by a single female peasant, accompanied
by "a chorus of voices" (419). These two poems effectively frame the poetic
absence formed by the Udolpho section, and by seeming to communicate
through it they suggest the importance of the poetic residue kept alive by
epigraphs and self-evacuation onto landscape. The peasant's song, which is
explicitly posed here as a quotation from deep within the culture by being
called a "traditional song," opens with an apostrophe to the sea nymph and
refers directly back to the last stanza of Emily's poem:

> O nymph! Who loves to float on the green wave,
> When Neptune sleeps beneath the moon-light hour,
> Lull'd by the music's melancholy pow'r.
> O nymph, arise from out thy pearly cave!   (420)

Communication of music or poetry is credited with the power to help one escape confinement: it is as though the peasant's own song has lulled Neptune, who here seems something like a prison guard, to sleep and so made it safe for the nymph to arise or escape. In the chorus, the solitary voice of the singer is joined by others who sing *"Arise! Arise!"* And they ask the nymph, once risen, to make her voice alleviate the loneliness of their own landscape – the "lonely silence" and the "solitary shore." As Beatrice Battaglia comments about another poem in *Udolpho*, "To a Sea-Nymph" transforms Emily's personal experience into a choral one.[68] The fourth and final stanza conjures an image of the land itself singing in harmony with the nymph:

> While the long coast in echo sweet replies,
> Thy soothing strains the pensive heart beguile,
> And bid the visions of the future smile,
> O nymph! from out thy pearly cave – arise!
>
> (Chorus) – *Arise!*
> (Semi-chorus) – *Arise!*   (420)

To "arise" is pointedly to "reply" (to rhyme or complete the pair): to arise is to enter once more into conversation and community. It is to move between subjectivities. The coast echoes the nymph's song here, which is in fact what the singers on the coast are already doing. This voice which is itself singing in "soothing strains" asks that "soothing strains" should the "pensive heart beguile," making the poem itself an endless series of songs and replies, with no way of saying which is the original, which the echo. Neither one, though, is alone, and Emily, the auditor of one song and the maker of the other, is released into (and by) a multiplicity of potent voices. Adela Pinch has shown that such displacement of origin is a general feature of *Udolpho*: "Almost any given moment in the novel earns its significance in relationship to other moments, past, future, or both."[69] In its penultimate line, "To a Sea-Nymph" moves on to imagine that this state of echo and re-echo could break through to something new, that it could create alternative "visions of the future." The final stanza also makes this state spacial and global, making different locations and mobile speakers call back and forth from coast to coast.

    In the light of these two poems, and the many other poetic calls and replies in *Udolpho*, it becomes apparent that interpolated verse, as much as quotation, participates in the development of feelings that ideally wander freely between people and that Radcliffe understands any voice as strongest when dissolved into a communal one. Despite the surface passivity even of

Emily's poetic compositions, the effect of interpolated poetry, whether it takes the form of citation or original composition, is of a "potent voice" which can potentially speak of a whole community. This community, Radcliffe's text implies, needs certain conditions, a certain level of freedom, if it is to continue to imaginatively bring itself into being. This communal voice needs not to be occupied by the demands of others but to be allowed to wander away from itself into new worlds and new thoughts.

Finally, then, what are we to make of the fact that this story of consolation and community in *Udolpho* appears in a form that virtually invites us not to read it? Why are we still, like the contemporary readers Barbauld was concerned about, inclined to skip over the poems in novels, and what are the consequences of this for Radcliffe's novel in particular? *Udolpho* poses two problems for the literary community it develops: one, that this community of the mind might become blocked by gothic terror; and two, that even if developed the possibility of community might be overlooked.

Readers' tendency to skip over the poems in *Udolpho* would seem to threaten the novel's development of a community founded on literary interaction. As Mark Blackwell rightly observes, encapsulating the now common understanding of the narrative tension that creates the distinctive atmosphere of Radcliffe's work:

> The bad guys in Radcliffe's work have goals for themselves and designs on others, plotting to get from point A to point B and move the story forward, while the good guys manifest a capacity to pause and enjoy nature … Radcliffe produces narrative suspense that compels us to read for plot … Yet at the same time, those moments of poetic elaboration that fail to advance the story … encourage us to linger, hinting that we should not pursue the plot at all, but revel in a plotless natural world wherein true meaning and unmitigated pleasure reside.[70]

Like Blackwell, other critics also tend to present the pictorial descriptions and poetry in novels as mechanisms by which authors slow the pace of their narratives and build suspense – the words "interrupt," "disrupt," and "arrest" are frequently used to describe how poetry works within narrative.[71] Yet *Udolpho* draws attention too, to the way in which the enforced journey of the narrative in fact constantly disrupts and breaks in upon the space of landscape description, quotation, and lyric. Even while offering us the comfort of literary company and the possibility of a different kind of meaning, *Udolpho* simultaneously shows that, like

Emily, in certain circumstances we may find it difficult to take advantage of this companionship, to "revel" is the space of the plotless. In certain circumstances, we too may only be able to read much as Emily describes landscape when imprisoned in Udolpho: using landscape for consolation and evacuation from our own pressing anxieties but unable to reflect for long enough to make anything new out of disquiet.[72] As readers of the gothic we cannot maintain the controlled, measured bipartite approach of the anthology reader. If *Udolpho* is akin to the "frantic novels" William Wordsworth censures in his Preface to *Lyrical Ballads* (1800), it is frantic because the experience – the enforced journey – it seeks to represent is frantic.[73]

While literary community offers only muted, intermittent opposition to the domination by the gothic plot in *Udolpho*, it is worth remembering that the central symbol of horror in the novel is also only partially recognized. The poems in *Udolpho*, in their very unreadability, balance and counteract the equally unknowable corpse in the castle. Like the unnamed corpse, interspersed poetry and interpolated quotations form ghostly parts of the text, never being fully present, but always haunting. Unlike the corpse, however, poems haunt in a way that is predominately soothing rather than terrifying. They work something like the "spectral images of those one loves"; the new ghosts of memory that Terry Castle has shown are also a vital part of the fabric of Radcliffean gothic.[74] Meanwhile, the need for this generic doubling in the novels of the period suggests a growing sense of the potential for any person to be either overwhelmed by too much interaction, or isolated by too little, and as a result seeks always to insert the single voice into a wider community of the imagination.

Sympathy and subjectivity in Radcliffe, then, is represented through what Miranda Burgess calls in a discussion of Sydney Owenson's *Wild Irish Girl: A National Tale* (1806), "the transpersonal circulation of affect."[75] Burgess sets this figuring of sympathy against that developed by Wordsworth in his Preface, but her discussion of Wordsworth's anxious conflation of the "accumulation of men in cities" and "the rapid communication of intelligence" with certain kinds of "frantic" reading could equally well be drawn from Cowper's many stagings of the troubling capacity of reading to keep "an unthinking multitude enthrall'd" (*Task*, 6.100).[76] For Wordsworth and Cowper, the potential for excessive mobility of feeling akin to Hume's contagious "transfusion" of emotions from one person to another creates the need for an alternate mode of engagement. Burgess argues that Wordsworth's privileging of a new version of sympathy founded on the recollecting poet, like Adam Smith's model of the impartial spectator, depends on a mixture of imagination and judgment, and works to confirm an individual subjectivity, albeit one highly capable of acts of sympathetic engagement with others.[77] But in Radcliffe things don't work out like this. Radcliffe's answer to the "frantic," demanding, mental mobility of the gothic works primarily on the level of form. Throughout this chapter, I have emphasized the many ways in which *Udolpho* works by echo and reecho, from Radcliffe's use of the conventionalized language of landscape descriptions, to double thinking between prose and verse, to the displacement of moments of origins, to the ways individual voices not only call on voices from outside the text but seem to communicate through the web of the text. This could easily be expanded into discussions of the explicit doubling of characters in the novel and the general sense of sameness in how characters express themselves. The result is a narrative form that represents an omnipresent mobility of feeling and a journey in which the heroine's involuntary movements mirror her porosity to the feelings of those around her as well as those she has read. There is little that is impartial or indifferent about character, individual subject, or text – at times dangerously so.

While Oliver Goldsmith makes collective experience necessarily expressed through the voice of the wanderer – the person of no fixed affiliation – and Charlotte Smith explores the difficulties in finding the space for this kind of experience, Radcliffe in *Udolpho* begins to define the particular conditions needed to make accessing or evoking this collective experience possible. She begins to make this a specific kind of community – and at points, a nation. In the politically charged atmosphere of the mid-1790s, *Udolpho* amounts to a historically situated argument for the need for imaginative freedom and its associated sympathies. At the same time, the presence of poetry in novels of the 1790s, in particular gothic novels, suggests both an anxiety about the seemingly onward, monolithic drive that was seen as becoming characteristic of the novel form, and a concern with the dictatorial mandates of the world of mobility outside novels. In *Udolpho*, as well as in other poetic novels of this period, neither lyric nor narrative seems sufficient. Together, perhaps, they represent something about the struggle going on in the wider world, reconstituting a grand journey in which moments of pause and reflection must repeatedly be sought. Taking up the invitation to try to pause over the poetic moments in *Udolpho* produces a whole new reading of this novel – one with a community of poetic imagination at its center. In rushing through novels in general we may miss both the extent of what a character (or reader) is threatened by, as well as that character's immense, energetic, and lyrical powers of self-expansion, creation, and inhabiting of an alternate community with an alternate story. Radcliffe encourages us to pay attention to gaps, pauses, silences and to moments of literal, imaginative, and textual wandering. From these she constructs a narrative form, and a journey through that form, based on an endless circulation of feeling between people and texts, eliding the very notion of a self-constructing subject or an individual self-directing traveler.

CHAPTER 4

"Take, O World! Thy Much Indebted Tear!"
Mary Wollstonecraft Travels

When Mary Wollstonecraft took her 3-month journey through Scandinavia in the summer and autumn in the year after *The Mysteries of Udolpho* (1794) was published, she was already well known as the author of *A Vindication of the Rights of Woman* (1792). She traveled the rocky coasts of Sweden and Norway by carriage and boat and visited Copenhagen and Hamburg, taking with her on much of the trip her first child, Fanny Imlay, then just 1 year old. For the first time in this book on reluctant wanderers, I turn to an actual travel narrative, the book Wollstonecraft based on her journey, *Letters Written During a Short Residence in Sweden, Norway, and Denmark* (1796). In this epistolary work, Wollstonecraft does something quite different with a figuration of the woman wanderer from what has been done in the work of any of the authors I have discussed so far: Wollstonecraft's wanderer escapes the constraints of the domestic space altogether and becomes a self-directing traveler. Wollstonecraft's independence is remarkable even for women travel writers of the period, and parts of her book are imbued with the sense of pleasure and expansiveness travel can offer.

At the outset, the main journey that *A Short Residence* recounts offers a tangible sense of relief, as the traveler moves away from England, and from the difficulties of her everyday life, toward a new situation. On first landing on the coast of Sweden in Letter I, Wollstonecraft vividly describes the sense of new hope that marks the beginning of her traveler's journey:

> I gazed around with rapture, and felt more of that spontaneous pleasure which gives credibility to our expectation of happiness, than I had for a long, long time before. I forgot the horrors I had witnessed in France, which had cast a gloom over all nature, and suffering the enthusiasm of my character, too often, gracious God! damped by the tears of disappointed affection, to be lighted up afresh, care took wing while simple fellow feeling expanded my heart.[1]

Here the new sights offered as part of the journey provide relief from "the horrors" of memory, and open up a space for "expectation" and a sense of "expansion," fusing personal and political feeling in a way that becomes characteristic of the text as a whole.[2]

A Short Residence is also as much characterized by the many contemplative walks within it as it is by an onward journey. As in *Udolpho*, we repeatedly find the traveler's sense of being "stifled" or "confined" by particular aspects of her main journey eased by her physically "escaping" to "wander" alone, "stray abroad," or simply take a "solitary evening's walk" (117, 63, 116, 64, 102). In *A Short Residence*, again as in *Udolpho*, it is precisely these walks that enable the kinds of mobile reveries that are such a feature of the texts of this period. Describing her traveler's stay at Tønsberg in Norway in Letter VIII, for instance, Wollstonecraft writes of how she "frequently strayed" on a nearby hilltop, looking down on the sea and letting her eye follow "vaguely curious," the sails of fishing boats (96–7). As her description of the movement of her eyes develops, the boundaries of the individual subject become increasingly permeable, making way for a sense of ecstatic and unlimited imagined movement:

> With what ineffable pleasure have I not gazed – and gazed again, losing my breath through my eyes – my very soul diffused itself in the scene – and, seeming to become all senses, glided in the scarcely-agitated waves, melted in the freshening breeze, or, taking its flight with fairy wing, to the misty mountains which bounded the prospect, fancy tript over new lawns, more beautiful even than the lovely slopes of the winding shore before me.——I pause, again breathless, to trace, with renewed delight, sentiments which entranced me . . . (97)

The gazing eyes become a kind of window out of which the reflexively "diffused" self flows: becoming "all senses" at once, the speaker's disembodied breath is released to become a part of the scene. The effect is of an almost ecstatic performance of expansion and mobile release, in which Wollstonecraft enacts, as Sara Mills puts it, "the disappearance of the notion of difference between herself and the landscape."[3] Wollstonecraft imagines moving without limits in such scenes, like Radcliffe's Emily in the sea-nymph poem, in which Emily wanders in imagination far from Montoni's realm to become one with the "sounding seas."[4] Like Ariel in *The Tempest* which underwrites this letter, Wollstonecraft's walker feels able to "glide," "melt," and "fly" beyond constraint, gliding *in* the waves and melting *in* the breeze, rather than merely moving *on* them.[5] We might also read this as an early version of the "reveries of flight" that become central to Romanticism, which as Paul de Man puts it, "not only express a desire to escape from earth-bound matter, to be relieved for a moment from the weight of gravity, but . . . they uncover a fundamentally new kind of relationship between nature and consciousness."[6]

Such evocations of unfettered movement also take on specific textual manifestations in *A Short Residence*, working on the level of punctuation as well as of intertextuality, which I return to later in this chapter. As I have argued elsewhere, on the level of the sentence, clusters of dashes are a distinctive feature of those passages in Wollstonecraft's text that involve imaginative wandering.[7] It is as though as Wollstonecraft describes the soul "diffusing" and "melting" her sentences enact this by breaking free from the confines of strict syntactical punctuation. As Mitzi Myers comments in an early work on what she calls Wollstonecraft's "running" style, "No one was more keenly aware of how ideological substance spills over into style."[8] In *A Short Residence*, Wollstonecraft's frequent use of dashes becomes part of the unfettered syntax of the wandering sentence, used deliberately in more meditative passages in the text (often enabled by literal wandering) to represent and perform particular kinds of mobile imaginative thinking.

In a way that is not true of Radcliffe, however, Wollstonecraft is distinctly wary of such wandering reveries, literature inspired or otherwise, as modes of relief: they frequently become just additional sources of her traveler's sorrow. Despite her radically altered starting point, the opening sentence of *A Short Residence* once again introduces readers to a troubled woman wanderer, "so exhausted" both by the physical hardship of the voyage to Sweden and by "other causes," only referred to in ominous, obscure tones at this point, that she can hardly even record her observations. The book ends abruptly on the traveler's arrival in Dover with the bleak declaration:

> Adieu! My spirit of observation seems to be fled – and I have been wandering round this dirty place, literally speaking, to kill time; though the thoughts, I would fain fly from, lie too close to my heart to be easily shook off, or even beguiled, by any employment, except that of preparing for my journey to London. – God bless you! (177)

It is no coincidence, I believe, that Wollstonecraft's most eloquent and moving work is voiced through the persona of a pained, heavily gendered, and reluctant wanderer – no coincidence that one of the most brilliant social analysts of the eighteenth century should find the trope of the reluctant wanderer especially expressive for extending her representations of women's position in society. As I noted earlier, in *Rights of Woman*

Wollstonecraft imagines the world according to a Cowperian prospect view: "Let me from an eminence survey the world . . . while my heart is still," she writes. Quickly, however, she relinquishes all claims to this position, descending from her "height" to feel herself instead, "hurried along the common stream": "The world cannot be seen by an unmoved spectator," she continues, "we must mix in the throng, and feel as men feel before we can judge of their feelings."[9] *A Short Residence* is in part an experiment with the consequences of this determination, demonstrating the complex difficulties that face a person, and in particular a woman, who writes and lives as a moving participant, rather than as an elevated, *un*moved, or *im*partial spectator. Wollstonecraft writes as a woman who dares to represent herself as unhoused, a position that has both pains and pleasures. Her representation of her traveler as an embodied, pained, and homeless figure involved in a series of encounters marks a radical shift in the position of the traveler, as radical a shift as Charlotte Smith's introduction within the space of the long poem of the embodied, displaced poet-wanderer in direct conversation with numerous homeless others. Both authors seem intent on finding a figure not only adequate to their own, gendered experiences, but also to the moment of historical crisis they see themselves as inhabiting and addressing. We can learn much about Wollstonecraft's text by placing it in the context of a longer literary tradition of the reluctant woman wanderer. And we can learn much about the potential politics of the tradition itself from paying close attention to one of its most eloquent practitioners.

Some of the critical intuitions in this chapter are grounded on Mary Favret's key insight that "As the *Short Residence* unfolds . . . the mobility of the subject, which had initially presented itself as both liberating and creative, modulates into something compromised, inescapable."[10] This can also be put in terms of the basic challenge of mobility studies scholarship, when it sets out to disentangle mobility from a necessary, and frequently ideological, equation with liberty.[11] Such disentangling is an especially complex undertaking in the context of women's movement, given that a generation of feminist scholars taught us to see women's escape from the domestic home as a sign of liberation. While Favret argues that the crisis of mobility in Wollstonecraft's text opens out into wider political analysis and a space in which the personal voice of Wollstonecraft's letter writer becomes communal and cultural, I see this text as ultimately unable to find a satisfactory way to generalize, and so to relieve or speak a personal sense of suffering.[12] By highlighting failures of sympathy in *A Short Residence*, as well as the wanderings, fragmentation, and increasingly reluctant referentiality of the text itself, I suggest we should be careful not to take a reading of Wollstonecraft's text as a successful rhetorical performance too far.[13] Underlying the difficulties explored in the text is also the related but separate problem of how, even if it can be found, a new voice is to be made audible, a new path visible. How is a new, and in some sense exiled, voice to continuously bring not just itself, but a new language, narrative, and even community of readers into being? How is one to find a new genre and syntax for this new story? While I give a partially non-redemptive reading of *A Short Residence*, I also draw out the elements of insight and defiance at the heart of this melancholic work.

"These Imperious Sympathies": Regendering the Sentimental Journey

In her Advertisement to *A Short Residence*, Wollstonecraft presents her travel book in seemingly modest terms as presenting an "unrestrained" account, based on "impression[s]" and the "effect" produced by different objects on her "mind and feelings" (51). The work itself is written as a series of twenty-five letters addressed, the reader gradually learns, to an unfaithful lover. For a long time, Wollstonecraft's opening statement as well as the work's structuring conceit based on her real relationship with American Gilbert Imlay was influential in *A Short Residence* being read predominantly as a biographical document rather than as a shaped epistolary narrative. This was compounded by the way in which her husband William Godwin, when she died in childbirth in August 1797, published both her private letters to Imlay and his intimate memoir of her life, *Memoirs of the Author of a Vindication of the Rights of Woman* (1798). Godwin's description of *A Short Residence* constructs it unambiguously, and influentially, as a series of love letters. In it, he writes, Wollstonecraft "speaks of her sorrows" in such a way that "[i]f ever there was a book calculated to make a man in love with its author, this appears to me to be the book."[14] All this set up *A Short Residence* to be read as a kind of real-life version of the tragic love stories familiar from contemporary sentimental novels, which were also often written in epistolary form. Godwin introduced the private letters Wollstonecraft actually sent to Imlay during her voyage as bearing "a striking resemblance to the celebrated romance of Werter," and indeed as having "superiority over the fiction of Goethe."[15] In Godwin's account, Wollstonecraft's private letters become a literary work, while her literary work appears to be a direct transcription of her feelings. The curious blending of the life and the work has had the odd effect of at once making Wollstonecraft a kind of character in a sentimental novel and of inviting a reading of her travel book that emphasizes its status as a peculiarly authentic biographical document.

As interest in travel writing has developed, however, and as scholars have turned less biographical and more literary attention to *A Short Residence*, attention sensitive to manipulations of genre and gender conventions and to the interplay of different personae, Wollstonecraft's text has come to be seen as a brilliant work in the genre, remaking discourses of political philosophy, landscape aesthetics, and sentimental travel, and marking a vital and influential moment in the history of both travel writing and autobiography.[16] Rather than being treated as a biographical document, *A Short Residence* has come to be seen as a virtuoso performance of self, both polemical and persuasive. In particular, over the past 15 years, many critics, most notably Mary Favret, Gregory Dart, Harriet Guest, Saba Bahar, and Deborah Weiss, have worked to show how self-consciously Wollstonecraft uses the language and tropes of sentimentality and feeling in *A Short Residence*, and how intimately the more seemingly personal moments in her text are intertwined with her wider political arguments.[17] This new note in Wollstonecraft's writing produces not only a new kind of "little hero," as she describes her persona in her Advertisement, but also an altered version of the sentimental journey.[18]

The way in which Wollstonecraft positions her travel book inside rather than outside sentimental discourse even as she reimagines it, is especially striking because of the way in which descriptions of women, and in particular of suffering women, feature in sentimental literature, and especially in the sentimental journey. As I suggested in the General Introduction, in *A Sentimental Journey through France and Italy* (1768), Laurence Sterne makes the very objects of his traveler's journey feminine: Yorick compares women to tourist sites he would like to enter and describes the purpose of his journey as being "to spy the *nakedness* of their hearts."[19] Scenes reminiscent of the emblematic sentimental encounter between Yorick and "poor Maria" reappear in texts such as Henry Mackenzie's *The Man of Feeling* (1771), where a lovely madwoman calls forth tears and a guinea from the eponymous hero, with her pretty face and its display of "a dejection of that decent kind, which moves our pity unmixed with horror."[20] In *Rights of Men*, Wollstonecraft directly critiques such gendered aesthetics of sensibility, drawing attention to the kind of pleasure it associates with sights of women in pain and arguing that this mode of engagement is only capable of paying attention to some forms of suffering. She depicts Edmund Burke in his *Reflections on the Revolution in*

France (1790), which her first *Vindication* answers, as a man of feeling, only sympathizing with visually pleasing spectacles such as the "downfall of queens . . .; whilst the distress of many industrious mothers . . . and the hungry cry of helpless babes, were vulgar sorrows that could not move your commiseration, though they might extort an alms." Wollstonecraft's defense of the Revolution in general revolves around the way in which the day-to-day "*inelegant* distress" and "continual miseries" of a society based on inequality can be overlooked in an economy of social feeling based on sentimental emotional exchange.[21] Wollstonecraft's in-depth and wide-ranging critique of what G. J. Barker-Benfield dubbed the "culture of sensibility" underpins many late twentieth- and early twenty-first-century critiques of the politics of sentimental literature, including the many works that encouraged their readers to shed tears – and little else – over the sufferings of distant others.[22] It also provides a natural point of origin for wider discussions of a feminist history of sympathy and affect.

This background makes Wollstonecraft's blending of a discourse of sentimentality and feeling with her political arguments in *A Short Residence* significant not only for understanding Wollstonecraft's development as a thinker and writer but also for understanding the important connections between imaginings of mobility and sympathy that emerged in this period. As Bahar puts it, if Wollstonecraft thought "vulgar sorrows," and in particular the distresses of "industrious mothers," had been too often overlooked, "the account of her voyage through the Scandinavian countries" provided the vehicle for an effort "to rectify this social and theatrical over-sight."[23] Mobility was the natural medium for extending her sustained challenge to the workings of sympathy. Wollstonecraft performs this reimagining in part by having her epistolary traveler notice the specific economic workings of households she visits. She makes detailed comments, for instance, on her observations of who does the family spinning and household washing (64–5, 70, 113, 122) and of how illegitimate children are financially supported (102). One of the most vivid asides in the text gives a description of how the hands of female servants get so cut by ice while washing clothes in the freezing winter rivers of Sweden that they bleed (65). More surprisingly, as Weiss in particular has explored, *A Short Residence* also redresses the imbalance in sentimental writing by restaging and reconfiguring the conventional sentimental tableau of the woman in distress in order to draw attention to the economic situation of working-class women.[24] Perhaps most emblematically, the traveler describes an encounter with a young wet nurse in Norway who has been left by the father of her own child. In an unmistakably sentimental mode, the "melancholy ditty sung by this poor girl" is described as exciting the letter writer's compassion (101) just as the melancholy songs of Sterne's "poor Maria" and Mackenzie's lovely maniac do to their male auditors. However, unlike conventional sentimental accounts of women in distress, in Wollstonecraft, the girl's melancholy is put very specifically in its material context. She is included in a paragraph that begins, "The wages are low, which is particularly unjust, because . . . ," and that continues to recount how the father of the woman's child has left her in order to escape the scarcely affordable expense of paying for their own child to be breast-fed by yet another woman, who is paid even less (101). As Weiss puts it, the political import of Wollstonecraft's self-conscious sentimental revisions in *A Short Residence* is that "if a woman's pain is caused not by chance, . . . but is rather the logical outcome of certain political and economic conditions, then female suffering might be alleviated through social progress."[25]

Wollstonecraft's foregrounding of the gender of her traveler also alters how she is able to present such encounters and she uses this very specific subject position to unsettle the conventional hierarchies associated with mobility and sympathetic exchange. In the encounter with the wet nurse, for instance, rather than sympathizing with the young woman as a kind of erotic object, aestheticizing her pain, or offering her either tears or money, the traveler's response is one of identification:

> There was something in this most painful state of widowhood which excited my compassion, and led me to reflections on the instability of the most flattering plans of happiness, that were painful in the extreme, till I was ready to ask whether this world was not created to exhibit every possible combination of wretchedness. I asked these questions of a heart writhing with anguish, whilst I listened to a melancholy ditty sung by this poor girl. It was too early for thee to be abandoned, thought I, and I hastened out of the house, to take my solitary evening's walk. – And here I am again, to talk of any thing, but the pangs arising from the discovery of estranged affection, and the lonely sadness of a deserted heart. (101–102)

Here her "reflections" turn her back on the condition of her own heart "writhing with anguish" so that the comments of the rest of the paragraph as much refer to her own situation as a mother alone as they do to that of the young wet nurse. In such scenes of staged sentimental encounter and mutual sympathy, Wollstonecraft seeks to develop a highly intimate form of what Bahar calls an "aesthetics of solidarity."[26]

One of the vital ways in which Wollstonecraft enacts this new senti-mental aesthetics is through her staging of her own story in the sentimental mode. In the scene quoted above, Wollstonecraft draws on the conventional language of desertion, constructing her letter writer alongside her young Norwegian companion as a female victim, virtuous and suffering. In the opening letter, the traveler describes how the very "idea of home, mingled with reflections respecting the state of society" makes her drop "a tear . . . on the rosy cheek" of her daughter (59). In a later letter, she contrasts her situation to that of a woman returning to her cottage with her family, a scene that evokes "a pang" that "only an unhappy mother could feel" (141). Wollstonecraft had begun *Rights of Woman* with the claim that "I plead for my sex – not for myself."[27] In *A Short Residence*, the foregrounding of a version of herself in motion becomes one of the ways in which she argues – or pleads – for women and presents the needs of those disadvantaged and uprooted in various ways. Late in *A Short Residence*, following some general comments on relations between the "two sexes" reminiscent of her treatises, she defends this continued focus in her work (much as Charlotte Smith defends a sameness of "tone" in her *Elegiac Sonnets*) with a new self-referentiality:

> Still harping on the same subject, you will exclaim – How can I avoid it, when most of the struggles of an eventful life have been occasioned by the oppressed state of my sex: we reason deeply, when we forcibly feel. (153)

This is justification both for the recurring focus within the text on the lives of women and for Wollstonecraft having made a version of herself the "hero of each tale." Her own particular "struggles" here become the basis for her observations and, more importantly, for both her sympathetic engagement and her reasoning.[28]

Like the published personal memoirs of her Revolutionary acquaintances, such as those Madame Roland wrote while imprisoned before her execution and that Wollstonecraft may have helped edit, Wollstonecraft's emphasis on the personal and gendered aspects of her new project now tends to be understood not as a turning away from the political but, at least in part, as an "indulgence in the personal as a means of intervening upon the political."[29] As Claudia Johnson has written of the literature of the 1790s in general, "In short, sentimentality is politics made intimate."[30] This is especially evident in the way in which the sentimental narrative is utilized within Wollstonecraft's critique of commerce. As *A Short Residence* progresses, the letter writer's unfaithful lover is increasingly presented as a financial speculator and as exemplar of the brutalizing effects that involvement in commerce has on social bonds. In the two letters written from the shipping ports of Hamburg and Altona, Wollstonecraft mounts a vehement attack on commerce, which becomes the dominant closing theme of *A Short Residence.* The neutral port of Hamburg was one of the largest ports in the world in the 1790s and had doubled its business in the year before her visit.[31] There she observes the huge profits – "mushroom fortunes" – being made by wartime speculators, comparing "these men" to "the owners of negro ships" who "never smell on their money the blood by which it has been gained" (171, 176). In a prescient critique, she presents this form of financial speculation as detrimental to society because it "embrutes" people until they consider "anxiety about the welfare of others, a search after misery, in which we have no concern" (172). This is precisely the kind of new, complex world system that constituted the conditions of mobility that became newly salient in this period, and Wollstonecraft presents a visceral demonstration of how central these could be to a developing understanding of a philosophical concept such as sympathy. Her critique is in part of a failure to imagine community across distance, and it is structured in its very conception by issues of mobility.

Against the abstracted, depersonalized, and ultimately modern image of the ceaseless circulation of goods and capital, Wollstonecraft positions her alternative model of intimate personal engagement. Commerce is made to function almost like the "other woman," as that which has taken her lover from her: "But you will say that I am growing bitter, perhaps, personal. Ah! shall I whisper to you – that you – yourself, are strangely altered, since you have entered deeply into commerce – more than you are aware of – never allowing yourself to reflect, and keeping your mind, or rather passions, in a continual state of agitation" (172). "A man ceases to love humanity, and then individuals, as he advances in the chase after wealth," she writes, until "all the endearing charities of citizen, husband, father, brother, become empty names" (174). Commercial circulation is bad, the logic runs, because it hurries and agitates, and because it abstracts, distancing cause and effect and in the process making people ("strange machines" as Wollstonecraft's calls us) incapable of more intimate engagements (174).

The success of both this depiction of the former lover and the letter writer's critique of commerce within the text more generally depends on the extent to which Wollstonecraft is able to stage the journey her text narrates as a sentimental one, editing out the specific commercial enter-prise that in fact drove her own travels.[32] The very mode in which Wollstonecraft expresses her "personal" opposition to a kind of excessive circulation emphasizes the fact that she means to present a sharp contrast between kinds of engagement. Her sentence, presented as a "whisper," is made to stumble or stutter on "you – that you – yourself," while the sentiments that follow this stuttered address then jump from one thought to the next, never quite breaking off. The effect is that, as with the epistolary novel, the reader has the feeling of eavesdropping on the most intimate of communications, expressed in the most sincere and unpremeditated terms. The way in which the letters in *A Short Residence* move between political observations and the informal intimacy of epistolary prose makes Wollstonecraft's critique work as an urgent personal appeal: the reader's sympathies are demanded by the self-revealing sentimental heroine, leaving little room for disagreement with either the letter writer's judgments of her lover or, more importantly, her accompanying political opinions. At the same time, through both the relationship between letter writer and her implied recipient and between the letter writer and the reader of the published text, Wollstonecraft models what an intimate, personal engagement based on sympathy might look and sound like.

"Sympathy Rises to Anguish": Feeling the Pain of Others

It is important, however, not to overemphasize *A Short Residence* as purely a rhetorical performance, successfully interweaving and reimagining a range of discourses. At points in her text, Wollstonecraft has clearly reached a kind of impasse in imagining how to travel through and, indeed, live in the world. Without reemphasizing the biographical too much, it is worth having in the frame the fact that Wollstonecraft's actual journey was bracketed by her two suicide attempts in May and October 1795, and that she prepared the text itself for publication in the final months of that year. Following her visit to Risør, during which she began to realize that her business negotiations on Imlay's behalf – the immediate reason for her entire journey – were not going to be successful, Wollstonecraft turned around and began literally to retrace her steps.[33] This turning back falls exactly halfway through the twenty-five letters that make up the published text. From this point onward *A Short Residence* no longer tells of a liberatory journey outward toward new possibilities, but of a journey back, of mobility that is a kind of painful repetition of places already seen, actions already performed.

Wollstonecraft's sense that this is not the journey homeward that would give shape to a more conventional travel narrative pervades the later parts of *A Short Residence*, structuring, I would argue, the shift in tone Mary Favret and others also locate around Letter XII.[34] Letter XII tells of the first steps of the return journey, from Risør back to Tønsberg where the traveler had previously spent time, and observes:

> Tonsberg was something like a home – yet I was to enter without lighting up
> pleasure in any eye – I dreaded the solitariness of my apartment and wished
> for night to hide the starting tears, or to shed them on my pillow, and close
> my eyes on a world where I was destined to wander alone. (119–20)

By the end of Wollstonecraft's sentence, the image of Tønsberg as the barely passable "something like a home" has been displaced by the image of an undifferentiated world through which the letter writer is destined to "wander alone." As the text develops, each description of arrival in each new town along the way becomes layered with past and future moments of disappointing arrival. After recounting her traveler's difficulty finding lodgings in Hamburg, where Imlay had originally planned to meet Wollstonecraft, Letter XXII generalizes, "After a long journey, with our eyes directed to some particular spot, to arrive and find nothing as it should be, is vexatious, and sinks the agitated spirits" (170). The passive formulation of the sentence implies that this has become the normative, endlessly repeated condition of arrival, so that when the traveler then refers to a particular instance in the immediate past, when she received "the cruelest of disappointments" on returning "to my home," this seems to be the condition of life itself (170). Conversely, when the letter writer does find someone or something to become attached to, the inevitability of onward motion becomes akin to an act of self-mutilation: parting is "– always a most melancholy, death-like idea – a sort of separation of soul; for all the regret which follows those from whom fate separates us, seems to be something torn from ourselves" (164). More generally, it is in these later parts of *A Short Residence* that it becomes increasingly clear that the unnamed "you" to whom the letters are addressed – who would form the most natural center of the journey, the point of origin and of return which would make each lesser parting bearable – has deserted his post. Imlay, or at least the addressee of the letters, is made to perform not only as a figure of rampant financial speculation in the later parts of the text but as a kind of aberrant Penelope. It is in a private letter from this time, which she echoes in *A Short Residence*, that Wollstonecraft writes the phrase with which I began this book: "I am weary of travelling – yet seem to have no home – no resting place to look to. – I am strangely cast off."[35]

Some of the most complex forms of homelessness evoked by *A Short Residence* involve ideas of the nation and of society itself. At various points, Wollstonecraft deliberately sets aside the nation, which might have offered a more generalized space through which to imagine "home." Instead of the epiphanies that typically follow first sightings of British soil in accounts by British travelers, in the final letter in *A Short Residence*, Wollstonecraft's traveler writes only, "at the sight of Dover cliffs, I wondered how any body could term them grand" (177). In a private letter Wollstonecraft adds, "I had a dislike of living in England."[36] Radcliffe, by contrast, in her travel book published a few months earlier exemplifies a more typical scene of homecoming: "There are, perhaps, few prospects of sea and shore more animated and magnificent than this ... And we landed in England under impressions of delight more varied and strong than can be conceived ... the love of our own country, greatly enhanced by all that had been seen of others."[37] In *A Short Residence*, Wollstonecraft refuses to fall back on this conventional trope of return to one's beloved nation. In her posthumously published second novel, *The Wrongs of Woman; or Maria* (1798), she would deny that women even have a nation, for "the laws of her country – if women have a country – afford her no protection or redress."[38]

The backward glance at the past does not structure the thinking of Wollstonecraft's travel narrative any more than does a backward glance at an imagined nation: elegy forms little part in the personal, political, or social hopes Wollstonecraft places in change. In her writings, home is very seldom imagined to exist even in ideal retrospective – as something lost – but explicitly exists only in future, prospective form. In *Rights of Woman*, Wollstonecraft distinguishes herself from Rousseau whom she suggests "exerts himself to prove that all *was* right originally," as well as from the "crowd of authors" who seek to show that "all *is* now right": she believes that "all will be right" only in the future.[39] In *A Short Residence*, this critique of the nostalgic strain in philosophical and political thought from Rousseau to Burke returns as "Rousseau's golden age of stupidity," a state Wollstonecraft declares not only undesirable but "physically impossible" (107). As numerous critics have observed, throughout her text she works to position Sweden, Norway, and Denmark according to a temporal geography on which to build a narrative about, and an argument for, the progress of civilization. As her letter writer travels further, Wollstonecraft's "progressive" voice becomes increasingly marked.[40] Her emphasis on inevitable social improvement becomes so naturalized within the discourse in *A Short Residence* that she can candidly inform her readers that she observes "the present state of morals and manners" only to "trace the progress of the world's improvement" (154).

This utopian belief in future worlds, however, only makes her individual wanderer's dependence on the outcome of the journey more acute than is the case for writers like Oliver Goldsmith, for whom, as we saw in

Chapter 1, like Rousseau, even when home is inaccessible it continues to function as an anchoring object of nostalgia for an idealized condition now past. Wollstonecraft, by contrast, wages the most sustained critique of nostalgia of any writer discussed in this book: if her traveler is an exile, it is from a home that does not yet exist and never has. The effect of this is to make all the more terrifying those moments in which, while "black melancholy hovers round my footsteps" in the present, hope in "future prospects" disappears (125). The fact that Wollstonecraft began her failed relationship with Imlay in Revolutionary Paris adds a political layer to her personal sense of homelessness. As Claudia Johnson writes: "[I]n the light of the hope that Wollstonecraft invested in republican masculinity in *Rights of Woman*, Imlay's derelictions spelled a disillusionment that was personal and political at the same time."[41] Traveling through Europe in 1795, after the French Constitution of 1791 had disappointed by having failed to grant the rights of citizenship to women, and the Terror of 1793 and 1794 had forced her to leave Paris, it is unclear even where someone like Wollstonecraft's political hopes and home would lie.[42] The radically unhoused situation she means to evoke is not even encompassed by the pathologized and medicalized eighteenth-century version of nostalgia, or motion travel sickness, which Kevis Goodman has shown was suffered by mariners and colonial soldiers and is characterized by Samuel Johnson as an "unconquerable desire of returning to one's native country."[43] Beyond the political, it is unclear even toward what a wanderer like Wollstonecraft should yearn.

The later letters in *A Short Residence*, written from this position of deep homelessness, oscillate between a self so preoccupied by her own cares as to be confined and almost incapacitated by them – obsessed with her own endless journey – and a self who seeks to negotiate an almost overwhelming awareness of the sufferings of others and the immense emotional mobility required to sympathize with them. At one extreme, her pain makes her incapable of sympathizing or generalizing; at the other, she appears so vulnerable and exposed that she seems in danger of losing herself altogether.

Reverie now marks one end of the spectrum, becoming confining rather than releasing. Early on characterized by expansive movements outward and upward, and once able to "transport" the speaker beyond care, reverie in the later parts of *A Short Residence* comes to be typified by unstoppable sinkings and fallings. Wollstonecraft's traveler in some sense collapses *into* herself in these moments of reverie, unable to "dilat[e] the emotions which were painfully concentrated" as she does on a walk in Letter I (58). By her pained Tønsberg letter, Letter XII, she finds that walking offers her only transient "forgetfulness," and that on her return she "cannot write composedly – I am every instant sinking into reveries – my heart flutters, I know not why. Fool! It is time thou wert at rest" (120). The syntax of the sentence itself stutters here, the dashes now merely serving to punctuate a list, rather than moving forward. Elsewhere the traveler becomes quite incapable of looking outside the cell of herself: en route to Copenhagen she finds that nothing she sees "took me out of myself"; on leaving Copenhagen some days later, she feels she "ought not to omit observing" but finds that despite this, "still I fell into reveries . . ." (145, 163–4). Katherine Turner dubs these passages of "guilty introspection," which invoke the empirical demands of travelogue as "unbearable pressure."[44] The act of writing the observations of travel become akin to reading in *Udolpho*, an outward facing gesture that at points becomes impossible. On the level of trope, at least, the traveler has reached the point so dreaded by Rousseau in *Reveries of the Solitary Walker* (1782), in which he feared "that my imagination, alarmed by my misfortunes, might end by filling my reveries with them, and the continual consciousness of my sufferings might gradually come to oppress my heart."[45] Wollstonecraft, like Radcliffe, Smith, and Frances Burney, is committed to exploring what happens when someone is placed in precisely this situation and denied access to the "peace" and "untroubled" "calm" that is offered by "steady and moderate motion" in accounts such as Rousseau's.[46]

But then something different happens in Wollstonecraft in terms of sympathy in Letter XVIII, which tells of the traveler's actual arrival in Copenhagen. Rather than being unable to observe, suddenly, on coming across the poorer refugees from a recent fire in the city, the pressure of the external world itself becomes extreme and unmanageable:

> here I was treading on live ashes. The sufferers were still under the pressure of the misery occasioned by this dreadful conflagration. I could not take refuge in the thought; *they have suffered – but they are no more!* a reflection I frequently summon to calm my mind, when sympathy rises to anguish: I therefore desired the driver to hasten to the hotel recommended to me, that I might avert my eyes, and snap the train of thinking which had sent me into all the corners of the city, in search of houseless heads. (145–6)

Wollstonecraft first lists the many conventional ways in which a traveler might safely contemplate a scene like this, from taking up the position of the aesthetic viewer of picturesque travel and looking for what might "attract the eye of taste," to meditating on the futility of human endeavor.

She finds each inadequate. The literal, physical warmth of the visceral image that follows, in which she describes herself as "treading on live ashes," then highlights just how inappropriate, as well as impossible, a disembodied, distanced response would be. In addition to giving a literal sense of the still-hot city immediately after the fire, this image conflates the recent dead with those living under its shadow, those "sufferers still under the pressure of misery," making the inhabitants of the city a kind of living dead themselves. There is no distancing mechanism for this situation, Wollstonecraft suggests, that would calm her traveler's mind, and as a result sympathy is transformed into the less manageable "anguish." "Anguish" is also the term Wollstonecraft uses in the wet-nurse scene. In the Copenhagen scene, she goes on to figure this emotional response of excessive sympathy as a form of endless, painful mental movement, as her traveler's thoughts move outward in a "train of thinking."

What exactly has gone wrong in these moments? Weiss and Bahar argue that Wollstonecraft's refiguring of "spectacles of female suffering" becomes, in Weiss's account, stimuli for social analysis, or, in Bahar's, the impetus for "collective political intervention."[47] But what Bahar terms Wollstonecraft's "aesthetics of solidarity," which blurs the distinction between the subject and the object of sympathy and seeks to depict two equal subjectivities, I believe collapses in the pivotal Copenhagen moment in particular, in a way that amounts to more than a staged refusal to view or represent distress.[48] What needs to be added to current critical analysis, as well as to discussions of the reimagining of hierarchies of seeing in women's travel writing more generally, is the pressing sense not just of suffering but of danger and vulnerability that pervades texts such as *A Short Residence*.[49] This is a new kind of traveler: a traveler who moves reluctantly without a center or a clear direction, a traveler who is unable and unwilling to ascend to the elevated height necessary to look down and pity people, and a traveler who knows that she possesses few means to relieve the sufferings of others. For such a traveler, sympathy becomes a dangerously exposing transaction.

Part of the problem Wollstonecraft depicts her traveler as encountering in regulating the movements of her sympathy in the complex Copenhagen passage is that the sufferings of others seem to chime *too* closely with her own. This is the flipside of Adam Smith and David Hume's idealized models of "mutual" or "*immediate*" sympathy. The thought of those made homeless by the fire incapacitates Wollstonecraft's vulnerable traveler precisely because their sufferings seem too much like those that occupy her internal reveries – herself arriving in yet another new city she feels for their "houseless heads." The reason for, and conditions of, the traveler's journey, Wollstonecraft shows, has a direct impact on her relations with others. Wollstonecraft's letter writer may refuse to depict these others as (merely) externalized objects of her pity, but imagining their equal subjectivities is also too overwhelming. Like Smith in *The Emigrants*, in the moment of collapse of the distance between homeless wanderer and homeless other, Wollstonecraft evokes the shock and subsequent unhoused insight of Lear on the heath: "Poor naked wretches, wheresoe'er you are, / . . . / How shall your houseless heads and unfed sides, /Your looped and windowed raggedness, defend you / From seasons such as these?"[50] Like Lear, and like Smith's wanderer-poet, and *unlike* William Cowper, for instance, Wollstonecraft's traveler's destabilizing anguish in contemplating the situation of the poor comes also from her own literal, as well as psychological, expulsion from any home. Here, Wollstonecraft develops the possible consequences of Charlotte Smith's radical reimagining of the social observer for the 1790s and her associated refiguring of what a stranger's "near approach" might mean: like Smith, Wollstonecraft registers the shock of a placeless, houseless, mobile speaker encountering a multitude of displaced others. In doing so, both women writers challenge on a basic level the valorizing of the sentimental encounter in work ranging from Adam Smith to Laurence Sterne, a valorization that re-emerges at times in mobility studies scholarship that, for instance, privileges Georg Simmel's notion of face-to-face connection. Wollstonecraft shows how such "face-to-face interaction" can certainly be productive of "intense affect," as John Urry suggests when he sets such interaction up as one of the "central features" of the mobilities paradigm,[51] but this affect can take multiple and troubling forms.

In reaction to experiencing an excess of communal pain in the Copenhagen passage, Wollstonecraft then momentarily reasserts the difference between "them" and her in what is presented as a peculiar act of self-defense. Her letter writer tells of how she hurried to her hotel to "avert" her eyes and "snap" the movement of her thoughts, just as she had "hastened" away from her encounter with the wet nurse. What Wollstonecraft seems to depict in such moments comes close to Susan Sontag's argument in *Regarding the Pain of Others* (2003) that people sometimes turn away from images of suffering not because of indifference, but rather, because they are afraid – both for themselves and for the fact that despite their compassion they may not be able to help.[52] The proximity or distance from which that suffering is viewed plays a key role in this. Wollstonecraft's account of hastening to her hotel might be read not just as a rhetorical refusal to represent suffering but as a demonstration of how very threatened her decentered traveler becomes in the presence of so many other, more desperate, homeless heads. This insight is helpful in understanding how differently people react to the presence, for instance, of refugees arriving in the place where they live, in which a lack of security or a sense of intense identification may lead to a less rather than a more compassionate response.

In *The Wrongs of Woman*, Wollstonecraft would place her hopes for social change in people using their personal struggles as a way into a wider understanding of the world, and in particular in women sympathizing with other women and so learning to generalize their sufferings. Her novel's heroine, Maria, who is locked up after confronting her husband with his attempt to prostitute her, finds that her pain "led me out of myself, to expatiate on the misery peculiar to my sex" (254). Similarly Jemima, Maria's prison guard and working-class counterpart, tells of how, "The anguish which was now pent up in my bosom, seemed to open a new world to me: I began to extend my thoughts beyond myself, and grieve for human misery" (194). This is precisely the language – "extend," "expatiate" – used by James Thomson to characterize the prospective view of the world in *The Seasons*, but in Wollstonecraft's *The Wrongs of Woman*, as in Goldsmith and Cowper, this is achieved though suffering and sympathy. What is importantly new in Wollstonecraft, and what draws on the tradition developed by writers like Charlotte Smith and Radcliffe, is the emphasis on both the *need* and the danger of moving "out of myself" or "beyond myself." The trope of moving beyond the self into a wider idea of collective experience is here made not only crucial to imagining society as a whole but, within this new tradition, necessary to counteract and alleviate the sufferings of individual experience.[53] The shared sense of suffering in *The Wrongs of Woman* finally forms the socializing bond by which both Maria and Jemima escape the highly symbolic madhouse and begin to make a new life together – a life founded on a quite different understanding of the world than that developed from the flawed politics and sentimental romantic reveries of the madhouse itself.

Little such transcendence through generalized sorrow, however, is offered in the bleaker late parts of *A Short Residence*. Besides the Copenhagen letter, at other times we even see the traveler hastening away from the "stench" of overcrowded houses, hurrying so as to see as little as possible (139).[54] The sense in which sympathy in suffering remains painfully and problematically earthbound in the later parts of *A Short Residence*, rather than opening "a new world" as it will in parts of

The Wrongs of Woman, is vividly represented in Letter XIII through metaphorical comparisons between the traveler's mind, an almost extinguished fire, and a bird that cannot fly:

> I can scarcely say why, my friend, but in this city [Christiania, now Oslo], thoughtfulness seemed to be sliding into melancholy, or rather dullness. – The fire of fancy, which had been kept alive in the country, was almost extinguished by reflections on the ills that harass such a large portion of mankind. – I felt like a bird fluttering on the ground unable to mount; yet unwilling to crawl tranquilly like a reptile, whilst still conscious it had wings. (128)

The dashes that open the second and third sentences in this passage suggest that each of these sentences modify or explain the experience of "melancholy, or rather dullness" named in the first. The warmth of fancy that characterizes the earlier parts of *A Short Residence* are put into dialogue here with reflections on the sufferings of others, and as a direct result are almost extinguished. These outwardly directed reflections might potentially offer, as *The Wrongs of Woman* will suggest, an alternative, more ethical and engaged, means of looking beyond the self to replace the move no longer offered by fancy. But here knowledge of the "ills that harass such a large portion of mankind" only has the effect of almost smothering the transformative potential of the "fire of fancy": reflections on the varieties of misery only produce a self who can no longer get airborne in imaginative or sympathetic flight. Wollstonecraft represents her imagination as virtually paralyzed by her awareness of suffering in the world. Rather than lifting the self out of herself – allowing her to "expatiate" or "extend" her personal sense of suffering – sympathy in *A Short Residence* becomes a weight of anguish, reducing mental movement to fluttering along the ground.

It is worth noting, though, that the fire is only "almost extinguished," the speaker "yet unwilling" to crawl and "still conscious" she has wings. The words "almost," "yet," and "still" in passages like this are vital as evidence of the sustained – if barely sustained – life of the imagination and of sympathy even in such moments. Reading this passage alongside that in *Udolpho* in which the "fire of the poet" becomes "cold, and dim" to Emily when she is imprisoned also brings into focus the fact that there, too, the fire of the imagination is not extinguished although it is crucially dimmed. Wollstonecraft's traveler refuses, metaphorically and linguistically, to crawl, that is, simply to accept things as they are without seeking to reach beyond or move forward. She may retreat to a hotel on first encountering the destruction of Copenhagen, but in the next paragraph she forces herself literally back out on the "straight road of observation" (153). We encounter her the next morning "walking round the town, till I am weary of observing the ravages" and commenting on the direct, preventable causes of the fire spreading through the city, while those not in immediate danger themselves did nothing about it till, "fear, like an electrical shock," roused them (146–7). Continuing to write and to try to observe keeps alive at least the potential for visionary flight and fully engaged sympathetic imagination. If we return to the passage in which the letter writer could not write composedly because her "heart flutters" not allowing her to rest, we might now see the pain of constant movement as forming a vital residue of a commitment not to rest, not to crawl, but to try to keep observing, and to try to keep moving forward.

"All the World Is a Stage, Thought I": Quoting Wollstonecraft

The struggle of being trapped in a framework of excessive involvement, or of repetition, not quite able to move in a new direction, is nowhere more painfully and evocatively performed than in the way in which Wollstonecraft's practice of quotation and allusion develops in the desolate second half of *A Short Residence*. In this part of the text, literary interaction takes on increasingly uncanny, at times gothic, qualities, at once being all too familiar, and at the same time expressing feelings that are not quite the speaker's own. I want to conclude my main discussion of Wollstonecraft's use of the figure of the wanderer with a return to quotation, but in an altered form from that analyzed in the previous chapter.

The notion of a porous, referential mind or text was an important and vexed one for Wollstonecraft, and one which she returns to repeatedly across a range of genres. "A great reader," she writes in her posthumously published *Hints* (notes for a second part of *Rights of Woman*), "is always quoting the description of another's emotions."[55] But in the case of her two *Vindications*, this takes the form of confrontational close readings, forming the basis, Susan Wolfson has argued, of what we now call feminist literary criticism.[56] In addition, in *Hints*, Wollstonecraft actually brings the "great reader" forward by way of contrast to a person in possession of a "strong imagination," which "delights to paint its own" emotions.[57] The ability to think and speak effectively in new and original ways is integral to both the utopian, transformative tenor of her political philosophy and to her literary theory. Women must become able, she reiterates throughout her *Vindications*, to think and act independently.[58] In her many reviews published in the *Analytical Review*, she consistently criticizes "imitators," and "copyists," who "borrow sentiments and arrange words."[59] Writers of genius, she writes in her final essay, "On Poetry, and Our Relish for the Beauties of Nature" (1797) which influenced Wordsworth's Preface to *Lyrical Ballads* (1800), should not need the aid of another writer to express themselves.[60] And in delineating her first heroine in *Mary; A Fiction* (1788), she placed herself among the few authors who "wish to speak for themselves, and not to be an echo – even of the sweetest sounds – ."[61] This context invites us to think again about what Wollstonecraft is doing by having her pained woman wanderer in *A Short Residence* use other voices to create or express her feelings at moments of most difficulty and suggests a very different understanding of quotation and communality from Radcliffe's. The most logical way to account for the difference between Radcliffe's and Wollstonecraft's practices of quotation is political, with associated aesthetic effects. Despite her association with reformers in the 1790s, Radcliffe still sits more comfortably within a dominant social order and literary tradition than does Wollstonecraft, who would have the world, including the literary tradition, made anew.

Wollstonecraft's practices of quotations and allusion have been seen predominantly as part of the self-constituting, performative agency by which Wollstonecraft generalizes her experience and stages herself for her readership in her letters and fiction as well as in *A Short Residence*. Mary Favret argues that much of the rhetorical power of *A Short Residence* comes from the way in which Wollstonecraft manages to exchange her own tale for that of various dramatic personae, so that "the drama," as Favret puts it, that Wollstonecraft presents "is not personal, it is communal and cultural."[62] Other critics have also drawn attention to the way in which across her work Wollstonecraft, ignoring any gender divide, "summons" the language of Shakespeare's tragic heroes in particular to, in Wolfson's words, "elevate her expressions of personal crisis and despair."[63] However, I would suggest that Wollstonecraft's multivocal dramatic performances are not, and are not meant to be, quite the consummate success that this critical consensus suggests, and are not necessarily figured as "elevating." In parts of *A Short Residence*, Wollstonecraft certainly uses or summons other voices, as Radcliffe does, to release her protagonist from confinement in the personal, and so to generalize her melancholy. The content of each quotation allows her to enter into conversation with other characters and writers, even when the source texts are unsettling. *The Tempest*, *Twelfth Night*, and *A Midsummer Night's Dream* feature especially prominently at moments of reverie in the early parts of *A Short Residence* along with their aura of a world imbued with more than can be seen.[64] In a quotation-fuelled evening boating scene in Letter XI, for instance, Wollstonecraft's letter writer evokes being figuratively "transported" from her real situation – in which she feels both physically and socially constrained in the Norwegian port of Risør – to the "magic island" of *The Tempest*, a location very much germane to the conjuring of imaginative worlds (and indeed, to the ultimate difficulties of such imaginative feats) (115, 119). Once there, she is joined by a host of "spirits unseen" who seem to "walk abroad ... to sooth my soul to peace" (119, and see also 64).[65] However, the configuration of quotations in the second more despairing part of *A Short Residence* in particular intimates that quotations can as easily invade, occupy, and limit a speaker as release her. Wollstonecraft's practice of quotation here performs, much as Smith's does in her late sonnets but in a different way, not an elevation of pain through entrance into the communal but an exacerbation of a sense of suffering, presenting another manifestation of a woman writer's fraught relationship with a community of the mind. Wollstonecraft's traveler's very need to quote provides further demonstration of the extremity of her situation.

Extending into the work of a number of eighteenth-century poets including Goldsmith and Edward Young, as well as into Shakespeare's tragedies, quotations and allusions become increasingly numerous as *A Short Residence* progresses, repeatedly closing – or closing down – individual letters, and becoming a central characteristic of the desolate fabric of the text itself. Letters XVIII, XXI, and XXIV all end on quotations. The move into quotation at the end of Letter XVIII, which gives the first description of the fire-damaged Copenhagen, is representatively bleak, as Wollstonecraft cites the despairing sentiments of blind Gloucester to reinforce her statements about injustice in society:

> 'As flies to wanton boys, are we to the gods;
> They kill us for their sport.'
> > Adieu!   (149)

Wollstonecraft had also ended the first edition of her *Rights of Men* – her first public statement on the state of the world – with reference to this passage.[66]

The shift in Wollstonecraft's use of literary reference as her text advances is graphically illustrated by the way the early letters invoke literary reference primarily by means of verbal echo and allusion, while the later letters use offset quotations. Rather than being absorbed into her letter writer's sentences as in the earlier letters and so made her own, the later quotations break up Wollstonecraft's prose and draw attention to themselves as distinct and separate voices – and to the emotions they express as not quite belonging to the woman who speaks them. In an evening scene in Letter X, no apparent relief is offered through the blending of voice and emotion with that of another. "Sitting then in a little boat on the ocean, amidst strangers, with sorrow and care pressing hard on me, – buffeting me about from clime to clime, – I felt," Wollstonecraft writes, and at this pivotal point she shifts into a quotation from Goldsmith's ever-present, *The Traveller, or A Prospect of Society* (1764):

> – I felt
>
> 'Like a lone shrub at random cast,
> That sighs and trembles at each blast!'
> On some of the largest rocks there were actually groves, the retreat of foxes and hares ...   (112)

Drawing attention to the implicit comparison Wollstonecraft makes here between herself and the "little boat on an ocean," as well as with Goldsmith's "lone shrub," Saba Bahar writes that Wollstonecraft's repeated images of being adrift "reveal both fragility and vulnerability. So do the broken grammar, the system of embedded tropes and the reported speech that contribute to her self-description. The syntax disrupts the cohesion of the speaking subject and as such considerably diminishes its otherwise expansive potential."[67] What Bahar identifies as syntax and reported speech is as much a symptom of quotation. There is no sociable plural ushered in by quotation here: the speaker remains resolutely alone, among but not accompanied by "strangers," and only "like" Goldsmith's lone shrub. While other, predominantly earlier, quotations conjure whole hosts of soothing spirits, this quotation is itself all about exposure, vulnerability, and above all loneliness, thus reinscribing rather than alleviating the speaker's sufferings. The inset quotation itself sits very differently on the page from the grammatically integrated reference to "spirits unseen" in an earlier evening passage. Wollstonecraft's speaker's explicit and active reaching for quotation – "I felt / 'Like ... ' " – is also distinct from the effect of quotation in the boat scene from *Udolpho* discussed in the previous chapter, where Emily's thoughts merge seamlessly in and out of James Thomson's without the act of quotation being ascribed to Emily herself. Meanwhile, in Wollstonecraft's passage, "sorrow and care" seem to come not from inside – not from her heart – but from the outside "pressing hard" on her and "buffeting" her about. Indeed, they push her "from clime to clime," in a vivid image of the movements of a reluctant traveler. This presentation of quotation has the effect that even while evocatively expressing something "like" the speaker's feelings, the quotation also forms a part of the battering she is undergoing by occupying the very space of what she feels. Becoming momentarily too weak to utilize a "strong imagination," Wollstonecraft's traveler becomes a space to be spoken by others, a copyist, a vessel for generalized already spoken pain rather than a template from which to generalize.

The link between quotation and a kind of haunted mental lassitude is perhaps most starkly demonstrated at the conclusion to the final letter from Copenhagen, Letter XXI, in which Wollstonecraft modulates the language of her traveler's heart into a (mis)quoted fragment from Hamlet:

> I have remained more at home, since I arrived at Copenhagen, than I ought to have done in a strange place; but the mind is not always equally active in search of information; and my oppressed heart too often sighs out,
> 'How dull, flat, and unprofitable
> Are to me all the usages of the world –
> That it should come to this!' –
> Farewell! Fare thee well, I say – if thou can'st, repeat the adieu in a different tone. (161–2)

The passage begins with her failure to observe properly during her stay in Copenhagen, where she had found herself almost too depressed – or "dull" – to leave her hotel. The next clause takes the initial juxtaposition of "home" and "strange place" that the sentence opens with to the level of mind, the implication being that her mind, also, has stayed too much "at home," having failed to be "active" in search of new information. In such moments, Wollstonecraft's traveler fails to correctly perform her role as empirical, Enlightenment traveler, seeking out information for her own and other's education, the kind of performed failure I explore in more detail in the context of Burney's *The Wanderer; or Female Difficulties* (1814) in the following chapter. In Wollstonecraft, as if to illustrate her traveler's situation of mental and emotional weakness, at this moment the "oppressed heart" does not even quite possess its own most intimate language, passively – perhaps as a gesture of exhaustion – yielding agency and expression to something both familiar and outside itself. In her private letters, Wollstonecraft returns repeatedly to this same quotation from Hamlet at those moments in her life in which she experiences what she calls a "listless kind of despair," most forcefully when she thinks she will be restricted to the life of a governess, unable to live in the new way she feels she is capable of living.[68] Instead, or as well as, being an elevation or diffusion of the personal, one might say, the drama Wollstonecraft stages is one of displacement of the particular personal by something more general which does not fully represent it. Wollstonecraft's practice of quotation functions as an intriguingly effective and expressive demonstration of precisely the misery that comes from the *sheer difficulty* of finding a position solid enough to speak in a new and original voice.

In Letter XXII, which describes the journey on from Copenhagen, Wollstonecraft evokes the world as a stage. This turns out to be not very different from her repeatedly evoked image of the world as a "vast prison," suitably, given her location, echoing Hamlet's "Denmark's a Prison," to which Rosenkrantz replies, "Then the world is one."[69] "All the world is a stage, thought I;" Wollstonecraft writes – herself unavoidably thinking in the words of another even as she attempts to make a claim for her own originality – continuing, "and few are there in it [the world] who do not play the part they have learnt by rote." Here the slight space allowed for those who seek not to play roles within already known parameters is described with evident bitterness: they "seem marks set up to be pelted at by fortune; or rather as sign-posts, which point out the road to others, whilst forced to stand still themselves amidst the mud and dust" (167). This is as different from her optimistically phrased declaration from a decade earlier that she was an original, "not born to tread in the beaten track," as it is from a strong-minded letter she would write to Mary Hays two years later, just before her death: "Those who are bold enough to advance before the age they live in, and to throw off, by the force of their own minds, the prejudices which the maturing reason of the world will in time disavow, must learn to brave censure."[70] Her bravery on this point seems to have reached a point of exhaustion in the final parts of *A Short Residence*.

In *A Short Residence*, Wollstonecraft depicts not treading the beaten track as feeling like simply being forced to stand still, only able to see and point out the new road without being quite able to move along it oneself. At the end of *The Wanderer*, Elinor, a Wollstonecraftian figure in Burney's novel and as much a wanderer as the central character, Juliet, wonders if she will eventually "find that she has strayed from the beaten road, only to discover that all others are pathless!"[71] This is a fear Wollstonecraft's wanderer faces with increasing intensity in the later parts of her journey. During this period, Wollstonecraft variously casts herself as Cassandra, her "warning voice" unheeded, and like Smith in *The Emigrants* as Sisyphus, "rolling a great stone up a hill" only to have it roll down again and to have to begin the work all over again.[72] This difficulty in moving forward, and of creating new languages and forms, goes to the heart of the tragedy *A Short Residence* seeks to enact. A tragedy, nonetheless, which even in its despair succeeds in demonstrating the oppressiveness of the conventional – the traditional, the conservative, the restrictive – thus converting the very performance of struggle against these things into yet another tool in Wollstonecraft's ongoing project of unmaking the assumptions of the world, as well as unmaking her readers' assumptions about travel, travel narratives, and the more general meanings of mobility. Unlike Elinor, whom Burney suggests will indeed be forced to return to the beaten path, Wollstonecraft continues to look ahead toward as yet uncharted roads.

A Final Tear: Weeping for the World

The penultimate letter of *A Short Residence*, like so many others, ends in citation. "Why should I weep for myself?" Wollstonecraft asks, before shifting into a direct quotation from Young's *Night Thoughts*, " – 'Take, O world! thy much indebted tear!' " (176). This would seem to signal a decisive move from personal grief into communal suffering, a reading reinforced by Wollstonecraft's allusion to the same line in her novel, *Mary*. Arriving back in England as a "forlorn wanderer" and seeing the "complicated misery" of the world for the first time, Mary "— Forgetting her own griefs, [ ] gave the world a much indebted tear; mourned for a world in ruins."[73] While the "world in ruins" by the end of *A Short Residence* has particularized in a number of ways, the mode of mourning is the same. Citation moves in to occupy the space left by the breakdown of a genre, the travel narrative, with its triumphant, or at least fond, return at its end.

But what are we to do with the fact that even the "tear" Wollstonecraft offers this world – and all the "ills that harass" it – is offered in the form of a quotation? It is notable just how many of the quotations in *A Short Residence* revolve around the topic of the ruin of the world, or of mankind, such as those from *King Lear* and *Hamlet*. In *A Short Residence*, unlike in *Mary*, Wollstonecraft uses punctuation to make sure we know this offering to the world is a quotation. Even her tear – understood as the most authentic gesture of the body – is presented as an already occupied or clichéd gesture, and in fact connected to a generalized sentimental stance that Wollstonecraft repeatedly rejected. A "tribute of some tears" is what MacKenzie's man of feeling and Sterne's Yorick pay to objects of pity – and often all they pay. Yorick offers his tears to the wandering Maria as a kind of balm: "Adieu, poor luckless maiden! – imbibe the oil and wine which the compassion of a stranger, as he journieth on his way, now pours into thy wounds. "[74] And it is precisely the kind of gesture Wollstonecraft had condemned in her response to Burke. Her *Rights of Men* ends with an apocalyptic vision of a world in which "[m]an preys on man," and "Hell stalks abroad," and with a declaration of the profound inadequacy of a sentimental response to such a situation:

> Such misery demands more than tears – I pause to recollect myself; and smother the contempt I feel rising for your rhetorical flourishes and infantine sensibility.

> - - - - - - - - - - -
> - - - - - - - - - - -.[75]

Even if these dashes can be read as textual tears, as some critics have suggested, they also express contempt for such gestures of grief. Even in her own *Mary*, which by 1797 she considered a "crude production," the tribute of tears is not followed by action but by a turning away in "disgust and horror" to find simpler comfort instead in "the smiling face of nature."[76]

On the other hand, if we read the "world" to whom Wollstonecraft offers her "much indebted tear" in *A Short Residence* as indicating, at least in part, her readers – and indeed ourselves – something interesting happens. In the same breath as offering up precisely the cliché tear her readers might expect of a suffering woman, Wollstonecraft, through offering this tear only in the form of a quotation, both separates herself from the conventionality of it and demonstrates just how oppressive, pervasive, and most importantly inadequate, such conventional gestures can be. Wollstonecraft's accomplishment, I have sought in this chapter to suggest, is in having found ways to perform the immense struggle involved in a woman finding both an adequate and a new position from which to feel, speak, and sympathize.

If we read "world" as audience we see, in addition, Wollstonecraft confronting her readers with the difficulty of making the particularities of any new position visible or audible – the difficulty of generalizing from, and so seeking sympathy for, an inherently marginal position. Adam Smith had warned that emotions which arise from "a certain situation or disposition of the body" as well as a "peculiar turn or habit" of the imagination, will be "little sympathized with," if they do not coincide with what the spectator himself feels (*TMS*, 31,38). One obvious reading of a "disposition of the body" is sex, in particular within Smith's matrix in which the normative subject is the upper-class man. Wollstonecraft, encountering what she saw as precisely such a problem in the response of George Dyson, and possibly of William Godwin also, to her final novel, protests, "I am vexed and surprised at your not thinking the situation of Maria sufficiently important, and can only account for this want of – shall I say it? delicacy of feeling, by recollecting that you are a man." She declares herself interested in delineating "the particular wrongs of woman": "For my own part I cannot suppose any situation more distressing. "[77] Beyond the reimagining of the sentimental encounter, through allusion in *A Short Residence* Wollstonecraft confronts the problem of the limits of sympathy in two additional ways: she dramatizes her sorrows through the voices of authoritatively representative subjects – Hamlet and Gloucester to Goldsmith and Young – and thus demands consideration for them; and at the same time draws attention to the violence this generalizing does to the particularities of her own marginalized story. This is precisely what makes quotation both so compelling and so problematic for Wollstonecraft: the voice of Hamlet – itself a rewrite of an older story – can certainly contextualize isolated grief, but it can never fully articulate the particular difficulties of a British woman writer traveling with her child in post-Revolutionary Europe. And a woman, Wollstonecraft implies in her letter to Dyson, should not need the assistance of a Hamlet or a Gloucester to make her particular difficulties sufficiently important.

Wollstonecraft was well aware that the "wrongs" that tortured her during the journey on which *A Short Residence* is based might of course attract interest in quite a different way. By declaring her "interesting," one critical review in the *Monthly Mirror* deftly sought to render Wollstonecraft a familiarly conventional, feminized object of pity, and in the process to undermine the radical political import and agency of her text and of her depiction of female wandering. *A Short Residence* appears, the reviewer writes, "to have been intended as an appeal to our feelings, and surely no object can be more interesting than that of an unhappy mother, wandering through foreign countries with her helpless infant." "Helpless" is applied to the infant, but the implication leaves its residue. Even this reviewer is aware that, as he puts it, "Mrs W., perhaps, will thank us little for our compassion," which he is careful to add is merely for her "private sorrows."[78] In a letter to Gilbert Imlay from this time Wollstonecraft had written, "I am not, I will not be, merely an object of compassion."[79] One of the chapters of *Rights of Woman* had taken up the topic of "Writers Who Have Rendered Women Objects of Pity, Bordering on Contempt."

Within *A Short Residence*, Wollstonecraft seeks to preempt such "compassionate" attacks: we owe her our sympathy, she suggests, precisely because there is nowhere unoccupied (or socially acceptable) for her to stand and speak her particular suffering. At the same time, Wollstonecraft refuses to present herself as an easily recognizable and untroubling object of pity, instead repeatedly confronting her readers with the social causes of women's pain, the conventionality of the tears they are expected to weep, the prescribed nature of the emotions they are expected to feel, reminding us, always, of the depth and complexity of what she is not (yet) able to express, and a road she is not (yet) able to travel. Unlike Adam Smith's imagined object of sympathy, Wollstonecraft cannot "communicate the cause" of her sorrow and be "relieved" by that (*TMS*, 18). There is no such simple solution. Nor does she exactly want to communicate in this way. As David Simpson suggests, Smith's model of sympathetic exchange is entirely dependent on a passionate yearning for sympathy on the part of the sufferer, and Smith's imagining of civil society is developed on this basis so that in his schema sympathy becomes "a function of a desire for sympathy, or the desire for consensus."[80] However, Wollstonecraft has little desire to be an object of compassion and she asserts that her experience falls outside a generalizable consensus. Like Charlotte Smith, she also refuses to "flatten" her emotions to a level of communicable "mediocrity," to use Adam Smith's terms again, which would make them fit for general consumption. Her performances of the inadequacies and failures of a system based on imaginings such as Adam Smith's, failures that she demonstrates through difficulties in occupying the position of either subject or object of sympathy, represent fundamental and far-reaching ruptures in imaginings of the social fabric, with economic and social as well as psychic effects. *A Short Residence* comes out of an impasse which Wollstonecraft only began to move beyond in *The Wrongs of Woman*, but out of this impasse she produces a kind of Pyrrhic victory. If her wanderings cannot be sympathized with, she will not stand still in order to be sympathized *at*. Wollstonecraft's traveler remains forever restlessly – if painfully and reluctantly – mobile, forever seeking that promised ground on which she hopes to one day be able to speak in a new voice, and live a new life. In Wollstonecraft, the voice of the woman wanderer becomes the voice of a woman unable to rest, to adequately express her pain, or to safely feel for others, but also a woman continuing to seek a satisfactory way to travel forward – and a way to feel and live.

CHAPTER 5

"No Motive of Choice"
Frances Burney and the Wandering Novel

Frances Burney's fourth, final, and longest novel, *The Wanderer; or, Female Difficulties* (1814) was eagerly awaited by nineteenth-century readers from Lord Byron to Jane Austen. It had been a long time coming – Burney began writing it in the 1790s. However, when it appeared well into the new century it received a chilly reception. William Hazlitt is typical in describing its plot as "teazing and tedious," and he scathingly suggests that the "difficulties in which she involves her heroine are indeed 'Female Difficulties' – they are difficulties created out of nothing." Byron dismissed it as "feminine trash."[1] A number of more recent critics have shown how *The Wanderer* suffered from a mistiming of publication. It is essentially a belated 1790s novel set at the height of the French Revolution and embroiled in Revolutionary-era debates about rights, national identity, the politics of movement, and women's situation.[2] It is also belated in being part of a tradition of writing about women's movement concentrated in the last decade of the eighteenth century.

Dismissals such as Hazlitt's echo criticisms of Mary Wollstonecraft's final novel, *The Wrongs of Woman, or Maria, A Fragment* (1798), which as I have discussed Wollstonecraft interpreted as implying that "the particular wrongs of woman" were considered by some as a subject not "sufficiently important" to bother writing about.[3] In the critical era of the late twentieth century, in which such particular difficulties were considered of the utmost importance, *The Wanderer* came to be seen by many as Burney's most interesting and ambitious work – as "essential reading for feminist literary historians" and for those interested in "the culture of revolution and reactions."[4] Over the last two centuries, though, many scholars have also agreed with the judgments of the novel's early reviewers, dubbing the novel practically unreadable, and the "style and language quite astonishingly bad."[5] This is not, then, just a case of a great read published at the wrong moment. What, precisely, is so difficult – so "unreadable" – about Burney's female difficulties? The peculiar aesthetics of this text, I argue, are inextricably linked to its narrative of female homelessness.

The Wanderer stars an articulate, Wollstonecraftian Jacobin, Elinor Joddrell, and a seemingly better-behaved emigrant heroine, Juliet Granville. Elinor is the wider ranging traveler; at points disguised as a man, she goes back and forth to the Continent, believing that the Revolution has "Ushered in a whole new world" and offers "a new road for life, when the old one was worn out."[6] As I suggested in the previous chapter, Burney has Elinor embody the fear that haunts Wollstonecraft's writing, that of eventually finding "she has strayed from the beaten road, only to discover that all others are pathless!" (873). In this chapter, I am principally interested in the movements of Juliet, the wanderer of Burney's title, who arrives in England in flight from a forced marriage to a commissioner in the new French Republic. Like Charlotte Smith with *The Emigrants* (1793), Burney had written an immediate response to the arrival of increasing numbers of French refugees into Britain in the 1790s. Her short pamphlet, *Brief Reflections Relative to the Emigrant French Clergy* (1793), was published shortly after her marriage to Alexandre D'Arblay, himself an émigré and a close associate of Germaine de Staël and other prominent liberal French politicians and intellectuals who sought asylum in Britain. Kirsty Carpenter argues that Burney should herself be treated as an "honorary émigré," and Toby Benis that *The Wanderer*, despite its publication date, is best read "specifically as a novel of the Emigration."[7] The novel is carefully dated in its first sentence to the bitter December of 1792, situating it, like Smith's *The Emigrants* (1793), in the winter that saw the greatest numbers of new arrivals on British shores. Whereas Smith imaginatively figures the situation of the houseless exile as the existential situation of the 1790s in *The Emigrants*, and Wollstonecraft explores a kind of "deep homelessness" in her Scandinavian travels, Burney casts a woman who is displaced in the most basic and literal terms as the center of her novel of wandering. Moreover, Burney does not limit this female wanderer to the coastlines or to foreign parts, but brings her deep into Britain, using her nameless, classless, jobless, nationless situation to test the limits of British conceptions of both travel and sympathy and to show what a woman wanderer's situation represents about women's situation more generally. In the process, Burney rethinks what mobility can mean, making Juliet's pained movements function as a radical reimagining of the standard domestic tour, and her life a radical reimagining of how the lives of women could be presented in fiction.

As with Smith's poet-speakers, Ann Radcliffe's gothic heroines, and Wollstonecraft's traveler, the suspense of Burney's work arises not from a marriage plot but from whether her wandering protagonist will find a means of physical and psychological survival, or as Julia Epstein writes of Juliet, "a way to exist in the world."[8] Unavailable for marriage for most of the novel, Juliet is a strange woman, an inassimilable stranger stuck in reluctant circulation.[9] If *The Wanderer* has a plot, it involves increasing pressure on Juliet and a gradual, episodic, encroachment of her external circumstances on her mind. It is as though once Burney has ejected her heroine from the domestic home she can take her novel (almost) anywhere, explore (almost) any of this situation's ramifications. Without a name, money, legible class markings, or a speakable story, Burney's Juliet is relentlessly forced to move from one location, one lodging, and one job to the next. Over the course of the novel, she travels from the coast of France to Dover, to London, then on to Lewes and Brighton, back to Lewes, back to London, then on to Salisbury by stagecoach and the New Forest on foot, to Wilton House and Stonehenge, and finally back to the coast. She seeks work as a harp teacher, a seamstress, a factory worker, and a lady's companion, but finds that none of these occupations offer either financial security or "mental freedom" (473). While Juliet spends the first seven books of the novel moving house and trying out different "species of subsistence" (49), she spends the final two books, after detection by her husband, literally running away and hiding.

Despite the novel's full title, *The Wanderer; or Female Difficulties*, and despite Burney describing Juliet as a "female Robinson Crusoe" (873), criticism has not tended to focus on Juliet's actual movements – on how Burney represents Juliet's reluctant wanderings in the novel and what they represent. Such a concentration on Juliet's specific movements is not quite the same as directing attention to the implications of her identity as an emigrant more broadly, or fixing, as does David Simpson in *Romanticism and the Question of the Stranger* (2013), for instance, on how the novel "incarnates the foreign woman as the compound stranger who tests out the integrity of the homeland."[10] It instead involves reading Juliet's actual journeying within Britain and the ways in which her incessant mobility is mapped onto generic female difficulties – from the difficulties associated with female labor to basic rights of self-determination over action and thought. In notes for a never published third edition Burney signaled an intention to capitalize the words "WANDERER" and "DIFFICULTIES" throughout the text, as if to refocus attention on the implied equivalence within the title.[11]

I read Burney's depiction of Juliet's movements as a lengthy, historically specific exploration of the ways in which, as John Urry writes in a basic statement of recent scholarship on mobility, where movement is coerced it generates economic and social deprivation and exclusion. If one of the widest claims of mobility studies in the social sciences is to provide "a different way of thinking through the character of economic, social and political relationships,"[12] then Burney's *The Wanderer*, like Wollstonecraft's *A Short Residence*, is a key early contribution to the effort to explicate these relationships using the lens of women's movement. Drawing on the new focus on mobility in contemporary scholarship, in turn, allows for a more acute sense of how mobility works in Burney's text and of what a prescient and strikingly modern novel *The Wanderer* turns out to be.

In writing *The Wanderer*, Burney set out to write the story of a different kind of heroine from those of her earlier novels and the time she took to write her suggests that the making of this new story was as difficult to articulate as the journeys the novel narrates. The question the tortured form of Burney's novel asks is how one can tell this different story. How can one construct the impossible identity of a female exile and wanderer? I read *The Wanderer* as Burney's magnum opus of digression and indirection, and as much an expressive failure of genre as Wollstonecraft's *Letters Written During a Short Residence in Sweden, Norway, and Denmark* (1796), which asks a version of the same question. It is no accident that Burney's story of a woman lacking destination, a home to return to, or an adequate way to earn a living is told in a novel that repeatedly performs the difficulty of forging a clear narrative path. This story comes with in-built potential for narrative difficulty and textual endlessness. Here I show the interpretative value of putting the geographical distances covered within this narrative in close relation to the (immense and digressive) distance traversed between the first cover of Burney's five-volume novel and the last. This reading necessitates not looking past Burney's "teasing and tedious" style in *The Wanderer*, but instead seeing what happens when we treat her style as an aesthetic inextricable from the subject and politics of her novel.

"No Motive of Choice"

The Wanderer begins with Juliet's voice calling from darkness, "O hear me! ... for the love of Heaven, hear me!" (11). Despite this early, urgent plea for an auditor, however, Burney withholds her wanderer's name and history even from the reader for most of the novel, and her emigrant heroine spends the bulk of the novel refusing, or unable, either to tell or to direct her story.[13] The novel's distinctive exclusion of the reader from the protagonist's mind is especially striking by contrast with Burney's earlier works, as well as with other works featuring roving protagonists, from *Robinson Crusoe* (1719) to *Tom Jones* (1749) to *A Sentimental Journey through France and Italy* (1768) and *Wilhelm Meister's Apprenticeship* (1795–1796). In Henry Fielding, for instance, we tend to know more about a protagonist's situation than he or she does, while the epistolary form of Burney's own *Evelina; or, A Young Lady's Entrance into the World* (1778) and its sentimental precursors gives the appearance of offering up the protagonist's mind directly. The first three paragraphs of *Cecilia; or, Memoirs of an Heiress* (1782), Burney's earliest novel in the third person, not only give the history and net worth of Cecilia, this "fair traveller" setting out into the world, but tell us the "secret prayer" she makes as she does so.[14]

The Wanderer works differently. Having set her first mature heroine on the road, Burney refuses to provide any kind of adventure of interiority. At the outset of the novel, Burney presents her readers not with a recognizable heroine as traveling companion but with a stranger, an *incognita*, who in the first few pages even appears with her face painted black. As this woman escapes from France on a boat bound for England, her readers are set alongside the wondering spectators within the novel, ignorant of the new passenger's name, class, intentions, or the meaning of her actions. Juliet yields only the "vivifying food of conjecture" and leaves readers guessing: rather than being admitted to Juliet's "secret prayer" as we are to Cecilia's, we learn only from another character's reported comment that she "seems to be at prayers" (12). Even in name, Juliet's character is performative – she is known variously as the Stranger, the Incognita, L.S. and Miss Ellis, before her identity as Juliet Granville is revealed. Her nationality, too, is unfixed, as she is English but was brought up in France. While we are gradually admitted to Juliet's thoughts and feelings, only near the end of the novel are we told her motives for disguise.[15]

Juliet doesn't just refuse to reveal where she is going, however; she herself doesn't know. From the opening chapter of *The Wanderer*, Burney systematically strips Juliet of anything that would help direct her precipitous journey. She has Juliet lose her purse at the moment she boards a British boat off the coast of France, making her loss of access to financial self-determination one of the trigger mechanisms by which the plot is put in motion. In parallel, Juliet also starts the novel with a destination and a plan, only to have both stripped away. She misses the friend she had planned to meet in London as well as the letters she had planned to pick up in Brighton and as a result becomes literally directionless, having failed to find, as she tells another character, "either the friend, or her direction, that I expected" (66). From this point onward, Juliet's lack of both home and destination are the symbiotic lacunae around which her increasingly random movements occur.

To put this in the terms of mobility studies, Burney sets her heroine up in a way that demonstrates what can happen to a person forced to be mobile, but excluded from what John Urry terms "network capital." Network capital, which Urry sets alongside economic and cultural capital as a form of capital by which certain people and groups accumulate emotional, financial, and practical benefits, is produced by such things as access to the travel documents and money that enable the movement of one's body from place to place, access to safe places to receive mail and to meet with others, access to others who can offer hospitality, and above all, time to coordinate and plan one's movements.[16] Juliet is lacking all these things, and it is from this that the many difficulties of her wandering stem.

But to return more directly to the question of the relationship between movement and interiority, *The Wanderer* is very much an eighteenth-century novel in the way in which it is saturated with descriptions of Juliet as directionless wanderer. Sandra Macpherson and Jesse Molesworth have shown that, contrary to what has been suggested in critical studies that focus on the *Bildung* model of the education of the protagonist or of the "adventure of interiority," eighteenth-century novels frequently display an overt obsession with randomness, displayed as the "causelessness of accident" over the "causality of narrative." They argue that in the process chance is frequently elevated above intention in these texts, clearing space for the narration of the fundamental instability of society and of human life.[17] Early on in *The Wanderer*, when faced with being cast out of her first temporary home, Juliet asks in the "deepest dismay," "Whither could she now wander?" (107). She is repeatedly forced, with ever-increasing regularity and dread, to "wander again alone" (363), to "be again a Wanderer" (655), "again, in search of a new asylum, [to] be[come] a Wanderer" (703), and to follow generally a "hazardous plan of lonely wandering" (671), if this can be called a plan at all. In the final two books of the novel, her wanderings become a matter of being pursued from place to place, moving on foot now, directed by nothing more than fear of detection. By the time she enters the New Forest in Book Eight, she has no "guides" but "fear" and "accident" (674–5). She follows "paths unknown to herself" (662), not even bothering to ask directions, "wholly ignorant what choice might bring security" (703). In her wanderings, Juliet must "commit to accident, since she had no motive of choice, the way she should go" (364).

Independent of Juliet's identity as a foreigner in flight, her situation as a solitary, nameless woman – whether in a boarding house, an inn, a factory, or alone in a forest at night – is represented as hazardous, or to use the novel's language, "little fitted to the female character, to female safety, and female propriety" (671). Without a speakable identity, Juliet's morality is constantly under suspicion and her body frequently in danger of attack, lending an extra layer of anguish to her repeated need to seek "strange succour, new faces, and unknown haunts; to expose her helplessness, plead her poverty, and confess her mysterious, nameless situation" (363). As a result, at every stage she tries to conceal what differentiates her movements from those of other travelers, that is "so extraordinary a circumstance, as that of beginning an excursion in utter ignorance where it might end" (655).[18] Throughout the final sections of the novel, Juliet attempts to move forward as though she knows where she is going, hoping to escape attracting attention by seeming to "pace her lonely way, with the quick steps of busy haste" (686). Burney has Juliet attempt to perform a simulation of positive intent, rather than simply reactive movement; she has her attempt to appear as the traveler she is not, rather than the dangerously vulnerable and directionless wanderer she is.

But while Juliet has been rendered homeless and nameless by chance rather than intent, Burney shows how such wanderers could be held strictly to account and punished for their houselessness. Within the novel as a whole, solitary female wandering is frequently perceived as actually criminal, punishable either by detention, or more counterintuitively, expulsion *to* wander. As is frequently the case with not easily categorized people, her mobility itself is conceived of as deviant. To put this in terms of Smithian equations between sympathy and moral judgment, because such movement is not understood and so cannot be sympathized with, it becomes a subject of moral disapproval. On arrival at the inn in Dover at the opening of the novel, one of Juliet's fellow-shipmates, Mrs. Maple, "angrily desire[s] the landlord to take notice, that a foreigner, of a suspicious character, had come over with them by force, whom he ought to keep in custody" (26). The seriousness of this declaration is suggested by Burney's notes for revision, which propose changing "to take notice" to "would send to the police."[19] Here Juliet's crime is as much that of being outside her country as outside her home. Mrs. Maple's threats are not idle. As Burney would have known, the Aliens Bill that was at that moment being debated in Parliament would soon legally require foreign nationals to register on arrival, while the newly strengthened legal provisions aimed at tightening regulations on vagrancy could subject both foreigners and Britons without means of financial support to punishment, imprisonment, or removal.[20] Jeremy Bentham, in his 1797–1798 articles on "Pauper Management," proposed that a simple question be put to suspected vagrants: "Have you any honest means of livelihood, and if so, what is it?" To answer in an unsatisfactory way, he argued, should lead to confinement in a panopticon industry house.[21] Even Elinor, the person most inclined to sympathize, assumes that Juliet must be "an adventurer" (33). Elinor asks whether one could "credit that any thing but a female fortune-hunter, would travel so strangely alone, or be so oddly without resource?" (30). The equation between lack of social ties and financial resources, and (criminal) guilt is made most explicitly, and tautologically, by Juliet's own relative, Mrs. Howel: "Innocent?" she asks Juliet, rhetorically, "without a name, without a home, without a friend? – Innocent?" She continues by asserting that Juliet will find that those "who have no ostensible means of existence, will be considered only as swindlers; and as swindlers be disposed of as they deserve" (133).[22] Later in the novel, Juliet will end up being advertised for in the newspaper as a "young female-swindler" (673). It is little wonder that Juliet's own language of fear expresses guilt within it, as she dreads having, once again, to "confess her mysterious, nameless situation" (363).[23]

The inherent problem with which Burney confronts her readers through Juliet's wanderings around Southern England is the inability of English society as a whole to imagine that, as Juliet puts it, "distress might be guiltless" (107), and that someone's actions and situation might not be of her own creation. The prevailing social assumption within the novel, reflected also in the new police and penal systems introduced in the 1790s, is that a person's "misfortunes" must be "the effect of their crimes" (37), if misfortunes are not, indeed, crimes in themselves. By contrast, Burney shows the world that Juliet actually experiences, and which she looks over in prospect view late in the novel, in ways that highlight the injustices and unpredictability of "uncertain existence": "failure without fault; success without virtue; sickness without relief; oppression in the very face of liberty; labour without sustenance; and suffering without crime" (701). This is not a world of just rewards but a world of frightening and bewildering randomness and of actual cruelty. This is the world in which the narrative of Juliet's nameless, mapless wanderings – her *Wanderjahr* – needs to be seen.

The Wanderer serves as a keystone in Deidre Lynch's rewriting of the history of novelistic character from Fielding to Jane Austen, where Lynch suggests that Juliet's assertion that she is "nobody" involves a new novelistic claim that "she has no social self, only an inner identity that transcends social determination" and capitalist exchange: Juliet is "invulnerable to other people's readings."[24] While Lynch's focus is on what is preserved by what she sees as the novel's refusal to yield up interiority to an outside gaze, critics whose work builds on and departs from her insights suggest, rather, that *The Wanderer* critiques the very demand for such "a picture of inner life," and does not work within a character model of "self-possessed autonomy."[25] This new critical approach to Burney's work fits well with new approaches to the eighteenth-century novel more generally such as Macpherson's and Molesworth's, which demonstrate the benefits of shifting attention beyond the post-Romantic focus on character, identity, interiority, and development still characteristic of much scholarship on the novel.[26] In relation to *The Wanderer*, I would argue additionally that the novel's reticence is not just a matter of not revealing interiority but also involves an exploration of a suppression or necessary move away from interiority itself, as happens, also, in Radcliffe's *The Mysteries of Udolpho* (1794), when a subject comes under extreme external pressure. There is a correlation between the difficulties Juliet encounters which strip her of choices, the increasing pressure that is brought to bear on her by her social situation, and the inaccessibility of any version of interiority or conscious desire at points in the novel. At the height of Burney's own misery during 5 years as a reluctant lady-in-waiting at the Royal Court, she wrote in her diary that in order to survive she must "wean myself from myself – to lessen all affections – to curb all my wishes – to deaden all my sensations," and later, "little *i* am fairly as one annihilated."[27] *The Wanderer* chronicles the necessity, and ultimately the pain, of such a suppression of self through its catalogue of Juliet's increasingly reluctant movements. Contrary to the 'discovery of the self' narrative charted by Lynch, Margaret Doody, and others in this novel, I see Juliet's journey as evolving from a suppression of conscious desires to a gradual emptying out of consciousness in the final two books of the novel.

The Syntax of Suppression; or, Burney's Johnsonese

The style of *The Wanderer* may seem "quite astonishingly bad," but the novel's signature extended sentences are also a fundamental means by which the novel's suppression of desire is performed. Burney's most unwieldy sentences recurrently appear at moments when Juliet is forced to move from one situation to another; whether these moves are of lodging, location, or occupation, they are almost always dictated by someone else. Cumulatively, these sentences link the novel's failure of narrative direction with the denial of Juliet's desires.

An early hint of the novel's suppression of desire and of Juliet's right to self-determination comes near the beginning of *The Wanderer*. Juliet, marooned on her arrival in Dover and known at this point merely as "the stranger," makes a reluctant decision to obey the querulous Mrs. Ireton's command that she accompanies her to London as a kind of lady's maid:

> The stranger, at first, refused to obey this imperious summons; but the wish of placing herself under female protection during her journey, presently conquered her repugnance. (39)

Juliet's subsequent decision to take up Mrs. Maple's equally unpalatable invitation to become an unwanted house guest is expressed using a similar grammatical formulation and identical phrasing:

> Nothing, to the stranger, could be less attractive at this moment; yet . . . the unspeakable dread of losing, in her helpless situation, all female countenance, conquered her repugnance. (68)

By the second iteration given here, Juliet is directed not by the positive "wish of placing herself under female protection" but by an "unspeakable dread of losing" it. More and more frequently in moments of apparent choice, Burney has Juliet "conquering" her "wishes," "feelings," "repugnance," or "reluctance," and deciding that "in a situation so defenceless, pride must give way to prudence; and nicer feelings must submit to necessity" (214, 224). Burney typically describes such moments of reluctant acceptance in especially long, ungainly sentences. Such sentences, strung together with multiple coordinating conjunctions which ultimately deny or shut down the feelings they initially express, become a distinctive feature of the style of *The Wanderer*, of how it moves or rather creeps forward. Burney even made a note to herself of the need in subsequent editions to cut down on all the "Buts," "Neverthelesses," and "Howevers," as though this feature of her style had become too excessively marked.[28]

Burney reserves one of the novel's most emblematic evocations of reluctant transition, rising now to the language of revolt, for the moment at the end of Book Five when Juliet returns full circle, being forced to take an ongoing position as companion to the vindictive Mrs. Ireton. Once again jobless, homeless, and now also pursued by a villainous Baronet, Juliet has no other options at this point in the novel. The paragraph in which she agrees to take the job consists of a single tortuous sentence:

> Juliet, instinctively, recoiled at the very name of that lady; yet a little reflection upon the dangers to which she was now exposed, through unprotected poverty; through the lawless pursuit of Sir Lyell Sycamore; and the vindictive calumnies of the Brinvilles, made the wish of solid safety repress the disgusts of offended sensibility; and, after a painful pause, she recommended herself to the support of Elinor: resolving to accept, for the moment, any proposition, that might secure her an honourable refuge from want and misconception. (474)

Juliet initially "recoils" from Elinor's suggestion that she takes a position with Mrs. Ireton, in an instinctive, embodied reaction. But then, once again "reflection" on her situation makes her "repress" her disgust and "offended sensibility." Juliet's journey from recoil and disgust to reluctant repressing of all feeling is performed clause by clause over the course of Burney's sentence. The extended sentence enacts the "painful pause" during which its mental action takes place. When Juliet eventually sets out "for her new destination" she does so, "[w]ith a mind revolting from a measure which, while prudence, if not necessity, dictated, choice and feeling opposed" (478). "[M]ind," as well as "choice" and "feeling" are lined up here, in syntactic revolution against the forced move Juliet makes. She becomes a subject literally, but not willingly, "dictated" (written) by the narrow, constricting demands of "prudence." Over the novel as a whole, Juliet's (and Burney's) repeated denial of desire cumulatively amounts to a knowing, and circumstantially necessary, suppression of conscious will or volition. Burney goes on to depict Juliet's situation in Mrs. Ireton's household where she works alongside a literal slave from the West Indies as a form of physical and mental "slavery" (474). Juliet's employer has ambitions to command her "liberty of speech and thought," while another character is moved to exclaim at the way in which Juliet is asked to become a kind of simulacrum of a human being, asking how one can, "Tell a human being that she must only move to and fro, like a machine? Only say what she is bid, like a parrot?" (524).[29]

It is the kind of sentence by which Juliet resolves to accept Mrs. Ireton's offer of employment, one presumes, that led Thomas Macaulay in a mid-nineteenth-century assessment of Burney's career, to call her late style, "the worst style that has ever been known among men," and "a sort of broken Johnsonese, a barbarous *patois*, bearing the same relation to the language of 'Rasselas' which the gibberish of the Negroes of Jamaica bears to the English of the House of Lords." He sets this in contrast with her early style, which he judges to be "true woman's English, clear, natural, and lively."[30] The race and gender assumptions of Macaulay's metaphors alone say much about the limited range of what might pass as an acceptable form of language – and from whom. But what is also revealing is his locating of Burney's style *as* language – as sentences. What we get in Samuel Johnson, and certainly what we might imagine a reader like Macaulay seeks, is an appearance of the weighing and balancing of thought; Samuel Johnson's balanced sentences perform reason as much as do Alexander Pope's rhyming couplets. Burney's sentences in her later novels, by contrast, perform a painful, enforced relinquishment of thought and agency. Burney's style is part of a syntactic and cognitive doubling going on in *The Wanderer*, which allows for both the expression and suppression of feeling, both the revelation and the denial of interiority and conscious desire. Burney's sentences reflect and perform the tortured movement of the thoughts they describe, taking the issue of "liberty of speech and thought" to the level of syntax. We might read her sentences, indeed, as a form of female style which contributes to the performance of female difficulties to which the novel is dedicated. We might read it, indeed, as a more challenging – less charming and more confronting – version of "true woman's English." The effect is that the novel is full of situations and syntax that read something like this: "Her immediate wish ... was to clear herself ...; but her wishes, tamed now by misfortune and disappointment, were too submissively under the control of fear and discretion, to suffer her to act from their first dictates ..." (421). The overwhelming feeling Burney develops is of a protagonist whose every impulse must be suppressed and whose every motion is directed by others; and of a correspondingly slow, reluctant, halting movement of the text itself, from the level of the sentence to the level of plot. The very length and indirection of each of the novel's sentences, then, might be read as a small-scale version of the length of the novel as a whole, while the reluctant state of mind these sentences seek to perform indicates the reasons for the length of both.

As an aside before moving on, it is worth registering that despite performing this relinquishment of agency, Burney makes sure that Juliet, like Radcliffe's Emily, and also like Jane Austen's ever-accommodating Fanny Price in *Mansfield Park* (1814), knows how to refuse demands. In fact much of the tension and energy of the text comes from the fact that while Juliet has little autonomy to direct her own movements, she sets clear limits on what she will do at another's command. Just how little weight Juliet's wishes carry within the world the novel depicts, however, is underscored by how often she is actually forgotten within scenes, so that other characters talk on for pages without registering her presence. In the jostle for what Alex Woloch calls "character-space," Juliet is frequently the loser.[31] All the same, Juliet is resistant enough to the demands of the world she inhabits to infuriate characters such as Mrs. Ireton, much as Fanny Price does Sir Thomas.

Much of the critical interest of *The Wanderer* lies in its ambivalent or contradictory politics, in the way in which it seems to be pulling in different ideological directions. Most obviously, this political ambivalence is evident in the way in which the narrative voice seems to disapprove of the radical Elinor's behavior and opinions but gives her ample room to speak. For some critics, this consists of the novel masking its "political insurgency by valorizing the 'conservative' ... while retaining signs of revolutionary sentiment," so that the novel needs to be read "against the grain of its author's ostensible politic sympathies."[32] For Claudia Johnson, it amounts, instead, to a novelistic "failure[] of mastery" in which, "Whatever race, class, gender, and political stripe are at stake, critique gets strangled in the plethora of the novel's counterexamples, and the novel's very immensity impedes rather than extends insight."[33] Bringing to the fore the connection between Burney's digressive, circumlocutory sentences, and her heroine's reluctant movements opens up a new direction for this discussion, which has failed to read Burney's digressive style in sufficiently political ways. To fully understand what is going on in *The Wanderer*, we need a mode of reading which explores Burney's corrupt "Johnsonese" for all its wandering, vacillating, contradictions. To quote a phrase Mark Blackwell uses to explain how Radcliffe uses syntactic suspension to evoke an experience of delay, we need to find ways of reading Burney's "grammatical infelicity as aesthetic achievement."[34] In *The Wanderer*, Burney's sentences play a dynamic role in allowing Juliet simultaneously to protest and to submit. They are a constituent part of Burney's performance of the signature situation of the novel, a situation in which a woman's desires and her movements are painfully opposed.

Revealing exceptions to this form of reluctant transition on the level of the sentence occurs during the interval in Books Three to Five in which Juliet attempts to earn a subsistence from various forms of labor. At this point in the novel, Juliet enters each new line of work decisively, with the hope that it might prove to be better than the last. Initially, the very "hope of self-dependence," "sweeten[s]" her sleep, while she approaches the move from private harp teacher to public performer with "courage and calmness," "Resolute in her plan" (220, 355). After this plan fails, as well as her subsequent effort to earn a living by taking in sewing with her refound friend, Gabriella, she takes a position in a milliner's shop "without murmuring; hoping to gain in security all that she lost in liberty" (425). When milliner's work, too, becomes "intolerable," Juliet's decision is as swift as the sentence which tells of it (swift in Burney terms, that is): "Without, therefore, a moment's hesitation, she determined to relinquish her present enterprise" (449). Having fully descended the social ladder, she now enters factory work, continuing to seek, Crusoe-like, a satisfactory form of "self-dependence" (220). The clear sentences in these moments of self-directed shift perform the decisiveness of the moves they describe.

Ultimately, however, Burney does not even allow her wanderer the curtailed freedom of choosing her line of work. Before the move to Mrs. Ireton's Juliet rejects Elinor's accusation that she has created her own difficulties by choosing to seek self-dependence through labor:

> [']Choice, Madam! Alas! deprived of all but personal resource, I fixed upon a mode of life that promised me, at least, my mental freedom. I was not then aware how imaginary is the independence, that hangs for support upon the uncertain fruits of daily exertions! Independent, indeed, such situations may be deemed from the oppressions of power, or the tyrannies of caprice and ill humour; but the difficulty of obtaining employment, the irregularity of pay, the dread of want, – ah! what is freedom but a name, for those who have not an hour at command from the subjection of fearful penury and distress?' (473–4)

Burney has Juliet find notions of "independence" and "freedom" as illusory as "choice," so that "independence" becomes only the insecurity of employment, and "freedom" a kind of ever-present fear that one may be reduced to immediate poverty. This is reminiscent of Wollstonecraft's ironizing of the word "independence" in *The Wrongs of Woman*, as something that consists for her working-class character, Jemima, of "choosing the street in which I should wander" as a prostitute. Like Juliet, Jemima is forced to relinquish even this level of independence, taking up the "servitude" of a brothel in order to escape from the brutal uncertainties associated with the autonomy of being a street walker.[35] Juliet, too, only takes up the "slavery" of being a lady's companion after the promise of other forms of labor have failed to provide either financial independence or space for the mind to have some "poor unshackled instants to itself" (453). Like Jemima, as both laborer and commodity in reluctant circulation, Juliet cannot afford the luxury of choice.

"Not Juliet": The Wanderer on Tour

As we have seen, Juliet is always on the move. Her "difficulties" arise from the fact that she is a wanderer – a woman without a home or identifiable class markings – and these difficulties in turn create more difficulties. In Books Eight and Nine, Burney heightens the desperation of Juliet's situation as wanderer, so that Juliet lacks food, shelter, and sleep, and is literally hunted from place to place along the open roads around Salisbury. The counterintuitive insight that emerges from paying close attention to the movement in this section of *The Wanderer* is that precisely as Burney's heroine's flight becomes increasingly desperate and seemingly undirected, her movements also become structured by an absolutely standard, pre-scripted tourist itinerary.[36] Burney places her fleeing female wanderer – who on the surface is moving as blindly as a hunted animal – repeatedly in contact with the kinds of places and experiences that a more conventional traveler would expect to take in. The careful parallels and distinctions Burney develops between tourist and reluctant wanderer in this section of the novel are, I argue, a continuation of an exploration and evocation of the availability – or relative unavailability – of an interiority under pressure to act or engage with the world around. In the process, this amounts to a rewriting of the literary meanings ascribed to mobility and sympathy.

Alongside the general shift to a more mobile society, tourism – and especially domestic tourism – saw a huge upsurge in the last two decades of the eighteenth century. An increasing number of Britons with new access to leisure and financial security were traveling in search of aesthetically pleasing or culturally informative sites, following relatively proscribed routes.[37] Travel within Britain became especially important from 1793 onward, when the Terror and the declaration of war effectively closed the Continent to Britons, while the pedestrian tour rose steadily in popularity, becoming intimately associated with ideas of independence and freedom from one's own biographical context.[38]

The final section of *The Wanderer*, when read as a kind of domestic tour, involves four key, if in this context unexpected, forms of tourist experience: Juliet visits the town of Salisbury and its gothic cathedral; encounters the picturesque beauties of nature in the New Forest on foot; visits the galleries of a country seat at Wilton; and encounters ancient ruins at Stonehenge.[39] Juliet's route approximately follows the itinerary Burney herself took on her "*Tour for Health*" in August 1791, immediately following her long desired release from her role as Second Keeper of the Robes at Court. Weak from a period of illness and a near breakdown, Burney expressed frustration in her journal that "when I cannot rest at will, I become languid and sick to a degree not merely irksome, but painful."[40] Through the movements of Juliet as homeless, pursued wanderer, never able to "rest at will," Burney superimposes a new experiential map onto old routes, showing the domestic tour as a nightmare version of itself. This "literary map," to use Franco Moretti's term, of Juliet's reluctant, pained, and relentless tour will form the itinerary for the rest of this chapter.[41]

Following Burney, I use the terms tourist and traveler interchangeably here to mean someone who sets out on a journey of their own volition and who expects to return home, and as distinct from exiles, refugees, or, in Burney's formulation at least, wanderers, who do not typically direct their own journeys and are often homeless. The same distinction is apparent in Burney's account of her own "tour" through Southern England in 1791 when she gives a long description of her first encounter with a group of French emigrants, whom she describes as "Poor Wanderers!"[42] In the pamphlet on the emigrant clergy she wrote 2 years later she casts her subjects as "destitute wanderers," much as Charlotte Smith depicts her Miltonic "ill-starr'd wanderers," as "Banish'd for ever" "to wander" "Thro' the wide World unshelter'd" (*Em*, 1.97,101,103; 2.436)[43] Burney's Juliet is figured as a wanderer in similar terms, but in more (and more realist) detail. *The Wanderer* was written and set in the decades in which modern understandings of tourism and the figure of the tourist were being forged, and the movements of Burney's reluctant tourist suggest a strikingly different history of travel from the one to which we are accustomed.

Town: Salisbury

Juliet is never more explicitly a failed or frustrated tourist than in her time in Salisbury, an important stopping point for travelers in the late eighteenth century, and, owing to its thirteenth-century cathedral,

a popular destination with the advent of the Gothic Revival.[44] Soon
after Juliet's unplanned arrival there Burney gives a virtual compendium of possible tourist activities her heroine might engage in, but
does not:

> To have seen and examined the famous cathedral; to have found out the
> walks; to have informed herself of the manufactures; and to have visited the
> antiquities and curiosities of this celebrated city, and its neighbourhood,
> might have solaced the anxiety of this moment; but discretion baffled
> curiosity, and fear took place of all desire of amusement. (661)

The language of tourism in this passage is predominantly the language of
disinterested information – "seen and examined," "found out," and
"informed herself" – in line with the educative, public role typically
assigned to the urban tour. Burney depicts visiting the cathedral as only
one of many activities in which an eighteenth-century urban tourist might
expect to partake.[45] In addition to information, she suggests, such activities
might, if necessary, offer "solace" or distraction. Burney's friend, Hester
Thrale Piozzi, when describing a continental tour she planned to take in
the spring of 1783, hoped that, "external Objects [may] supply the room of
internal Felicity."[46] But in Burney's account of Salisbury she only lists
these as possible activities not taken up. Burney is careful to show that
Juliet's lack of activity is not simply due to fear of discovery: the final clause
of the sentence suggests, using the peculiar verb "baffled" with its connotations of being muffled from the world, that in Juliet, the curiosity so
vital to the traveler has been lost or bewildered.[47] Burney replaces "desire of
amusement" with fear. Her characteristic sentence structure, in which the
final clause negates the possibilities expressed in the opening of the
sentence, is familiar by this point in the novel. Juliet's precarious, wandering situation, and her experience of repeated repression of any desire on her
own part have left her without the "curiosity" – which Edmund Burke
describes as the "simplest emotion which we discover in the human
mind" – necessary to engage properly as a tourist.[48]

Burney tempers her depiction of Juliet's lack of interest later in the
Salisbury section when Juliet ends up in the gardens of Salisbury Cathedral
by accident. At first, what is directly in front of her is "nearly lost to her
sight, from the misery and preoccupation of her mind." Soon, however, the
immediate proximity of the sight/site overcomes this preoccupation, so
that,

> in defiance of all absorption, the magnetic affinity, in a mind natively pious,
> of religious solemnity with sorrow, made the antique grace of this wonderful

edifice, catch, even in this instant of terrour and agitation, the admiring eye of Juliet; whose mind was always open to excellence, even when most incapable of receiving any species of pleasure. (663)

Here Burney distinguishes between an ability to perceive "excellence" and an ability to take pleasure in it: the first of which Juliet is (just) capable of in this state of mind and the second of which she is not. In addition, the church "catches" Juliet's attention – in a grammatical construction which makes the church rather than Juliet active – precisely because its "religious solemnity" is the same as her "sorrow." Juliet values the cathedral, in other words, for harmonizing with her own state of mind, rather than for taking her out of herself. And even this moment in which Juliet becomes a tourist, albeit an emotionally crippled one, is truncated so that by the end of the following paragraph her world has narrowed again, and we are told that "every feeling was transient, that led not to immediate escape; every reflection was momentary, that turned, not to personal safety" (663). Anything but thoughts of immediate security is markedly absent.

Country: The New Forest

Burney has Juliet's country interlude in the New Forest follow a similar structure, this time involving a momentary opening up to the landscape and to the requisite prospect view, a standard trope of the picturesque tour, before shutting it down again. At first Juliet enters the forest as the antithesis both of picturesque traveler and prospect viewer, literally running from the road and straight into the trees followed closely by her husband's emissaries (676). Such movement leaves little space for what William Gilpin describes in his key essay on picturesque travel as the traveler's "first source of amusement," that of the "*pursuit*," "hunt," or "chase" after his object, in this case what he would describe as the "beauties of nature."[49] Burney neatly inverts picturesque theory's heavily gendered conceit of the traveler as hunter: Juliet enters the forests of the picturesque as the object of a hunt, becoming almost bestial in the process. This has implications for how she sees, and initially fails to see, the "beauties" by which she is quickly, and unknowingly, surrounded. The chapter in which Juliet enters deep into the forest begins:

> The terrified eagerness with which Juliet sought personal security, made her enter the New Forest as unmoved by its beauties, as unobservant of its prospects, as the 'Dull Incurious', who pursue their course but to gain the

place of their destination; unheeding all they meet on their way, deaf to the songsters of the wood, and blind to the pictures of 'God's Gallery', the country. (674)

"Dull Incurious" is from near the beginning of James Thomson's *The Seasons*, a poem which, as we saw in Chapter 1, is deeply and influentially concerned with making distinctions between those few fitted for curiosity, or for prospective vision – in this particular part of the poem, those in possession of the "sage-instructed Eye" – and those who make their "blind way" through the world. Like the few women who appear in *The Seasons*, who move with "downcast Eyes," Juliet enters the forest "without daring to raise her eyes" (674).[50] Burney uses a similar formulation later in the novel, when she has Juliet proceed unknowingly toward Stonehenge with "eyes bent upon the turf" (765). In both cases, Juliet is explicitly not a picturesque traveler but instead someone who moves only to get to her destination, while at the same time, of course, not even having a destination. The "terrified eagerness" (674) with which she moves here, and the similarly "utterly deplorable" (765) state of mind with which she later approaches Stonehenge, provide a suggestive contextual gloss to why some subjects more than others might not have the capacity to stop and look at the view – and indeed to engage with those they meet along the way. Mrs. Thrale observed that Samuel Johnson was a poor traveling companion, and by implication a poor traveler, because he appreciated neither music, painting, nor prospects: "he was almost as deaf as he was blind."[51] Burney, unlike Mrs. Thrale, situates the metaphorical condition of deafness and blindness squarely in the lap of circumstance: her wanderer's lack of personal security, like that of Radcliffe's Emily, leads to lack of freedom to see beyond her immediate concerns, which in turn leads to an inability to take visual pleasure. Burney had rehearsed this situation with a slightly different emphasis in *Camilla*, where on an excursion to Southampton in despair of her lover's affections, Camilla finds that "The journey, though in itself short and pleasant, proved ... long and wearisome; the beauties of the prospect were acknowledged by her eye, but her mind, dead to pleasure, refused to give them their merited effect."[52]

As in the scene in the Salisbury churchyard, Burney then gradually allows Juliet's self-absorption to release. Burney carefully demarcates, and almost exaggerates, the conditions that make a prospect view possible, allowing Juliet a short, but vital, interval of "undisturbed repose," after which her eyes "recover their functions," and she begins to "cast them around" (676). Taking notice now of the "prospect" around her, she "mounted a hillock to take a general survey of the spot, and thought all paradise was opened to her view" (676). There is nothing modest about the prospect Burney grants her wandering heroine when she finally grants her one: the scene takes in the "variegated woods" of "aged oaks," rises in "lofty grandeur" to the sky, and takes in the setting sun, which seems to "irradiate" "the world."[53] The language is a mix of loco-descriptive, picking up on Thomsonian periphrastic constructions such as "feathered race," and of something closer to divine inspiration, so that bird song strikes "her ear as sounds celestial, issuing from the abode of angels" (676). This vision of an apparently harmonious, and indeed glorious, natural world seems to offer Juliet an ability to feel released from the oppressiveness of the present moment as well as the need for human society in general:

> Here, for the first time, she ceased to sigh for social intercourse: she had no void, no want; her mind was sufficient to itself; Nature, Reflection, and Heaven seemed her own! Oh Gracious Providence! she cried . . . Religion! source and parent of resignation! under thy influence how supportable is every earthly calamity! how supportable, because how transitory becomes all human woe, where heaven and eternity seem full in view!
>   Thus, in soul-expanding contemplation, Juliet composed her spirits and recruited her strength . . . (676–7)

In this moment, one of the very few in which Juliet is allowed to be alone in *The Wanderer*, she has no need of "social intercourse"; she needs nothing, and no one, but is "sufficient" unto herself.[54] There is nothing merely adequate about this self-sufficiency, which takes in this world (Nature) and the next (Heaven), as well as something which seems to sit in between (Reflection). The apparent consolation of this moment of asocial self-absorption comes from the fact that it makes no less than "all human woe" seem almost inconsequential, because "transitory."

As a number of critics point out, Juliet finds some consolation in this New Forest scene, and momentarily feels her own strength and potential expansiveness. Deidre Lynch, for instance, understands Juliet's "soul-expanding contemplation" (676) as a move in the "final phase of her narrative of self-recovery."[55] But Burney's emphasis on a feeling of self-sufficiency and detachment from all "social intercourse," while celebrated, also brings to the surface the isolated, amoral position of the prospective, and aesthetic, viewer. Burney explicitly, and systematically, undercuts the efficacy and accessibility of all three tenets of the traveler's prospect view: disinterestedness, disembodiment, and distance. The effect, to use

Elizabeth Bohls's description of Wollstonecraft's revision of aesthetic discourse in her travel writing, is that of "profoundly subverting the world view that informs aesthetic discourse."[56] Juliet may "take a general survey" of the "aged oaks," as Burney echoes travel writing's language of expert observation, prospect poets from Alexander Pope to Thomson, and theorists of the ideal aesthetic subject and of the picturesque from Joshua Reynolds to Gilpin, but Juliet's gaze is far from disinterested (or impartial). What she sees is a body of trees that she hopes will offer her "shelter from the storms of life" (676) or, more literally, a hiding place.

Nor is she disembodied for long. Burney quickly dismantles the sense that her female wanderer has been able to occupy unproblematically the generalized position of the prospect viewer, even for an instant. A mere five paragraphs after Juliet's eyes have "recover[ed] their functions," and she has begun to look around her, Burney has her back on the high road, and within "a few minutes," and a single paragraph, she is being accosted by a carter. This brief encounter could be passed over as comic relief, but the few paragraphs of reported dialect, in which the carter and his companion familiarly comment on Juliet's "bonnet of old" and her slim figure, then refer to her as a "jeade" and a "wench," have the effect of abruptly transforming Juliet from contemplative observer, from seeing eye who takes in the world as "her own," to embodied spectacle – that is, back into a woman to be looked at, commented on, and approached (677). Scenes such as this one bring to the fore the fact that, as Anne Wallace puts it, "Special difficulties faced women walkers, especially if they walked alone, because their peripateia translated as sexual wandering."[57] These New Forest scenes also highlight precisely the kinds of difficulties that women face when they try to take up the position of the aesthetic subject as explored in work by Bohls, Jacqueline Labbe, and Elizabeth Dolan.[58] Juliet's (re)embodiment in this moment is all the more startling and forceful because, as readers we too have for a brief moment been allowed (persuaded) to forget her female body – and almost to enter her mind. Burney makes quite certain we *see* Juliet again, "coarse" bonnet and all (665), and presents us with a visual image of her female wanderer as an object of a male gaze. This specifically female figure can only be disruptively superimposed on the contemplative tableau of the preceding prospect scene.

Juliet's encounter with the carter is further complicated by the fact that he thinks she is someone else. Juliet is accosted because she is mistaken for Debby Dyson, the village girl whose bonnet she borrows. This misrecognition makes her doubly disqualified as a prospect viewer, not a suitable aesthetic subject by virtue of her gender and of the class position she seems to inhabit. It also suggests that any woman walker is substitutable for any other. A considerable amount of Burney scholarship examines the exposure Burney's heroines face in public places, which also often happen to be tourist destinations. Their exposure frequently centers around class and identity confusions, which take on moral overtones.[59] At Vauxhall and Marylebone Gardens, Evelina is mistaken for an actress or prostitute. On her first arrival at Southhampton, Camilla is mistaken for a thief.[60] On the rural roadside, and repeatedly in the same section of the novel, Juliet is mistaken for a village girl of loose morals. Debby is described as a "wilful . . . victim to pleasure" (665), and a "hussy" (702), and the men who see Juliet walking on the open road, and who think she is Debby, assume that their attentions will be welcomed. Paradoxically, then, Burney shows us that her female wanderer's seemingly secluded, picturesque location in the New Forest is in fact as publicly exposing for a woman as the city tourist destinations that feature in her earlier novels, in addition to being more immediately physically dangerous. Burney implies by the intimate juxtaposition of these two scenes (prospect and pursuit) that the solitary situation of the prospect viewer or pedestrian tourist is an entirely different proposition for a female traveler than for a male one: a female traveler is every moment at risk of becoming the object of view rather than the viewer, the quarry rather than the hunter. This remakes the countryside as a space of ceaseless movement and labor, rather than a place rich in "pausibility," to again borrow this term from mobility studies scholarship, a notion which works strikingly well as a description of how the landscape is imagined within more conventional texts of picturesque travel in the eighteenth and early nineteenth centuries.[61]

Burney develops the logical extension of the threat contained in Juliet's encounters as Debby, and indeed in her many moments as a vulnerable wanderer, in a later parallel scene. As Juliet tries to make her way through the New Forest itself, "alone and unaided" – a kind of nightmare version of a traveler in search of the picturesque – she encounters two young farm laborers. This scene poses the most imminent threat of rape of any in the novel – a novel filled, and indeed driven, by that threat. Faced with the men's demand for a kiss Juliet fears "a danger more dreadful" than any she has yet encountered, "the danger of personal and brutal insult" (688). On entering the New Forest, she hoped to find "asylum" (685) and "shelter" (676), but in this situation the forest offers her worse than nothing: "She looked around vainly for succour or redress; the woods and the heavens were alone within view and within hearing" (688).

Finally, Burney also dismantles the distance from the "sublimely picturesque" forest, as seen in prospective overview. Juliet enters the woods and
finds there a "reality" as gothic as anything in Radcliffe, involving blood on
the walls of a forest hut, and what she mistakenly takes to be a murder.
Soon she is running from the forest almost as fast as she had entered it.
At this point, the novel returns in retrospect directly to Juliet's first,
idealized "prospect," made plural now so as to invoke, also, her vain
expectations and hopes in that earlier moment:

> Where, now, was the enchantment of its [the New Forest's] prospects?
> Where, the witchery of its scenery? All was lost to her for pleasure, all was
> thrown away upon her as enjoyment; she saw nothing but her danger, she
> could make no observation but how to escape what it menaced. (685–6)

These sentiments are far removed from the earlier feeling that the prospect
view grants Juliet that human suffering is supportable, because transitory.
The original prospect, described elsewhere as having "charmed her, visually
and intellectually" (692), is rendered just that – a charm, an enchantment,
a kind of witchery that had led her to false hope. Pleasure, enjoyment, and
again, even the ability to observe are once more denied her, as her mind
narrows to how to deal with her immediate situation. Burney dismisses the
efficacy or possibility of the prospect as Juliet returns to the terrified (deaf
and blind) condition in which she had first entered the forest. Now,
however, the forest itself has become a part of that terror.

Burney explores the problem of prospective distance enacted in the
framing sections of the New Forest section most directly in the final
chapters of Book Eight, in which Juliet, still in hiding, tries out
a number of modes of rural existence, becoming a kind of sociologist of
rural life. Here Juliet looks, Rasselas-like, "with an intelligent desire of
information, upon every new scene of life, that was presented to her view;
and every class of society, that came within her knowledge" (700).
The novel is never more encyclopedic, never more like "a dissertation on
the inequalities of the sexes" or classes than in these chapters.[62] It is also
never more like contemporary travel accounts. Notably, the "view"
obtained as a result of this experience is radically different from that
acquired from the hilltop, and is, instead, an extension of Juliet's working
life in Brighton. She comes to understand, we are told in a disquisition
upon the merits of detail versus distance, the "fallacy, alike in authors and
in the world, of judging solely by theory." Critiquing those who judge the
lives of others, and in particular the lives of the rural working poor, "at
a distance," Juliet (and Burney) addresses her readers directly: "O ye, she

cried, who view them through your imaginations! were ye to toil with them but one week! to rise as they rise, feed as they feed, and work as they work! like mine, then, your eyes would open" (700–1). We might remember, here, that Adam Smith's model of sympathetic vision is founded on imagination, as well as remember Wollstonecraft's contrary declaration in the second of her *Vindications* of the need for descent from an elevated position and from the position of an "unmoved spectator."[63] As Margaret Doody puts it, Burney asks in this section of her novel, "whether there has not been too great a disparity between the vision" of the "enlightened rambler, or affluent possessor" and that of the laborer.[64] The hilltop view that immediately follows, and seems to be enabled by and representative of these new observations, now moves beyond that of a picturesque tourist or prospect viewer, and contains everything that the previous prospect view lacked, most strikingly people and human suffering. Juliet's gesture toward immortality here is sharply outweighed by her enumeration of the different forms of "human woe" (676) elided in the previous view. The list is worth repeating: "failure without fault; success without virtue; sickness without relief; oppression in the very face of liberty; labour without sustenance; and suffering without crime" (701).

It is tempting to read this scene as the real prospect that Burney means to put forward in *The Wanderer* and the insight she means to grant Juliet; and indeed it is a key statement of the political and aesthetic arguments of the novel. Burney herself saw it as "The Best Chapter in the Work."[65] It is certainly the most succinct statement the novel contains of the injustice of the world it depicts – of a world gone awry, in which cause and effect fail to function. But Burney also presents this version of prospective vision and wide understanding as unsustainable and as impossible for Juliet to fully own. This world "view" ends a chapter, and Burney almost comically insists that her gendered wanderer is not able to inhabit this position for any longer than she can that of the prospect viewer. In the first paragraph of the next chapter, the wife of a neighboring farmer appears angrily with the object by which each of Juliet's moments of vision in this section of the novel is dismantled or undercut: "bearing in her hand the bonnet of Debby Dyson, which she flung scornfully upon a table" (702). Juliet's obscure identity, and so the ease with which she is associated with women of "light company" such as Debby, costs her even the protection of other women. Feared now for a kind of contagious ability to bring her new companions "to ruin," Juliet is expelled from her rural retreat and "again, in search of a new asylum, became a Wanderer" (702–3).

Country House: Wilton

Leaving the prospective picturesque behind as a kind of false "enchantment" or hopeful "witchery," and having found rural life as tedious, painful, and unsustainable as any other, Juliet as sightseer quickly ends up at Wilton, the country house of the Earl of Pembroke. A day trip from Salisbury, taking in Wilton and Stonehenge, had been a well-established circuit since the early-mid-century, and Wilton was especially famous for its sculpture collection and for its collection of Van Dykes.[66] The seriousness of her situation is demonstrably escalating: in between the New Forest and her country house visit, Juliet is nearly abducted from an inn by her husband and sees herself advertised for in the newspaper as a runaway wife. By this point, Juliet's situation and resultant state of mind makes her unable to respond not to the sites of a town or the picturesque beauties of nature ("God's Gallery") but to art. Again, as in the Salisbury scene, Burney gives a catalogue of the things a sight-seer could view – "figures of the noblest sculpture; busts of historical interest; ... marbles, alabasters, spars, and lavers of all colours, and in all forms" (760) – only to have them "solicit" Juliet's attention in vain. Juliet dumbly follows her temporary escort, the Baronet Sir Jasper, and a guide, around the galleries:

> Not as Juliet she followed; Juliet whose soul was delightedly 'awake to tender strokes of art', whether in painting, music, or poetry; who never saw excellence without emotion; and whose skill and taste would have heightened her pleasure into rapture, her approbation into enthusiasm, in viewing the delicious assemblage of painting, statuary, antiques, natural curiosities, and artificial rarities, of Wilton; – not as Juliet, she followed; but as one to whom every thing was indifferent; whose discernment was gone, whose eyes were dimmed, whose powers of perception were asleep, and whose spirit of enjoyment was annihilated. (759–60)

The sentence reads like the inevitable consequence of all those earlier repressive sentences in the novel. In this scene, Juliet suffers from what is called in the following paragraphs, "morbid insensibility," and a "nearly torpid state," in which her mind no longer responsive even to "excellence." Juliet's numbed condition is reminiscent of mental states I discussed in Chapters 2 and 3, where the speaker in Smith's later sonnets becomes excluded from the community of quotation, and where Radcliffe's Emily, at the height of her terror when imprisoned in the castle of Udolpho, finds herself unable to read. In *Udolpho*, Emily finds that her state of intense anxiety about what is going to happen to her renders the "fire" of "the poet" "cold, and dim."[67] Correspondingly, Juliet finds herself "indifferent" to the art she walks past, unable to view it with "discernment," "percep-tion," or "enjoyment." As in the New Forest scene, she is presented as almost blind to her surroundings, her eyes "dimmed." Burney's vocabulary of insensibility, sleep, morbidity, and annihilation, as well as the repetition of the phrase "she followed," emphasizing that Juliet is not directing her own movements, suggests a kind of waking faint, or an act of death-like sleep walking, in which Juliet's movements are little different from those of an automaton. She becomes like the "machine" Mrs. Ireton had tried to command her to be (524). This insensibility, combined with the repeated statement that she follows "not as Juliet," suggests an alienation from self under extreme pressure reminiscent of the gothic mode. Denied the respite that might allow her a "spirit at ease," she is, on the contrary, in a state of "deep distress." In this moment, Juliet becomes both unable to respond to anything around her and in some way absent from herself. This wandering woman, no longer even wearing someone else's bonnet but with her hair hanging loose now, in a sign of either lax morals or female madness,[68] is not Juliet.

Country house tours, like urban tours, prospect views, and picturesque sight-seeing trips, contained a strong ideological component, and as Susan Lamb puts it, "overwhelmingly tended to celebrate the puissance, glory, and fitness of the governing or socially prominent elite."[69] Burney sidesteps any role in this celebration by having Juliet walk insensibly through Wilton, with her satirically depicted aging beau delivering a long "harangue" (761) in which he fancies himself a part of every art work. Gilpin, who visited Wilton in the late 1790s, asserted that the "grand collection of statues in Wilton-house entitle it very deservedly to the attention of every traveller," and dutifully made a lengthy inventory, running over ten pages.[70] In the journal of her own tour, Burney writes of Wilton House's "noble, noble collection."[71] Juliet, by contrast, does not, or cannot, acknowledge this entitlement. She has "as little desire to see as to be seen" (759), and if anything the house – with the help of Sir Jasper – assaults her with its demands for admiration. As in the Salisbury and New Forest sections, an instant of respite suggests an innate, but dormant, ability to respond. Notably, though, by this point in the novel the eruption of feeling is not even given a full paragraph, or even a full sentence. Noticing Van Dyke's portrait of three children of King Charles I by "accident," Juliet begins to experience, "unconsciously, some pleasure, when the sound of a carriage" is heard.[72] This sound announces the arrival of a new group of visitors, which includes her former employer Mrs. Ireton, the character who more than any other thinks it possible to control people's liberty of action and thought

(760–1). With Mrs. Ireton's arrival, Wilton becomes as inhospitable and dangerous a location for Burney's female wanderer as the New Forest. Suitably, Juliet spends her remaining time hiding in an anteroom below a Salvator Rosa painting of barely clothed banditti, far removed from the staged court portraits of the main gallery rooms.

Ruin: Stonehenge

The peculiar domestic tour the novel takes us on does not end here. In the next chapter we follow Juliet on an accidental visit to Stonehenge, where for most of the episode she doesn't even comprehend where she is. The novel is in the territory of the Burkean sublime by this point, as Juliet wanders alone through the "wild edifice" struck with "wonder," perceiving the spot as "grand," "awful," and "terrific" (765). As Gilpin, whose party also visited Stonehenge on the same day they viewed Wilton, comments, "Wonderful" as Stonehenge is, "it is totally void . . . of every idea of picturesque beauty."[73] In this scene, Burney reimagines the sublime in the context of her wanderer's pained travels just as she has the picturesque. Like Radcliffe and Wollstonecraft, she emphasizes the terrors of the sublime encounter for a female wanderer more than the sublime's capacity for producing moments of transcendence.

In order to survey her new location, Juliet mounts on a stone to see a view matched to both the location itself and to her own personal "prospects":

> She discerned, to a vast extent, a boundless plain, that, like the ocean, seemed to have no term but the horizon; but which, also like the ocean, looked as desert as it was unlimited. Here and there flew a bustard, or a wheat-ear, all else seemed unpeopled air, and uncultivated waste. (765)

What she "discern[s]" here is a vast, limitless emptiness. Even Gilpin was moved to describe this view as one of "waste after waste," "*like the ocean*," and so vast that "the eye is carried, if I may so phrase it, *out of sight*."[74] Despite Gilpin's pedantic wording, he highlights the sense of limitless space associated with Stonehenge and brought out in Burney's description. That for Juliet, this view is as bleak as it is frighteningly boundless is suggested by Burney's adjectival use of "desert," perhaps meant to encompass both the literal noun (as in, a dry place) and the adjective "deserted." The location's emptiness is underscored by the repeated negative, "unpeopled air" and "uncultivated waste." The landscape is a void, defined by what it lacks.

Doody sees Juliet's Stonehenge visit as the wild heart of the novel, signaling a moment of strength, relief, and an entrance into a kind of Romantic "inner self." "The narrative here seeks some images of the mind itself," Doody writes, "Feeling, as Juliet does, a permanent alien, a stranger in the world, she finds solace and rests upon the strangeness of the world . . . In the little time in which Juliet is alone in the 'wild edifice,' she is free."[75] If the Stonehenge scene is one of freedom or escape, though, it takes a peculiar form. The language of Burney's passage evokes unsettling echoes, for instance, of narratives of encounter with the New World. Like accounts of *terra incognita*, Burney's description draws on the figure of litotes to evoke the intense disorientation of an encounter with seeming emptiness and immense unknowns. Juliet's Salisbury Plains have what Jonathan Lamb calls the "ghostly specificity" of particularized absences that characterize early descriptions of the American prairies and voyagers' accounts of the Pacific.[76] Like voyagers and colonists subject to extreme conditions of social isolation and fear, Juliet experiences a destabilization of self in the face of the unknown so that, as with bewildered voyages as described by Lamb, "the self suffers a sea change into something odd and strange."[77] Unlike even these voyagers, however, and unlike both the poet-speaker at the opening of Oliver Goldsmith's *The Traveller, or A Prospect of Society* (1764), or the exile at his poem's close discussed in Chapter 1, Juliet does not even have a home locale she can be safely nostalgic for, nowhere to which her "heart untravelled fondly turns," and certainly nowhere "where England's glories shine" (*Tr*, 8, 421).[78] Even Thomson's "dark way-faring Stranger," who eventually becomes fatally lost to "black Despair" in a "formless" "trackless Plain" in *The Seasons*, has "the Thoughts of Home; the Thoughts of Home" to help him onward (*W*, 178, 281–6). As Wollstonecraft does with her traveler and Smith with her late sonnet-speaker, Burney strips even these thoughts away.

Rather than presenting an image of an "inner self," the "unpeopled air" of Salisbury Plains might be read as an external representation of the "unpeopled" absence that Juliet has become at this late point in the novel, under extreme, relentless, multifaceted pressure. The view from Stonehenge can be read as a companion piece to the "unpeopled" tourist – the "not Juliet" – who visits Wilton. Juliet's response to the plains surrounding Stonehenge is very different from her earlier response to the New Forest prospect, which had left her relieved by the sight of external objects, at least momentarily. At Stonehenge,

In a state of mind so utterly deplorable as that of Juliet, this grand, uncouth monument of ancient days had a certain sad, indefinable attraction, more congenial to her distress, than all the polish, taste, and delicacy of modern skill ... the nearly savage, however wonderful work of antiquity, in which she was now rambling; placed in this abandoned spot, far from the intercourse, or even view of mankind, with no prospect but of heath and sky; blunted, for the moment, her sensibility, by removing her wide from all the objects with which it was in contact; and insensibly calmed her spirits; though not by dissipating her reverie. Here, on the contrary, was room for 'meditation even to madness'; nothing distracted the sight, nothing broke in upon attention, nor varied the ideas. Thought, uninterrupted and uncontrouled, was master of the mind. (765–6)

There is a clumsiness about this passage, in which Burney seems intent on making some fine distinctions. Like Salisbury Cathedral, Stonehenge is "congenial," or suited to Juliet's sadness. But rather than attracting her attention by virtue of its quiet "religious solemnity" (663), the "indefinable attraction" of Stonehenge is to the "uncouth," the "nearly savage," and to absence, or lack of civilization. The fact that Juliet needs to be removed from "all the objects" with which she has been in contact apart from "heath and sky" suggests the extent to which the whole world has come to be seen as part of what is persecuting her. This prospect is "no prospect."

The "mind sufficient to itself" of the New Forest prospect takes on dark undertones here, reinforced by the quotation at its core from Calista in Nicholas Rowe's tragedy, *The Fair Penitent* (1703), which in its original context reads, "here's room for meditation even to madness / Till the mind burst with thinking."[79] Rowe's play was popular throughout the eighteenth century and Burney likely saw Mrs. Siddons performing the role of Calista in 1782.[80] Suggestively, a number of contemporary novels also pick up this specific phrase, in two cases evoking the state of mind of a character locked in a dark room and subject to both real and imagined terrors.[81] Juliet's view from Stonehenge over Salisbury Plain, in its unvaried extensiveness, might be seen by striking analogy as a dark cell. The phrase "Thought, uninterrupted and uncontrolled" which then closes the paragraph and which, subject to no "distraction," becomes "master" of the mind, echoes the "unpeopled air" and "uncultivated waste" that closes the previous paragraph. In other words thought, and the landscape that corresponds to it, are in this moment identically vast, limitless and boundless – and horrifically so. If the mind is free here, it is also perilously unanchored. This moment is a descendant of the unsettling moment in *The Seasons* in which the prospective "wandering Eye" momentarily loses track of its center and, becoming "Unfixt, is in a verdant Ocean lost"(*Su*, 692–3). However, whereas in *The Seasons* this frightening moment of disorientation is transitory, in *The Wanderer* it is the logical climax of a state developed incrementally over Burney's entire novel – and developed more broadly in this tradition of writing about wandering as a whole. The crisis in Burney is also not precipitated by the extensiveness of empire as in Thomson but by an experience deep within Britain itself.

The evocation of this state of extreme difficulty is, in some way, the point of *The Wanderer*, as it is also of Smith's most desolate sonnets and of Wollstonecraft's travel narrative. If earlier in Burney's novel, external objects (traveler's distractions) such as Salisbury Cathedral and a view over the New Forest offer at least some respite from internal torment, Stonehenge only replicates the full horror of the wanderer's prospects. The desolate endlessness of Juliet's wanderings leaves her mind "blunted," "nearly savage," and almost mad. I see this as a moment of psychic disintegration (or evacuation) rather than discovery of an "inner self." Or, to quote critic Nicholas Roe's phrase about William Wordsworth, a kind of " 'black hole' of the spirit; a collapsed spot of time," precisely the kind of "vortex," Roe suggests, that is carefully excluded from the story of the growth of a mind in *The Prelude*.[82] One might think, instead, of Juliet's friend Gabriella's lament about the "hard necessity of toiling, when death has seized upon the very heart, merely to breathe, to exist, after life has lost all its charms!" (388). Or even of the unpublished ending of William Godwin's *Things as They Are; or, the Adventures of Caleb Williams* (1794), another novel about a relentlessly persecuted wanderer, in which Caleb declares himself reduced to a "BLANK! . . . a stone – a GRAVESTONE! – an obelisk to tell you, HERE LIES WHAT WAS ONCE A MAN!"[83] By this key point in *The Wanderer* and in this tradition, wandering has become a form of exile, deracination, or deep homelessness, in psychological as well as material terms.

Scholars both critique and celebrate Burney's Stonehenge scene as a move into the mythic. Doody writes that in its "context in this novel about history – and about the *pain* of history – Stonehenge is a release from history," while Claudia Johnson sees it, less positively, as part of a wider effort in the final sections of the novel to "bypass politics."[84] If this scene does elide history and politics, however, it is illuminating to see that it does so, again, in the gothic mode. Earlier I drew a parallel between the moment in *Udolpho* when Emily becomes unable to read and Juliet's inability to look at the art in Wilton. The Stonehenge scene works alongside the moment of horror in *Udolpho*, when Emily thinks she sees a dead body and faints under the extreme pressure of the horror of this sight and of what is happening to her more generally. In this moment in *Udolpho*, horror excludes "for a time, all sense of past, and dread of future misfortune."[85] The Stonehenge scene in *The Wanderer* is atemporal in a similar way, as Juliet enters a kind of "deep time."[86] But as in *Udolpho*, Juliet's experience comes closer to the aspects of the sublime associated with "horror" than with "terror" as Radcliffe defines them, the second of which "expands the soul, and awakens the faculties to a high degree of life," while the first "contracts, freezes, and nearly annihilates them."[87] The wasteland around Juliet is an externalization, a *vision*, of a Radcliffian faint. If we see the ending of *Tess of the D'Urbervilles* (1891) as a reading of this moment in *The Wanderer*, then Thomas Hardy makes explicit the deathliness only linguistically implied in Burney's Stonehenge passage. This deathliness might be read as the real ending of Burney's great novel of wandering. The Stonehenge scene works as the novel's most vivid demonstration of what can happen to a mind when put under extreme pressure, relentlessly persecuted, and gradually denied everything for which it yearns.

The experience of reading *The Wanderer* – the journey from the first cover to the last – is as difficult and challenging as its difficult gestation and subject matter portends. It is a "painful pleasure" as Andrea Henderson might describe it,[88] and a pleasure that requires appreciation of the novel's alternative – and often strange – aesthetics. Burney offers little of the compensatory consolation Radcliffe proffers in *Udolpho*. "Difficulty" is one of Burke's categories of the sublime: he uses the example of Stonehenge for this category, noting that, "When any work seems to have required immense force and labour to effect it, the idea is grand."[89] In the preface to *The Wanderer*, Burney casts her novel as an epic, marked by "the grandeur, yet singleness of the plan" (7). If we bring these two arguments together, *The Wanderer* appears as both female epic and sublime object. The vacillating, accidental, wandering nature of the narrative itself, embodied in the tortuous journeying of the novel's reluctant wanderer, and enacted from extended sentences to endless plot, is both part of the social critique the novel seeks to make, and vital to the puzzling fascination involved in encountering this strange text. Of course, Burney's digressive and verbose style also means she courts the possibility that her audience will encounter her text as overwhelming and annihilating rather than transcendent. However, I would argue that if the immense bulk – and indeed difficulty – of Burney's novel almost suffocates the very voice it means to speak, the novel's painful indirection is also her female wanderer's most eloquent instrument. *The Wanderer* begins with the voice of an unknown woman calling from darkness, "O hear me! . . . for the love of Heaven, hear me!" (11). The bulk of the rest of the novel demonstrates just how difficult it is for such a single, unsupported, voice to direct and speak its own narrative.

Reading *The Wanderer* as a novel that rewrites the journey, then, throws new and challenging light on the still influential notion of travel as a vehicle of freedom and Romantic self-discovery, as well as highlighting the narrowness of reading the novel of the journey as analogous to the *Bildungsroman* or the novel of development. Burney's novel represents an exaggerated version of the experiences of those who do not have access to the privilege that makes travel – and its associated experiences – a source of improvement and self-development. As such, *The Wanderer* involves sophisticated early thinking about how identity and locale affect how mobility is experienced. Moreover, if the journey through the world is associated with a discovery of the "self," and if Burney suggests that access to this journey is limited for a woman wanderer, then "wandering" represents a radical and far-reaching form of "female difficulty." This difficulty leads to difficulties on the level of thought process, of interaction, of syntax, and of narrative, as well as of literal movement in the world.

Coda
"He Could Afford to Suffer": Losses and Gains

The territory traversed in this book has been wide ranging, following women's wanderings through long poems, sonnet sequences, novels, and travel narratives, and taking up a number of different modes of wandering, from literal, to imaginative, to textual. What holds these explorations together is a desire on the part of these wartime women writers to find ways of evoking experiences of marginality, coercion, difficulty, and desolation. The ways they discover to evoke these frequently gendered experiences are aesthetically experimental and often strange, performing failures of sympathy and the imagination, and corresponding failures of genre. Paying attention to the literal wanderings at the center of texts such as *The Emigrants*, *Elegiac Sonnets*, *Udolpho*, *A Short Residence*, and *The Wanderer* opens up new ways of thinking about the distinctive formal and textual indirections of the literary works of this period – and about movement's possible paths.

I want to end this exploration by asking how we might rethink the influential Romantic transformation of movement in light of the tradition of the reluctant woman wanderer. I pose this question with a focus on William Wordsworth as the poet most closely associated in time, as well as in intellectual formation, with the group of women authors who are the primary focus of this book. It is unnecessary to rehearse the many ways in which Wordsworth's idea of "the poet" came into being on the back of gendered imaginings, an understanding that has been reinscribed and complicated in recent years by work such as Susan Wolfson's on the feminine language of men's feeling in Wordsworth's 1790s work. We know this. What the tradition of the woman wanderer in women's writing helps to show is the precise terrors such Romantic imaginings of suffering women allude to. As a result, this overlooked female tradition also shows why it is so vital for Wordsworth and other Romantics to invoke these female figures of abjection and loss.

As noted at the outset, Wordsworth turns almost compulsively to depictions of women wanderers, from the female beggar in *An Evening Walk* (1793), to the female vagrants of the Salisbury Plains poems and *Lyrical Ballads* (1798 and 1800), to Margaret in *The Ruined Cottage* (1798) and Book One of *The Excursion*, "The Wanderer" (1814). These frequently analyzed women are far more important in Wordsworth's work than the female bit players in the eighteenth-century version of the sentimental journey. Many of them look and sound much like exaggerated versions of the pained, reluctant women wanderers examined in this book. When a woman wanderer first appears with arresting dissonance in Wordsworth's oeuvre, in *An Evening Walk*, she is painfully embodied, in striking contrast to the wandering male poet-speaker of the poem, whose activities are associated throughout with what is "pleasant." Denied shelter and condemned to the public road, this female beggar is depicted dragging her children "along the weary way," with "stark o'er labour'd bones," "lock'd joints, and step of pain." Summer's "breathless ray" afflicts her, and winter storms freeze her, until she is left to die with her two children "coffin'd" in her arms.[1] The woman in "The Female Vagrant" of *Lyrical Ballads* is pained in a similar way. Over thirty stanzas she tells a tale of displacement, poverty, hunger, and socially enforced movement as she transitions from daughter of a cottager, to army wife and mother "wading at the heels of war," to widow and vagrant.[2] By the point at which she comes to tell her story, she is as uncertain of where she is going as she is unable to complete her own narrative. The poem ends:

> Three years a wanderer, often have I view'd
> In tears, the sun towards that country tend
> Where my poor heart lost all its fortitude:
> And now across this moor my steps I bend –
> Oh! tell me whither—for no earthly friend
> Have I. —She ceased, and weeping turned away,
> As if because her tale was at an end
> She wept; – because she had no more to say
> Of that perpetual weight which on her spirit lay.[3]

Margaret, too, of *The Ruined Cottage* and Book One of *The Excursion* spends her days "travelling far," "knowing this / Only, that what I seek I cannot find."[4] Like the female vagrant, she sinks ever deeper into poverty and loss, as her soldier husband and her child also die. Wordsworth represents the disorder of Margaret's mind through her increasing neglect of her cottage. In the past of the poem, the cottage functions as an anchoring domestic space for the eponymous male Wanderer who tells

Margaret's story, as she, Penelope-like, welcomes the Wanderer on each return. By the point in the poem when Margaret has herself become a wanderer and is near death, the distinction between inside and outside has collapsed, so that Margaret is chilled and her clothes "ruffled by the wind; / Even at the side of her own fire," as exposed to the elements in her own home as the female beggar of *An Evening Walk* is on the open road.[5] As Mary Favret comments, "For poor, abandoned Margaret, the security and exemption Cowper found in his retreat are far past."[6]

There are important differences, however, between the representations of such female figures in Wordsworth and those focused on in this book. Women wanderers in women's texts such as Wollstonecraft's are "the little hero[es] of each tale," the center of their own texts and narratives, while in Wordsworth another mind is usually brought in to be custodian, and indeed writer, of the woman wanderer's story.[7] The *Evening Walk*'s abrupt return from its troubling vision of the dying female beggar to the "sweet" sounds heard by the evening walker is joltingly awkward, and necessitates what Robin Jarvis calls "an element of crisis management" in the poem.[8] The second line of "The Female Vagrant" also reports her speech, signaling that it comes to us through an intermediary rather than being spoken directly: "(The Woman thus her artless story told)."[9] Like Laurence Sterne's story of Maria of Moulines, the stories of Wordsworth's women wanderers are imagined as being told to a listener who meets her in the course of his own wanderings. Her now "artless" story is partially (re)-bracketed in such Romantic situations. Favret is right to observe that, "Against Cowper's more privileged newspaper reader, sitting at home while the world turns submitted to his view, these characters are externally and internally moved, unsettled, sent wandering from home."[10] However, it is important to hold on to the distinction in the degree to which "these characters," the male Wanderer and his female counterparts, suffer as a result of this unsettlement. Their narratives of movement perform different work within the structure of Wordsworth's poems. While never quite addressing the gender differential involved in these repeated scenes, Jarvis some time ago observed how the (male) poet/wanderer and the (female) beggar/wanderer, in the many and varied forms they take in Wordsworth, repeatedly represent "positive and negative inflections," or "counterbalancing elements within the overall structure" of Wordsworth's poems.[11] Or as Wolfson writes of "The Thorn" (1798), although the derangement is slightly less marked in poems such as "The Female Vagrant," "Gender makes a critical difference: he speaks, she cries; he arranges, she's deranged."[12]

The effect of this repeated structure in Wordsworth is that women wanderers become in some way expendable in these poems – free either to die, go mad, or collapse into tears. Their framed stories can end because another (usually male) traveler's journey implicitly continues. The woman wanderer's voice is stopped by tears at the end of "The Female Vagrant" in precisely the way Wollstonecraft refuses (or is unable) to let hers stop at the end of *A Short Residence*. Neither Emily in *Udolpho*, nor Juliet in *The Wanderer*, nor even the desolate persona Smith assumes in *The Emigrants* or her *Elegiac Sonnets*, could afford to dissolve in this way (I will come back to the term "afford" in a moment). These authors also refuse to solve their wanderers' situations by narrating their deaths. As Smith's desolate additions to her sonnet sequence over 16 years of her life attests, there is always more to say. The ill-fated women wanderers of Wordsworth's poems, whose narratives do cease, and the male auditors of these women's stories, who explicitly or implicitly continue along the road after each encounter, might be read as representing poles on either side of the women's journeys at the center of texts in the tradition of the reluctant woman wanderer. Wanderers such as Burney's laboring Juliet can no more afford to stop or to go mad than they can afford to engage with the stories of others or look at the view.

In many ways, the masculine figure of the Romantic wanderer in poems such as Wordsworth's would seem to represent a reaching back to attributes of the prospect view, and a reconnection of the wanderer with the kind of stability and detachment still present, if weakened, in poems such as Goldsmith's *The Traveller* and Cowper's *The Task*. The Romantic figure bears a genealogical relationship to Adam Smith's sympathizing but carefully impartial spectator, as well as to James Thomson's "Man of philosophic Eye," who "Curious surveys" the world directly, and who is carefully distinguished from those lost in the maze of their own concerns (*A*, 1133, 1135).

The arranging wanderer figure in Wordsworth (along with his deranging female counterpart) reaches its most representative form in *The Excursion*. In the emblematic Wanderer of this poem, the new version of the visionary, generalizing, all-inclusive prospect view imagined in the eighteenth century through sympathy and wandering reaches its logical conclusion. Wordsworth represents this wanderer as a teller of tales and a keeper of other people's stories. His mind "unclouded by the cares / Of ordinary life," is so free to understand the minds of others that he appears, "like a Being made / Of many Beings":

Unoccupied by sorrow of it's own,
His heart lay open; and, by Nature tuned
And constant disposition of his thoughts
To sympathy with Man, he was alive
To all that was enjoyed where'er he went;
And all that was endured; for, in himself
Happy, and quiet in his chearfulness,
He had no painful pressure from without
That made him turn aside from wretchedness
With coward fears. He could *afford* to suffer
With those whom he saw suffer. Hence it came
That in our best experience he was rich,
And in the wisdom of our daily life.[13]

This wanderer, much like the prospect surveyor from the early eighteenth century, gathers the experiences of others without seeming to be threatened by their pain in the way that Wollstonecraft's traveler, for instance, most certainly is. Wordsworth's wanderer's itinerancy allows him to be both sympathetic and detached, so that, as Wolfson puts it, despite some "unspecified vulnerability," the Wanderer of *The Excursion* is represented as "a spectator *ab extra* on the world of human events."[14] He travels endlessly because he "can *afford* to suffer" with those he meets, implying emotional and economic resources unavailable to both Margaret whose story he tells, and to the women wanderers at the center of texts such as Burney's *The Wanderer*, published in the same year, and composed over the same period. Wordsworth suggests that his wanderer may be able to feel for others because he is "Unoccupied" by sorrows of his own, again in direct contrast to Margaret who, "[s]elf-occupied," sees everything through the prism of her own suffering.[15]

It is impossible to imagine the Wanderer of a poem like *The Excursion*, or his many Wordsworthian predecessors, coming into being without also evoking the feelings embodied by figures such as Margaret. By the same token, it should be as impossible to imagine the predominantly masculine tradition of the Romantic wanderer without seeing how it engages with, draws on, and to an extent suppresses, elements of the tradition of the reluctant woman wanderer as explored in women's writing. By 1793, Wordsworth and Charlotte Smith were reading each other closely, and Wordsworth may also have read *A Short Residence* by 1797 when he was composing *The Ruined Cottage*, which would become *The Excursion*.[16] We know that both *Elegiac Sonnets* and *A Short Residence*, along with the works of "Mother Radcliffe" as John Keats called her, were read and reread by the Romantics.[17] It seems little coincidence that Romantic female figures of abjection such as Margaret achieve a level of psychological complexity wholly absent in Sterne's Maria but developed by Charlotte Smith, Wollstonecraft, and Burney in particular. "The Female Vagrant," a figure Wordsworth first conceived of immediately after reading Smith's *The Emigrants*, has been read as his "first history of an individual mind."[18] As an aside, it is also interesting to note that *The Excursion*, perhaps Wordsworth's poem with the most intimate, if vexed, relationship to this female tradition, presents similar formal difficulties to the ones posed by texts such as *Elegiac Sonnets* and Burney's *The Wanderer*. Francis Jeffrey famously saw *The Excursion* as "beyond the power of criticism"; when William Hazlitt reviewed it 6 months after condemning Burney's novel he was almost equally unimpressed; and generations of critics have seen its sprawling bulk, which gives little sense of narrative progression, as virtually unavailable to analysis.[19] Efforts at textual arrangement are in some sense pushed aside in *The Excursion*.

The tradition of the reluctant woman wanderer offered more than a way to write women, however, or more widely a way to use female figures to represent the terrors of displacement. Elements of deep homelessness, vulnerability, and an emphasis on the fraught nature of sympathy associated with male figures of wandering in Romantic poetry also owe much to this alternative tradition. Most directly, the gendered tradition of reluctant movement is indispensable to Romanticism's self-imagining because it develops the potential of mobility on the margins. This literal and psychological location and activity remains vital to both Romantic wanderer and Romantic poet, even when it is paradoxically recombined with an elevation and generalizability reminiscent of much earlier figures. Wordsworth's new version of the wanderer as someone in possession of almost Thomsonian, all-encompassing view of humanity, starts from a position of marginality which would have been difficult to imagine without the transitional precedent of the reluctant woman wanderer. The Romantic wanderer also tends to be represented as visionary not only by virtue of being mobile but because he has nothing – or almost nothing. The Wanderer of *The Excursion* is a marginal figure just as much as Margaret is, and is marginal in a way that is clearly distinct from Sterne's affluent Yorick and other eighteenth-century sentimental travelers. Wordsworth's male wanderer's close identification with marginalized figures of abjection – and his potential vulnerability despite his claims to vision – is underscored by the fatal ghosting of his aimless wanderings in those of Margaret. This ghosting is once again far more marked and developed than Maria's ghosting of Yorick's movements in *A Sentimental*

Journey. The male Romantic wanderer moves always in close proximity to his darker, feminized double, knowing always that being able to "*afford* to suffer" is a fragile privilege. In taking up the position of the "suffering traveler,"[20] I would argue, the canonical male writers of Romanticism are also taking up, if remaking, a potentially female subject position – and in the process exposing themselves *to* suffering, or registering that they are already exposed.

Indeed arguments such as Celeste Langan's in *Romantic Vagrancy: Wordsworth and the Simulation of Freedom* (1995) have suggested that even as poems such as *The Excursion* inscribe a gender difference, and a difference between wanderers, the structure of these Romantic poems can simultaneously seem to encourage us to overlook these distinctions. These poems encourage us to focus instead on an overriding relationship of equivalent displacement between different wanderers.[21] Each wanderer appears to be exchangeable for each other wanderer. This has its problems. Langan argues that in the stock encounters between different types of walkers that are such a feature of Romantic poetry, and especially important within *The Excursion*, the mobility of vagrants and wanderers of various sorts is "abstracted from their determining social conditions" in order to forge an idea of "human community" based on shared movement:

> within the structure of the poem, both the poet and the vagrant render an account of their comings and goings. This rendering of accounts is the chief method by which the poem produces a figurative identity – an analogy – between the poet and the vagrant . . . Even where origin and destination are included in these accounts, however, what matters is the fact of traveling; it is on the basis of *actual* mobility rather than *intentional* mobility (desire) that figurative identity – and political equality – is achieved.[22]

Langan shows how this constructed equivalence between different kinds of walkers (and wanderers), which obfuscates the issue of choice (intention and desire), can make *all* movement within Romanticism appear to be undertaken by choice. The way in which Langan describes the workings of this relationship between different kinds of wanderers represents a radical rethinking of understandings of what had been seen as merely "counterbalancing elements" in poems such as Wordsworth's.[23] We are back to something like Cowper's equally all-encompassing position that we are all wanderers gone astray, which likewise obscures the fact that there is a difference between feeling like a wanderer while sitting at home by the fire and being outside lost in a snow storm. There is a difference between being forced to migrate for economic reasons and taking a tour of Europe.

As Langan puts it in relation to Wordsworth, "The poet as private episte-mological subject, released from his political identity, encounters the vagrant, released from *economic* affiliations."[24] For Langan, Romanticism's obfuscating analogy is the foundation of what is most troubling in modern liberalism's claims to social equality, and is part of why it is difficult to see concepts such as vagrancy and economic insecurity outside the context of positive understandings. Mobility studies work further extends this thinking to show how central the suggestion of equal access to, and experience of, mobility has become to neoliberal politics, and the serious implications of this pivotal underpinning. As Peter Adey summarizes, "ideologically charged mobility politics and policies ... fail to assume that mobilities are incredibly uneven and differentiated."[25] Such failures not only overlook but create real hardships for some, ranging from insecurity of work, to inequality of access to transport routes, to the prosecution of the homeless or of refugees. A deeper understanding of the history of mobility through the figure of the reluctant woman wanderer may help us to tease apart this important ideology.

At the same time, this tradition of the reluctant wandering may also help us to be still more precise about the most complex stagings of social interaction in Wordsworth, which may, as I suggested in the Introduction drawing on David Simpson, actually question the limits of sympathy and critique rather than accept a notion of equivalence of all displacements. When a poem like *The Excursion* is read in the light of texts such as Charlotte Smith's and Wollstonecraft's, and even many of Wordsworth's own 1790s poems, it becomes apparent the extent to which the specificity, as well as the responsibility, of sympathy gets lost in his Wanderer's narration of movement and encounter. We are forced to ask what we are to make of a figure who can describe someone's sadness, in this case Margaret's, which it "would have grieved / Your very soul to see," and then claim to carry on with his journey, seemingly unaffected.[26] Like Sterne's Yorick, having dwelt on the sorrow of a woman wanderer's fate long enough for the "purposes of wisdom" Wordsworth's Wanderer says he, "turned away / And walked along my road in happiness."[27] More obviously than Sterne, Wordsworth stages and invites us to notice such breaks in sympathy.[28] The Wanderer in *The Excursion*, Wordsworth suggests, is in some sense only able to see everything, and to wander without pain, because he contains nothing within and reacts to nothing in particular without. In being neither the comfortable middle-class tra-veler of *A Sentimental Journey* nor quite the same as the pained women wanderers of Smith's sonnets, Radcliffe's gothic, Wollstonecraft's *A Short*

Residence, or Burney's final novel, this wanderer is nobody in particular. "Unoccupied," and suffering from "no painful pressure," he is in some sense emptied out of any specific content. Although Byron's Childe Harold is an entirely different kind of wanderer again, the same might be said of him. Such emptiness is highlighted by the fact that, by contrast, the consciousness at the center of texts such as *Elegiac Sonnets* and *A Short Residence* explicitly filter all prospects through the clouds and cares of ordinary life. Only through in some way setting aside the subjectivity of the wanderer – by making him once again a figure for society rather than the individual – can Wordsworth, at least in *The Excursion*, (re)grant him the voice of prospective authority. And Wordsworth's poem asks us to consider whether as a wide view is gained, aspects of an intimate one may be lost. In contrast to the "easy chearfulness" of the Wanderer himself, Wordsworth's Poet figure in *The Excursion* who narrates the second frame narrative responds to the Wanderer's tale of Margaret with a "heart-felt chillness."[29] This chill might be as much a response to the Wanderer's continued cheerfulness as it is to the tale he tells.

The Wanderer's encounter with Margaret in *The Excursion* has been at the center of critical discussions of the complex problem of sympathy in Wordsworth, as well as at the center of efforts to make sense of Romanticism's recurring uses of "distressed women." It provides the occasion for Simpson's argument that we crucially "mistake Wordsworth's distinctive historical intelligence by attributing his condition of arrested concern – his awareness of problems he seems to be unable to handle – to some sort of moral inadequacy."[30] In Wordsworth's simultaneously historically specific and modern depictions of wandering, Simpson argues, the ideal of sympathy (either along the Smithian model of hierarchical human interaction or of desired sentimental exchange) is something Wordsworth repeatedly both stages and undermines. Wordsworth's use of the language of commerce in *The Excursion* would even suggest that the "expense" of Margaret's life would seem to "subsidize" the Wanderer's "spiritual profit."[31] Of the parallel encounter with the leech-gather in "Resolution and Independence" Simpson writes, "This is not the standard picaresque or charitable interaction in which some bond is established between strangers that models or presages the initiation of a social contract. Instead, the poem presents an anatomy of how hard it can be to take that step."[32] In the case of *The Excursion*, Simpson asks if Wordsworth means to present the price of his wanderer's insulation from sorrow, which means he does not *need* to "turn aside from wretchedness," as also "the loss of a self-involvement that might have proved more positive and made him more than a mere listener to Margaret's story."[33] The poem would seem to suggest that while the Wanderer's detached approach may be the only possible way to look on suffering without being overwhelmed by it, such detachment has social consequences. If we accept this reading of Wordsworth's radical questioning, then it is not quite Wordsworth's own poetry that creates the problems with understandings of mobility canvassed by Langan and Adey. These problems come rather from the influence of aspirations such as Wordsworth's (and Goldsmith's and Cowper's and Charlotte Smith's) to a feeling of "human community" through a common sense of homelessness, which overlook how frequently Wordsworth himself (as well as Charlotte Smith and Wollstonecraft and even Cowper at times) actually stage the possibly insurmountable difficulty of achieving this community in a meaningful way. Wordsworth in fact radically departs from Adam Smith's imaginings of sympathy by which mobile subjects produce themselves as suitable products for emotional exchange, but by which no redistribution of goods happens that would redress a situation in which some can "afford to suffer" and some cannot even afford to live.

Simpson concludes that, "In this way Wordsworth offers what I take to be the first comprehensively modern formulation of the aporias of human interaction in a society of dispersed populations governed by the operations of commodity form, the first one in which the rhetoric of resolution is so fully withheld" and which so fully investigates "failed communication and unmade community."[34] Here the commodity form can also stand in for the ubiquitous, and potentially bewildering, circulation of goods, bodies, and feelings that mobility studies theorists locate as the beginning of the modern in this period. Wordsworth's wanderers thus need to be understood as both "historically embodied" in the discharged soldiers, beggars, and wandering widows of the 1790s and beyond, and as "proleptic, looking forward to a future in which questions of home and homelessness – and of home *as* homelessness – would become more and more urgent and obsessive."[35] However, they also need to be understood in relation to the precursive and contemporaneous engagements with the same complex problems of mobility and society in Charlotte Smith, Wollstonecraft, and Burney in particular. The literary heritage of Wordsworth's wanderers goes beyond the off-cited masculine pantheon of Odysseus, Aeneas, the Wandering Jew, and Milton's Satan, finding its most crucial vulnerabilities, sympathies, and formal innovations in the more immediately contemporary.[36] It is this immediate literary context of the writings of reluctant women's wanderings that also suggests new directions for more complete understandings of Romanticism's recurrence to narratives of women in distress, not so much as sentimental figurings, but as sources of radical rupture in the fabric of a society that seeks to understand itself through sympathy. The contemporary tradition of the reluctant woman wanderer provides crucial, as yet missing, material for understanding the absolutely central role that "distressed women" played in signaling the potential consequences of an increasingly mobile world.

Smith, Radcliffe, Wollstonecraft, and Burney's mobilizations of the figure of the wanderer bring to the surface the difficulty, the sublimity even, of many journeys – and of many lives. In a very real sense, the female poetic speakers, travelers, and characters depicted at the center of these texts cannot afford to suffer with those they see suffer, themselves feeling persistently threatened by the task of encountering the wider world from vulnerable, socially and economically unstable, positions. The tradition of the reluctant woman wanderer begins to mark out exactly what individual vulnerability might mean to a person moving through a world they cannot control, fully understand, or perhaps even adequately feel for. In their work, equivalence in suffering is demonstrably both difficult to manage and inadequate as a response – or as an explanation of response. Paying attention to this wider framework in explorations of literal, metaphorical, and textual wandering in literary works of this period helps to bring into focus what is suppressed each time an apparent remastering of mobility – of exile, of circulation, of wandering – occurs. The wanderings taken up through this book embody the ghostly opposites contained in claims to vision, exploring what it means to move about here below without necessarily having access to the elevation, the eminence, or the detachment which might produce the implicitly political power to generalize one's experience.

The female figures at the center of these texts are nothing if not "self-occupied" wanderers, and their authors frequently show that not only is this self-occupation the result of political and social realities, but that it is the only possible approach to social sympathy. Rather than being able to leave all the specifics of her own situation behind, and so becoming "rich" in "our best experience," the reluctant wanderer journeys onward accompanied always by herself. Her victory is the same as her defeat – it lies in preparing for the next leg, in continuing to seek engagement with those around her even when this seems almost impossible, in keeping on moving, and in keeping on trying to find forms and ways to tell this story.

Notes

Introduction

1. Mary Wollstonecraft "To Gilbert Imlay" September 6, [1795], Letter 201, *The Collected Letters of Mary Wollstonecraft*, ed. Janet Todd (New York: Columbia University Press, 2003), 320, echoed, for instance, in Mary Wollstonecraft, *Letters Written During a Short Residence in Sweden, Norway, and Denmark* (1796), ed. Ingrid Horrocks (Peterborough, ON: Broadview, 2013), 120.

2. Ann Radcliffe, *The Romance of the Forest* (1791), ed. Chloe Chard (Oxford: Oxford University Press, 1986), 58.

3. Georg Simmel, "The Adventurer," *On Individuality and Social Forms*, ed. Donald N. Levine (Chicago: University of Chicago Press, 1971), 189.

4. Odysseus is still described as "the appropriate archetype for the traveller, and by extension for the travel writer," in the introduction to *The Cambridge Companion to Travel Writing*, ed. Peter Hulme and Tim Youngs (Cambridge: Cambridge University Press, 2002), 2.

5. Samuel Johnson, *Rasselas*, in *Rasselas, Poems, and Selected Prose*, ed. Bertrand H. Bronson (Fort Worth: Harcourt, 1971), 638–9.

6. John Milton, *Paradise Lost* (1674), in *The Riverside Milton*, ed. Roy Flannagan (Boston: Houghton, 1998), 11.282–4. In Milton, of course, this is also a function of her culpability.

7. Laurence Sterne, *A Sentimental Journey through France and Italy* (1768), new edn., ed. Ian Jack and Tim Parnell (Oxford: Oxford University Press, 2003), 95–6.

8. Sterne, *A Sentimental Journey*, 96–7.

9. Susan Wolfson, *Romantic Interactions: Social Being and the Turns of Literary Action* (Baltimore: Johns Hopkins University Press, 2010), 11.

10. William Wordsworth, *The Excursion*, ed. Sally Bushell, James A. Butler, and Michael C. Jaye (Ithaca: Cornell University Press, 2007), Book One, lines 399–400.

11. James Chandler, *An Archaeology of Sympathy: The Sentimental Mode in Literature and Cinema* (Chicago: University of Chicago Press, 2013), 176. See also, in particular, 163–89.

12. Julie Ellison "Sensibility," *A Handbook of Romanticism Studies*, ed. Joel Faflak and Julia M. Wright (Oxford: Blackwell, 2012), 41.

13. Sterne, *A Sentimental Journey*, 41.

14. Ellison, "Sensibility," 48.

15. G. J. Barker-Benfield, *The Culture of Sensibility: Sex and Society in Eighteenth-Century Britain* (Chicago: University of Chicago Press, 1992). For early understandings of sensibility as less complicatedly enabling to women writers see, for instance, Stuart Curran, "Romantic Poetry: The I Altered," *Romanticism and Feminism*, ed. Anne K. Mellor (Bloomington: Indiana University Press, 1988), 185–207; and Jerome McGann, *The Poetics of Sensibility: A Revolution in Literary Style* (Oxford: Clarendon, 1996).

16. Claudia L. Johnson, *Equivocal Beings: Politics, Gender, and Sentimentality in the 1790s: Wollstonecraft, Radcliffe, Burney, Austen* (Chicago: University of Chicago Press, 1995), especially 1–14; Julie Ellison *Cato's Tears and the Making of Anglo-American Emotion* (Chicago: University of Chicago Press, 1999), especially Introduction and 18–20.

17. Wollstonecraft, *A Short Residence*, 145; Ann Radcliffe, *The Mysteries of Udolpho* (1794), ed. Bonamy Dobree (Oxford: Oxford University Press, 1998), 248–9.

18. Edmund Burke, *A Philosophical Enquiry into the Origin of Our Ideas of the Sublime and the Beautiful* (1757), ed. James T. Boulton (Notre Dame: University of Notre Dame Press, 1958), 44.

19. D.D. Raphael, *The Impartial Spectator: Adam Smith's Moral Philosophy* (Oxford: Clarendon, 2007), 14.

20. Raphael, *The Impartial Spectator*, 17–18.

21. David Hume, *An Enquiry Concerning the Principles of Morals* (1751–1777), ed. Tom L. Beauchamp (Oxford: Clarendon, 1998), 44.

22. David Hume, "Of National Characters," *Essays, Moral and Political* (London, 1748), 273, *Eighteenth Century Collections Online (ECCO)*, Gale, web. April 9, 2016; Mary Fairclough, *The Romantic Crowd: Sympathy, Controversy and Print Culture* (Cambridge: Cambridge University Press, 2013), 2.

23. Raphael, *The Impartial Spectator*, 34.

24. Raphael, *The Impartial Spectator*, 34.

25. Raphael, *The Impartial Spectator*, 42. The new formulations, "impartial spectator" and "supposed impartial spectator" first appeared in Part VI, "Of the Character of Virtue," added to the Sixth Edition of *The Theory of Moral Sentiments* in 1790 (Raphael, 34–5).

26. David Simpson, *Wordsworth, Commodification and Social Concern: The Poetics of Modernity* (Cambridge: Cambridge University Press, 2009), 34–5.

27. Simpson, *Wordsworth*, 34.
28. Simpson, *Wordsworth*, see in particular 34–9, 50–1.
29. Simmel, "On Sociability," *On Individuality*, 133.
30. Simpson, *Wordsworth*, 50–1.
31. Simpson, *Wordsworth*, 35.
32. Simpson, *Wordsworth*, 27, 35.
33. Simpson, *Wordsworth*, 25.
34. I am thinking here, for example, of Gayatri Spivak, "Can the Subaltern Speak?" (1988), *The Post-Colonial Studies Reader*, ed. Bill Ashcroft, Gareth Griffiths, and Helen Tiffin (London: Routledge, 1995), 24–8; Homi K. Bhabha, *The Location of Culture* (New York: Routledge, 1994); and Judith Butler, *Excitable Speech: A Politics of the Performative* (New York: Routledge, 1997).
35. Dorothy Mermin, *Elizabeth Barrett Browning: The Origins of a New Poetry* (Chicago: University of Chicago Press, 1989), 6.
36. Charlotte Dacre, *Zofloya, or, the Moor* (1806), ed. Kim Ian Michasiw (Oxford: Oxford University Press, 2000), 28, 166, 246.
37. Percy Bysshe Shelley, *Zastrozzi, A Romance* (1810), *Zastrozzi, a Romance and St. Irvyne; or, the Rosicrucian: A Romance*, ed. Stephen C. Behrendt (Peterborough, ON: Broadview, 2002), 111, 82, 86.
38. Jane Austen, *Mansfield Park* (1814), ed. John Wiltshire (Cambridge: Cambridge University Press, 2005), 114–16.
39. Dacre, *Zofloya*, 119.
40. Frances Burney, *The Wanderer; or, Female Difficulties* (1814), ed. Margaret Doody, Robert L. Mack, and Peter Sabor (Oxford: Oxford University Press, 1991), 37.
41. This conceptualization is influenced by Mary A. Favret's work, in which she argues for the need to place something other than (or at least additional to) the French Revolution at the center of understandings of this period. She defines "modern wartime" as the experience of those living through, but not in, war (Favret, *War at a Distance: Romanticism and the Making of Modern Wartime* [Princeton: Princeton University Press, 2010], especially 9 and 37).
42. Kirsty Carpenter, *Refugees of the French Revolution: Émigrés in London, 1789–1802* (Basingstoke: Macmillan, 1999), 39–44.
43. Carpenter, *Refugees*, 29–31.
44. David Parker, *A Charitable Morsel of Unleavened Bread, for the Author of a Letter to The Rev. William Romaine; Entitled, Gideon's Cake of Barley Meal: Being a Reply to that Pamphlet* (London, 1793), 5; *Letter of a Freeholder to Mr. Johnes, Member of Parliament for the County of Denbigh, on the Subject of his Motion against the French Emigrants* (London, 1798), 19.

45. Carpenter, *Refugees*, 35–9.
46. Roger Wells, *Wretched Faces: Famine in Wartime England 1793–1801* (Gloucester: Sutton, 1988).
47. Quentin Bailey, *Wordsworth's Vagrants: Police, Prisons, and Poetry in the 1790s* (Farnham: Ashgate, 2011), 118, 155.
48. Albert Goodwin, *The Friends of Liberty: The English Democratic Movement in the Age of the French Revolution* (London: Hutchinson, 1979), 387–95. See also John Barrell, *Imagining the King's Death: Fantasies of Regicide, 1793–1796* (Oxford: Oxford University Press, 2000).
49. Burney, *The Wanderer*, 474.
50. Mary Wollstonecraft, *The Wrongs of Woman, or Maria* (1798), ed. Michelle Faubert (Peterborough, ON: Broadview, 2012), 248.
51. Anne D. Wallace, *Walking, Literature, and English Culture: The Origins and Uses of the Peripatetic in the Nineteenth Century* (Oxford: Clarendon, 1993), especially 27–31; Robin Jarvis, *Romantic Writing and Pedestrian Travel* (Basingstoke: Macmillan, 1997), especially 22–4.
52. Samuel Johnson, "to tra'vel," *Dictionary of the English Language* (London, 1755). In his emblematic 1760 *Idler* essay, Johnson describes the "useful traveller" as one who "brings home something by which his country may be benefited" ("Idler 97" [1760], *The Yale Edition of the Works of Samuel Johnson*, ed. W. J. Bate, vol. 2 [New Haven: Yale University Press, 1963], 300).
53. Johnson, "to wa'nder," *Dictionary*. Johnson's second definition of wandering is equally negative – "To deviate; to go astray" – and his examples link this directly to moral transgression.
54. These include Wallace, *Walking*, and Jarvis, *Romantic Writing*, as well as Gary Harrison, *Wordsworth's Vagrant Muse: Poetry, Poverty and the Poor* (Detroit: Wayne State University Press, 1994); Celeste Langan, *Romantic Vagrancy: Wordsworth and the Simulation of Freedom* (Cambridge: Cambridge University Press, 1995); and Toby R. Benis, *Romanticism on the Road: The Marginal Gains of Wordsworth's Homelessness* (Basingstoke: Macmillan, 2000). There are also a number of more popular and wide-ranging histories of walking, most notably, Rebecca Solnit, *Wanderlust: A History of Walking* (London: Verso, 2002) and Frederic Gros, *A Philosophy of Walking*, trans. John Howe (London: Verso, 2014).
55. Wallace's study highlights the comparative safety of the "peripatetic," focusing on "excursive walking" characterized by local, bounded movements out into the world followed by a return to familiar territory: "unwandering wandering," as she puts it at one point (Wallace, *Walking*, 180). Jarvis defines his peripatetic slightly differently from Wallace's as that of, "the more fluid, improvised, open-ended

walking typified by the pedestrian tour," but his use of the words "improvised" and "tour" alert us to the fact that this is no less a self-directed form of movement within circumscribed limits than Wallace's concept (Jarvis, *Romantic Writing*, 90). For Jarvis, influenced by both Romanticism's own claims, and early-1990s philosophical histories of travel, the pedestrian tour undertaken by well-educated, mainly middle-class, men in this period involves nothing less than "a radical assertion of autonomy": "a desired freedom from context, however partial, temporary or illusory that freedom might be: freedom from the context of their upbringing and education ... Freedom, finally, from a culturally defined and circumscribed self" (Jarvis, *Romantic Writing*, 28). Eric C. Leed, who Jarvis draws on, contends that the Romantic period essentially laid out what "remain the characteristics of the modern conception of travel": "– the voluntariness of departure, the freedom implicit in the indeterminacies of mobility, the pleasure of travel free from necessity, the notion that travel signifies autonomy and is a means for demonstrating that one 'really' is independent of one context or set of defining associations –" (Leed, *The Mind of the Traveler: From Gilgamesh to Global Tourism* [New York: Basic, 1991], 13–14). George Dekker locates the same state of mind in Romantic tourism and the Romantic novel, which he suggests cultivate an aesthetic "that effectively defined both tour and novel as privileged spaces exempt from the boring routines and hampering contingencies of ordinary life and rich with opportunities for imaginative transport," an argument I contest in relation to Radcliffe in Chapter 3 (George G. Dekker, *The Fictions of Romantic Tourism: Radcliffe, Scott, Mary Shelley* [Stanford: Stanford University Press, 2005], 3). Meanwhile, for Quentin Bailey, Wordsworth's figuring of the mobile poor within a sphere of economic indeterminacy is a deliberate response to the systematizing new penal systems by which their movements were in fact increasingly being policed (*Wordsworth's Vagrants*, 10).

56. Carl Thompson, *The Suffering Traveller and the Romantic Imagination* (Oxford: Oxford University Press, 2007), 1–11.

57. Langan, *Romantic Vagrancy* (and for a summary of this position, see especially 19).

58. Toby R. Benis, *Romantic Diasporas: French Émigrés, British Convicts, and Jews* (New York: Palgrave, 2009), 1; Michael Wiley, *Romantic Migrations: Local, National, and Transnational Dispositions* (New York: Palgrave, 2008). Benis' career might be seen as representative of the shift in scholarship on movement, which also redirects attention to different sets of texts: she has progressed from a reading of homelessness

focused on Wordsworth's recuperations of wandering to a more literally wide-ranging work on the novel, which focuses directly on depictions of the radically displaced, and aims to place Romantic period literary culture in a global context. Rather than taking Wordsworth as a point of origin for conceptions of recuperative displacement, Benis's new work, like my own, focuses on 1790s texts with entirely different starting points for understanding what constitutes travel and what it represents (Benis, *Romanticism on the Road* [2000]; Benis, *Romantic Diasporas* [2009]).

59. Benis, *Romantic Diasporas*, 7.
60. "reluctant, adj. and n.," *OED Online*, September 2013, Oxford University Press, web. November 24, 2013.
61. James Clifford, *Routes: Travel and Translation in the Late Twentieth Century* (Cambridge, MA: Harvard University Press, 1997), 34. Elizabeth A. Bohls and Ian Duncan discuss this quote in their Introduction to *Travel Writing, 1700–1830: An Anthology* (Oxford: Oxford University Press, 2005), xvi. Bohls and Duncan also note that while Paul Fussell's *The Norton Book of Travel Writing* (New York: Norton, 1987) defines "real travel" as "movement from one place to another" according to some "impulse of non-utilitarian pleasure," they want to ask, "But what about those whose movement is not so free, not so secure? Do sailors, soldiers, servants, slaves, emigrants, exiles, transported convicts, military and diplomatic wives, count as travelers?" (Fussell, *The Norton Book of Travel Writing*, 21; Bohls and Duncan, Introduction, *Travel Writing*, xvi–xvii). See also Susan Roberson's introduction to her anthology of critical thinking about travel, *Defining Travel: Diverse Visions* (Jackson: Mississippi University Press, 2001), xi–xxvi. Roberson contrasts new understandings of travel to those of earlier theorists such as Fussell, Dean MacCannell, and Jean Baudrillard, who, she suggests, define travel in ways that "tend to universalize travel around models of pleasure and escape" (*Defining Travel*, xiii).
62. For a summary of how mobility studies work has played out in different disciplines, in particular as influenced by the work of human geographer Doreen Massey, see Peter Adey, *Mobility* (London: Routledge, 2010), 91–104.
63. Stephen Greenblatt, Introduction, *Cultural Mobility: A Manifesto*, ed. Greenblatt et al. (Cambridge: Cambridge University Press, 2010), 17.
64. Tim Cresswell, *On the Move: Mobility in the Modern Western World* (New York: Routledge, 2006), 3.
65. John Urry, *Mobilities* (Cambridge: Polity Press, 2007), 194–210.
66. Cresswell, *On the Move*, 20.

67. Cresswell, *On the Move*, 18–19. Figures such the nomad and the *flâneur* are subjects of intense scrutiny and frequent critique in mobility studies literature. See, for example, Caren Kaplan, *Questions of Travel: Postmodern Discourses of Displacement*, 2nd edn. (Durham: Duke University Press, 2005); as well as Adey's summary of debates around the figures, in particular in relation to Deleuze and Guattari's work (*Mobility*, 57–71).
68. Simpson, *Wordsworth*, 3.
69. Cresswell, *On the Move*, 16.
70. Cresswell, *On the Move*, 14–15.
71. Urry, *Mobilities*, 66–70, 77–81.
72. "[C]onditions of mobility" is Burgess' phrase ("On Being Moved: Sympathy, Mobility, and Narrative Form," *Poetics Today* 32.2 [Summer 2011]: 303).
73. Cresswell, *On the Move*, 6–7; Urry, *Mobilities*, 18, 46–8.
74. See, for example, Burgess' discussions of changes in global transportation systems ("On Being Moved," 304–5; and "Transport: Mobility, Anxiety, and the Romantic Poetics of Feeling," *Studies in Romanticism* 49.2 [Summer 2010]: 235–8); Alan Bewell's accounts of "mobilized nature" and of the "unique form of exile" brought about by enclosure ("Erasmus Darwin's Cosmopolitan Nature," *English Literary History* 76.1 [March 2009]: 21; "John Clare and the Ghosts of Natures Past," *Nineteenth-Century Literature* 65.4 [March 2011]: 550; and see also "Traveling Natures," *Nineteenth-Century Contexts* 29.2–3 [June/September 2007]: 89–110).
75. Burgess, "On Being Moved," 306.
76. Burgess, "Transport," 234; Kevis Goodman, "'Uncertain Disease': Nostalgia, Pathologies of Motion, Practices of Reading," *Studies in Romanticism* 49.2 (Summer 2010): 202–7; Jonathan Lamb, *Preserving the Self in the South Seas, 1680–1840* (Chicago: University of Chicago Press, 2001), 120–8. Lamb examines the intense homesickness experienced by sailors on South Sea voyages (in part as a result of scurvy), so nostalgia as exhibited by people who are literally excessively mobile.
77. Goodman, "Nostalgia," 207; Burgess, "Transport," 241.
78. Deidre Lynch, *The Economy of Character: Novels, Market Culture, and the Business of Inner Meaning* (Chicago: Chicago University Press, 1998), 118, and see also especially chapter 5: Jane Austen and the Social Machine; Adela Pinch, *Strange Fits of Passion: Epistemologies of Emotion, Hume to Austen* (Stanford: Stanford University Press, 1996); and Dror Wahrman, *The Making of the Modern Self: Identity and Culture in Eighteenth-Century England* (New Haven: Yale University Press, 2004), see especially chapter 7. Central to both Lynch and Wahrman's studies is an examination of the more fluid, mutable concepts of identity and literary "character" which preceded

new conceptions of a bounded self. This critical work is indebted also to histories of the relationship between sensibility and the public and private spheres such as Markman Ellis, *The Politics of Sensibility: Race, Gender, and Commerce in the Sentimental Novel* (Cambridge: Cambridge University Press, 1996).

79. David Hume, *A Treatise of Human Nature: A Critical Edition* (1739–1740), ed. David Fate Norton and Mary J. Norton (Oxford: Clarendon, 2007), 1.386.

80. Hume, "Of National Characters," 275.

81. Hume, *Enquiry*, 9, 43.

82. Pinch, *Fits of Passion*, 19.

83. Fairclough, *Romantic Crowd*, 26–7.

84. David Marshall, *The Surprising Effects of Sympathy: Marivaux, Diderot, Rousseau and Mary Shelley* (Chicago and London: Chicago University Press, 1988), 4–5.

85. Burgess, "On Being Moved," 300; Fairclough, *Romantic Crowd*, 27–8.

86. Burgess, "Transport," 231. Despite her attunement to mobility and metaphors of transport, Burgess's own structuring metaphors tend to keep her subjects of emotion themselves pretty much at home. This is exemplified by her discussion of how the development of inland canals worked to "erase the difference between self and other, home and away" and "lent new urgency to existing transport metaphors" such as Adam Smith's. Here, the body of a stationary nation or subject becomes penetrated by movement from elsewhere ("Transport" 237–8).

87. Paula Backscheider, *Eighteenth-century Women Poets and their Poetry: Inventing Agency, Inventing Genre* (Baltimore: Johns Hopkins University Press, 2005); Susan Staves, *A Literary History of Women's Writing in Britain, 1660–1789* (Cambridge: Cambridge University Press, 2006); Stephen C. Behrendt, *British Women Poets and the Romantic Writing Community* (Baltimore: Johns Hopkins University Press, 2009). Other recent studies focused on women's writing, which for the most part concentrate on the novel, include Angela Keane, *Women Writers and the English Nation in the 1790s: Romantic Belongings* (Cambridge: Cambridge University Press, 2000); Leanne Maunu, *Women Writing the Nation: National Identity, Female Community, and the British-French Connection, 1770–1820* (Lewisburg: Bucknell University Press, 2007); and Fiona L. Price, *Revolutions in Taste 1773–1818: Women Writers and the Aesthetics of Romanticism* (Farnham: Ashgate, 2009).

88. Staves, *Women's Writing*, 3; Johnson, *Equivocal Beings*, 1; see also, in particular, Behrendt, *British Women Poets*, especially 298–302.

89. Backscheider, *Women Poets*, 24.

90. On the exceptional woman narrative in imaginings of women's travel, see Shirley Foster and Sara Mills, Introduction, *An Anthology of Women's Travel Writing* (Manchester: Manchester University Press, 2002), 1. Susan Bassnett describes this as an old way of marginalizing women's achievements ("Travel Writing and Gender," *The Cambridge Companion to Travel Writing*, 228).

91. Mary A. Favret, "*Letters Written During a Short Residence in Sweden, Norway, and Denmark*: Traveling with Mary Wollstonecraft," *The Cambridge Companion to Mary Wollstonecraft*, ed. Claudia L. Johnson (Cambridge: Cambridge University Press, 2002), 213. See also Roberson, who notes that "Relations to place, power, and identity, often based on racial, class, and ethnic backgrounds, make up part of the baggage that the traveler carries" (*Defining Travel*, xiv).

92. Kaplan, *Questions of Travel*, 2.

93. Wallace, *Walking*, 30. See also Roberson, *Defining Travel*, xiv.

94. Foster and Mills, *Women's Travel Writing*, 1. For other books that start from this point, see, for example, Zoë Kinsley, *Women Writing the Home Tour, 1682–1812* (Aldershot: Ashgate, 2008) and Sara Mills, *Discourses of Difference: An Analysis of Women's Travel Writing and Colonialism* (London: Routledge, 2002).

95. "Background," *MONK: Metadata Offer New Knowledge*, n.p., n.d., web. November 20, 2013 (http://monkproject.org). MONK, now discontinued, was a digital environment designed to help humanities scholars discover and analyze patterns. Behrendt, in his challenge to the coming generation of critics to develop a new, revisionist aesthetics for assessing the literature of this period, notes that this new work will need to draw on newly available technologies in ways that allow for new forms of primary textual scholarship (Behrendt, *British Women Writers*, 298–302).

96. Franco Moretti's model of "distant reading" aims to approach "*a specific form of knowledge*" by focusing on fewer elements in order to give "a sharper sense of their overall interconnection. Shapes, relations, structures" (Moretti, *Graphs, Maps, Trees: Abstract Models for a Literary History* [London: Verso, 2005], n.p.). My "distant reading" is based on a content analysis of a corpus of 186 novels, and just under 22 million words, representing all the novels published from 1720 to 1820 that were available in 2010 through Chadwyk-Healey's Literature Online (153 novels), Brown Women Writers Project (6 novels), and the Chawton House Library Novels Online archive (27 novels). Each novel in the sample was downloaded, converted into a text file, and uploaded to the lexical analysis software, Wordsmith 5.0, produced by Oxford University Press. It was necessary to work across databases because of the relative lack of women-authored texts available through Chadwyk-Healey's source. My specific approach draws on

social science methodology, by which content analysis is defined as "the systematic, objective, quantitative analysis of message characteristics," primarily involving "*counts* of key categories" (Kimberly A. Neuendorf, *The Content Analysis Guidebook* [Thousand Oaks, CA: Sage, 2002], 1, 14). It works on the assumption that shifts in manifest language and word use, although in some ways a crude measure, can nonetheless help to plot the trajectory of shifts in ideas and understandings, or the emergence of new paradigms. Such methodologies are of most use in identifying texts and passages worth *further* investigation in relation to specific ideas – in particular in texts we do not yet know well. I do not, therefore, mean to lay over much emphasis on the findings of this small, focused study in a book that for the most part uses very different methodologies. It needs to be acknowledged, for example, that the results have not been through tests for statistical significance, and in addition, that the usefulness of keyword searches are limited, especially for literary texts. As Robin Valenza remarks, "keyword techniques depend overmuch on specific verbal configurations, and natural language (such as English) depend on significant variability in the way that similar ideas can be expressed" (Valenza, "How Literature becomes Knowledge: A Case Study," *English Literary History* 76.1 [2009]: 225). As Moretti himself notes, quantitative research "provides *data*, not interpretation" (Moretti, *Graphs, Maps, Trees*, 9). This project works on the assumption that even beyond interpretation, to be truly informative any quantitative analysis of literary texts needs to be combined with other methods of textual analysis. The second step in this distant reading involved focused readings of the group of novels identified in the preliminary quantitative stage as featuring the terms for wandering with a notable degree of frequency.

97. Eliza Haywood, *Adventures of Eovaii, Princess of Ilaveo* (1736); Samuel Johnson, *The History of Rasselas, Prince of Abissinia* (1759); Henry Mackenzie, *Julia de Roubigné* (1777); William Beckford, *Vathek* (1786); Elizabeth Sophia Tomlins, *The Victim of Fancy* (1787); Mary Wollstonecraft, *Mary* (1788); Anna Maria Bennett, *Agnes De-Courci* (1789); Anna Maria Mackenzie, *Monmouth* (1790); Ann Radcliffe, *A Sicilian Romance* (1790); Ann Radcliffe, *The Romance of the Forest* (1791); Ann Radcliffe, *The Mysteries of Udolpho* (1794); Mrs.Rowson, *The Inquisitor; or, the Invisible Rambler* (1794); Mary Hays, *Memoirs of Emma Courtney* (1796); Mary Robinson, *Walsingham, or, the Pupil of Nature* (1797); Mary Hays, *The Victim of Prejudice* (1799); Mrs. Martin, *The Enchantress* (1801); Charlotte Dacre, *Zofloya, or, The Moor* (1806); Sydney Owenson, Lady Morgan, *The Wild Irish Girl* (1806); Anonymous. *The Monk and the Vine-Dresser* (1809); Anna Maria

Mackenzie, *The Irish Guardian* (1809); Percy Bysshe Shelley, *Zastrozzi, A Romance* (1810); Percy Bysshe Shelley, *St. Irvyne; or, The Rosicrucian: A Romance* (1811); Augusta Amelia Stuart, *Cava of Toledo* (1812); Maria Susanna Cooper, *The Wife* (1813); Mary Shelley *Frankenstein* (1818); Charles Robert Maturin, *Melmoth the Wanderer* (1820). Of the next twenty novels from the main corpus which feature wandering only slightly less than those featured here, only two are published prior to 1790, Sarah Fielding and Jane Collier's joint production, *The Cry* (1754), and Penelope Aubin's *Madame de Beaumont* (1739).

98. Mary Wollstonecraft, *Mary, A Fiction* (1788), ed. Michelle Faubert (Peterborough ON: Broadview, 2012), 130; Mary Hays, *Memoirs of Emma Courtney* (1796), ed. Eleanor Ty (Oxford: Oxford University Press, 1996), 116; Charlotte Smith, *The Old Manor House* (1793), ed. Jacqueline M. Labbe (Peterborough, ON: Broadview, 2002), 397, 410, 457, 508; Augusta Amelia Stuart, *Cava of Toledo; or, the Gothic Princess. A Romance* (London, 1812), *Chawton House Library Novels Online*, n.d., vol. 4. chapter 2, web. December 8, 2013; Anna Maria Mackenzie, *Irish Guardian, or, Errors of Eccentricity* (London, 1809), *Chawton House Library Novels Online*, web. December 8, 2013; Radcliffe, *A Sicilian Romance* (1790), ed. Alison Milbank (Oxford: Oxford University Press), 56.

99. Burney, *The Wanderer*, 655.

100. Jarvis, *Romantic Writing*, 82–3, 30.

101. Ina Ferris, "Mobile Words: Romantic Travel Writing and Print Anxiety," *Modern Language Quarterly: A Journal of Literary History* 60.4 (1999): 458.

102. John Richetti, "Formalism and Eighteenth-Century English Fiction: An Introduction," *Eighteenth-Century Fiction* 24.2 (2011–2012): 158.

103. Stephen C. Behrendt, "Response Essay: Cultural Transitions, Literary Judgments, and the Romantic-Era British Novel," *Enlightening Romanticism, Romancing the Enlightenment: British Novels from 1750 to 1832*, ed. Miriam L. Wallace (Surrey: Ashgate, 2009), 201. See also, for example, A. C. Toner, who takes J. Paul Hunter's arguments that there is an inherent anti-formalism in the eighteenth-century novel, and an immense tolerance for unpredictable endings among eighteenth-century readers, as her starting point (Toner, "Anna Barbauld on Fictional Form in *The British Novelists* [1810]," *Eighteenth-Century Fiction* 24.2 [2011–2012]: 175–7).

104. Sandra Macpherson, *Harm's Way: Tragic Responsibility and the Novel Form* (Baltimore: Johns Hopkins University Press, 2010); Jesse Molesworth, *Chance and the Eighteenth-Century Novel: Realism, Probability, Magic* (Cambridge: Cambridge University Press, 2010).

105. Georg Lukács, *The Theory of the Novel: A Historico-Philosophical Essay on the Forms of Great Epic Literature*, trans. Anna Bostock (Cambridge: MIT Press), in *Theory of the Novel: A Historical Approach*, ed. Michael McKeon (Baltimore: Johns Hopkins University Press, 2000), 204.

106. Geoffrey Hartman's is one classic argument for poetry as a "drama of consciousness," while Jarvis's work exemplifies this approach to both poetry and travel (Hartman, *Wordsworth's Poetry, 1787–1814* [New Haven: Yale University Press, 1964]; Jarvis, *Romantic Writing*).

107. See, for example, Kate Parker and Courtney Weiss Smith, eds. *Eighteenth-Century Poetry and the Rise of the Novel Reconsidered* (Lewisburg: Bucknell University Press, 2014).

108. Andrea Henderson, *Romanticism and the Painful Pleasures of Modern Life* (Cambridge: Cambridge University Press, 2008), 2.

109. Burney, *The Wanderer*, 364.

110. Of the seventy-five pieces in Harriet Devine Jump's 2003 anthology of central works of criticism on Wollstonecraft, only two are dedicated to *A Short Residence* (*Mary Wollstonecraft and the Critics: 1788–2001*, ed. Harriet Devine Jump, 2 vols. [London: Routledge, 2003]). The same year a whole collection of essays appeared on the work, and it has since been the subject of a number of significant articles and book chapters (Anka Ryall and Catherine Sandbach-Dahlström, eds. *Mary Wollstonecraft's Journey to Scandinavia: Essays* [Stockholm: Almqvist, 2003]).

111. In relation to the focus on the woman's novel, two foundational texts include Jane Spencer, *The Rise of the Woman Novelist: From Aphra Behn to Jane Austen* (Oxford: Blackwell, 1986) and Janet Todd, *The Sign of Angellica: Women, Writing and Fiction, 1660–1800* (New York: Columbia University Press, 1989). Harriet Guest and Susan Staves make similar comments to my own on the limitations of this focus on the novel (Guest, *Small Change: Women, Learning, Patriotism, 1750–1810* [Chicago: University of Chicago Press, 2000], 15; Staves, *Women's* Writing, see especially 7).

112. Ferris, "Mobile Words," 452–3.

113. Ingrid Horrocks, "Creating an 'Insinuating Interest': Mary Wollstonecraft's Travel Reviews and *A Short Residence*," *Studies in Travel Writing* 19.1 (2015): 1–15.

114. Erinç Özdemir, "Hidden Polemic in Wollstonecraft's *Letters from Norway*: A Bakhtinian Reading," *Studies in Romanticism* 47.3 (2008): 321. For a similar reading to Özdemir's, see Christine Chaney, "The Rhetorical Strategies of 'Tumultuous Emotions': Wollstonecraft's *Letters Written in Sweden*," *Journal of Narrative Theory* 34.3 (2004): 277–303, or for a wider discussion of the ways in which Wollstonecraft is understood to have created a hybrid literary form in this text, see Horrocks, Introduction, *A Short Residence*, 13–42.

115. Ferris, "Mobile Words," 458–9.
116. Jonathan Lamb, *Preserving the Self in the South Seas, 1680–1840* (Chicago: University of Chicago Press, 2001) and Jonathan Lamb, *The Things Things Say* (Princeton: Princeton University Press, 2011).
117. Ferris, "Mobile Words," 453. See also Susan Lamb, *Bringing Travel Home to England: Tourism, Gender, and Imaginative Literature in the Eighteenth Century* (Newark: University of Delaware Press, 2010), 110.
118. The quotation on Radcliffe is from Dekker (*Romantic Tourism*, 92); on Smith see Backscheider, *Women Poets*, 335–6; and for a discussion of accusations of plagiarism which places them in a wider context of Romantic period reviewing, see Behrendt, *British Women Poets*, 9–11.
119. Ralph Waldo Emerson, "Self-reliance," *The Collected Works of Ralph Waldo Emerson*, ed. Joseph Slater, vol. 2 (Cambridge: Belknap Press, 1979), 47.
120. Jennie Batchelor, "Introduction: Influence, Intertextuality and Agency: Eighteenth-Century Women Writers and the Politics of Remembering," *Women's Writing* 20.1 (2013): 1–12. The issue of precedence in literary works, of which practices of quotation and allusion forms a part, of course has a long and important critical history, tied to debates about originality and influence in poetry in particular, as well as to ideas about cultural capital and canon formation. In recent years, the ground has generally shifted to an understanding that writers' relationships with their predecessors can be as much a relationship of "energy and gratitude," to use Christopher Ricks' phrase, as one of debilitation and Harold Bloom's "great defeat" (Ricks, *Allusion to the Poets* [Oxford: Oxford University Press, 2002], 12; Bloom, *The Anxiety of Influence: A Theory of Poetry* [New York: Oxford University Press 1973], 10).
121. Wolfson, *Romantic Interactions* 2. See Jacqueline M. Labbe's work on Smith and Wordsworth's shared experimentation for an extended example of a critical approach focused on how authors come into being in relation to each other (*Writing Romanticism: Charlotte Smith and William Wordsworth, 1784–1807* [Basingstoke: Palgrave, 2011]).
122. Behrendt, *British Women Poets*, 11
123. Wolfson, *Romantic Interactions*, 9.
124. Wolfson, *Romantic Interactions*, 2.
125. Cresswell, *On the Move*, 16.

1 "Circling Eye" to "Houseless Stranger"

1. John Barrell, *English Literature in History, 1730–1780: An Equal, Wide Survey* (London: Hutchinson, 1983), 35.

2. John Sitter traces the critical conception of the eighteenth-century poet as melancholy wanderer back to Eleanor M. Sickel's *The Gloomy Egoist: Moods and Themes of Melancholy from Gray to Keats* (1932), published half a century before his own book (*Literary Loneliness in Mid-Eighteenth Century England* [Ithaca: Cornell University Press, 1982], 85).

3. Mary Wollstonecraft, *A Vindication of the Rights of Woman* (1792), *A Vindication of the Rights of Men and A Vindication of the Rights of Woman*, ed. D. L. Macdonald and Kathleen Scherf (Peterborough, ON: Broadview, 1997), 239–40.

4. Kevis Goodman, *Georgic Modernity and British Romanticism: Poetry and the Mediation of History* (Cambridge: Cambridge University Press, 2004), 64.

5. See Roger Lonsdale's account of the textual history of the poem in *The Poems of Thomas Gray, William Collins, and Oliver Goldsmith*, ed. Lonsdale (London: Longman, 1969), especially 624.

6. Paula R. Backscheider, *Eighteenth-Century Women Poets and Their Poetry: Inventing Agency, Inventing Genre* (Baltimore: Johns Hopkins University Press, 2005), xxi; David Fairer, *English Poetry of the Eighteenth Century, 1700–1789* (London: Pearson, 2003), ix–x.

7. Backscheider, *Women Poets*, xvii–xviii.

8. Here I am not so interested in the specific 1730s meaning of the word "Patriot" in this period, which associates it with the group of oppositional Whig politicians that included Bolingbroke, Lyttleton, and Chesterfield, but as a more general term that would be picked up by poets later in the century, in particular by Goldsmith. For an analysis of the shifting meaning of the term, see Dustin Griffin, *Patriotism and Poetry in Eighteenth-Century Britain* (Cambridge: Cambridge University Press, 2002), 16–22, 74–5.

9. Alexander Pope, *Windsor Forest*, in *Alexander Pope*, ed. Pat Rogers (Oxford: Oxford University Press, 1993), 234–7.

10. Thomas Nagel, *The View from Nowhere* (New York: Oxford University Press, 1986).

11. Sitter, *Literary Loneliness*, 85.

12. John Barrell, *Poetry, Language and Politics* (Manchester: Manchester University Press, 1988), 109, 108–18.

13. Fairer, *English Poetry*, 192–3.

14. This forms part of what Barrell describes as "the *notion* of mobility" that characterized the experience of those who had encountered and could easily imagine other landscapes, and the relationships between different places. Barrell distinguishes those in possession of this attitude from the laboring poor (John Barrell, *The Idea of Landscape and the Sense of Place 1730–1840: An Approach to the Poetry of John Clare* (Cambridge: Cambridge University Press, 1972), 63.

15. Tim Fulford, *Landscape, Liberty and Authority: Poetry, Criticism and Politics from Thomson to Wordsworth* (Cambridge: Cambridge University Press, 1996); Jacqueline M. Labbe, *Romantic Visualities: Landscape, Gender, and Romanticism* (Basingstoke: Macmillan, 1998); Suvir Kaul, *Poems of Nation, Anthems of Empire: English Verse in the Long Eighteenth Century* (Charlottesville: University Press of Virginia, 2000); Rachel Crawford, *Poetry, Enclosure, and the Vernacular Landscape, 1700–1830* (Cambridge: Cambridge University Press, 2002).

16. Dennis Desroches, "The Rhetoric of Disclosure in James Thomson's *The Seasons*; or, on Kant's Gentlemanly Misanthropy." *The Eighteenth Century* 49.1 (2008): 1–24; Goodman, *Georgic Modernity*, 12, 41. Kaul's suggestion that we should focus on the "social and ethical indigestion" of empire, as much as on its greed, sets a similar critical agenda (*Poems of Nation*, 35). Other Thomson criticism that starts with a departure from the prospect includes Evan Gottlieb, "The Astonished Eye: The British Sublime and Thomson's 'Winter,'" *The Eighteenth Century* 42.1 (2001): 42–57; Zoë Kinsley, "Landscapes 'Dynamically in Motion': Revisiting Issues of Structure and Agency in Thomson's *The Seasons*," *Papers on Language and Literature* 41.1 (2005): 3–25; and Heather Keenleyside, "Personification for the People: On James Thomson's *The Seasons*," *English Literary History* 76.2 (2009): 447–72.

17. Labbe, *Romantic Visualities*, xiii.

18. See, for example, *Spring*, 944–9 and *Autumn*, 195–6.

19. *The Seasons'* frequent recurrence to "mazes" echoes and evokes the hell of Milton's *Paradise Lost*, where the fallen angel's thoughts are similarly "in wandring mazes lost" (*Paradise Lost* [1674], in *The Riverside Milton*, ed. Roy Flannagan [Boston: Houghton, 1998], 2.561).

20. David Hume, *A Treatise of Human Nature: A Critical Edition* (1739–1740), ed. David Fate Norton and Mary J. Norton (Oxford: Clarendon, 2007), 386. On the 1790s context see Mary Fairclough, *The Romantic Crowd: Sympathy, Controversy and Print Culture* (Cambridge: Cambridge University Press, 2013).

21. See also *Winter*, 179–80.

22. Fulford, *Landscape*, 24, 26, see also especially 18–19. For a still earlier version of this argument, although without Fulford's critique of the politics it assumes, see Ralph Cohen, *The Unfolding of the Seasons* (Baltimore: Johns Hopkins University Press, 1970), 256–8.

23. Barrell, *Idea of Landscape*, 30; Kinsley, "Landscapes," 19.

24. Kaul, *Poems of Nation*, 134, 157.

25. Richard Savage, *The Wanderer*, in *Various Poems* (London: 1761), canto 1. 99–103.

26. Oliver Goldsmith, *The Deserted Village* (1770), in *The Poems of Gray, Collins, and Goldsmith*, ed. Roger Lonsdale, lines 37–9.

27. Fairer, *English Poetry*, 99.

28. Dustin Griffin, *Literary Patronage in England, 1650–1800* (Cambridge: Cambridge University Press, 1996), see especially 123–9, 225–6.

29. Oliver Goldsmith, "An Enquiry into the Present State of Polite Learning in Europe" (1759), *Collected Works of Oliver Goldsmith*, ed. Arthur Friedman, vol. 1 (Oxford: Clarendon, 1966), 310–11. For wider discussions of Goldsmith's views on the commercialization of print culture and the position of the author, see Griffin, *Patriotism and Poetry*, 208–9, 217–19 and Megan Kitching, "The Solitary Animal: Professional Authorship and Persona in Goldsmith's *The Citizen of the World*," *Eighteenth-Century Fiction* 25.1 (2012), 175–98.

30. Goldsmith, "Enquiry into the Present State," 317.

31. Griffin, *Patriotism and Poetry*, 213.

32. Oliver Goldsmith, "A Comparative View of Races and Nations" (1760), vol. 3, *Collected Works of Oliver Goldsmith*, 68.

33. For a discussion of how Goldsmith's argument for "comparative history" works, see Kaul, *Poems of Nation*, 112–16.

34. Samuel Johnson, *Rasselas, Poems, and Selected Prose* (1759), ed. Bertrand H. Bronson (Fort Worth: Harcourt, 1971), 628–9.

35. Pat Rogers, "The Dialectic of *The Traveller*," *The Art of Oliver Goldsmith*, ed. Andrew Swarbrick (Totowa: Barnes, 1984), 114. See also Marshall Brown, *Preromanticism* (Stanford: Stanford University Press, 1991), 123.

36. John Denham, *Coopers Hill*, line 13, quoted in W. B. Carnochan, *Confinement and Flight: An Essay on English Literature of the Eighteenth Century* (Berkeley: University of California Press, 1977), 111–12.

37. Robin Jarvis, *Romantic Writing and Pedestrian Travel* (Basingstoke: Macmillan, 1997), 78. Jarvis traces the emergence of the subject-in-motion in poetic form through the work of John Denham, John Dyer, William Crowe, and William Cowper to its culmination in William Wordsworth.

38. Brown identifies fullness turning into emptiness as a general characteristic of *The Traveller*, although he sees this as the effect of the linear logic of the satirist, that is, of the "narrator of decline and cataloguer of lost glories." This emptiness, he argues, is always in turn creating a space to be brought back to life by the poetic voice (*Preromanticism*, 137).

39. Thomas Gray, "Ode on a Distant Prospect of Eton College" (1747), *The Poems of Gray, Collins, and Goldsmith*, line 1.

40. The poet in *The Traveller* at times occupies a curious double position, occasionally failing to maintain his separation from the blinded patriot: "Such is the patriot's boast where'er *we* roam" (74, my emphasis), he

concedes, thus including himself in this boast through the first-person plural. Lonsdale identifies this as a moment in which Goldsmith, caught in the complexities of the position he has been creating for the poet, begins to play down the subjective aspect of the poem (" 'A Garden and a Grave': The Poetry of Oliver Goldsmith," *The Author in His Work: Essays on a Problem in Criticism*, ed. Louis Martz and Aubrey Williams [New Haven: Yale University Press, 1978], 15). However, if this is the case it is done awkwardly: the switch between "we" and "his" in these two lines makes the merging of the poet with the patriot, the specific individual with the generality, uncertain even in the moment it is stated. Ironically, it is precisely at the moment that the traveler is actually faced with the strangeness and otherness of foreign patriots that he retreats into remembrance and vindication of his own home.

41. Richard Savage, "The Lament" (1724), quoted in Richard Holmes, *Dr Johnson and Mr Savage* (London: Harper, 1993), 79.

42. Lonsdale, "A Garden and a Grave," 15.

43. Alexander Pope, *Eloisa to Abelard* in *Alexander Pope* (1717), line 208.

44. Goldsmith, *The Deserted Village*, line 192.

45. Goldsmith's original version of the poem ends two lines later. The published ending, with its shift away from this material, was written by Johnson. See Brown's discussion of Johnson's rewriting of Goldsmith's endings (*Preromanticism*, 113–40).

46. David Hume, *A Treatise of Human Nature: A Critical Edition* (1739–1740), ed. David Fate Norton and Mary J. Norton (Oxford: Clarendon, 2007), 385.

47. Crawford, *Poetry, Enclosure*, 12–13; and see also Raymond Williams, *The Country and the City* (New York: Oxford University Press, 1973), 9–12.

48. Deidre Lynch, "Homes and Haunts: Austen's and Mitford's English Idylls," *Representing Place in British Literature and Culture, 1660–1830: From Local to Global*, ed. Evan Gottlieb and Juliet Shields (Farnham, UK and Burlington, VT: Ashgate, 2013), 183.

49. On the shifting meaning of nostalgia, see Kevis Goodman, " 'Uncertain Disease': Nostalgia, Pathologies of Motion, Practices of Reading," *Studies in Romanticism* 49.2 (Summer 2010): 197–227.

50. Katherine Turner, *British Travel Writers in Europe, 1750–1800: Authorship, Gender and National Identity* (Aldershot: Ashgate, 2001), 13–16; Mary Wollstonecraft, *Letters Written During a Short Residence in Sweden, Norway and Denmark* (1796), ed. Ingrid Horrocks (Peterborough, ON: Broadview, 2013), 112.

51. Ann Radcliffe, *The Mysteries of Udolpho* (1794), ed. Bonamy Dobree (Oxford: Oxford University Press, 1998), 161.

52. Leonore Davidoff and Catherine Hall, *Family Fortunes: Men and Women of the English Middle Class, 1780–1850* (London: Hutchinson, 1987), 155–66; and, see also, Andrew Elfenbein, *Romantic Genius: The Prehistory of a Homosexual Role* (New York: Columbia University Press, 1999), especially 71–7. As Elfenbein points out, the fact that Cowper was a bachelor complicates this role.

53. Goodman, *Georgic Modernity*, 69; Mary A. Favret, *War at a Distance: Romanticism and the Making of Modern Wartime* (Princeton: Princeton University Press, 2010), 24. Favret goes so far as to describe Cowper's contribution in *The Task* as being to "construct[ ] a poetic form adequate to his consciousness of modern, global warfare" (54).

54. Julie Ellison, "Sensibility," *A Handbook of Romanticism Studies*, ed. Joel Faflak and Julia M. Wright (Oxford: Blackwell, 2012), 44.

55. Brown, *Preromanticism*, 60.

56. Sarah Houghton-Walker, "William Cowper's Gypsies," *Studies in English Literature, 1500–1900* 48.3 (2008), 659, 667. Goodman reads these figures as "anti-Lucretian spectators" who work as uncanny and unsettling doubles of the speaker (*Georgic Modernity*, 92–5).

57. See Goodman, *Georgic Modernity*, Favret, *War*, and Julie Ellison, "News, Blues, and Cowper's Busy World," *Modern Language Quarterly* 62.3 (2001): 219–37.

58. Goodman, *Georgic Modernity*, 91–2.

59. David Higgins, *Romantic Englishness: Local, National, and Global Selves, 1780–1850* (Basingstoke: Palgrave, 2014), 18, 42.

60. Anne D. Wallace, *Walking, Literature, and English Culture: The Origins and Uses of the Peripatetic in the Nineteenth Century* (Oxford: Clarendon, 1993), 86.

61. Favret, *War*, 55.

62. See Goodman for an extended reading of these "chains of silence" (*Georgic Modernity*, 80–3).

63. Brian William Cowan, "Mr. Spectator and the Coffeehouse Public Sphere," *Eighteenth-Century Studies* 37.3 (Spring 2004): 349–56.

64. Richard Steele, *The Tatler*, no. 178, ed. Donald F. Bond, vol. 2 (Oxford: Oxford University Press, 1987), 469, 471.

65. Brown, *Preromanticism*, 60; Houghton-Walker, "Cowper's Gypsies," 672, 653.

66. See also the end of the newspaper scene, where Cowper evokes "Winter" in a lyric passage which forms a kind of antidote to the impossible, quick-moving demands made on the subject by reading the news (*Task*, 4. 120–9).

67. Goodman, *Georgic Modernity*, 90. Earlier readings of this passage, such as Brown's, tend to emphasize, rather, this passage as a moment in which "consciousness becomes autonomous, independent of the world in which the conscious being lives" (*Preromanticism*, 69).

68. Goodman, *Georgic Modernity*, 92.

69. Favret, *War*, 66; and, see also Fulford, *Landscape*, 41–5.

70. Miranda Burgess, "On Being Moved: Sympathy, Mobility, and Narrative Form," *Poetics Today* 32.2 (Summer 2011): 301; David Simpson, *Wordsworth, Commodification and Social Concern: The Poetics of Modernity* (Cambridge: Cambridge University Press, 2009), 33–4.

71. *Paradise Lost*, 12. 648–9, 587.

72. *Paradise Lost*, 11. 283–4. Cowper uses the word "snug" in his letters in descriptions of a parlor that resembles that in *The Task*. See, for example, "To William Unwin" [October 6, 1781], *The Letters and Prose Works of William Cowper*, ed. James King and Charles Ryskamp, vol. 1 (Oxford: Clarendon, 1984), 527.

73. Burgess' phrase from, "Transport: Mobility, Anxiety, and the Romantic Poetics of Feeling," *Studies in Romanticism* 49.2 (Summer 2010), 234.

74. Elfenbein, *Romantic Genius*, 83–4.

75. "To Thomas Cadell, Sr." [December 16, 1792], *The Collected Letters of Charlotte Smith*, ed. Judith Stanton (Bloomington: Indiana University Press, 2003), 55.

76. On Smith's strategic dating of the two books of *The Emigrants* in the context of the Alien Act of 1793 in particular, see Harriet Guest, *Unbounded Attachment: Sentiment and Politics in the Age of the French Revolution* (Oxford: Oxford University Press, 2013), 27–9.

77. *Speeches of the Right Honourable Charles James Fox, in the House of Commons* vol. 4 (London: Longman, 1815), 418–28.

78. Loraine Fletcher, *Charlotte Smith: A Critical Biography* (New York: St Martin's, 1998), 161–3.

79. "To Thomas Cadell, Sr." [December 16, 1792]; "To Joseph Cooper Walker" [February 20, 1793], *Collected Letters of Charlotte Smith*, 54 and 61.

80. See, for example, Ellison, "News," 236–7; Jacqueline M. Labbe, *Charlotte Smith: Romanticism, Poetry and the Culture of Gender* (Manchester: Manchester University Press, 2003), 31; and, Stephen C. Behrendt, *British Women Poets and the Romantic Writing Community* (Baltimore: Johns Hopkins University Press, 2009), 164–7.

81. Dedication to "The Emigrants," *Charlotte Smith: Major Poetic Works*, ed. Claire Knowles and Ingrid Horrocks (Peterborough, ON: Broadview, 2017), 127.

82. Dedication to "The Emigrants," *Charlotte Smith: Major Poetic Works*, 128.

83. Susan Wolfson, *Romantic Interactions: Social Being and the Turns of Literary Action*, (Baltimore: Johns Hopkins University Press, 2010), 32.

84. "To William Hayley" [April 1, 1793], *Letters and Prose Works of William Cowper*, 318–19.

85. "To William Hayley" [April 23, 1793]; "To Charlotte Smith," [July 25, 1793], *Letters and Prose Works of William Cowper*, 324, 373. See also 308–9.

86. "To Lady Hesketh" [September 9, 1792], *Letters and Prose Works of William Cowper*, 190.

87. Stuart Curran, Introduction, *The Poems of Charlotte Smith*, ed. Curran (New York: Oxford University Press, 1993), xxiv.

88. As Michael Wiley's juxtaposition of the views of Sarah Zimmerman and Judith Pascoe suggests, critics read Smith's identification of her own sufferings with those of the emigrants in two different directions. Zimmerman, for instance, sees Smith as lending her own authority and capacity to generate sympathy to the emigrants, and as modeling the kind of sympathetic response that she wants her readers to imitate, while Pascoe argues that Smith uses the emigrants to universalize her own suffering, which as Stuart Curran puts it, is "inflated to mythic status" (Wiley, "The Geography of Displacement and Replacement in Charlotte Smith's *The Emigrants*," *European Romantic Review* 17.1 [2006]: Footnote, 13; Pascoe, *Romantic Theatricality: Gender, Poetry, and Spectatorship* [Ithaca: Cornell University Press, 1997], 109; Zimmerman, *Romanticism, Lyricism, and History* [New York: State University of New York Press, 1999], 57; Curran, "Romantic Poetry: The I Altered," *Romanticism and Feminism*, ed. Anne K. Mellor [Bloomington: Indiana University Press, 1988], 201). Jacqueline M. Labbe's new work provides a fresh way into this discussion by focusing on failures of symbolism in the poem and by suggesting the problem of creating transcendent emblems as one of the works generating poetic questions (Labbe, *Writing Romanticism: Charlotte Smith and William Wordsworth, 1784–1807* [Basingstoke: Palgrave, 2011], 17).

89. For a discussion of Smith's inhabiting of Milton's great closing lines, see Wolfson, *Romantic Interactions*, 52, and also 38–42.

90. Labbe, *Charlotte Smith*, 121.

91. Amy Garnai, *Revolutionary Imaginings in the 1790s: Charlotte Smith, Mary Robinson, Elizabeth Inchbald* (Basingstoke: Palgrave, 2009), 25–6. Garnai is referring to Hannah More, *Prefatory Address to the Ladies &C of Great Britain and Ireland in Behalf of the French Clergy* (1793); and, [Frances Burney], *Brief Reflections Relative to the Emigrant French Clergy: Earnestly Submitted to the Humane Consideration of the Ladies of Great Britain* (1793).

92. "To Lady Hesketh" [May 21, 1793], *Letters and Prose Works of William Cowper* 336; Judith Stanton, *Collected Letters of Charlotte Smith*, 61, footnote 1.

93. Translation of dedication from Curran, *Poems of Charlotte Smith*, 149, endnote to epigraph.

94. Garnai, *Revolutionary Imaginings*, 26, 29.

95. Kari E. Lokke, " 'The Mild Dominion of the Moon': Charlotte Smith and the Politics of Transcendence," *Rebellious Hearts: British Women Writers and the French Revolution*, ed. Adriana Craciun and Lokke (Albany: State University of New York Press, 2001), 85–106, especially 93. See also Labbe, Introduction, *The Works of Charlotte Smith*, vol. 14 (London: Pickering, 2007), xiv–xv.

96. Cowper in fact rejects this specific cottage, like Smith welcoming back society. But in Smith the domestic home and the cottage seem to function in roughly the same way as each other, not allowing for Cowper's distinction.

97. On the buildings surrounding the Royal Pavilion, see Curran, *Poems of Charlotte Smith*, 138, footnote lines 87–9.

98. Favret, *War*, 78.

99. "To Joel Barlow" [November 3, 1792], in *Collected Letters of Charlotte Smith*, 49; see also "To Joseph Cooper Walker" [February 20, 1793], in *Collected Letters of Charlotte Smith*, 61–2.

100. This draws on James Chandler's definition of sentiment as "distributed feeling": "It is emotion that results from social circulation, passion that has been mediated by a sympathetic passage through a virtual point of view" (*An Archaeology of Sympathy: The Sentimental Mode in Literature and Cinema* [Chicago: University of Chicago Press, 2013], 11–12).

101. Michael Wiley, *Romantic Migrations: Local, National, and Transnational Dispositions* (New York: Palgrave, 2008), 16–17.

102. "The Female Exile, Written at Brighthelmstone in November 1792," lines 35–56, *Charlotte Smith: Major Poetic Works*.

103. For discussion of the still present power imbalance, see Wiley, *Romantic Migrations*, 19.

104. Edmund Burke, *A Philosophical Enquiry into the Origin of Our Ideas of the Sublime and the Beautiful* (1757), ed. James T. Boulton (Notre Dame: University of Notre Dame Press, 1958), 44–5. Burke, it should be acknowledged, is not entirely convinced that our feeling for the sufferings of others is quite so influenced by our reason, but he argues strongly that such sufferings do cause a degree of "delight" (45).

105. Simpson, *Wordsworth*, 61.

106. Labbe, *Charlotte Smith*, 130. Adriana Craciun writes that Smith creates Britain as "a mirror of *ancien régime* corruption" ("Citizens of the World: Émigrés, Romantic Cosmopolitanism, and Charlotte Smith," *Nineteenth-Century Contexts* 29.2–3 [2007]: 174).

107. Wolfson, *Romantic Interactions*, 32; Labbe, *Charlotte Smith*, 118, 126; Lokke, "Mild Dominion," 92; Behrendt, *British Women Poets*, 165.
108. Favret, *War*, 79–80.
109. Wolfson, *Romantic Interactions*, 42–3.
110. *King Lear* (Conflated Text) 3.4.29–33, in *The Norton Shakespeare*, ed. Stephen Greenblatt (New York: Norton, 1997).

2 The Desolations of Wandering

1. Stephen C. Behrendt, *British Women Poets* (Baltimore: Johns Hopkins University Press, 2009), 118–19. *Elegiac Sonnets* is now regularly recognized as the "most important volume of women's poems" of the last part of the eighteenth century, and Smith herself as "the best woman poet" of the period (Susan Staves, *A Literary History of Women's Writing in Britain, 1660–1789* [Cambridge: Cambridge University Press, 2006], 396; Paula R. Backscheider, *Eighteenth-Century Women Poets and Their Poetry: Inventing Agency, Inventing Genre* [Baltimore: Johns Hopkins University Press, 2005], 317). In recent work, Jacqueline M. Labbe argues that Charlotte Smith was a greater influence on William Wordsworth than Samuel Taylor Coleridge (*Writing Romanticism: Charlotte Smith and William Wordsworth, 1784–1807* [Basingstoke: Palgrave, 2011]).

2. For examples of the earlier critical understanding, see early work by Stuart Curran and Sarah M. Zimmerman (Curran, *Poetic Form and British Romanticism* [New York: Oxford University Press, 1986], 30; Zimmerman, *Romanticism, Lyricism, and History* [New York: State University of New York Press, 1999], 57). William Richey makes a somewhat similar argument in "The Rhetoric of Sympathy in Smith and Wordsworth," *European Romantic Review* 13.4 (2002): 427–43. The more recent shift in critical approach is illustrated most clearly by the development within the work of preeminent Smith scholar, Jacqueline M. Labbe: in her *Charlotte Smith: Romanticism, Poetry and the Culture of Gender* (Manchester: Manchester University Press, 2003), Labbe describes *Elegiac Sonnets* as a "compendium" and gives little sense of shift over time, but by *Writing Romanticism* (2011) she observes that readings that locate Smith's political work only in her novels "miss the political tinge" of the later poems in *Elegiac Sonnets* (Labbe, *Charlotte Smith*, 112; Labbe, *Writing Romanticism*, 50). In addition, Backscheider has done important work to show why we need to learn to read *Elegiac Sonnets* more closely as a sonnet *sequence* – and, in the opening few poems in the sequence, even as a sonnet chain, "united in myriad ways, both repetitive of words, images, and ideas and substantively varied as it demonstrates how creatively and nonrepetitively the theme and tone can be actualized" (*Women Poets*, 329, 331, 328).

3. For examples of recent discussions of this problem in reading *The Seasons*, see, for example, Sandro Jung, *The Fragmentary Poetic: Eighteenth-Century Uses of an Experimental Mode* (Bethlehem: Lehigh University Press, 2009); and Dennis Desroches, "The Rhetoric of Disclosure in James Thomson's *The Seasons*; or, on Kant's Gentlemanly Misanthropy," *The Eighteenth Century* 49.1 (2008): 1–24.

4. Neil Fraistat, *The Poem and the Book: Interpreting Collections of Romantic Poetry* (Chapel Hill: University of North Carolina Press, 1985), 8. Fraistat also first showed how important the idea of the collection was to Romantic era poets.

5. Stuart Curran, "Romantic Poetry: The I Altered," *Romanticism and Feminism*, ed. Anne K. Mellor (Bloomington: Indiana University Press, 1988), 200. On Smith's figuring of her poet-speaker as wanderer, see also, for example, Backscheider, *Women Poets*, especially 326, footnote 34.

6. Backscheider, *Women Poets*, 326.

7. Backscheider, *Women Poets*, 329.

8. Quotations from Smith's poems, prefaces and notes are all taken from *Charlotte Smith: Major Poetic Works*, ed. Claire Knowles and Ingrid Horrocks (Peterborough, ON: Broadview, 2017). Prose is cited by page number, and poetry by title (or abbreviated title), book number when applicable, and line number.

9. Anna Seward, quoted in Curran, Introduction, *The Poems of Charlotte Smith*, ed. Stuart Curran (New York: Oxford University Press, 1993), xxv; Anne Bannerman, *Poems*, new edn. (Edinburgh: 1807), 220, *Google Books*, web. April 4, 2012. I am grateful to Backscheider's work for bringing Bannerman's book to my attention.

10. Melissa Sodeman, "Charlotte Smith's Literary Exile," *English Literary History* 76.1 (2009), 135.

11. Charlotte Smith "To Sarah Rose" [June 15, 1804], *The Collected Letters of Charlotte Smith*, ed. Judith Stanton (Bloomington: Indiana University Press, 2003), 625.

12. William Cowper "To William Haley" [January 29, 1793], *Letters and Prose Works of William Cowper*, ed. James King and Charles Ryskamp, vol. 4, (Oxford: Clarendon, 1984), 281.

13. See Loraine Fletcher, *Charlotte Smith: A Critical Biography* (New York: St Martin's, 1998), and the increasingly autobiographical prefaces to *Elegiac Sonnets*. Most famously, Smith's financial worries were also caused by the law courts, in which her children's inheritance from their grandfather was held up for over 30 years.

14. Sodeman, "Charlotte Smith's Literary Exile," 135, 147.

15. *King Lear* (Conflated Text), 4.7.47, in *The Norton Shakespeare*, ed. Stephen Greenblatt (New York: Norton, 1997). Tellingly, the moment in

King Lear comes when Lear is brought in off the heath and greeted by Cordelia, but has become incapable of even recognizing that he is in his own kingdom – that is, at home.

16. Alan Bewell, "John Clare and the Ghosts of Natures Past," *Nineteenth-Century Literature* 65.4 (March 2011), see, in particular, 551 and 554.

17. Samuel Taylor Coleridge, "Introduction to the Sonnets," *Poems*, 2nd edn. (London, 1797), 71–2. *Eighteenth Century Collections Online (ECCO)*, Gale, web, December 9, 2013.

18. These plates first appeared in the fifth edition of 1789. Smith was closely involved in the design of the plates, providing instructions for their production and they work as an integral part of the text. For further discussion, see Zimmerman, *Romanticism*, 44–7 and Labbe, *Charlotte Smith*, 32–44.

19. Edward Young, *The Revenge, A Tragedy* (London: 1721), 1.1.5–7. *Eighteenth Century Collections Online (ECCO)*, Gale, web, December 9, 2013.

20. Zimmerman argues that by the end of *Elegiac Sonnets* this privacy has become "so complete" that Smith's speakers "lose contact with other human beings, their environment, and their own identity," charting an "interiority that becomes pathology" ("Varieties of Privacy in Charlotte Smith's Poetry," *European Romantic Review* 18.4 [2007], 489).

21. Curran, "The I Altered," 200. Curran deals exclusively with Sonnet 44 in relation to Smith in this landmark essay.

22. Adela Pinch, *Strange Fits of Passion: Epistemologies of Emotion, Hume to Austen* (Stanford: Stanford University Press, 1996), 59. See also, Behrendt, *British Women Poets*, 122; and, Curran, General Introduction, *The Works of Charlotte Smith*, vol. 1 (London: Pickering, 2005), xiii. Sonnet 44 has been dealt with by almost all modern critics of *Elegiac Sonnets*, generally being read as emblematic of the Gothicism, "morbidity" and "famously gruesome" aspects of Smith's sonnets (Pinch, *Fits of Passion*, 59; Daniel Robinson, "*Elegiac Sonnets*: Charlotte Smith's Formal Paradoxy," *Papers on Language and Literature: A Journal for Scholars and Critics of Language and Literature* 39.2 [Spring 2003]: 192). For Labbe and Behrendt the poem's "poetic perfection" and "remarkable aesthetics" in the end serve to "regularize[] its macabre content" and "vitiate the emotional charge by calling attention to the sonnet's nature as a work of artifice, of deliberate craft" (Labbe, "Revisiting the Egotistical Sublime: Smith, Wordsworth, and the Romantic Dramatic Monologue," *Fellow Romantics: Male and Female British Writers, 1790–1835*, ed. Beth Lau [Surrey: Ashgate, 2009], 25; Behrendt, *British Women Poets*, 122).

23. Esther Schor, *Bearing the Dead: The British Culture of Mourning from the Enlightenment to Victoria* (Princeton: Princeton University Press, 1994), 65–6.

24. Diana Fuss, "Corpse Poem," *Critical Inquiry* 30.1 (2003), 13. Fuss draws on Katherine Verdery's work in *The Political Lives of Dead Bodies: Reburial and Postsocialist Change* (New York: Columbia University Press, 1999), and by "corpse poem" means specifically poems in which corpses are given voice.

25. Labbe, *Charlotte Smith*, 13–14, 97, 104.

26. Smith also felt that her financial difficulties had directly contributed to the death of her eldest daughter, Anna Augusta, for whom she lacked the money to help with medical expenses. On Anna Augusta's death, see Fletcher, *Charlotte Smith: A Critical Biography*, 238–9.

27. John Urry, *Mobilities* (Cambridge: Polity Press, 2007), 80; Rebecca Solnit, *Wanderlust: A History of Walking* (London: Verso, 2002), 97–103.

28. See Kerri Andrews for a discussion of the significance of the three poems dated 1792 in Volume Two, and Susan Wolfson for Smith's careful re-writing of the moment from *The Emigrants* in "The Female Exile" (Andrews, " 'Herself... Fills the Foreground': Negotiating Autobiography in the *Elegiac Sonnets* and *The Emigrants*," *Charlotte Smith in British Romanticism*, ed. Jacqueline M. Labbe [London: Pickering, 2008], 23–4; Wolfson, *Romantic Interactions: Social Being and the Turns of Literary Action* [Baltimore: Johns Hopkins University Press, 2010], 53).

29. Labbe's 2007 edition (which appeared as part of Smith's Collected Works brought together by Curran), as well as Claire Knowles and my own 2017 edition, go some way toward helping with these issues, both including the plates and presenting the poems according to the 1800 edition, which clearly distinguishes between Volume One and Volume Two (*Elegiac Sonnets, Volumes I and II*, in *The Works of Charlotte Smith*, ed. Jacqueline Labbe, vol. 14 [London: Pickering, 2007], 1–115; *Charlotte Smith: Major Poetic Works*, ed. Knowles and Horrocks (Peterborough, ON: Broadview, 2017). In addition, the 2017 Broadview edition provides the full Tables of Contents for all nine editions, making it clear which poems were added when (*Charlotte Smith: Major Poetic Works*, Appendix F).

30. Fletcher, *Charlotte Smith: A Critical Biography*, 237–8.

31. Charlotte Smith, *The Banished Man, A Novel*, vol. 2 (London: 1794), 34, *Eighteenth Century Collections Online (ECCO)*, Gale, web, December 9, 2013. John Barrell and Harriet Guest have written of *The Emigrants*, which also comes out of this moment, that it is a difficult work because "it has to articulate a difficult set of beliefs and attitudes... Smith now wants to defend the revolution as it had been in the 3 years before the ascendancy of the Jacobins, and wishes to believe that the Jacobin terror, and the execution of Louis, were not its inevitable outcome" ("Thomson in the 1790s," *James Thomson: Essays for the Tercentenary*, ed. Richard Terry [Liverpool: Liverpool University Press, 2000], 232).

32. Charlotte Smith "To Joseph Cooper Walker" [October 9, 1793], *Collected Letters of Charlotte Smith*, 78.
33. Labbe, *Writing Romanticism*, 51–6.
34. John Milton, *Samson Agonistes* (1671), in *The Riverside Milton*, ed. Roy Flannagan (Boston: Houghton, 1998), 79–80, 100–3.
35. Sonnet 62, "Written on passing by moon-light through a village, while the ground was covered with snow," first appeared as the production of Orlando Somerive in Charlotte Smith's novel, *The Old Manor House* (1794) (*The Old Manor House*, ed. Jacqueline M. Labbe [Peterborough, ON: Broadview, 2002], 450–1).
36. Sonnet 52, "The Pilgrim," first appeared in Smith's novel *Celestina* (1791).
37. In Sonnet 52 Smith's speaker imagines an "unhappy Pilgrim" who, like her, "[j]ourneys alone," thus imagining her psychological state through, and connecting it with, the physical journey of an actual traveler just as Goldsmith and William Cowper do (*ES*, 52.1,4). Smith's allusion to Goldsmith, which evokes an archetypal and allegorical style of language as much as it does a style of movement, then extends this identification further, so that her speaker in effect travels "Alone" not only like her sonnet's own "unhappy Pilgrim," but also like Goldsmith himself, like his traveler-poet, and like his imagined "pensive exile" (*Tr*, 419). Smith's speaker may be existentially and literary alone, in other words, but rhetorically and poetically she has company. At the same time Smith represents the past in the form of the village dead and various traditions and laws which have marginalized her sonnet-speaker, as one of her wanderers' many problems. In sonnets like this one Smith both inserts her speaker into a community of solitary wanderers, and suggests a rupture within the analogy itself.
38. From the first edition, *Elegiac Sonnets* contains a number of sonnets entitled "From Petrarch" as well as sonnets in the voice of Goethe's Werther, engaging directly in the kind of generalizing "creative recycling of familiar materials" that Stephen Behrendt notes, "has always been a part of the sonnet tradition" (Behrendt, *British Women Poets*, 147). It is "richly allusive" poems such as these that lead Backscheider, along with Behrendt, to place Smith at the heart of discussions of the inherent sociability of the sonnet (Backscheider, *Women Poets*, 335). Curran comments of Smith's practices of quotation in general, "I know of no other writers in the later eighteenth century, whether in prose or verse, who so continually and so extensively incorporate other voices within their texts" ("Charlotte Smith: Intertextualities," *Charlotte Smith in British Romanticism*, ed. Jacqueline M. Labbe [London: Pickering, 2008], 179). More generally, from the best early critical work on *Elegiac Sonnets* from Schor and Adela Pinch, through Labbe and Claire Knowles,

much of the achievement of Smith's sonnets has been attributed to her manipulations of the interplay between the personal and the conventional. See in particular Schor, *Bearing the Dead*, 62; Pinch, *Fits of Passion*, 8, 69; and Labbe, *Charlotte Smith*; as well as Behrendt, *British Women Poets*, 120, Backscheider, *Women Poets*, 328; and Claire Knowles, *Sensibility and Female Poetic Tradition, 1780–1860: The Legacy of Charlotte Smith* (Farnham, England: Ashgate, 2009), 45–72.

39. Wolfson, *Romantic Interactions*, 9, 18.
40. Wolfson, *Romantic Interactions*, 2.
41. Sodeman, "Charlotte Smith's Literary Exile," 145.
42. Pinch, *Fits of Passion*, 60.
43. Labbe notes that the earlier plates "narrate a fiction of feminine attractiveness," which both associates this figure with "Charlotte Smith" the poet, and distinguishes the idealized images from the author (*Charlotte Smith* 32, and see also 32–44 and 14–17).
44. William Wordsworth, *The Excursion*, ed. Sally Bushell, James A. Butler, and Michael C. Jaye (Ithaca: Cornell University Press, 2007), Book One, lines 462–3.
45. *King Lear* (Conflated Text), 3.4.98–99.
46. Wordsworth, "Lines Written a Few Miles Above Tintern Abbey, on Revisiting the Banks of the Wye During a Tour, July 13, 1798" (1798), *Lyrical Ballads 1798 and 1800*, ed. Michael Gamer and Dahlia Porter (Peterborough, ON: Broadview, 2008), lines 142–3.
47. Behrendt, *British Women Poets*, 45.
48. Mary Wollstonecraft, *Mary, a Fiction; and the Wrongs of Woman, or Maria* (1788, 1798), ed. Michelle Faubert (Peterborough, ON: Broadview, 2012), 130.

3 "The Irresistible Force of Circumstances"

1. Ellen Moers, "Traveling Heroinism: Gothic for Heroines," *Literary Women* (London: W.H. Allen, 1976), 126.
2. Ann Radcliffe, *The Romance of the Forest*, ed. Chloe Chard (Oxford: Oxford University Press, 1986), 5; Ann Radcliffe, *The Mysteries of Udolpho*, ed. Bonamy Dobree (Oxford: Oxford University Press, 1998), 151. Hereafter cited parenthetically in text.
3. Moers, "Traveling Heroism," 126. In one of many recent modifications on Moers' argument, which still nonetheless sees the journey as enabling, Robert Miles argues that Radcliffe's use of the journey allows her to place her heroines "in situations of isolation and scenery where sublimity and other expressions of genius come naturally – indeed, spontaneously" (" 'Mother Radcliffe': Ann Radcliffe and the Female Gothic," *The Female Gothic: New Directions*, ed. Diana Wallace and Andrew Smith [Basingstoke: Palgrave, 2009], 50). Angela

Keane, who usefully divides journeys in Radcliffe's novels up into those motivated by a "recreational search for health and change of scene" and "journeys which the protagonists take against their will, in the thrall of kidnappers; or flights to liberty, often in fear of pursuit," still concludes that the "imaginative investments made in the course of the picturesque journeys have an improving effect on the travellers … the journeys in these texts, however meandering, are always purposive" (*Women Writers and the English Nation in the 1790s: Romantic Belongings* [Cambridge: Cambridge University Press, 2000], 41–2).

4. Tim Cresswell, *On the Move: Mobility in the Modern Western World* (New York: Routledge, 2006), 3.

5. David Morley, *Home Territories: Media, Mobility and Identity* (London: Routledge, 2000), 199. See also Peter Adey, *Mobility* (London: Routledge, 2010), 91–5, 104.

6. George G. Dekker, for instance, comments that "In novels that follow an unabashed flight-and-pursuit pattern, the action tends to alternate between frenetic movement and comparative stasis" (*The Fictions of Romantic Tourism: Radcliffe, Scott, Mary Shelley* [Stanford: Stanford University Press, 2005], 94), and Mark R. Blackwell shows how Radcliffe creates suspense in part through slowing down her narratives through digression ("The Gothic: Moving in the World of Novels," *A Concise Companion to the Restoration and Eighteenth Century*, ed. Cynthia Wall [Malden: Blackwell, 2005], 144–61).

7. In *The Romance of the Forest*, by contrast, poems proliferate when the heroine Adeline lives in perfect, sympathetic harmony with her adopted family, the La Lucs. One chapter in this section, for instance, contains four poems in only twice as many pages (*The Romance of the Forest*, Chapter XVIII, 282–90). While in *The Romance of the Forest* Radcliffe explores the conditions necessary for poetry through its presence, *Udolpho* investigates these conditions by marking poetry's absence.

8. Review of *The Mysteries of Udolpho*, *British Critic* 4 (August 1794): 110–21, rpt. in *The Critical Response to Ann Radcliffe*, ed. Deborah D. Rogers (Westport, CN: Greenwood Press, 1994), 20.

9. Anna Laetitia Barbauld, "Mrs Radcliffe," *The British Novelists; with An Essay; and Prefaces, Biographical and Critical by Mrs Barbauld*, vol. 43 (London: Rivington, 1810), viii.

10. Samuel Taylor Coleridge, Review of *The Mysteries of Udolpho*, *Critical Review* 2nd ser. 11 (August 1794), 369. Leah Price has shown that Coleridge was typical of contemporary reviewers of poetic novels in excising the lyric moments and considering them on their own merits (Price, *The Anthology and the Rise of the Novel: From Richardson to George Eliot* [Cambridge: Cambridge University Press, 2000], 94–7).

11. Mary Wollstonecraft, Review of *Emmeline, the Orphan of the Castle*, by Charlotte Smith, *Analytical Review* 1 (June 1788) rpt. in *The Works of Mary Wollstonecraft*, ed. Janet Todd and Marilyn Butler, vol. 7 (London: Pickering, 1989), 27.

12. On the gothic as most expressive when seemingly most inarticulate see, for instance, Eve Kosofsky Sedgwick, *The Coherence of Gothic Conventions* (New York: Arno Press, 1980); and David Punter, "Ceremonial Gothic," *Spectral Readings: Towards a Gothic Geography*, ed. Punter and Glennis Byron (New York: St Martin's, 1999), 40; and Blackwell, "The Gothic."

13. Charlotte Lennox makes the heroine of *The Life of Harriot Stuart, Written by Herself* (London, 1751) a poet, and includes more than a dozen original poems in the novel. My claim about the dearth of poetic novels pre-1780 is most specifically based on analysis of the ninety-six novels published between 1705 and 1780 that were available through the Chadwyck-Healey's Eighteenth-Century Fiction database in 2007.

14. Jane Barker, *A Patch-Work Screen for the Ladies; or, Love and Virtue Recommended: in a Collection of Instructive Novels. Related after a Manner Entirely New, and Interspersed with Rural Poems, Describing the Innocence of a Country-Life* (London, 1723), iv, *Eighteenth Century Collections Online (ECCO)*, Gale, web, December 9, 2013; Jane Barker, *The Lining of a Patch-work Screen; Design'd for the Farther Entertainment of the Ladies* (London, 1726), n.p. *Eighteenth Century Collections Online (ECCO)*, Gale, web, December 9, 2013.

15. E. J. Clery, *Women's Gothic: From Clara Reeve to Mary Shelley*, 2nd edn. (2000: Tavistock: Northcote House, 2004), 57.

16. *British Critic 4* (1794): 110–21, rpt. in *The Critical Response to Ann Radcliffe*, 20.

17. See in particular Ann Wierda Rowland, "Romantic Poetry and the Romantic Novel," *The Cambridge Companion to British Romantic Poetry*, ed. James Chandler and Maureen N. McLane (Cambridge: Cambridge University Press, 2008), 117–35; Marcie Frank, "Fairy Time from Shakespeare to Scott," *Shakespeare and the Eighteenth Century*, ed. Peter Sabor and Paul Yachnin (Aldershot: Ashgate, 2008), 103–117; and, Angela Wright, *Britain, France and the Gothic, 1764–1820: The Import of Terror* (Cambridge: Cambridge University Press, 2013), 88–119.

18. Terry Castle draws attention to what she calls the "crude focus on the so-called Gothic core" of *Udolpho* in modern criticism, which Moers had also noted 20 years earlier (Castle, *The Female Thermometer: Eighteenth-Century Culture and the Invention of the Uncanny* [New York: Oxford University Press, 1995], 121; Moers, "Traveling Heroism," 134). A number of studies published around the time of Castle's own began the work of redressing and rethinking

this imbalance. See in particular Claudia L. Johnson, *Equivocal Beings: Politics, Gender and Sentimentality in the 1790s, Wollstonecraft, Radcliffe, Burney, Austen* (Chicago: University of Chicago Press, 1995), 95–116; and Adela Pinch, *Strange Fits of Passion: Epistemologies of Emotion, Hume to Austen* (Stanford: Stanford University Press, 1996), 111–36.

19. Mary A. Favret, "Telling Tales About Genre: Poetry in the Romantic Novel," *Studies in the Novel* 26.2 (Summer 1994): 162; Price, *The Anthology*, 93; G. Gabrielle Starr, *Lyric Generations: Poetry and the Novel in the Eighteenth Century* (Baltimore: Johns Hopkins University Press, 2004), 142. Starr suggests that what gives identity to lyric once it is placed in the context of the novel is its subjection to rules that lie beyond it – that is to novelistic rules. In discussions of mid-century novels, Starr shows that this can have the effect of making lyric moments, which act by "focusing emotion," appear as episodic, rather than active, within novels (*Lyric Generations*, 142). Rachel Crawford provides a useful analogy for this understanding of the role of the lyric in the novel: "One of the attributes of the lyric moment in epic and georgic poetry . . . is its extractability from its contexts, its capacity to exist in isolation from the rest of the text as an antinarrative" (*Poetry, Enclosure and the Vernacular Landscape, 1700–1830* [Cambridge: Cambridge University Press, 2002], 177).

20. Price, *The Anthology*, 5. Favret, Price, Clery, and Starr all draw attention to the way writers of the 1790s assign different cultural and aesthetic labor to each genre, even as they bring them together.

21. Mary Robinson, *Walsingham: or, the Pupil of Nature. A Domestic Story*, vol. 1 (London: Longman, 1797), n.p.; Matthew Lewis, *The Monk, a Romance*, vol. 1 (London: Bell, 1796), n.p. Smith also republished the poems that appeared in her novels in *Elegiac Sonnets*, in the process inserting them within multiple, divergent frameworks and drawing attention to how narrative contexts effect how lyric is read. Radcliffe's poems were later detached from their context within her novels and published as *The Poems of Mrs. Ann Radcliffe* (London: 1816).

22. Price, *The Anthology*, 96.

23. See in particular Rowland, "Romantic Poetry," Frank, "Fairy Time," and Beatrice Battaglia, "The 'Pieces of Poetry' in Ann Radcliffe's *The Mysteries of Udolpho*," *Romantic Women Poets: Genre and Gender*, ed. Lilla Maria Crisafulli and Cecilia Pietropoli (Amsterdam: Rodopi, 2007), 137–51.

24. John Urry, *Mobilities* (Cambridge: Polity Press, 2007), 74–5. Urry is drawing here on the work of L. Demerath and D. Levinger (2003).

25. Price, *The Anthology*, 7.

26. Shelley King, " 'To Delineate the Human Mind in Its Endless Varieties': Integral Lyric and Characterization in the Tales of Amelia Opie." *Eighteenth-*

Century Poetry and the Rise of the Novel Reconsidered. ed. Kate Parker and Smith Courtney Weiss. (Lewisburg: Bucknell University Press, 2014), 65–6.

27. Morley, *Home Territories*, 199.

28. Edmund Burke, *A Philosophical Enquiry into the Origin of Our Ideas of the Sublime and the Beautiful* (1757), ed. James T. Boulton (Notre Dame: University of Notre Dame Press, 1958), 57. I have developed a longer reading of this aspect of the veil scene in *Udolpho* in Ingrid Horrocks, "More Than a Gravestone: *Caleb Williams, Udolpho*, and the Politics of the Gothic," *Studies in the Novel* 39.1 (2007): 31–47.

29. Ann Radcliffe, "On the Supernatural in Poetry" (c. 1802.1826), rpt. in *Gothic Readings: the First Wave, 1764–1840*, ed. Rictor Norton (London: Leicester University Press, 2000), 315.

30. Robert Miles, *Gothic Writing, 1750–1850: A Genealogy*, 2nd edn. (1993: Manchester: Manchester University Press, 2002), 3. See also Sedgwick, *Gothic Conventions*, and Punter, "Ceremonial Gothic."

31. See, for example, *Udolpho* 284 and 355. Keane has commented on the importance of the many scenes of reading in Radcliffe's work, "What epistolary fiction had done for writers, fictionalizing and putting into discourse the mechanisms of a newly privatised, yet professionalised activity, Radcliffe did for the reader. … Radcliffe puts the reading and viewing subject into fiction, tracing her (and sometimes, his) interior reactions to varieties of aesthetic experience" (*Women Writers*, 23).

32. The figure of the reader is frequently drawn on by Adam Smith, Hume, and Burke. For a discussion of its continued centrality within contemporary theorizations of affect, including in Sedgwick's work, see Miranda Burgess, "Transport: Mobility, Anxiety, and the Romantic Poetics of Feeling," *Studies in Romanticism* 49.2 (Summer 2010): 294–5.

33. Angela Wright, "In Search of Arden: Ann Radcliffe's William Shakespeare," *Gothic Shakespeares*, ed. John Drakakis, Dale Townshend, and Jerrold E. Hogle (New York: Routledge, 2008), 114, 127.

34. Burke, *Sublime and the Beautiful*, 44.

35. Charlotte Lennox, *The Female Quixote: or, The Adventures of Arabella*, ed. Margaret Dalziel (Oxford: Oxford University Press, 1998), 355.

36. Mary Robinson, *Walsingham, or, The Pupil of Nature* (1797), ed. Julie Shaffer (Peterborough, ON: Broadview, 2003), 245.

37. Robinson, *Walsingham*, 312.

38. W. B. Carnochan, *Confinement and Flight: An Essay on English Literature of the Eighteenth Century* (Berkeley: University of California Press, 1977), see especially 111–14.

39. Dekker, *Romantic Tourism*, 9, and see also especially 73–4. Critics now tend to treat the indebtedness of Radcliffe's landscape descriptions as an aspect of her

aesthetic innovation, by which her landscapes perform their failure to function as descriptions of any particular locale in a way that draws attention to their identity as linguistic constructions. See, for example, Jayne Lewis, "'No Color of Language': Radcliffe's Aesthetic Unbound," *Eighteenth-Century Studies* 39.3 (2006): 377–90; Katarina Gephardt, "Hybrid Gardens: Travel and the Nationalization of Taste in Ann Radcliffe's Continental Landscapes," *European Romantic Review* 21.1 (2010): 3–28; and Alice Labourg, " 'Exhibiting Awful Forms': Mountains and the Pictorial Framing of the Gothic in Ann Radcliffe's the Mysteries of Udolpho," *Mountains Figured and Disfigured in the English-Speaking World*, ed. Françoise Besson (Newcastle: Cambridge Scholars, 2010), 317–33. Marshall Brown discusses Radcliffe's landscapes in terms of Freud's theory of the expressive function of cliché (*The Gothic Text* [Stanford: Stanford University Press, 2005], 161–82).

40. Coleridge, *Critical Review*, 362. The reviewer in the *Analytical Review* comments that "her descriptions sometimes partake too much of uniformity," and that in the *British Critic*, that, "The lady's talent for description leads her to excess. We have somewhat too much of evening and morning; of woods, and hills, and vales, and streams" (*Analytical Review* 19 [June 1794]: 140–5 and *British Critic* 4 [1794]: 110–21, rpt. in *The Critical Response to Ann Radcliffe*, 19, 20).

41. Rowland, "Romantic Poetry," 129, see also 117. Rowland argues that poetic quotations within novels have a greater social function than our twenty-first-century expectations have led us to expect.

42. See Rictor Norton for a league table of who gets quoted how many times across all Radcliffe's work. After Shakespeare comes Thomson, followed by Milton, William Collins, and James Beattie. Radcliffe hardly quotes from writers of her own generation, but when she does, it is mainly from women writers, including Hannah More, Anna Laetitia Barbauld, Anna Seward, and Charlotte Smith (Norton, *Mistress of Udolpho: The Life of Ann Radcliffe* [London: Leicester University Press, 1999], 49–50).

43. In a discussion of this scene, Eric Miller makes a similar argument for the role of the picturesque in Radcliffe to the one I make for poetry as a social event ("Radcliffe's Reveries of a Social Walker," *Dalhousie Review* 83.1 [2003], see especially 39–41).

44. James Thomson, *Britannia, A Poem* (London, 1729), p. 8. The original quote begins "With Him the Sailor sooths" and "him" within the context of the poem is Peace.

45. John Barrell and Harriet Guest, "Thomson in the 1790s," *James Thomson: Essays for the Tercentenary*, ed. Richard Terry (Liverpool: Liverpool University Press, 2000), 217–35.

46. The quotation within *Udolpho* comes from Thomson, *Britannia*, p. 4.

47. Deidre Lynch, "Gothic Libraries and National Subjects," *Studies in Romanticism* 40.1 (Spring 2001): 42.

48. Miles, *Gothic Writing*, 131–2.

49. Rowland, "Romantic Poetry," 130.

50. John Barrell, *Imagining the King's Death: Figurative Treason, Fantasies of Regicide 1793–1796* (Oxford: Oxford University Press, 2000), see in particular 30 and 306.

51. William Godwin, April 23, 1794, *Diaries*, Oxford, Bodleian Library, MS Abinger e.6, fol 27. See Horrocks, "More than a Gravestone." Compared to Smith, Wollstonecraft, and Burney, relatively little is known about Radcliffe's political views, but Rictor Norton and Robert Miles have done work that shows her links to dissenting culture in Britain. Her husband, William Radcliffe, was editor of the *English Chronicle*. See Norton, *Mistress of Udolpho* (especially 9, 60–1, 66); and, Miles, *Ann Radcliffe: The Great Enchantress* (Manchester: Manchester University Press, 1995). Godwin's diary records seven visits or attempted visits with "Radcliffe" over the crucial months of March–May 1794 (*The Diary of William Godwin*, ed. Victoria Myers, David O'Shaughnessy, and Mark Philp [Oxford: Oxford Digital Library, 2010], web. November 27, 2013, http://godwindiary.bodleian .ox.ac.uk).

52. William Godwin, *Things as They Are: or, the Adventures of Caleb Williams* (1794).

53. Wright, *Britain, France and the Gothic*, 107 and 112. Wright reads the scene of failed reading I discuss above as a specific use of Shakespeare as "England's national literary treasure" within the context of Anglo-French hostilities. Wright's work draws out the subversiveness of Radcliffe's suggestion that under certain circumstances even the national genius becomes powerless to console: "War, revolutionary paranoia and the pending suspension of habeus corpus in England all undermined Shakespeare's ability to enchant" (106–7).

54. As is often the case, this is a slight misquotation: the original line reads, "With many a foul and midnight murther fed." In the original it refers to the "Towers of Julius" – the Tower of London – believed to be the site of a number of secret murders, making it a fitting analogy for Udolpho. Thomas Gray, "The Bard," in *The Poems of Thomas Gray, William Collins, and Oliver Goldsmith*, ed. Roger Lonsdale (London: Longman, 1969), line 88.

55. See Wright, *Britain, France, and the Gothic*, 106.

56. This has the effect, Favret argues, of making the lyrics appear as "parenthetical" and detachable from the novel as a whole (Favret, "Telling Tales About Genre," 162–3). Favret argues that in general, "One is led to believe that poetry is an entirely common occurrence in the world of the

novel, practiced by nearly anyone upon nearly any premise" (162). But in the case of *Udolpho*, Montoni never quotes anyone and neither does his wife. Those who cite or compose poetry are all part of Emily's extended family of feeling: Emily herself, St. Aubert, Emily's lover Valancourt, Valancourt's double, Du Pont, and Emily's double, Lady Blanche. For a related argument to Favret's, see Clery's discussion of Radcliffe's use of epigraphs (*Women's Gothic*, 59). Ellen Arnold, Battaglia, and Frank all argue, by contrast, for the "transgressive" aspects and "suggestive power" of the poems in *Udolpho*, and for their value as "counter-text," linked to a "feminine" way of knowing, and an "essential element of Radcliffe's narrative technique" (Arnold, "Deconstructing the Patriarchal Palace: Ann Radcliffe's Poetry in *The Mysteries of Udolpho*," *Women and Language* 19.2 [Fall 1996] *Proquest*, web. December 9, 2004; Battaglia, " 'Pieces of Poetry'," 143; Frank, "Fairy Time," 103).

57. Charlotte Smith, *Desmond*, ed. Antje Blank and Janet Todd (Hamilton, ON: Broadview, 2001), 192, 334, 244, 243.
58. Smith, *Desmond*, 235–41, 243, 250.
59. Smith, *Desmond*, 241.
60. As Olivia Murphy comments, Jane Austen integrates the traces of her literary influences deep within her texts in a way that "renders them deliberately obscure or ambivalent" (Murphy, *Jane Austen the Reader: The Artist as Critic* [Basingstoke: Palgrave, 2013], 93). This does not, however, as Murphy assumes, make her allusive strategies entirely distinct from that of her contemporaries.
61. Jane Austen, *Northanger Abbey*, ed. Barbara M. Benedict and Deirdre La Faye (Cambridge: Cambridge University Press, 2006), 7.
62. Jane Austen, *Persuasion*, ed. Janet Todd and Antje Blank (Cambridge: Cambridge University Press, 2006), 90.
63. Jane Austen, *Mansfield Park*, ed. John Wiltshire (Cambridge: Cambridge University Press, 2005), 183.
64. Austen, *Persuasion*, 91.
65. William Collins, "An Ode on the Popular Superstitions of the Highlands of Scotland, Considered as the Subject of Poetry," *The Poems of Gray, Collins, and Goldsmith*, ed. Roger Lonsdale (London: Longman, 1969), lines 16–17.
66. Barbauld, "Mrs. Radcliffe," viii. Barbauld selects the "Song to a Spirit" and "The Sea Nymph" for particular praise as "exquisitely sweet and fanciful," while Coleridge quotes "The Sea Nymph" in full across three pages (Barbauld, "Mrs. Radcliffe," vii; Coleridge, *Critical Review*, 369–71). See Frank for an in-depth discussion of Radcliffe's association of Emily's voice with that of Ariel ("Fairy Time," 108–9).

67. Gary Kelly, *English Fiction of the Romantic Period, 1789–1830* (London: Longman, 1989), 54. Radcliffe, showing her roots in the eighteenth century, understands the lyric – in Romanticism regarded as the most inward of literary practices – as that which opens up solitude to the communal. As Jonathan Culler has shown, definitions of the lyric such as M. H. Abrams' influential one, that a lyric is "any fairly short, nonnarrative poem presenting a single speaker who expresses a state of mind or a process of thought and feeling," immediately become problematic when put into contact with lyrics whose voice is not individualized, or which participate in a bardic tradition (M. H. Abrams, *A Glossary of Literary Terms*, 4th edn. [New York: Holt, 1981], 249, as quoted in Culler, "Changes in the Study of the Lyric," *Lyric Poetry: Beyond New Criticism*, ed. Chaviva Hošek and Patricia Parker [Ithaca: Cornell University Press, 1985], 38–54).

68. Battaglia, " 'Pieces of Poetry'," 148.

69. Pinch, *Fits of Passion*, 121.

70. Blackwell, "The Gothic," 151.

71. Starr writes of the "potential for *disruption* involved in the use of poetry in prose" (*Lyric Generations*, 133); Rowland that poetry within 1790s novels in general teaches "readers how poetry fits into the rest of what one does – poetry as the experience of intense emotion that *interrupts* the business of living" ("Romantic Poetry," 132); and Frank, more specifically, that "The poems, which repeatedly *interrupt* the narrative flow of *The Romance of the Forest* and *The Mysteries of Udolpho*, would seem to be very much at odds with the heavily plot-driven forward momentum of Gothic" ("Fairy Time," 103). Melissa Sodeman argues that quotations and landscape descriptions in Smith's novels tend to "*arrest* narrative progress and to forestall the forward march of plot" ("Charlotte Smith's Literary Exile," English Literary History 76.1 [2009]: 140). (Emphasis added in all cases).

72. Of course *Udolpho* may simply show us that as readers of novels we are actually just more interested in the tyranny and tortures of Montoni's realm, than in the more liberatory meditations that frame the terrors of the Udolpho section. The obsessive fascination with this section of the novel in criticism of *Udolpho* for so many years would certainly suggest this. Radcliffe may, inadvertently, show that as readers we are like Montoni, or the controller of a gothic plot, in our interest in (obsession with, addiction to) power rather than community, to speed rather than more leisurely, and perhaps in some sense more difficult, reflective experience.

73. William Wordsworth, Preface (1800), *Lyrical Ballads 1798 and 1800*, ed. Michael Gamer and Dahlia Porter (Peterborough, ON: Broadview, 2008), 177.

74. Castle, *Female Thermometer*, 123.
75. Miranda Burgess, "On Being Moved: Sympathy, Mobility, and Narrative Form," *Poetics Today* 32.2 (Summer 2011): 308.
76. Wordsworth, Preface, 176–7.
77. Burgess, "On Being Moved," 311.

4   "Take, O World! Thy Much Indebted Tear!"

1. Mary Wollstonecraft, *Letters Written During a Short Residence in Sweden, Norway, and Denmark*, ed. Ingrid Horrocks (Peterborough, ON: Broadview, 2013), 57. Hereafter cited parenthetically in text.
2. Harriet Guest, *Small Change: Women, Learning, Patriotism, 1750–1810* (Chicago: University of Chicago Press, 2000), 305.
3. Sara Mills, "Written on the Landscape: Mary Wollstonecraft's *Letters Written During a Short Residence in Sweden, Norway and Denmark*," *Romantic Geographies: Discourses of Travel, 1775–1844*, ed. Amanda Gilroy (Manchester: Manchester University Press, 2000), 31. The brilliant figurative mobility of Wollstonecraft's reveries in *A Short Residence*, as well as their link to literal walks, is a well-covered critical territory. See, in particular, Mary A. Favret, "Traveling with Mary Wollstonecraft," *The Cambridge Companion to Mary Wollstonecraft*, ed. Claudia L. Johnson (Cambridge: Cambridge University Press, 2002), 214–17.
4. Ann Radcliffe, *The Mysteries of Udolpho*, ed. Bonamy Dobree (Oxford: Oxford University Press, 1998), 179.
5. *The Tempest* in *The Norton Shakespeare*, ed. Stephen Greenblatt (New York: Norton, 1997), 1.2.191–4.
6. Paul de Man, "Intentional Structure of the Romantic Image," *The Rhetoric of Romanticism* (New York: Columbia University Press, 1984), 14.
7. A survey of *A Short Residence* focused on identifying passages in which dashes proliferate produces a virtual compendium of the most critically discussed and influential passages in the text as a whole, including Wollstonecraft's meditations on death in Letter VII, her most engaged landscape descriptions such as that quoted above from Letter VIII, and the description of the cataract above Frederikstad in Letter XV. I have made this argument about Wollstonecraft's use of punctuation in *A Short Residence* at more length in, Ingrid Horrocks, "'——Pugh!': Re-Reading Punctuation through Wollstonecraft's *Letters Written During a Short Residence*," *Women's Writing* 21.4 (2014): 488–508. This argument draws in particular on the work of Janine Barchas, *Graphic Design, Print Culture, and the Eighteenth-Century Novel* (Cambridge: Cambridge University Press, 2003); and, Kathryn Sutherland, *Jane Austen's Textual Lives: From Aeschylus to Bollywood* (Oxford: Oxford University Press, 2005).

8. Mitzi Myers, "Sensibility and the 'Walk of Reason': Mary Wollstonecraft's Literary Reviews as Cultural Critique," *Sensibility in Transformation: Creative Resistance to Sentiment from the Augustans to the Romantics*, ed. Syndy M. Conger (Rutherford: Fairleigh Dickinson University Press, 1990), 132–3.

9. Mary Wollstonecraft, *A Vindication of the Rights of Woman* (1792), *A Vindication of the Rights of Men and a Vindication of the Rights of Woman*, ed. D. L. Macdonald and Kathleen Scherf (Peterborough, ON: Broadview, 1997), 237–40.

10. Favret, "Traveling with Mary Wollstonecraft," 209.

11. See, for example, Peter Adey, *Mobility* (London: Routledge, 2010), 85–8.

12. For moments of summary of this aspect of Favret's argument, see Favret, "Traveling with Mary Wollstonecraft," 219; and Favret, *Romantic Correspondence: Women, Politics and the Fiction of Letters* (Cambridge: Cambridge University Press, 1993), 111 and 115.

13. The emphasis on the rhetorical performance of the text that is a feature of much criticism of *A Short Residence* is exemplified in recent Bakhtinian readings. Christine Chaney, for instance, writes that Wollstonecraft "models the 'rational creature' of her polemical texts from the moment she hits the beach in Gothenburg and combines the powerfully emotional discourse of her self-narration with the ideological persuasiveness of an ethical appeal" (Chaney, "The Rhetorical Strategies of 'Tumultuous Emotions': Wollstonecraft's *Letters Written in Sweden*," *Journal of Narrative Theory* 34.3 [2004]: 288). See also Erinç Özdemir, "Hidden Polemic in Wollstonecraft's *Letters from Norway*: A Bakhtinian Reading," *Studies in Romanticism* 47.3 (2008): 321–49. An exception to this critical emphasis on the success of *A Short Residence* is to be found in the work of Katherine Turner, who presents a brief reading of the text based on an argument that it is "more illuminating to explore how the *Letters* actually describe and embody failure, of a genre and of a set of cultural beliefs" (*British Travel Writers in Europe, 1750–1800: Authorship, Gender and National Identity* (Aldershot: Ashgate, 2001), 229.

14. William Godwin, *Memoirs of the Author of a Vindication of the Rights of Woman* (1798), ed. Pamela Clemit and Gina Luria Walker (Peterborough, ON: Broadview, 2001), 95.

15. William Godwin, Preface, *Posthumous Works of the Author of a Vindication of the Rights of Woman*, vol. 3 (London: 1798).

16. Favret and Elizabeth A. Bohls first performed the important task of shifting readings of *A Short Residence* away from equating its persona simply with a recognizable biographical self. Favret reads *A Short Residence* as a performative text forged from an interplay between intimacy and publicity by the end of which Wollstonecraft performs for her public rather than for any

particular "you" (*Romantic Correspondence*, 96–132). Bohls persuasively argues for *A Short Residence* as an anti-Burkean, "politically motivated revision of aesthetic discourse," which continues the work Wollstonecraft had begun in her *Rights of Men* (*Women Travel Writers and the Language of Aesthetics, 1716–1818* [Cambridge: Cambridge University Press, 1995], 141, and see also 140–69).

17. Favret, *Romantic Correspondence*; Gregory Dart, *Rousseau, Robespierre and English Romanticism* (Cambridge: Cambridge University Press, 1999); Guest, *Small Change*; Saba Bahar, *Mary Wollstonecraft's Social and Aesthetic Philosophy: "An Eve to Please Me"* (Basingstoke: Palgrave, 2002); Deborah Weiss, "Suffering, Sentiment, and Civilization: Pain and Politics in Mary Wollstonecraft's *Short Residence*," *Studies in Romanticism* 45.2 (2006): 199–221. On Wollstonecraft's reimagining of the value of the emotions, see also John Whale, *Imagination under Pressure, 1789–1832: Aesthetics, Politics and Utility* (Cambridge: Cambridge University Press, 2000), and for this strand in Wollstonecraft's work more generally, Julie A. Carlson, *England's First Family of Writers: Mary Wollstonecraft, William Godwin, Mary Shelley* (Baltimore: Johns Hopkins University Press, 2007), especially 30–40.

18. Weiss, "Suffering, Sentiment, and Civilization"; Horrocks, Introduction, *A Short Residence*, 33–42. Wollstonecraft came to travel writing after extensive work as a reviewer of travels for the *Analytical Review*, during which she developed a theory for the deliberate, rhetorical use of the first person in travel writing (Horrocks, "Creating an 'insinuating interest': Mary Wollstonecraft's Travel Reviews and *A Short Residence*," *Studies in Travel Writing* 19.1 [2015], 1–15).

19. Laurence Sterne, *A Sentimental Journey through France and Italy* (1768), *A Sentimental Journey and Other Writings*, new edn., ed. Ian Jack and Tim Parnell (Oxford: Oxford University Press, 2003), 70.

20. Henry MacKenzie, *The Man of Feeling* (1771), ed. Brian Vickers (London: Oxford University Press, 1967), 33.

21. Wollstonecraft, *A Vindication of the Rights of Men*, ed. Macdonald and Scherf, 45, 39, 95.

22. G. J. Barker-Benfield, *The Culture of Sensibility: Sex and Society in Eighteenth-Century Britain* (Chicago: University of Chicago Press, 1992); and see also, for example, Claudia L. Johnson, *Equivocal Beings: Politics, Gender and Sentimentality in the 1790s, Wollstonecraft, Radcliffe, Burney, Austen* (Chicago: University of Chicago Press, 1995).

23. Bahar, *Wollstonecraft's Philosophy*, 145.

24. Weiss, "Suffering, Sentiment, and Civilization," 202–3, 209–16; see also Bahar, *Wollstonecraft's Philosophy*, 146–7. As Guest points out, Wollstonecraft is also building on the ways in which the language of sensibility has been transformed by women writers of the 1770s and 1780s (*Small Change*, 291).

25. Weiss, "Suffering, Sentiment, and Civilization," 218.
26. Bahar, *Wollstonecraft's Philosophy*, 166. This passage forms a stark contrast to the moments in *A Short Residence* when the traveler assumes a voice closer to that of the *Vindications*, as, for instance, when she comments on the "total want of chastity in the lower class of women" and how this renders them unfit even to be wet nurses (70).
27. Wollstonecraft, *A Vindication of the Rights of Woman*, ed. Macdonald and Scherf, 101.
28. As Weiss has argued, in *A Short Residence* reason and feeling are brought into an intimate relationship not seen previously in Wollstonecraft's work so that feeling, rather than being opposed to reason, is now made productive of the deepest reasoning (Weiss, "Suffering, Sentiment, and Civilization," see especially 220).
29. Dart, *Rousseau*, 131, see also especially 122–23, 136; Janet Todd, *Mary Wollstonecraft: A Revolutionary Life* (London: Weidenfel, 2000), 303; Weiss, "Suffering, Sentiment, and Civilization," 208; Chaney, "Rhetorical Strategies," 277–303.
30. Johnson, *Equivocal Beings*, 2.
31. Wil Verhoeven, *Gilbert Imlay: Citizen of the World* (London: Pickering, 2008), 189.
32. The complicated commercial back story of *A Short Residence*, which goes unmentioned in the published text and was excised from the private letters upon publication, is now well rehearsed. See Per Nyström, *Mary Wollstonecraft's Scandinavian Journey*, trans. George R. Otter (Gothenburg: Kungl. Vetenskaps, 1980), 18–32; Richard Holmes, Introduction, *A Short Residence in Sweden, Norway and Denmark, by Mary Wollstonecraft; and, Memoirs of the Author of "The Rights of Woman," by William Godwin* (London: Penguin, 1987), 21–6; Todd, *Mary Wollstonecraft*, 303–50; Lyndall Gordon, *Mary Wollstonecraft: A New Genus* (London: Little, Brown, 2005), 232–37, 256–81; and, Verhoeven, *Gilbert Imlay*.
33. Biographical work seeking to account for the darkening in the tone as *A Short Residence* progresses also assigns importance to letters Wollstonecraft received from Imlay on her return from Norway to Sweden. These letters effectively put an end to their relationship by informing her that he would not be joining her in Hamburg as planned (Todd, *Mary Wollstonecraft*, 340; Gordon, *Mary Wollstonecraft*, 270). Todd also discusses an earlier batch of five letters received in Tønsberg before Wollstonecraft set out for Risør (333). For Godwin's important original account of this correspondence, see his *Memoirs*, 94–6. This information is gathered from Wollstonecraft's responses as Imlay's own letters have been lost.

34. Favret locates the crucial turning point in *A Short Residence* in this letter at the moment at which the letter writer "confesses that the movement of fancy incapacitates her," and as a result, according to Favret's account which I depart from at this point, "abandons her flights and concentrates more on the worldly movements that keep her restless – especially economics and war" ("Traveling with Mary Wollstonecraft," 219). See also Guest, *Small Change*, 308–9.

35. Mary Wollstonecraft "To Gilbert Imlay" [September 6, (1795)], Letter 201, *Collected Letters of Mary Wollstonecraft*, 320. Echoed in *A Short Residence*, 120.

36. Mary Wollstonecraft "To Gilbert Imlay" August 26, [1795], Letter 200, *Collected Letters of Mary Wollstonecraft*, 319. In a similar way, when the eponymous heroine of Wollstonecraft's *Mary* returns to England as a "forlorn wanderer," she looks around only to find that "her affections were not attracted to any particular part of the Island" (130).

37. Ann Radcliffe, *A Journey Made in the Summer of 1794, through Holland and the Western Frontier of Germany* (Dublin: 1795), 369–70.

38. Mary Wollstonecraft, *The Wrongs of Woman, or Maria* (1798), ed. Michelle Faubert (Peterborough, ON: Broadview, 2012), 248. Hereafter cited parenthetically in text. In *The Wrongs of Woman*, a condition of peculiarly female homelessness which forces one to be constantly and painfully on the move even within one's own country reaches a new level of violent resonance. Before being imprisoned in the madhouse Maria is "hunted, like an infected beast" about London, much as Burney's Juliet would be in *The Wanderer*. Independence for Maria's working-class counterpart, Jemima, is reduced to "choosing the street in which I should wander": as a prostitute she nightly experiences a brutalized version of the episodic erotic encounters key to texts such as Sterne's *A Sentimental Journey* (1768) and Mackenzie's *The Man of Feeling* (1771) (*The Wrongs of Woman*, 266, 196).

39. Wollstonecraft, *A Vindication of the Rights of Woman*, ed. Macdonald and Scherf, 121.

40. Dart, *Rousseau*, 131.

41. Johnson, *Equivocal Beings*, 60.

42. In a letter to her friend, Ruth Barlow, Wollstonecraft exclaimed, "The French will carry all before them – but, my God, how many victims fall beneath the sword and the Guillotine! – My blood runs cold, and I sicken at thoughts of a Revolution which costs so much blood and bitter tears" (Mary Wollstonecraft "To Ruth Barlow" [July 8, (17)94], Letter 150, *Collected Letters of Mary Wollstonecraft*, 255).

43. Samuel Johnson's *Dictionary* quoted in Kevis Goodman, " 'Uncertain Disease': Nostalgia, Pathologies of Motion, Practices of Reading," *Studies in*

Romanticism 49.2 (Summer 2010): 205. Johnson uses a quotation from Goldsmith to exemplify the workings of the condition.

44. Turner, *British Travel Writers*, 232.

45. Jean-Jacques Rousseau, *Reveries of the Solitary Walker* (1782), trans. Peter France (Harmondsworth: Penguin, 1979), 107.

46. In the Fifth Walk, so evidently influential on the releasing reveries in Wollstoneraft's early letters, Rousseau defines the specific conditions that make reverie possible (or impossible): "The heart must be at peace and its calm untroubled by any passion," he writes, before modifying this statement using a metaphor of movement: "There must be neither a total calm nor too much movement, but a steady and moderate motion, with no jolts or breaks" (*Reveries*, 89).

47. Weiss, "Suffering, Sentiment, and Civilization," especially 217; Bahar, *Wollstonecraft's Philosophy*, 166, see also, in particular 145–54.

48. Bahar, *Wollstonecraft's Philosophy*, 8, 154.

49. On the dismantling of hierarchies of seeing in women's travel writing I am thinking here of work like Bohls, *Women Travel Writers*; Labbe, *Romantic Visualities: Landscape, Gender, and Romanticism* (Basingstoke: Macmillan, 1998); and Elizabeth A. Dolan, *Seeing Suffering in Women's Literature of the Romantic Era* (Aldershot: Ashgate, 2008).

50. *King Lear* (Conflated Text) 3.4.29–33. Wollstonecraft also quotes from this speech in Letter XV (133).

51. John Urry, *Mobilities* (Cambridge: Polity Press, 2007), 49, and see also 24.

52. Susan Sontag, *Regarding the Pain of Others* (New York: Farrar, 2003), 101–2.

53. It is worth noting that Jemima is only able to extend her thoughts beyond her own situation until she discovers the severity of that situation: "till I discovered, with horror – ah! what horror! – that I was with child" (*The Wrongs of Woman*, 194).

54. See Bohls for a discussion of how Wollstonecraft's "contradictory mixture of liberal concern and bourgeois condescension" disintegrates by Letter XVI. Bohls argues that Wollstonecraft's reintegration of the bodily into the language of aesthetics collapses in these moments, which reveal a disgust of the body (*Women Travel Writers*, 156). Even more problematically, such moments hardly credit the Norwegians that Wollstonecraft views with being human.

55. Wollstonecraft, *Hints*, No 31, in *A Vindication of the Rights of Men and A Vindication of the Rights of Woman*, ed. Macdonald and Scherf, 415.

56. Susan Wolfson summarizes Wollstonecraft's mode of critique as, "a resistant reading of argument and its ideological grain; sharp attention to language and its cultural information; and a reflection on herself as both victim and theorist of male prejudice" (*Romantic Interactions: Social Being and the Turns of Literary Action* [Baltimore, Johns Hopkins University Press, 2010], 69).

57. Wollstonecraft, *Hints*, No 31, 415.

58. See, for instance, Wollstonecraft's contention that "the grand end of [women's] exertions should be to unfold their own faculties," *A Vindication of the Rights of Woman*, 134.

59. See, for example, Mary Wollstonecraft, Review of *A View of England towards the Close of the Eighteenth Century, Analytical Review* 11 (February 1791) in *The Works of Mary Wollstonecraft*, ed. Janet Todd and Marilyn Butler, vol. 7 (London: Pickering, 1989): 347.

60. Mary Wollstonecraft, "On Poetry, and Our Relish for the Beauties of Nature," *Works of Mary Wollstonecraft*, vol. 7:7–11. In "On Poetry," Wollstonecraft criticizes modern writers for producing images that come not from "sensations" connected with the world but are "servilely copied" "selected from books." We might say, she accuses them of being merely readers, quoters of old images and emotions rather than writers – makers of new ones (9). For a discussion of the development of Wollstonecraft's idea of the "imagination" in this essay, see Harriet Devine Jump, "'A Kind of Witchcraft': Mary Wollstonecraft and the Poetic Imagination," *Women's Writing* 4.2 (1997): 235–45; and on Wollstonecraft's influence on William Wordsworth, see Wolfson, *Romantic Interactions*, 60–1, 87–8.

61. Mary Wollstonecraft, *Mary, A Fiction* (1788), ed. Michelle Faubert (Peterborough ON: Broadview, 2012), 75. Barbara Taylor links this to Wollstonecraft's commitment to female personal authenticity at odds with the masquerade of femininity to please men (*Mary Wollstonecraft and the Feminist Imagination* [Cambridge: Cambridge University Press, 2003], 33).

62. Favret, *Romantic Correspondence*, 115; see also 110–16. In "Traveling with Mary Wollstonecraft," Favret acknowledges that "luminaries" such as Milton, Shakespeare and Young, may "undermine the writer's sovereignty while illuminating her path" (217).

63. Susan Wolfson, "Mary Wollstonecraft and the Poets," *Cambridge Companion to Wollstonecraft*, ed. Claudia L. Johnson (Cambridge: Cambridge University Press, 2002), 164. See also Claudia Johnson for a discussion of the "pervasive intertextual presence" of *Hamlet* in *The Wrongs of Woman*, where she writes "Hamlet's alienation is Maria's birthright" (*Equivocal Beings*, 62). The practices of quotation which these critics describe are subtly different from Wollstonecraft's habit, which is more familiar from her two *Vindications*, of direct critique through quotation and close reading.

64. *The Tempest*, in particular, was one of Wollstonecraft's favorite Shakespeare plays. See the prominent role she gives it in her anthology, *The Female Reader: Or Miscellaneous Pieces, in Prose and Verse* (1789) (*Works of Mary Wollstonecraft*, vol 4.).

65. Other referential moments are less explicit in their sourcing but just as much a feature of *A Short Residence*. A number of critics have shown the direct and important influence of Rousseau's *Reveries of the Solitary Walker* (1782) on the passages of meditative reverie in *A Short Residence*, in particular his Fifth Walk. This correspondence would have been unmistakable to anyone familiar with Rousseau's work, and subtle differences would also have been evident to those prepared to read closely, as Wollstonecraft tends ultimately to shift away from Rousseau's alienated mode and to look back toward society. For discussions, see Favret, *Romantic Correspondence*, 104–7; John Whale, "Death in the Face of Nature: Self, Society and Body in Wollstonecraft's *Letters Written in Sweden, Norway, and Denmark*," *Romanticism* 1.2 (1995), 177–92. ; and Dart, *Rousseau*, 133–6.

66. [Wollstonecraft], *A Vindication of the Rights of Men, in a Letter to the Right Honourable Edmund Burke; Occasioned by his Reflections on the Revolution in France*, 1st edn. (London, 1790), 149–50.

67. Bahar, *Wollstonecraft's Philosophy*, 163.

68. Mary Wollstonecraft "To Everina Wollstonecraft" March 24, [1787], Letter 55, *Collected Letters of Mary Wollstonecraft*, 113; see also Mary Wollstonecraft "To the Reverend Henry Dyson Gabell" [c. early 1787], Letter 50, 103; and "To Gilbert Imlay" June 29, [1795], Letter 189, 307.

69. *Hamlet, The Norton Shakespeare*, 2.2.239–40.

70. Mary Wollstonecraft "To Everina Wollstonecraft" November 7, [1787], Letter 67, *Collected Letters of Mary Wollstonecraft*, 140; "To Mary Hays?" [c. April 1797], Letter 322, *Collected Letters of Mary Wollstonecraft*, 410.

71. Frances Burney, *The Wanderer; or, Female Difficulties* (1814), ed. Margaret Doody, Robert L. Mack, and Peter Sabor (Oxford: Oxford University Press, 1991), 873.

72. She casts herself as Cassandra in *A Short Residence*, 174; and Sisyphus in Mary Wollstonecraft "To Gilbert Imlay" [January 1, 1794], Letter 136, *Collected Letters of Mary Wollstonecraft*, 238.

73. Wollstonecraft, *Mary*, 130.

74. MacKenzie, *Man of Feeling*, 34; Sterne, *Sentimental Journey*, 97.

75. [Wollstonecraft], *A Vindication of the Rights of Men*, 1st ed. (London, 1790), 144–5.

76. Mary Wollstonecraft "To Everina Wollstonecraft" March 22, [1797], Letter 314, *Collected Letters of Mary Wollstonecraft*, 404; *Mary*, 130.

77. Mary Wollstonecraft "To George Dyson," [May 16, 1797], Letter 325, *Collected Letters of Mary Wollstonecraft*, 412. In her letter, Wollstonecraft mentions "yours and Mr G's criticism," and she transcribed a copy for Godwin (412).

78. The reviewer's claim in *The Monthly Mirror* that "we cannot … be charged with intrusion on her private sorrows, since her work was designed for publication before it was penned," implies that *A Short Residence* is an almost indecent *publication* of *private* sorrows. All the reviews of *A Short Residence* display an anxiety about the proper limits of sympathy. The *Monthly Review*'s oddly negative configuration, that readers "will seldom see reason to censure her feelings, and will never be inclined to withhold their sympathy," hints, or perhaps threatens, that there are some feelings that should not be sympathized with; while the review in the *British Critic*, after admitting that often the reader will find "their hearts beat in unison with that of the writer," considers it all the more its "duty" to censure a book in which "a woman so far outsteps her proper sphere." Only the *Analytical Review* suggests that the most appropriate response to the plight of the writer would be to deplore "that state of society" which made her sufferings possible, and thus credits her private sufferings with general importance (Reviews in *Monthly Mirror* 1 [March 1796]; *Monthly Review* 20 [July 1796]; *British Critic* 7 [June 1796]; *Analytical Review* 22 [January–June 1796], rpt. in *Mary Wollstonecraft and the Critics: 1788–2001*, ed. Harriet Jump Devine, vol. I (London: Routledge, 2003), 153, 157, 142, 146–7, 140). See Favret for a related discussion of the afterlife of *A Short Residence*, and in particular the problem of the female imagination being too marketable (*Romantic Correspondence*, 128–32).
79. Mary Wollstonecraft "To Gilbert Imlay," August 26, [1795], Letter 200, *Collected Letters of Mary Wollstonecraft*, 319.
80. David Simpson, *Wordsworth, Commodification and Social Concern: The Poetics of Modernity* (Cambridge: Cambridge University Press, 2009), 34.

5 "No Motive of Choice"

1. William Hazlitt, Review of *The Wanderer; or, Female Difficulties*, by Madame D'Arblay [Frances Burney], *Edinburgh Review* 24 (1815): 337; George Gordon Byron "To John Murray" [July 24, 1814], *Byron's Letters and Journals*, ed. Leslie Marchand, vol. 4 (London: Murray, 1975), 146. On the contemporary response to *The Wanderer*, see Margaret Doody, *Frances Burney: The Life in the Works* (New Brunswick: Rutgers University Press, 1988), 332–5; and Claudia L. Johnson, *Equivocal Beings: Politics, Gender, and Sentimentality in the 1790s: Wollstonecraft, Radcliffe, Burney, Austen* (Chicago: University of Chicago Press, 1995), 166–7, 170, 180–2. Jocelyn Harris also makes an argument for Jane Austen's rebuttal of *The Wanderer*'s most critical reviews in *Persuasion* (*A Revolution Almost Beyond Expression: Jane Austen's Persuasion* [Newark: University of Delaware Press, 2007], 20–7).

2. See Doody, *Frances Burney*, 332; Johnson, *Equivocal Beings*, 166–7; and Robert L. Mack, "The Novelist and the Critics: Frances Burney's Manuscript Corrections and Additions to *The Wanderer; or, Female Difficulties*," *Journal X: A Journal in Culture and Criticism* 9.1 (2004): 24.

3. Mary Wollstonecraft "To George Dyson" [May 16, 1797], Letter 325, *The Collected Letters of Mary Wollstonecraft*, ed. Janet Todd (New York: Columbia University Press, 2003), 412.

4. Johnson, *Equivocal Beings*, 167. Along with work by Doody, Mack, and Johnson, early work in the rehabilitation of *The Wanderer* includes Kristina Straub, *Divided Fictions: Fanny Burney and Feminine Strategy* (Lexington: University Press of Kentucky, 1987) and Julia Epstein, *The Iron Pen: Frances Burney and the Politics of Women's Writing* (Madison: University of Wisconsin Press, 1989).

5. Claire Harman, *Fanny Burney: A Biography* (London: Harper, 2000), 328.

6. Frances Burney, *The Wanderer; or, Female Difficulties* (1814), ed. Margaret Doody, Robert L. Mack, and Peter Sabor (Oxford: Oxford University Press, 1991), 156. Hereafter cited parenthetically in text.

7. Kirsty Carpenter, *Refugees of the French Revolution: Émigrés in London, 1789–1802* (Basingstoke: Macmillan, 1999), 134; Toby R. Benis, *Romantic Diasporas: French Émigrés, British Convicts, and Jews* (New York: Palgrave, 2009), 60.

8. Julia Epstein, "Marginality in Frances Burney's Novels," *The Cambridge Companion to the Eighteenth-Century Novel*, ed. John Richetti (Cambridge: Cambridge University Press, 1996), 207.

9. Andrea Henderson, *Romanticism and the Painful Pleasures of Modern Life* (Cambridge: Cambridge University Press, 2008), 114–15; David Simpson, *Romanticism and the Question of the Stranger* (Chicago: University of Chicago Press, 2013), 209.

10. Simpson, *The Question of the Stranger*, 229; and see also Benis, *Romantic Diasporas*.

11. Frances Burney, *The Wanderer; or Female Difficulties* (London 1814), First Edition, with holograph manuscript corrections for the Third Edition (never published) in the Berg Collection, New York Public Library: leaves opposite vols. 2.263, 3.48, 4.175, 4.193, 4.227.

12. John Urry, *Mobilities* (Cambridge: Polity Press, 2007), 6.

13. The novel's reticence is one of its most discussed features. See, for example, Deidre Lynch, *The Economy of Character: Novels, Market Culture, and the Business of Inner Meaning* (Chicago: University of Chicago Press, 1998), 200; Helen Thompson, "How *The Wanderer* Works: Reading Burney and Bourdieu," *ELH* 68.4 (2001): 965–89; and Suzie Park, "Resisting Demands for Depth in *The Wanderer*," *European Romantic Review* 15.2 (2004): 307–15.

14. Frances Burney, *Cecilia; or, Memoirs of an Heiress* (1782), ed. Peter Sabor and Margaret Doody (Oxford: Oxford University Press, 1988), 5. The identity of the heroines of Burney's earlier novels, however, is neither set nor simple. Questions about identity have long been at the forefront of scholarship on all Burney's novels, in large part due to the many performances and misunderstandings she stages which ask us to pay attention to identity's constructedness.

15. Benis argues that if we read *The Wanderer* specifically as a novel of the emigration, then Juliet's plight becomes specifically historicized in a way that explains why she must withhold information. This does not fully account, though, for why the information is withheld from the reader (Benis, *Romantic Diasporas*, 61–3).

16. Urry, *Mobilities*, 194–8.

17. Jesse Molesworth, *Chance and the Eighteenth-Century Novel: Realism, Probability, Magic* (Cambridge: Cambridge University Press, 2010), 171. Sandra Macpherson draws on Franco Moretti and Georg Lukacs' models when describing the novel's supposed "adventure of interiority," in which the content of the novel is "the story of the soul that goes to find itself, that seeks adventures in order to be proved and tested by them, and, by proving itself, to find its own essence" (*Harm's Way: Tragic Responsibility and the Novel Form* [Baltimore: Johns Hopkins University Press, 2010], 6).

18. See also the moment at which Juliet decides to flee Brighton (*The Wanderer*, 364).

19. *The Wanderer*, holograph corrections to Berg edition, leaf opp. 37; Mack, "The Novelist and the Critics," 31.

20. Carpenter, *Refugees*, 35–44; Quentin Bailey, *Wordsworth's Vagrants: Police, Prisons, and Poetry in the 1790s* (Farnham: Ashgate, 2011), 155.

21. Jeremy Bentham, "Outline of a Work Entitled Pauper Management Improved," *Annals of Agriculture* 30 (1798), 493, quoted in Bailey, *Wordsworth's Vagrants*, 156.

22. At one point in the novel two poor women help Juliet and offer her a place to stay, at which point the narrative comments that "often lonely travellers themselves, [the women] saw nothing in such a situation to excite distrust" (660). This lack of suspicion of the situation is an exception. In the sequence that precedes this scene in the novel, Juliet has been denied lodgings by both rich and poor as a result of being an "unknown traveller" (660).

23. This is, of course, complicated by the fact that Juliet, as an eloped wife, is potentially guilty of a legal crime.

24. Lynch, *Economy of Character*, 200.

25. For Thompson and Park, Burney's critique of the demand for depth is played out in the formal shape of the novel, so that Juliet's untold story becomes less important than the reticence that keeps it alive, revelation less important than the repeated actions that reveal and yet don't reveal. So, for example, while the end of the novel presents documents to prove Juliet's identity, it has already been withheld and revealed so many times that the notion of a fixed identity has come to seem unworkable (Thompson, "How *The Wanderer* Works," 987; Park, "Resisting Demands," 309).

26. See also, Jonathan Lamb, *The Things Things Say* (Princeton: Princeton University Press, 2011).

27. Frances Burney, *Diary and Letters of Madame D'Arblay (1788–1840)*, as edited by her niece Charlotte Barrett, with Preface and Notes by Austin Dobson, vol 3. (London: Macmillan, 1904–1905), 9, 43.

28. Burney, *The Wanderer*, holograph corrections to Berg edition, interleaf opp. Dedication. In only a very few instances does Burney actually cross out specific words within the original text. However, in the few instances when she does, these tend to be of embedded clauses which evoke contradictory emotions in close syntactic proximity, for example, "And here, ~~shocked, yet relieved, and happy, however forlorn~~, she remained," and "OFFENDED, indignant; ~~escaped, yet without safety; free, yet without refuge~~; Juliet hurried into the noble mansion" (1.67; 3.413). Mack notes, in his general assessment of the edits proposed in the Berg Collection's copy of *The Wanderer*, that "such coordinating conjunctions and conjunctive adverbs ... tend necessarily to qualify and delimit the novel's narrative prose, to retreat and to qualify meaning," while Burney's desire to edit them is "part of a clear desire on the part of the author to move her narrative forward at a swifter and less cluttered pace" (Mack, "The Novelist and the Critics," 33). I do not see Burney's intention as quite as clear cut as this.

29. For discussions of figurations of women as automaton in Burney's earlier novels, see Lynch (*Economy of Character*, 192–4) and Julie Park ("Pains and Pleasures of the Automaton: Frances Burney's Mechanics of Coming Out," *Eighteenth-Century Studies* 40.1 [2006]: 23–50). Thomas Macaulay wrote of Burney's own situation as the Queen's dresser, "The principle of the arrangement was, in short, simply this, that Frances Burney should become a slave, and should be rewarded by being made a beggar" (Macaulay, *Critical and Historical Essays Contributed to the Edinburgh Review*, vol. 2. [London: Longman, 1854], 300.)

30. Macaulay, *Critical and Historical Essays*, vol. 2:287, 315.

31. Alex Woloch, *The One Vs. The Many: Minor Characters and the Space of the Protagonist in the Novel* (Princeton: Princeton University Press, 2003). In her notes for revision, Burney indicates the need to reduce the space

taken up by minor characters, to the point of cutting whole chapters. This is particularly the case in the first two volumes, which feature a vast number of minor characters. Burney seems to have intended to omit most of the first six chapters of Book Four, for instance, which are dominated by the speeches of Mr. Giles Arbe (*The Wanderer*, holograph corrections to Berg edition).

32. Darryl Jones, "Radical Ambivalence: Frances Burney, Jacobinism, and the Politics of Romantic Fiction," *Women's Writing* 10.1 (2003): 19; Cathrine Frank, "Wandering Narratives and Wavering Conclusions: Irreconciliation in Frances Burney's *The Wanderer* and Walter Scott's *Waverley*," *European Romantic Review* 12.4 (2001): 438.

33. Johnson, *Equivocal Beings*, 168, 170; and see also, Sara Salih, "*Camilla* and *The Wanderer*," *Cambridge Companion to Frances Burney*, ed. Peter Sabor (Cambridge: Cambridge University Press, 2007): 39–53.

34. Mark R. Blackwell, "The Gothic: Moving in the World of Novels," *A Concise Companion to the Restoration and Eighteenth Century*, ed. Cynthia Wall (Malden: Blackwell, 2005), 155.

35. Mary Wollstonecraft, *The Wrongs of Woman, or Maria* (1798), ed. Michelle Faubert (Peterborough, ON: Broadview, 2012), 197.

36. On the standard itinerary, see Ian Ousby, *Englishman's England: Taste, Travel and the Rise of Tourism* (Cambridge: Cambridge University Press, 1990), especially 69.

37. Domestic tourism was intricately linked to a consolidation of British identity, and in the second half of the eighteenth century and on into the nineteenth visits to native scenery and to medieval rather than classical ruins became increasingly popular. See Susan Lamb, *Bringing Travel Home to England: Tourism, Gender, and Imaginative Literature in the Eighteenth Century* (Newark: University of Delaware Press, 2010); and Ousby, *Englishman's England*.

38. Robin Jarvis, *Romantic Writing and Pedestrian Travel* (Basingstoke: Macmillan, 1997), see especially 15, 28; Anne D. Wallace, *Walking, Literature, and English Culture: The Origins and Uses of the Peripatetic in the Nineteenth Century* (Oxford: Clarendon, 1993).

39. In the earlier sections of *The Wanderer*, Burney also depicts the underbelly of Brighton, itself a major tourist destination. In her enumeration of sites, Burney returns, albeit in a different style, to the mode of Evelina's account of the sites of London in her "town journal."

40. Frances Burney, "To Mrs. Phillips *and* The Lockes of Norbury Parke" [for August 1791], Letter 3, *The Journals and Letters of Fanny Burney (Madame D'Arblay)*, ed. Joyce Hemlow with Curtis D. Cecil and Althea Douglas., vol. 1 (Oxford: Clarendon, 1972), 18, 26.

41. Franco Moretti, *Graphs, Maps, Trees: Abstract Models for a Literary History* (London: Verso, 2005), 35.

42. Frances Burney, "To Mrs. Phillips *and* The Lockes of Norbury Parke" [for August 1791], Letter 3, *The Journals and Letters of Fanny Burney*, vol. 1:18.

43. [Frances Burney], By the Author of Evelina and Cecilia, *Brief Reflections Relative to the Emigrant French Clergy: Earnestly Submitted to the Humane Consideration of the Ladies of Great Britain* (London: Cadell, 1793), 3–4.

44. John Chandler, *Salisbury: History Around Us* (Salisbury: Hobnob Press, 2004).

45. For discussions of the range of objects of tourist enquiry and available discourses in this period, see Susan Lamb and Katherine Turner (Lamb, *Bringing Travel Home*, 101–18; Turner, *British Travel Writers in Europe, 1750–1800: Authorship, Gender and National Identity* [Aldershot: Ashgate, 2001], 49–51).

46. Mrs. [Hester Lynch] Thrale, *Thraliana: The Diary of Hester Lynch Thrale (Later Mrs. Piozzi)*, ed. Katharine C. Balderston (Oxford: Clarendon, 1942), 586.

47. Nigel Leask notes that the term curiosity "appears with almost mechanical regularity in travel writing throughout the period," denoting "an inclination to knowledge which will lead the observer to a rational, philosophical articulation" (Leask, *Curiosity and the Aesthetics of Travel Writing, 1770–1840* [Oxford: Oxford University Press, 2002], 4–5).

48. Edmund Burke defines curiosity in the first two lines of his treatise as "whatever desire we have for, or whatever pleasure we take in novelty" (*A Philosophical Enquiry into the Origin of Our Ideas of the Sublime and Beautiful* [1757], ed. James. T. Boulton [Notre Dame: University of Notre Dame Press, 1958], 31).

49. William Gilpin, "Essay on Picturesque Travel," *Three Essays: On Picturesque Beauty; on Picturesque Travel; and, on Sketching Landscape* (London: 1792), 47–8, *Eighteenth Century Collections Online* (*ECCO*), Gale, web, December 9, 2013. Gilpin had written about the New Forest in *Remarks on Forest Scenery* (London: 1791), *Eighteenth Century Collections Online* (*ECCO*), Gale, web, December 9, 2013.

50. See Thomson, *Sp*, lines 227–8, 210, 485.

51. Hester Thrale Piozzi, *Anecdotes of the Late Samuel Johnson, LL.D., During the Last Twenty Years of His Life*, ed. S. C. Roberts (Cambridge: Cambridge University Press, 1925), 66, quoted in Susan Lamb, *Bringing Travel Home*, 94.

52. The passage from *Camilla* continues, "A fine country, and diversified views, may soften even the keenest affliction of decided misfortune, and tranquillise the most gloomy sadness into resignation and composure; but suspense rejects the gentle palliative; ... exclusive in its despotism ... little short of torture"

(Frances Burney, *Camilla, or a Picture of Youth* [1796] [Oxford: Oxford University Press, 1972], 605).

53. The modesty of climbing a mere "hillock" is in line with the more reticent claims of the picturesque, which registered unease with the more elevated view of prospect writing from earlier in the eighteenth century (Malcolm Andrews, *The Search for the Picturesque: Landscape Aesthetics and Tourism in Britain, 1760–1800* [Aldershot: Scolar, 1989], 63). Meanwhile, the "aged oaks" Juliet "survey[s]" evoke an image of a timeless Britain, which at this moment promises to be more accommodating than the actual British people she has come into contact with have proven to be. In Alexander Pope's *Windsor Forest*, a view of "tow'ring oaks" is enough to make "future navies" appear (*Alexander Pope*, ed. Pat Rogers [Oxford: Oxford University Press, 1993], lines 219–20).

54. But as Claudia Johnson has pointed out in a different context, *The Wanderer* is a novel profoundly uncomfortable with such self-sufficiency. Harleigh calls it "desolate," and asks, using a somewhat punitive vocabulary, "who is permitted to act by the sole guidance of their own perceptions or notions?" (*The Wanderer*, 296). Within the novel more generally Elinor mistakenly desires self-sufficiency (Johnson, *Equivocal Beings*, 185).

55. Lynch, *Economy of Character*, 203.

56. Elizabeth A. Bohls, *Women Travel Writers and the Language of Aesthetics: 1716–1818* (Cambridge: Cambridge University Press, 1995), 149.

57. Wallace, *Walking*, 29. More generally, the simple act of walking is itself exposing, with its still strong associations with, "poverty, unrespectability, and possible criminal intent" (Jarvis, *Romantic Writing*, 22–3, and see also Wallace, *Walking*, 33).

58. Bohls, *Women Travel Writers*; Jacqueline M. Labbe, *Romantic Visualities: Landscape, Gender, and Romanticism* (Basingstoke: Macmillan 1998); Elizabeth A. Dolan, *Seeing Suffering in Women's Literature of the Romantic Era* (Aldershot: Ashgate, 2008).

59. Susan Lamb, *Bringing Travel Home*, 70; Epstein, "Marginality in Frances Burney's Novels," 202–9. In Lynch's account, Burney's heroines do not just risk being mistaken for other people in these locations but for objects of consumption (Lynch, *Economy of Character*, 165–86).

60. Frances Burney, *Evelina, or, a Young Lady's Entrance into the World. In a Series of Letters* (1779), ed. Susan Kubica Howard (Peterborough, ON: Broadview, 2000), 317–18, 359; *Camilla*, 608.

61. On the social implications of the "pausibility" of places, see Urry, *Mobilities*, 74–5. Urry discusses this idea only in relation to cities, despite the following section in his book being focused on leisure walking in the countryside.

62. Tracy Edgar Daugherty, *Narrative Techniques in the Novels of Fanny Burney* (New York: Peter Lang, 1989), 164–5, quoted in Tamara Wagner, "Nostalgia for Home or Homelands: Romantic Nationalism and the Indeterminate Narrative in Frances Burney's *The Wanderer*," *Cardiff Corvey: Reading the Romantic Text* 10 (June 2003), web. September 9, 2009: 51.

63. Mary Wollstonecraft, *A Vindication of the Rights of Woman (1792)*, in *A Vindication of the Rights of Men and A Vindication of the Rights of Woman*, ed. D. L. Macdonald and Kathleen Scherf (Peterborough, ON: Broadview, 1997), 239–40.

64. Doody, *Frances Burney*, 360.

65. *The Wanderer*, Berg edition, leaf opposite 4.339, at the end of Book Eight, Chapter 75.

66. See, for example, William Gilpin's *Observations on the Western Parts of England, Relative Chiefly to Picturesque Beauty* (London: 1798), *Eighteenth Century Collections Online (ECCO)*, Gale, web, December 9, 2013. Since the early eighteenth century, Wilton had been among half-a-dozen country houses that figured as major tourist attractions. According to Ousby, when one visitor, Mrs. Lybbe Powys, signed the visitor's book in 1776, she noted that 2324 people had already visited that year (Ousby, *Englishman's England*, 79).

67. Ann Radcliffe, *The Mysteries of Udolpho* (1794), ed. Bonamy Dobree (Oxford: Oxford University Press, 1998), 383.

68. "According to the conventional visual shorthand of paintings in the period, loose hair indicates female madness or sexual looseness . . . " (Susan Lamb, *Bringing Travel Home*, 174).

69. Susan Lamb, *Bringing Travel Home*, 123, drawing on Carole Fabricant, "The Literature of Domestic Tourism and the Public Consumption of Private Property," *The New Eighteenth Century: Theory, Politics, English Literature*, ed. Felicity Nussbaum and Laura Brown (New York: Methuen, 1987), 254–75; and Adrian Tinniswood, *A History of Country House Visiting: Five Centuries of Tourism and Taste* (Oxford: Blackwell, 1989).

70. Gilpin, *Observations on the Western Parts of England*, 102, 104–15.

71. Frances Burney "To Mrs. Phillips *and* The Lockes of Norbury Parke" [for August 1791], Letter 3, *The Journals and Letters of Fanny Burney*, vol. 1:22.

72. Burney is referring to the version of Anthony Van Dyke's *Children of Charles I (Group Portrait of Charles, Prince of Wales, James Duke of York and Princess Mary, the three eldest children of King Charles I and Henrietta Maria)*, still hung at Wilton House.

73. Gilpin, *Observations on the Western Parts of England*, 81.

74. Gilpin, *Observations on the Western Parts of England*, 83, 90.

75. Doody, *Frances Burney*, 363–5, 362–4.

76. Jonathan Lamb, *Preserving the Self in the South Seas, 1680–1840* (Chicago: University of Chicago Press, 2001), 111–12.
77. Jonathan Lamb, *Preserving the Self*, 12.
78. In the opening lines of *The Traveller*, Goldsmith's poet-speaker encounters a landscape not unlike Burney's Stonehenge: "Campania's plain forsaken lies, /A weary waste expanding to the skies" (*Tr*, 5–6).
79. Nicholas Rowe's *The Fair Penitent* (1703), ed. Malcolm Goldstein (London: Edward Arnold, 1969), 5.1.21.
80. Thomas Campbell, *Life of Mrs Siddons* (London: Edward Moxon, 1839), 97.
81. Fielding, *The History of Ophelia* (1760), ed. Peter Sabor (Peterborough, ON: Broadview, 2004), 155; Moser, "Adventures of Mohamet: The Wandering Sultan … Written in 1796," *The European Magazine and Monthly Review* 55 (January 1890 to June 1809): 9. Smith also quotes it in several of her novels, most notably in *The Banished Man* when the banished man of the title, D'Alonville, reflects on the cruel treatment of French emigrants in London (*The Banished Man, A Novel* vol. 2 [London: 1794], 87, *Eighteenth Century Collections Online* [*ECCO*], Gale, web, December 9, 2013).
82. Nicholas Roe, *The Politics of Nature: Wordsworth and Some Contemporaries* (Basingstoke: Macmillan, 1992), 36.
83. William Godwin, "The Original Manuscript Ending of the Novel," *Caleb Williams*, ed. Gary Handwerk and A. A. Markley (1794; Peterborough ON: Broadview, 2000), 442–3.
84. Doody, *Frances Burney*, 364; Johnson, *Equivocal Beings*, 186–8.
85. Radcliffe, *Udolpho*, 249.
86. The phrase "deep time" is from Doody (*Frances Burney*, 364).
87. Ann Radcliffe, "On the Supernatural in Poetry" (1826), rpt. *Gothic Readings: The First Wave, 1764–1840*, ed. Rictor Norton (London: Leicester University Press, 2000), 315.
88. Henderson, *Romanticism and the Painful Pleasures of Modern Life*.
89. Burke, *Sublime and the Beautiful*, 77.

Coda

1. William Wordsworth, *An Evening Walk* (1793), ed. James Averill (Ithaca: Cornell University Press, 1984), lines 97, 243–7, 300.
2. William Wordsworth, "The Female Vagrant" (1798), *Lyrical Ballads 1798 and 1800*, ed. Michael Gamer and Dahlia Porter (Peterborough, ON: Broadview, 2008), line 124.
3. Wordsworth, "The Female Vagrant," lines 262–70.

4. William Wordsworth, *The Excursion*, ed. Sally Bushell, James A. Butler, and Michael C. Jaye (Ithaca: Cornell University Press, 2007), Book One, lines 800–1.

5. Wordsworth, *The Excursion*, lines 1.944–5.

6. Mary A. Favret, *War at a Distance: Romanticism and the Making of Modern Wartime* (Princeton: Princeton University Press, 2010), 28.

7. Mary Wollstonecraft, Advertisement, *Letters Written During a Short Residence in Sweden, Norway, and Denmark* (1796), ed. Ingrid Horrocks (Peterborough, ON: Broadview, 2013), 51.

8. Robin Jarvis, *Romantic Writing and Pedestrian Travel* (Basingstoke: Macmillan, 1997), 95.

9. Wordsworth, "The Female Vagrant," line 2. This interlocutor never actually appears within the poem except through references like these, but within the context of *Lyrical Ballads*, so filled with meetings on the road, the reader is invited to imagine this poem as a version of one of these.

10. Favret, *War*, 28.

11. Jarvis, *Romantic Writing*, 96, 111.

12. Susan Wolfson, *Romantic Interactions: Social Being and the Turns of Literary Action* (Baltimore: Johns Hopkins University Press, 2010), 135.

13. Wordsworth, *The Excursion*, lines 1. 385–6, 462–3, 390–402.

14. Susan Wolfson, *The Questioning Presence: Wordsworth, Keats, and the Interrogative Mode in Romantic Poetry* (Ithaca: Cornell University Press, 1986), 102–3.

15. Wordsworth, *The Excursion*, lines 1.391 and 833.

16. On William Wordsworth's and Charlotte Smith's reading of each other, see Jacqueline M. Labbe, *Writing Romanticism: Charlotte Smith and William Wordsworth, 1784–1807* (Basingstoke: Palgrave, 2011), especially 12–14, 43–4, 58–61. Wordsworth visited Smith in 1791, and his copy of the 1789 edition of *Elegiac Sonnets* contained transcriptions of sonnets which did not appear until later editions, possibly transcribed during his visit (Labbe, *Writing Romanticism*, 12). On Wordsworth's reading of Wollstonecraft, see Duncan Wu, *Wordsworth's Reading 1770–1799* (New York: Cambridge University Press, 1993), 152–3. He certainly owned a copy of the 1802 edition of *A Short Residence*.

17. John Keats, *Letters of John Keats*, ed. Robert Gittings (Oxford: Oxford University Press, 1970), 214.

18. Paul D. Sheats, *The Making of Wordsworth's Poetry, 1785–1798* (Cambridge: Harvard University Press, 1973), 87, quoted in Wolfson, *Romantic Interactions* 309, footnote 26. On the timing of the poem's composition see Labbe, *Writing Romanticism*, 58.

19. Francis Jeffrey, *Contributions to the Edinburgh Review* (Philadelphia: Carey and Hart, 1846), 458, quoted in Alison Hickey *Impure Conceits: Rhetoric and*

Ideology in Wordsworth's "Excursion" (Stanford: Stanford University Press, 1997), 3. For a discussion of Hazlitt's response as well as that of subsequent critics, see also Hickey, especially 1–8.

20. Carl Thompson, *The Suffering Traveller and the Romantic Imagination* (Oxford: Oxford University Press, 2007).

21. In both versions, as *The Ruined Cottage* and *The Excursion*, this poem tends to be read as the emblematic statement of Romantic wandering, and of its tautological equation between walking and freedom. See, in particular, Celeste Langan, *Romantic Vagrancy: Wordsworth and the Simulation of Freedom* (Cambridge: Cambridge University Press, 1995), chapter 4, "The Walking Cure"; but also Anne D. Wallace, *Walking, Literature, and English Culture: The Origins and Uses of the Peripatetic in the Nineteenth Century* (Oxford: Clarendon, 1993), 12; and Jarvis, *Romantic Writing*, 109.

22. Langan, *Romantic Vagrancy*, 3 and 15–17.

23. Jarvis, *Romantic Writing*, 111.

24. Langan, *Romantic Vagrancy*, 19.

25. Peter Adey, *Mobility* (London: Routledge, 2010), 87. These concerns about ideological equations of equivalence run parallel to others' unease about universalizing moves in postmodern theory. For instance, Caren Kaplan, in discussing Gilles Deleuze and Felix Guattari's key theoretical terms, "deterritorialization" ("one term for the displacement of identities, persons, and meanings that is endemic to the postmodern world system") and "the nomadic subject," cautions against "a form of theoretical tourism on the part of the first world critic, where the margin becomes a linguistic and critical vacation, a new poetics of the exotic." The effect, Kaplan suggests, just as Langan does of Romantic vagrancy, is that everyone becomes the same – or comes to seem so (Caren Kaplan, "Deterritorializations: the Rewriting of Home and Exile in Western Feminist Discourse," *Cultural Critique 6* [Spring 1987], 187–98, rpt. Susan Roberson, *Defining Travel: Diverse Visions* [Jackson: Mississippi University Press, 2001], 191–3). Kaplan expands on these ideas in *Questions of Travel: Postmodern Discourses of Displacement* (Duke University Press, 2005).

26. Wordsworth, *The Excursion*, lines 1.811–12.

27. Wordsworth, *The Excursion*, lines 1.968 and 983–4.

28. As Wolfson and many others have argued, this moment invites us to query "psychic distance and the detachment that affords pleasure in tales of sorrow" (Wolfson, *The Questioning Presence*, 110).

29. Wordsworth, *The Excursion*, lines 1.637 and 649. Even the male wanderer in Book I of *The Excursion* needs someone else, the Poet-figure, to tell his story (*The Excursion* lines 1.106–11, 985–98). Like "The Female Vagrant" this poem ends with the central wanderer handing over his story to someone else: "He ceased . . ." (line 1.985).

30. David Simpson, *Wordsworth, Commodification and Social Concern: The Poetics of Modernity* (Cambridge: Cambridge University Press, 2009), 7, 40.
31. Simpson, *Wordsworth*, 45.
32. Simpson, *Wordsworth*, 25.
33. Simpson, *Wordsworth*, 45.
34. Simpson, *Wordsworth*, 27–8.
35. Simpson, *Wordsworth*, 59.
36. This is the male literary heritage in which Simpson situates Wordsworth's wanderers (*Wordsworth*, 59).

Bibliography

Adey, Peter. *Mobility*. London: Routledge, 2010.

Andrews, Kerri. " 'Herself . . . Fills the Foreground': Negotiating Autobiography in the *Elegiac Sonnets* and *The Emigrants*." *Charlotte Smith in British Romanticism*. Ed. Jacqueline M. Labbe. London: Pickering, 2008. 13–27.

Andrews, Malcolm. *The Search for the Picturesque: Landscape Aesthetics and Tourism in Britain, 1760–1800*. Aldershot: Scolar, 1989.

Arnold, Ellen. "Deconstructing the Patriarchal Palace: Ann Radcliffe's Poetry in *The Mysteries of Udolpho*." *Women and Language* 19.2 (1996): 21–9.

Austen, Jane. *Mansfield Park*. 1814. Ed. John Wiltshire. Cambridge: Cambridge University Press, 2005.

Northanger Abbey. 1818. Ed. Barbara M. Benedict and Deirdre La Faye. Cambridge: Cambridge University Press, 2006.

Persuasion. 1817. Ed. Janet Todd and Antje Blank. Cambridge: Cambridge University Press, 2006.

"Background." *MONK: Metadata Offer New Knowledge*. n.p. n.d. Web. November 20, 2013. http://monkproject.org.

Backscheider, Paula R. *Eighteenth-Century Women Poets and Their Poetry: Inventing Agency, Inventing Genre*. Baltimore: Johns Hopkins University Press, 2005.

Bahar, Saba. *Mary Wollstonecraft's Social and Aesthetic Philosophy: "An Eve to Please Me."* Basingstoke: Palgrave, 2002.

Bailey, Quentin. *Wordsworth's Vagrants: Police, Prisons, and Poetry in the 1790s*. Farnham: Ashgate, 2011.

Bannerman, Anne. *Poems*. New ed. Edinburgh, 1807. *Google Books*. Web. April 4, 2012.

Barbauld, Anna Laetitia. " 'Mrs Radcliffe': Introduction to *The Romance of the Forest*." *The British Novelists; with an Essay; and Prefaces, Biographical and Critical by Mrs Barbauld*. Vol. 43. London: Rivington, 1810. i–viii.

Barchas, Janine. *Graphic Design, Print Culture, and the Eighteenth-Century Novel*. Cambridge: Cambridge University Press, 2003.

Barker, Jane. *The Lining of a Patch-Work Screen; Design'd for the Farther Entertainment of the Ladies*. London, 1726. *Eighteenth Century Collections Online (ECCO)*. Gale. Web. December 9, 2013.

A Patch-Work Screen for the Ladies; or, Love and Virtue Recommended: In a Collection of Instructive Novels. Related after a Manner Entirely New, and Interspersed with Rural Poems, Describing the Innocence of a Country-Life. London, 1723. *Eighteenth Century Collections Online (ECCO).* Gale. Web. December 9, 2013.

Barker-Benfield, G. J. *The Culture of Sensibility: Sex and Society in Eighteenth-Century Britain.* Chicago: University of Chicago Press, 1992.

Barrell, John. *English Literature in History, 1730–1780: An Equal, Wide Survey.* London: Hutchinson, 1983.

The Idea of Landscape and the Sense of Place, 1730–1840: An Approach to the Poetry of John Clare. Cambridge: Cambridge University Press, 1972.

Imagining the King's Death: Figurative Treason, Fantasies of Regicide, 1793–1796. Oxford: Oxford University Press, 2000.

Poetry, Language and Politics. Manchester: Manchester University Press, 1988.

Barrell, John and Harriet Guest. "Thomson in the 1790s." *James Thomson: Essays for the Tercentenary.* Ed. Richard Terry. Liverpool: Liverpool University Press, 2000. 217–46.

Bassnett, Susan. "Travel Writing and Gender." *The Cambridge Companion to Travel Writing.* Ed. Peter Hulme and Tim Youngs. Cambridge: Cambridge University Press, 2002. 225–41.

Batchelor, Jennie. "Introduction: Influence, Intertextuality and Agency: Eighteenth-Century Women Writers and the Politics of Remembering." *Women's Writing* 20.1 (2013): 1–12.

Battaglia, Beatrice. "The 'Pieces of Poetry' in Ann Radcliffe's *The Mysteries of Udolpho.*" *Romantic Women Poets: Genre and Gender.* Ed. Lilla Maria Crisafulli and Cecilia Pietropoli. Amsterdam: Rodopi, 2007. 137–51.

Behrendt, Stephen C. *British Women Poets and the Romantic Writing Community.* Baltimore: Johns Hopkins University Press, 2009.

"Response Essay: Cultural Transitions, Literary Judgments, and the Romantic-Era British Novel." *Enlightening Romanticism, Romancing the Enlightenment: British Novels from 1750 to 1832.* Ed. Miriam L. Wallace. Surrey: Ashgate, 2009. 189–206.

Benis, Toby R. *Romantic Diasporas: French Émigrés, British Convicts, and Jews.* New York: Palgrave, 2009.

Romanticism on the Road: The Marginal Gains of Wordsworth's Homeless. Basingstoke: Macmillan, 2000.

Bewell, Alan. "De Quincey and Mobility." *Poetica* 76 (2011): 1–19.

"Erasmus Darwin's Cosmopolitan Nature." *English Literary History* 76.1 (March 2009): 19–48.

"John Clare and the Ghosts of Natures Past." *Nineteenth-Century Literature* 65.4 (March 2011): 548–78.

"Traveling Natures." *Nineteenth-Century Contexts* 29.2–3 (June/September 2007): 89–110.

Bhabha, Homi K. *The Location of Culture.* New York: Routledge, 1994.

Blackwell, Mark R. "The Gothic: Moving in the World of Novels." *A Concise Companion to the Restoration and Eighteenth Century.* Ed. Cynthia Wall. Malden: Blackwell, 2005. 144–61.

Bloom, Harold. *The Anxiety of Influence: A Theory of Poetry.* New York: Oxford University Press, 1973.

Bohls, Elizabeth A. *Women Travel Writers and the Language of Aesthetics, 1716–1818.* Cambridge: Cambridge University Press, 1995.

Bohls, Elizabeth A. and Ian Duncan. Eds. *Travel Writing, 1700–1830: An Anthology.* Oxford: Oxford University Press, 2005.

Brown, Marshall. *The Gothic Text.* Stanford: Stanford University Press, 2005.

Preromanticism. Stanford: Stanford University Press, 1991.

Burgess, Miranda. "On Being Moved: Sympathy, Mobility, and Narrative Form." *Poetics Today* 32.2 (Summer 2011): 289–321.

"Transport: Mobility, Anxiety, and the Romantic Poetics of Feeling." *Studies in Romanticism* 49.2 (Summer 2010): 229–60.

Burke, Edmund. *A Philosophical Enquiry into the Origin of Our Ideas of the Sublime and Beautiful.* 1757. Ed. James T. Boulton. Notre Dame: University of Notre Dame Press, 1958.

Reflections on the Revolution in France. 1790. Ed. Frank M. Turner. New Haven: Yale University Press, 2003.

[Burney, Frances]. By the Author of Evelina and Cecilia. *Brief Reflections Relative to the Emigrant French Clergy: Earnestly Submitted to the Humane Consideration of the Ladies of Great Britain.* London: Cadell, 1793.

Burney, Frances. *Camilla, or, a Picture of Youth.* 1796. Ed. Edward A. Bloom and Lillian D. Bloom. Oxford: Oxford University Press, 1972.

Cecilia; or, Memoirs of an Heiress. 1782. Ed. Peter Sabor and Margaret Doody. Oxford: Oxford University Press, 1988.

Diary and Letters of Madame D'Arblay (1788–1840). Ed. Charlotte Barrett, with Preface and Notes by Austin Dobson. Vol. 3. London: Macmillan, 1904–5.

Evelina; or, a Young Lady's Entrance into the World. In a Series of Letters. 1779. Ed. Susan Kubica Howard. Peterborough, ON: Broadview, 2000.

The Journals and Letters of Fanny Burney (Madame D'Arblay). 1791–1792. Ed. Joyce Hemlow with Curtis D. Cecil and Althea Douglas. Vol. 1. Oxford: Clarendon, 1972.

The Wanderer; or Female Difficulties. London, 1814. First Edition, with holograph manuscript corrections for the Third Edition (never published) in the Berg Collection, New York Public Library. 5 vols.

The Wanderer; or, Female Difficulties. 1814. Ed. Margaret Doody, Robert L. Mack, and Peter Sabor. Oxford: Oxford University Press, 1991.

Butler, Judith. *Excitable Speech: A Politics of the Performative.* New York: Routledge, 1997.

Byron, George Gordon. *Byron's Letters and Journals.* Ed. Leslie Marchand. Vol. 4. London: Murray, 1975.

Campbell, Thomas. *Life of Mrs. Siddons.* London: Edward Moxon, 1839.

Carlson, Julie A. *England's First Family of Writers: Mary Wollstonecraft, William Godwin, Mary Shelley*. Baltimore: Johns Hopkins University Press, 2007.

Carnochan, W. B. *Confinement and Flight: An Essay on English Literature of the Eighteenth Century*. Berkeley: University of California Press, 1977.

Carpenter, Kirsty. *Refugees of the French Revolution: Émigrés in London, 1789–1802*. Basingstoke: Macmillan, 1999.

Castle, Terry. *The Female Thermometer: Eighteenth-Century Culture and the Invention of the Uncanny*. New York: Oxford University Press, 1995.

Chandler, James. *An Archaeology of Sympathy: The Sentimental Mode in Literature and Cinema*. Chicago: University of Chicago Press, 2013.

Chandler, John. *Salisbury: History Around Us*. Salisbury: Hobnob Press, 2004.

Chaney, Christine. "The Rhetorical Strategies of 'Tumultuous Emotions': Wollstonecraft's *Letters Written in Sweden*." *Journal of Narrative Theory* 34.3 (2004): 277–303.

Clery, E. J. *Women's Gothic: From Clara Reeve to Mary Shelley*. Tavistock: Northcote, 2000.

Clifford, James. *Routes: Travel and Translation in the Late Twentieth Century*. Cambridge, MA: Harvard University Press, 1997.

Cohen, Ralph. *The Unfolding of The Seasons*. Baltimore: Johns Hopkins Press, 1970.

Coleridge, Samuel Taylor. "Introduction to the Sonnets." *Poems*. 2nd edn. London, 1797. 71–4. *Eighteenth Century Collections Online (ECCO)*. Gale. Web. December 9, 2013.

Coleridge, Samuel Taylor. "Review of *The Mysteries of Udolpho*." *Critical Review*. 2nd ser. 11 (August 1794): 361–72.

Cowan, Brian William. "Mr. Spectator and the Coffeehouse Public Sphere." *Eighteenth-Century Studies* 37.3 (Spring 2004): 345–66.

Cowper, William. *The Letters and Prose Works of William Cowper*. Ed. James King and Charles Ryskamp. 5 vols. Oxford: Clarendon, 1984.

The Task and Selected Other Poems. Ed. James Sambrook. London: Longman, 1994.

Craciun, Adriana. "Citizens of the World: Émigrés, Romantic Cosmopolitanism, and Charlotte Smith." *Nineteenth-Century Contexts* 29.2–3 (2007): 169–85.

Cresswell, Tim. *On the Move: Mobility in the Modern Western World*. New York: Routledge, 2006.

Culler, Jonathan. "Changes in the Study of the Lyric." *Lyric Poetry: Beyond New Criticism*. Ed. Chaviva Hošek and Patricia Parker. Ithaca: Cornell University Press, 1985. 38–54.

Curran, Stuart. "Charlotte Smith: Intertextualities." *Charlotte Smith in British Romanticism*. Ed. Jacqueline M. Labbe. London: Pickering, 2008. 175–88.

"General Introduction." *The Works of Charlotte Smith*. Ed. Stuart Curran. Vol. 1. London: Pickering, 2005. vii–xxvii.

"Introduction." *The Poems of Charlotte Smith*. Ed. Stuart Curran. New York: Oxford University Press, 1993. xi–xxiv.

Poetic Form and British Romanticism. New York: Oxford University Press, 1986.

"Romantic Poetry: The I Altered." *Romanticism and Feminism*. Ed. Anne K. Mellor. Bloomington: Indiana University Press, 1988. 185–207.

Dacre, Charlotte. *Zofloya, or, the Moor*. 1806. Ed. Kim Ian Michasiw. Oxford: Oxford University Press, 2000.

Dart, Gregory. *Rousseau, Robespierre and English Romanticism*. Cambridge: Cambridge University Press, 1999.

Davidoff, Leonore and Catherine Hall. *Family Fortunes: Men and Women of the English Middle Class, 1780–1850*. London: Hutchinson, 1987.

Dekker, George G. *The Fictions of Romantic Tourism: Radcliffe, Scott and Mary Shelley*. Stanford: Stanford University Press, 2005.

de Man, Paul. "Intentional Structure of the Romantic Image." *The Rhetoric of Romanticism*. New York: Columbia University Press, 1984. 1–17.

Desroches, Dennis. "The Rhetoric of Disclosure in James Thomson's *The Seasons*; or, on Kant's Gentlemanly Misanthropy." *The Eighteenth Century* 49.1 (2008): 1–24.

Dolan, Elizabeth A. *Seeing Suffering in Women's Literature of the Romantic Era*. Aldershot: Ashgate, 2008.

Doody, Margaret. *Frances Burney: The Life in the Works*. New Brunswick: Rutgers University Press, 1988.

Elfenbein, Andrew. *Romantic Genius: The Prehistory of a Homosexual Role*. New York: Columbia University Press, 1999.

Ellis, Markman. *The Politics of Sensibility: Race, Gender, and Commerce in the Sentimental Novel*. Cambridge: Cambridge University Press, 1996.

Ellison, Julie. *Cato's Tears and the Making of Anglo-American Emotion*. Chicago: University of Chicago Press, 1999.

  "News, Blues, and Cowper's Busy World." *Modern Language Quarterly* 62.3 (2001): 219–37.

  "Sensibility." *A Handbook of Romanticism Studies*. Ed. Joel Faflak and Julia M. Wright. Oxford: Blackwell, 2012. 37–53.

Emerson, Ralph Waldo. "Self-Reliance." *The Collected Works of Ralph Waldo Emerson*. Ed. Joseph Slater. Vol. 2. Cambridge: Belknap Press, 1979. 25–52.

Epstein, Julia. *The Iron Pen: Frances Burney and the Politics of Women's Writing*. Madison: University of Wisconsin Press, 1989.

  "Marginality in Frances Burney's Novels." *The Cambridge Companion to the Eighteenth-Century Novel*. Ed. John Richetti. Cambridge: Cambridge University Press, 1996. 198–211.

Fabricant, Carole. "The Literature of Domestic Tourism and the Public Consumption of Private Property." *The New Eighteenth Century: Theory, Politics, English Literature*. Ed. Felicity Nussbaum and Laura Brown. New York: Methuen, 1987. 254–75.

Fairclough, Mary. *The Romantic Crowd: Sympathy, Controversy and Print Culture*. Cambridge: Cambridge University Press, 2013.

Fairer, David. *English Poetry of the Eighteenth Century, 1700–1789*. London: Pearson, 2003.

Favret, Mary A. "*Letters Written During a Short Residence in Sweden, Norway, and Denmark*: Traveling with Mary Wollstonecraft." *The Cambridge Companion to Mary Wollstonecraft.* Ed. Claudia L. Johnson. Cambridge: Cambridge University Press, 2002. 209–27.

Romantic Correspondence: Women, Politics and the Fiction of Letters. Cambridge: Cambridge University Press, 1993.

"Telling Tales about Genre: Poetry in the Romantic Novel." *Studies in the Novel* 26.2 (Summer 1994): 153–72.

War at a Distance: Romanticism and the Making of Modern Wartime. Princeton: Princeton University Press, 2010.

Ferris, Ina. "Mobile Words: Romantic Travel Writing and Print Anxiety." *Modern Language Quarterly: A Journal of Literary History* 60.4 (1999): 451–68.

Fielding, Sarah. *The History of Ophelia.* 1760. Ed. Peter Sabor. Peterborough, ON: Broadview, 2004.

Fletcher, Loraine. *Charlotte Smith: A Critical Biography.* New York: St Martin's, 1998.

Foster, Shirley and Sara Mills, Eds. *An Anthology of Women's Travel Writing.* Manchester: Manchester University Press, 2002.

Fox, Charles James. *Speeches of the Right Honourable Charles James Fox, in the House of Commons.* Vol. 4. London: Longman, 1815.

Fraistat, Neil. *The Poem and the Book: Interpreting Collections of Romantic Poetry.* Chapel Hill: University of North Carolina Press, 1985.

Frank, Cathrine. "Wandering Narratives and Wavering Conclusions: Irreconciliation in Frances Burney's *The Wanderer* and Walter Scott's *Waverley.*" *European Romantic Review* 12.4 (2001): 429–56.

Frank, Marcie. "Fairy Time from Shakespeare to Scott." *Shakespeare and the Eighteenth Century.* Ed. Peter Sabor and Paul Yachnin. Aldershot: Ashgate, 2008. 103–17.

Freeholder. *Letter of a Freeholder to Mr. Johnes, Member of Parliament for the County of Denbigh, on the Subject of His Motion against the French Emigrants.* London, 1798.

Fulford, Tim. *Landscape, Liberty and Authority: Poetry, Criticism and Politics from Thomson to Wordsworth.* Cambridge: Cambridge University Press, 1996.

Fuss, Diana. "Corpse Poem." *Critical Inquiry* 30.1 (2003): 1–30.

Fussell, Paul. *The Norton Book of Travel.* New York: Norton, 1987.

Garnai, Amy. *Revolutionary Imaginings in the 1790s: Charlotte Smith, Mary Robinson, Elizabeth Inchbald.* Basingstoke: Palgrave, 2009.

Gephardt, Katarina. "Hybrid Gardens: Travel and the Nationalization of Taste in Ann Radcliffe's Continental Landscapes." *European Romantic Review* 21.1 (2010): 3–28.

Gilpin, William. *Observations on the Western Parts of England, Relative Chiefly to Picturesque Beauty.* London: 1798. *Eighteenth Century Collections Online (ECCO).* Gale. Web. December 9, 2013.

Remarks on Forest Scenery. London: 1792. *Eighteenth Century Collections Online (ECCO).* Gale. Web. December 9, 2013.

Three Essays: On Picturesque Beauty; on Picturesque Travel; and, on Sketching Landscape. London: 1792. *Eighteenth Century Collections Online (ECCO)*. Gale. Web. December 9, 2013.

Godwin, William. *Caleb Williams*. 1794. Ed. Gary Handwerk and Arnold. A. Markley. Peterborough, ON: Broadview, 2000.

Diaries, 1788–1836. Oxford, Bodleian Library. MS. Abinger e. 6, fols. 1–48.

The Diary of William Godwin. Ed. Victoria Myers, David O'Shaughnessy, and Mark Philp. Oxford: Oxford Digital Library, 2010. Web. November 27, 2014, http://godwindiary.bodleian.ox.ac.uk.

Memoirs of the Author of The Vindication of the Rights of Woman. 1798. Ed. Pamela Clemit and Gina Luria Walker. Peterborough, ON: Broadview, 2001.

"Preface." *Posthumous Works of the Author of a Vindication of the Rights of Woman*. Ed. William Godwin. Vol. 3. London: 1798.

Caleb Williams. 1794. Ed. Gary Handwerk and A. A. Markley. Peterborough, ON.: Broadview, 2000.

Goldsmith, Oliver. "A Comparative View of Races and Nations." 1760. *Collected Works of Oliver Goldsmith*. Ed. Arthur Friedman. Vol. 3. Oxford: Clarendon, 1966. 69–86.

"An Enquiry into the Present State of Polite Learning in Europe." 1759. *Collected Works of Oliver Goldsmith*. Ed. Arthur Friedman. Vol. 1. Oxford: Clarendon, 1966. 253–341.

Goodman, Kevis. *Georgic Modernity and British Romanticism: Poetry and the Mediation of History*. Cambridge: Cambridge University Press, 2004.

" 'Uncertain Disease': Nostalgia, Pathologies of Motion, Practices of Reading." *Studies in Romanticism* 49.2 (Summer 2010): 197–227.

Goodwin, Albert. *The Friends of Liberty: The English Democratic Movement in the Age of the French Revolution*. London: Hutchinson, 1979.

Gordon, Lyndall. *Mary Wollstonecraft: A New Genus*. London: Little, Brown, 2005.

Gottlieb, Evan. "The Astonished Eye: The British Sublime and Thomson's 'Winter'." *The Eighteenth Century* 42.1 (2001): 42–57.

Gray, Thomas, William Collins, and Oliver Goldsmith, *The Poems of Thomas Gray, William Collins and Oliver Goldsmith*. Ed. Roger Lonsdale. London: Longman, 1969.

Greenblatt, Stephen et al. Ed. *Cultural Mobility: A Manifesto*. Cambridge: Cambridge University Press, 2010.

Griffin, Dustin. *Literary Patronage in England, 1650–1800*. Cambridge: Cambridge University Press, 1996.

Patriotism and Poetry in Eighteenth-Century Britain. Cambridge: Cambridge University Press, 2002.

Gros, Frederick. *A Philosophy of Walking*. Trans. John Howe. London: Verso, 2014.

Guest, Harriet. *Small Change: Women, Learning, Patriotism, 1750–1810*. Chicago: University of Chicago Press, 2000.

Unbounded Attachment: Sentiment and Politics in the Age of the French Revolution. Oxford: Oxford University Press, 2013.

Harman, Claire. *Fanny Burney: A Biography*. London: Harper, 2000.

Harris, Jocelyn. *A Revolution Almost Beyond Expression: Jane Austen's Persuasion*. Newark: University of Delaware Press, 2007.

Harrison, Gary. *Wordsworth's Vagrant Muse: Poetry, Poverty and the Poor*. Detroit: Wayne State University Press, 1994.

Hartman, Geoffrey. *Wordsworth's Poetry, 1787–1814*. New Haven: Yale University Press, 1964.

Hays, Mary. *Memoirs of Emma Courtney*. 1796. Ed. Eleanor Ty. Oxford: Oxford University Press, 1996.

Hazlitt, William. "Review of *The Wanderer; or, Female Difficulties* by Madame D'Arblay." *Edinburgh Review* 24 (1815): 320–38.

Henderson, Andrea. *Romanticism and the Painful Pleasures of Modern Life*. Cambridge: Cambridge University Press, 2008.

Hickey, Alison. *Impure Conceits: Rhetoric and Ideology in Wordsworth's "Excursion."* Stanford: Stanford University Press, 1997.

Higgins, David. *Romantic Englishness: Local, National, and Global Selves, 1780–1850*. Basingstoke: Palgrave, 2014.

Holmes, Richard. *Dr Johnson and Mr Savage*. London: Harper, 1993.

"Introduction." *A Short Residence in Sweden, Norway and Denmark, by Mary Wollstonecraft; and Memoirs of the Author of "The Rights of Woman," by William Godwin*. Ed. Richard Holmes. London: Penguin, 1987. 9–55.

Horrocks, Ingrid. "Creating an 'Insinuating Interest': Mary Wollstonecraft's Travel Reviews and *A Short Residence*." *Studies in Travel Writing* 19.1 (2015): 1–15.

"Introduction." *Letters Written During a Short Residence in Sweden, Norway, and Denmark*, by Mary Wollstonecraft. Ed. Ingrid Horrocks. Peterborough, ON: Broadview, 2013. 13–42.

"More Than a Gravestone: *Caleb Williams*, *Udolpho*, and the Politics of the Gothic." *Studies in the Novel* 39.1 (2007): 31–47.

"'——Pugh!': Rereading Punctuation Through Wollstonecraft's *Letters Written During a Short Residence*." *Women's Writing* 21.4 (2014): 488–508.

Houghton-Walker, Sarah. "William Cowper's Gypsies." *Studies in English Literature, 1500–1900* 48.3 (2008): 653–76.

Hulme, Peter and Tim Youngs. "Introduction." *The Cambridge Companion to Travel Writing*. Ed. Peter Hulme and Tim Youngs. Cambridge: Cambridge University Press, 2002. 1–13.

Hume, David. *An Enquiry Concerning the Principles of Morals*. 1751–1777. Ed. Tom L. Beauchamp, Oxford: Clarendon, 1998.

A Treatise of Human Nature: A Critical Edition. 1739–1740. Ed. David Fate Norton and Mary J. Norton. Oxford: Clarendon, 2007.

Essays, Moral and Political. London, 1748. *Eighteenth Century Collections Online (ECCO)*. Gale. Web. December 9, 2013.

Jarvis, Robin. *Romantic Writing and Pedestrian Travel*. Basingstoke: Macmillan, 1997.

Johnson, Claudia L. Ed. *The Cambridge Companion to Mary Wollstonecraft*. Cambridge: Cambridge University Press, 2002.

Equivocal Beings: Politics, Gender, and Sentimentality in the 1790s: Wollstonecraft, Radcliffe, Burney, Austen. Chicago: University of Chicago Press, 1995.

Johnson, Samuel. *Dictionary of the English Language*. London, 1755.

"Idler 97." 1760. *The Idler and the Adventurer*. Ed. Walter J. Bate. Vol. 2. *The Yale Edition of the Works of Samuel Johnson*. New Haven: Yale University Press, 1963. 298–300.

Rasselas, Poems, and Selected Prose. 1759. Ed. Bertrand H. Bronson. Fort Worth: Harcourt, 1971.

Jones, Darryl. "Radical Ambivalence: Frances Burney, Jacobinism, and the Politics of Romantic Fiction." *Women's Writing* 10.1 (2003): 3–25.

Jump, Harriet Devine. " 'A Kind of Witchcraft': Mary Wollstonecraft and the Poetic Imagination." *Women's Writing* 4.2 (1997): 235–45.

Ed. *Mary Wollstonecraft and the Critics, 1788–2001*. 2 vols. London: Routledge, 2003.

Jung, Sandro. *The Fragmentary Poetic: Eighteenth-Century Uses of an Experimental Mode*. Bethlehem: Lehigh University Press, 2009.

Kaplan, Caren. *Questions of Travel: Postmodern Discourses of Displacement*. 2nd edn. Durham: Duke University Press, 2005.

"Deterritorializations: the Rewriting of Home and Exile in Western Feminist Discourse," *Cultural Critique* 6 (Spring 1987), 187–98. Rpt. Susan Roberson. *Defining Travel: Diverse Visions*. Jackson: Mississippi University Press, 2001. 190–9.

Kaul, Suvir. *Poems of Nation, Anthems of Empire: English Verse in the Long Eighteenth Century*. Charlottesville: University Press of Virginia, 2000.

Keane, Angela. *Women Writers and the English Nation in the 1790s: Romantic Belongings*. Cambridge: Cambridge University Press, 2000.

Keats, John. *Letters of John Keats*. Ed. Robert Gittings. Oxford: Oxford University Press, 1970.

Keenleyside, Heather. "Personification for the People: On James Thomson's *The Seasons*." *English Literary History* 76.2 (2009): 447–72.

Kelly, Gary. *English Fiction of the Romantic Period, 1789–1830*. London: Longman, 1989.

King, Shelley. " 'To Delineate the Human Mind in Its Endless Varieties': Integral Lyric and Characterization in the Tales of Amelia Opie." *Eighteenth-Century Poetry and the Rise of the Novel Reconsidered*. Ed. Kate Parker and Smith Courtney Weiss. Lewisburg: Bucknell University Press, 2014. 65–86.

Kinsley, Zoë. "Landscapes 'Dynamically in Motion': Revisiting Issues of Structure and Agency in Thomson's *The Seasons*." *Papers on Language and Literature* 41.1 (2005): 3–25.

Women Writing the Home Tour, 1682–1812. Aldershot: Ashgate, 2008.

Kitching, Megan. "The Solitary Animal: Professional Authorship and Persona in Goldsmith's *The Citizen of the World*." *Eighteenth-Century Fiction* 25.1 (2012): 175–98.

Knowles, Claire. *Sensibility and Female Poetic Tradition, 1780–1860: The Legacy of Charlotte Smith*. Farnham: Ashgate, 2009.

Labbe, Jacqueline M. *Charlotte Smith: Romanticism, Poetry and the Culture of Gender*. Manchester: Manchester University Press, 2003.

"Introduction." *The Works of Charlotte Smith*. Ed. Stuart Curran. Vol. 14: *Elegiac Sonnets, Volumes I and II, The Emigrants, Beachy Head: With Other Poems, Uncollected Poems*. Ed. Jacqueline M. Labbe. London: Pickering, 2007. vii–xx.

"Revisiting the Egotistical Sublime: Smith, Wordsworth, and the Romantic Dramatic Monologue." *Fellow Romantics: Male and Female British Writers, 1790–1835*. Ed. Beth Lau. Surrey: Ashgate, 2009. 17–38.

Romantic Visualities: Landscape, Gender, and Romanticism. Basingstoke: Macmillan, 1998.

Writing Romanticism: Charlotte Smith and William Wordsworth, 1784–1807. Basingstoke: Palgrave, 2011.

Labourg, Alice. " 'Exhibiting Awful Forms': Mountains and the Pictorial Framing of the Gothic in Ann Radcliffe's *The Mysteries of Udolpho*." *Mountains Figured and Disfigured in the English-Speaking World*. Ed. Françoise Besson. Newcastle: Cambridge Scholars, 2010. 317–33.

Lamb, Jonathan. *Preserving the Self in the South Seas, 1680–1840*. Chicago: University of Chicago Press, 2001.

The Things Things Say. Princeton: Princeton University Press, 2011.

Lamb, Susan. *Bringing Travel Home to England: Tourism, Gender, and Imaginative Literature in the Eighteenth Century*. Newark: University of Delaware Press, 2010.

Langan, Celeste. *Romantic Vagrancy: Wordsworth and the Simulation of Freedom*. Cambridge: Cambridge University Press, 1995.

Leask, Nigel. *Curiosity and the Aesthetics of Travel Writing, 1770–1840*. Oxford: Oxford University Press, 2002.

Leed, Eric J. *The Mind of the Traveler: From Gilgamesh to Global Tourism*. New York: Basic, 1991.

Lennox, Charlotte. *The Female Quixote: or, The Adventures of Arabella*. 1752. Ed. Margaret Dalziel. Oxford: Oxford University Press, 1998.

Lewis, Jayne. " 'No Color of Language': Radcliffe's Aesthetic Unbound." *Eighteenth-Century Studies* 39.3 (2006): 377–90.

Lewis, Matthew. *The Monk, a Romance*. 3 vols. London: Bell, 1796.

Lokke, Kari E. " 'The Mild Dominion of the Moon': Charlotte Smith and the Politics of Transcendence." *Rebellious Hearts: British Women Writers and the French Revolution*. Ed. Adriana Craciun and Kari E. Lokke. Albany: State University of New York Press, 2001. 85–106.

Lonsdale, Roger. " 'A Garden, and a Grave': The Poetry of Oliver Goldsmith." *The Author in His Work: Essays on a Problem in Criticism*. Ed. Louis Martz and Aubrey Williams. New Haven: Yale University Press, 1978. 3–30.

Lynch, Deidre Shauna. *The Economy of Character: Novels, Market Culture, and the Business of Inner Meaning.* Chicago: University of Chicago Press, 1998.

"Gothic Libraries and National Subjects." *Studies in Romanticism* 40.1 (2001): 29–48.

"Homes and Haunts: Austen's and Mitford's English Idylls." *Representing Place in British Literature and Culture, 1660–1830: From Local to Global.* Ed. Evan Gottlieb and Juliet Shields. Farnham: Ashgate, 2013. 173–84.

Macaulay, Thomas. *Critical and Historical Essays Contributed to the Edinburgh Review.* Vol. 2. London: Longman, 1854.

Mack, Robert L. "The Novelist and the Critics: Frances Burney's Manuscript Corrections and Additions to *The Wanderer; or, Female Difficulties.*" *Journal X: A Journal in Culture and Criticism* 9.1 (2004): 17–51.

Mackenzie, Anna Maria. *Irish Guardian, or, Errors of Eccentricity.* London: 1809. *Chawton House Library Novels Online.* Web. December 8, 2013.

Mackenzie, Henry. *The Man of Feeling.* 1771. Ed. Brian Vickers. London: Oxford University Press, 1967.

Macpherson, Sandra. *Harm's Way: Tragic Responsibility and the Novel Form.* Baltimore: Johns Hopkins University Press, 2010.

Marshall, David. *The Surprising Effects of Sympathy: Marivaux, Diderot, Rousseau and Mary Shelley.* Chicago: Chicago University Press, 1988.

Maunu, Leanne. *Women Writing the Nation: National Identity, Female Community, and the British-French Connection, 1770–1820.* Lewisburg: Bucknell University Press, 2007.

McGann, Jerome. *The Poetics of Sensibility: A Revolution in Literary Style.* Oxford: Clarendon, 1996.

McKeon, Michael, Ed. *Theory of the Novel: A Historical Approach.* Baltimore: Johns Hopkins University Press, 2000.

Mermin, Dorothy. *Elizabeth Barrett Browning: The Origins of a New Poetry.* Chicago: University of Chicago Press, 1989.

Miles, Robert. *Ann Radcliffe: The Great Enchantress.* Manchester: Manchester University Press, 1995.

Gothic Writing, 1750–1820: A Genealogy. 2nd edn. Manchester: Manchester University Press, 2002.

" 'Mother Radcliffe': Ann Radcliffe and the Female Gothic." *The Female Gothic: New Directions.* Ed. Diana Wallace and Andrew Smith. Basingstoke: Palgrave, 2009. 42–69.

Miller, Eric. "Radcliffe's Reveries of the Social Walker." *Dalhousie Review* 83.1 (2003): 29–50.

Mills, Sara. *Discourses of Difference: An Analysis of Women's Travel Writing and Colonialism.* London: Routledge, 2002.

"Written on the Landscape: Mary Wollstonecraft's *Letters Written During a Short Residence in Sweden, Norway and Denmark.*" *Romantic Geographies: Discourses of Travel 1775–1844.* Ed. Amanda Gilroy. Manchester: Manchester University Press, 2000. 19–34.

Milton, John. *The Riverside Milton* Ed. Roy Flannagan. Boston: Houghton, 1998.

Moers, Ellen. "Traveling Heroinism: Gothic for Heroines." *Literary Women*. London: W.H. Allen, 1976. 122–40.

Molesworth, Jesse. *Chance and the Eighteenth-Century Novel: Realism, Probability, Magic*. Cambridge: Cambridge University Press, 2010.

Moretti, Franco. *Graphs, Maps, Trees: Abstract Models for a Literary History*. London: Verso, 2005.

Morley, David. *Home Territories: Media, Mobility and Identity*. London: Routledge, 2000.

Moser, Joseph. "Adventures of Mohamet: The Wandering Sultan . . . Written in 1796." *The European Magazine and Monthly Review* 54 (August 1808)–59 (May 1811).

Murphy, Olivia. *Jane Austen the Reader: The Artist as Critic*. Basingstoke: Palgrave, 2013.

Myers, Mitzi. "Sensibility and the 'Walk of Reason': Mary Wollstonecraft's Literary Reviews as Cultural Critique." *Sensibility in Transformation: Creative Resistance to Sentiment from the Augustans to the Romantics*. Ed. Syndy M. Conger. Rutherford: Fairleigh Dickinson University Press, 1990. 120–44.

Nagel, Thomas. *The View from Nowhere*. New York: Oxford University Press, 1986.

Neuendorf, Kimberly A. *The Content Analysis Guidebook*. Thousand Oaks, CA: Sage, 2002.

Norton, Rictor. *Mistress of Udolpho: The Life of Ann Radcliffe*. London: Leicester University Press, 1999.

Nyström, Per. *Mary Wollstonecraft's Scandinavian Journey*. Trans. George R. Otter. Gothenburg: Kungl. Vetenskaps, 1980.

Ousby, Ian. *Englishman's England: Taste, Travel and the Rise of Tourism*. Cambridge: Cambridge University Press, 1990.

Özdemir, Erinç. "Hidden Polemic in Wollstonecraft's *Letters from Norway*: A Bakhtinian Reading." *Studies in Romanticism* 47.3 (2008): 321–49.

Park, Julie. "Pains and Pleasures of the Automaton: Frances Burney's Mechanics of Coming Out." *Eighteenth-Century Studies* 40.1 (2006): 23–50.

Park, Suzie. "Resisting Demands for Depth in *The Wanderer*." *European Romantic Review* 15.2 (2004): 307–15.

Parker, David. *A Charitable Morsel of Unleavened Bread, for the Author of a Letter to the Rev. William Romaine; entitled, Gideon's Cake of Barley Meal: being a Reply to that Pamphlet*. London, 1793.

Parker, Kate and Courtney Weiss Smith, Eds. *Eighteenth-Century Poetry and the Rise of the Novel Reconsidered*. Lewisburg: Bucknell University Press, 2014.

Pascoe, Judith. *Romantic Theatricality: Gender, Poetry, and Spectatorship*. Ithaca: Cornell University Press, 1997.

Pinch, Adela. *Strange Fits of Passion: Epistemologies of Emotion, Hume to Austen*. Stanford: Stanford University Press, 1996.

Pope, Alexander. *Alexander Pope*. Ed. Pat Rogers. Oxford: Oxford University Press, 1993.

Price, Fiona L. *Revolutions in Taste 1773–1818: Women Writers and the Aesthetics of Romanticism*. Farnham: Ashgate, 2009.

Price, Leah. *The Anthology and the Rise of the Novel: From Richardson to George Eliot*. Cambridge: Cambridge University Press, 2000.

Punter, David. "Ceremonial Gothic." *Spectral Readings: Towards a Gothic Geography*. Ed. David Punter and Glennis Byron. New York: St Martin's, 1999. 37–53.

Radcliffe, Ann. *A Journey Made in the Summer of 1794, through Holland and the Western Frontier of Germany*. Dublin, 1795.

    The Mysteries of Udolpho. 1794. Ed. Bonamy Dobree. Oxford: Oxford University Press, 1998.

    "On the Supernatural in Poetry." *Gothic Readings: The First Wave, 1764–1840*. 1802/1826. Ed. Rictor Norton. London: Leicester University Press, 2000. 311–16.

    The Poems of Mrs. Ann Radcliffe. London, 1816.

    The Romance of the Forest. 1791. Ed. Chloe Chard. Oxford: Oxford University Press, 1986.

    A Sicilian Romance. 1790. Ed. Alison Milbank. Oxford: Oxford University Press, 1993.

Raphael, D. D. *The Impartial Spectator: Adam Smith's Moral Philosophy*. Oxford: Clarendon, 2007.

Richetti, John. "Formalism and Eighteenth-Century English Fiction: An Introduction." *Eighteenth-Century Fiction* 24.2 (2011–2012): 157–60.

Ricks, Christopher. *Allusion to the Poets*. Oxford: Oxford University Press, 2002.

Roberson, Susan. "Introduction." *Defining Travel: Diverse Visions*. Jackson: Mississippi University Press, 2001. xi–xxvi.

Robinson, Daniel. "*Elegiac Sonnets*: Charlotte Smith's Formal Paradoxy." *Papers on Language and Literature: A Journal for Scholars and Critics of Language and Literature* 39.2 (Spring 2003): 185–220.

Robinson, Mary. *Walsingham: Or, The Pupil of Nature. A Domestic Story*. Vol. 1. London: Longman, 1797.

    Walsingham: Or, The Pupil of Nature. 1797. Ed. Julie Shaffer. Peterborough, ON: Broadview, 2003.

Roe, Nicholas. *The Politics of Nature: Wordsworth and Some Contemporaries*. Basingstoke: Macmillan, 1992.

Rogers, Deborah D. Ed. *The Critical Response to Ann Radcliffe*. Westport: Greenwood, 1994.

Rogers, Pat. "The Dialectic of *The Traveller*." *The Art of Oliver Goldsmith*. Ed. Andrew Swarbrick. Totowa: Barnes, 1984. 107–25.

Rousseau, Jean Jacques. *Reveries of the Solitary Walker*. 1782. Trans. Peter France. Harmondsworth: Penguin, 1979.

Rowe, Nicholas. *The Fair Penitent*. 1714. Ed. Malcolm Goldstein. London: Edward Arnold, 1969.

Rowland, Ann Wierda. "Romantic Poetry and the Romantic Novel." *The Cambridge Companion to British Romantic Poetry*. Ed. James Chandler and Maureen N. McLane. Cambridge: Cambridge University Press, 2008. 117–35.

Ryall, Anka and Catherine Sandbach-Dahlström, Eds. *Mary Wollstonecraft's Journey to Scandinavia: Essays*. Stockholm: Almqvist, 2003.

Salih, Sara "*Camilla* and *The Wanderer*." *Cambridge Companion to Frances Burney*. Ed. Peter Sabor. Cambridge: Cambridge University Press, 2007. 39–53.

Savage, Richard. *Various Poems*. London, 1761.

Sedgwick, Eve Kosovsky. *The Coherence of Gothic Conventions*. New York: Arno Press, 1980.

Schmidgen, Wolfram. "Undividing the Subject of Literary History: From James Thomson's Poetry to Daniel Defoe's Novels." *Eighteenth-Century Poetry and the Rise of the Novel Reconsidered*. Ed. Kate Parker and Courtney Weiss Smith. Lewisburg: Bucknell University Press, 2014. 87–104.

Schor, Esther. *Bearing the Dead: The British Culture of Mourning from the Enlightenment to Victoria*. Princeton: Princeton University Press, 1994.

Shakespeare, William. *The Norton Shakespeare*. Ed. Stephen Greenblatt. 2nd edn. New York: Norton, 1997.

Shelley, Percy Bysshe. *Zastrozzi, a Romance and St. Irvyne; or, the Rosicrucian: A Romance*. 1810 and 1811. Ed. Stephen C. Behrendt. Peterborough, ON: Broadview, 2002.

Simmel, Georg. *On Individuality and Social Forms*. Ed. Donald N. Levine. Chicago: University of Chicago Press, 1971.

Simpson, David. *Romanticism and the Question of the Stranger*. Chicago: University of Chicago Press, 2013.

  Wordsworth, Commodification and Social Concern: The Poetics of Modernity. Cambridge: Cambridge University Press, 2009.

Sitter, John. *Literary Loneliness in Mid-Eighteenth Century England*. Ithaca: Cornell University Press, 1982.

Smith, Adam. *The Theory of Moral Sentiments*. 1759. Ed. Knud Haakonssen. Cambridge: Cambridge University Press, 2002.

Smith, Charlotte. *The Banished Man*. London, 1794. *Eighteenth Century Collections Online (ECCO)*. Gale. Web. December 9, 2013.

  Charlotte Smith: Major Poetic Works. Ed. Claire Knowles and Ingrid Horrocks. Peterborough, ON: Broadview, 2017.

  The Collected Letters of Charlotte Smith. Ed. Judith Stanton. Bloomington: Indiana University Press, 2003.

  Desmond. 1792. Ed. Janet Todd and Antje Blank. Peterborough, ON: Broadview, 2001.

  The Old Manor House. 1793. Ed. Jacqueline M. Labbe. Peterborough, ON: Broadview, 2002.

  The Poems of Charlotte Smith. Ed. Stuart Curran. New York: Oxford University Press, 1993.

  The Works of Charlotte Smith. Ed. Stuart Curran. Vol. 14: *Elegiac Sonnets, Volumes I and II, The Emigrants, Beachy Head: With Other Poems, Uncollected Poems*. Ed. Jacqueline M. Labbe. London: Pickering, 2007.

Sodeman, Melissa. "Charlotte Smith's Literary Exile." *English Literary History* 76.1 (2009): 131–52.

Solnit, Rebecca. *Wanderlust: A History of Walking*. London: Verso, 2002.

Sontag, Susan. *Regarding the Pain of Others*. New York: Farrar, 2003.

Spencer, Jane. *The Rise of the Woman Novelist: From Aphra Behn to Jane Austen*. Oxford: Blackwell, 1986.

Spivak, Gayatri. "Can the Subaltern Speak?" 1988. *The Post-Colonial Studies Reader*. Ed. Bill Ashcroft, Gareth Griffiths, and Helen Tiffin. London: Routledge, 1995. 24–8.

Starr, G. Gabrielle. *Lyric Generations: Poetry and the Novel in the Eighteenth Century*. Baltimore: Johns Hopkins University Press, 2004.

Staves, Susan. *A Literary History of Women's Writing in Britain, 1660–1789*. Cambridge: Cambridge University Press, 2006.

Steele, Richard. *The Tatler*. Ed. Donald F. Bond. 3 Vols. Oxford: Oxford University Press, 1987.

Sterne, Laurence. *A Sentimental Journey through France and Italy*. 1768. *A Sentimental Journey and Other Writings*. New edn. Ed. Ian Jack and Tim Parnell. Oxford: Oxford University Press, 2003.

Straub, Kristina. *Divided Fictions: Fanny Burney and Feminine Strategy*. Lexington: University Press of Kentucky, 1987.

Stuart, Augusta Amelia. *Cava of Toledo; or, the Gothic Princess. A Romance*. 5 Vols. London: 1812. *Chawton House Library Novels Online*. n.d. Web. December 8, 2013.

Sutherland, Kathryn. *Jane Austen's Textual Lives: From Aeschylus to Bollywood*. Oxford: Oxford University Press, 2005.

Taylor, Barbara. *Mary Wollstonecraft and the Feminist Imagination*. Cambridge: Cambridge University Press, 2003.

Thompson, Carl. *The Suffering Traveller and the Romantic Imagination*. Oxford: Oxford University Press, 2007.

Thompson, Helen. "How *The Wanderer* Works: Reading Burney and Bourdieu." *English Literary History* 68.4 (2001): 965–89.

Thomson, James. *Britannia, a Poem*. London, 1729.

The Seasons. 1726–1746. Ed. James Sambrook. Oxford: Clarendon, 1981.

Thrale, Hester Lynch. *Thraliana: The Diary of Hester Lynch Thrale (Later Mrs. Piozzi)*. Ed. Katharine C. Balderston. Oxford: Clarendon, 1942.

Tinniswood, Adrian. *A History of Country House Visiting: Five Centuries of Tourism and Taste*. Oxford: Blackwell, 1989.

Todd, Janet. *Mary Wollstonecraft: A Revolutionary Life*. London: Weidenfeld, 2000.

The Sign of Angellica: Women, Writing and Fiction, 1660–1800. New York: Columbia University Press, 1989.

Toner, A. C. "Anna Barbauld on Fictional Form in *The British Novelists* (1810)." *Eighteenth-Century Fiction* 24.2 (2012): 171–93.

Turner, Katherine. *British Travel Writers in Europe, 1750–1800: Authorship, Gender and National Identity*. Aldershot: Ashgate, 2001.

Urry, John. *Mobilities*. Cambridge: Polity Press 2007.

Valenza, Robin. "How Literature Becomes Knowledge: A Case Study." *English Literary History* 76.1 (2009): 215–45.

Verhoeven, Wil. *Gilbert Imlay: Citizen of the World*. London: Pickering, 2008.

Wagner, Tamara. "Nostalgia for Home or Homelands: Romantic Nationalism and the Indeterminate Narrative in Frances Burney's *The Wanderer.*" *Cardiff Corvey: Reading the Romantic Text* 10 (June 2003): Web. September 9, 2009. 45–62.

Wahrman, Dror. *The Making of the Modern Self: Identity and Culture in Eighteenth-Century England*. New Haven: Yale University Press, 2004.

Wallace, Anne D. *Walking, Literature, and English Culture: The Origins and Uses of the Peripatetic in the Nineteenth Century*. Oxford: Clarendon, 1993.

Weiss, Deborah. "Suffering, Sentiment, and Civilization: Pain and Politics in Mary Wollstonecraft's *Short Residence.*" *Studies in Romanticism* 45.2 (2006): 199–221.

Wells, Roger. *Wretched Faces: Famine in Wartime England, 1793–1801*. Gloucester: Sutton, 1988.

Whale, John C. "Death in the Face of Nature: Self, Society and Body in Wollstonecraft's Letters Written in Sweden, Norway, and Denmark." *Romanticism* 1.2 (1995): 177–92.

Imagination Under Pressure, 1789–1832: Aesthetics, Politics and Utility. Cambridge: Cambridge University Press, 2000.

Wiley, Michael. "The Geography of Displacement and Replacement in Charlotte Smith's *The Emigrants.*" *European Romantic Review* 17.1 (2006): 55–68.

Romantic Migrations: Local, National, and Transnational Dispositions. New York: Palgrave, 2008.

Williams, Raymond. *The Country and the City*. New York: Oxford University Press, 1973.

Wolfson, Susan. "Mary Wollstonecraft and the Poets." *Cambridge Companion to Mary Wollstonecraft*. Ed. Claudia L. Johnson. Cambridge: Cambridge University Press, 2002. 160–88.

The Questioning Presence: Wordsworth, Keats, and the Interrogative Mode in Romantic Poetry. Ithaca: Cornell University Press, 1986.

Romantic Interactions: Social Being and the Turns of Literary Action. Baltimore: Johns Hopkins University Press, 2010.

Wollstonecraft, Mary. *The Collected Letters of Mary Wollstonecraft*. Ed. Janet Todd. New York: Columbia University Press, 2003.

Letters Written During a Short Residence in Sweden, Norway, and Denmark. Ed. Ingrid Horrocks. Peterborough, ON: Broadview, 2013.

Mary, a Fiction; and the Wrongs of Woman, or Maria. 1788, 1798. Ed. Michelle Faubert. Peterborough, ON: Broadview, 2012.

A Vindication of the Rights of Men, in a Letter to the Right Honourable Edmund Burke; Occasioned by His Reflections on the Revolution in France. 1st edn. London: Johnson, 1790.

A Vindication of the Rights of Men and A Vindication of the Rights of Woman.
1790, 1792. Ed. D. L. Macdonald and Kathleen Scherf. Peterborough, ON:
Broadview, 1997.

The Works of Mary Wollstonecraft. Ed. Janet Todd and Marilyn Butler. 7 vols.
London: Pickering, 1989.

Woloch, Alex. *The One Vs. The Many: Minor Characters and the Space of the
Protagonist in the Novel.* Princeton: Princeton University Press, 2003.

Wordsworth, William. *An Evening Walk.* 1793 Ed. James Averill. Ithaca: Cornell
University Press, 1984.

The Excursion. 1814. Ed. Sally Bushell, James A. Butler, and Michael C. Jaye.
Ithaca: Cornell University Press, 2007.

Wordsworth, William and Samuel Taylor Coleridge. *Lyrical Ballads 1798 and 1800.*
Ed. Michael Gamer and Dahlia Porter. Peterborough, ON: Broadview,
2008.

Wright, Angela. *Britain, France and the Gothic, 1764–1820: The Import of Terror.*
Cambridge: Cambridge University Press, 2013.

"In Search of Arden: Ann Radcliffe's William Shakespeare." *Gothic
Shakespeares.* Ed. John Drakakis, Dale Townshend, and Jerrold E. Hogle.
New York: Routledge, 2008. 111–30.

Wu, Duncan. *Wordsworth's Reading 1770–1799.* New York: Cambridge University
Press, 1993.

Young, Edward. *The Revenge.* London, 1721. *Eighteenth Century Collections Online
(ECCO).* Gale. Web. December 9, 2013.

Zimmerman, Sarah M. *Romanticism, Lyricism, and History.* New York: State
University of New York Press, 1999.

"Varieties of Privacy in Charlotte Smith's Poetry." *European Romantic Review*
18.4 (2007): 483–502.

Index

CAMBRIDGE STUDIES IN ROMANTICISM

General Editor

JAMES CHANDLER, *University of Chicago*